APPLIED
DYNAMIC PROGRAMMING

Applied
Dynamic Programming

BY

RICHARD E. BELLMAN

AND

STUART E. DREYFUS

1962

PRINCETON UNIVERSITY PRESS

PRINCETON, NEW JERSEY

To the Memory of
JOHN VON NEUMANN
Inspiration and Friend

Introduction

In the period following World War II, it began to be recognized that there were a large number of interesting and significant activities which could be classified as multistage decision processes. It was soon seen that the mathematical problems that arose in their study stretched the conventional confines of analysis, and required new methods for their successful treatment. The classical techniques of calculus and the calculus of variations were occasionally valuable and useful in these new areas, but were clearly limited in range and versatility, and were definitely lacking as far as furnishing numerical answers was concerned.

The recognition of these facts led to the creation of a number of novel mathematical theories and methods. Among these was the theory of dynamic programming, a new approach based on the use of functional equations and the principle of optimality, with one eye on the potentialities of the burgeoning field of digital computers.

The first task we set ourselves in the development of the theory was the examination of a variety of activities in the engineering, economic, industrial, and military domains with the aim of seeing which could be formulated in dynamic-programming terms and with what level of complexity. This is not always a routine operation, since in the description of an optimization process there is a good deal of leeway permitted in the choice of state variables and criteria. It often happens that one type of mathematical model is well suited to one type of analytic approach and not to another. Generally, the three principal parts of a mathematical model, the conceptual, analytic, and computational aspects, must be considered simultaneously and not separately. Consequently, a certain amount of effort is involved in translating verbal problems posed in such vague terms of efficiency, feasibility, cost, and so on, into precise analytic problems requiring the solutions of equations and the determination of extrema.

Once various translations had been effected, it was essential to study the relation between the solutions of the functional equations obtained and the optimal policies of the original decision process. This study of the existence and uniqueness of solutions is required before one can engage in any computational solution or structural analysis. Fortunately, in a number of significant cases, the demonstration of existence and uniqueness was readily carried out so that we could, with confidence, turn to the study of the nature of optimal policies and of the maximum return, using the basic functional equations.

Initially, we focussed on those processes which were specifically posed as multistage decision processes. Subsequently, we indulged in the mathematical license of studying any process which could be considered to be a multistage decision process. In this way we became extensively involved in the study of various parts of the calculus of variations, and, in particular, with trajectory processes and feedback control.

After this initial period of exploration and consolidation of territory, we felt that it was time to perform some computational studies. Although we had had this goal in mind from the very beginning, and had constantly examined the feasibility of our procedures from this viewpoint, it was absolutely necessary to carry out detailed numerical solutions. Those who have had even brief encounter with digital computers soon learn to be wary of proposed solutions, no matter how elegant. Until every single part of a numerical solution of a problem is carefully checked and tested in practice, one cannot be sure that considerations of accuracy and stability, storage or time, will not block a complete solution.

Secondly, it is soon realized that no solution of a particular problem is routine. Taking advantage of individual structural features, one can always cut down on the time required, increase the accuracy, add more realistic features at no cost in time, and so on. The theory of dynamic programming is specifically designed to exploit the idiosyncrasies of specific processes.

In 1955, we began a systematic study of the computational feasibility of dynamic programming. We collected a number of optimization problems from many different fields and applied our methods in many different ways.

Pursuing this course, we showed that dynamic programming could indeed be used to resolve a number of vexing variational and optimization problems of some interest and significance in applications. Some of these could be handled only with difficulty by other techniques, some only on a trial-and-error and "educated guess" basis, and some seemed completely to escape alternative methods.

The advantage of having a reasonably "turn-of-the-crank" technique for some large classes of problems in the fields of pure and applied mathematics is multiple. In the first place, in connection with guidance and control, or in scheduling and inventory control, we have a systematic means of obtaining precise numerical answers to specific numerical questions. Secondly, we have a means of getting exact answers which can be used as yardsticks for the approximate results obtained in other, perhaps simpler and quicker, ways. Thus, we can test the efficacy of approximate techniques.

When facing new classes of mathematical problems which cannot initially be treated by means of existing analytical devices, it is extremely important to be able to examine classes of numerical solutions in the hope of discerning patterns of behavior. These may furnish valuable clues to the analytic structure of the solutions, and so guide our investigation into profitable directions. After all, mathematics started as an experimental field. If we do not wish to suffer the usual atrophy of armchair philosophers, we must occasionally roll up our sleeves and do some spadework. With the aid of dynamic programming and digital computers we can methodically engage in mathematical experimentation.

Finally, let us note that in many cases we are more interested in the nature of optimal policies than we are in the precise numerical values which furnish the maximum or minimum of the criterion function. The exact optimal policies obtained in the study of simple decision processes can be used to furnish simple approximate policies for more complex decision processes.

Let us now sketch the contents of the various chapters.

The basic functional equation of dynamic programming has the form

(1) $$f(p) = \max_{q} [H(p, q, f(T(p, q)))].$$

The subject can be partitioned in several ways, either with respect to the precise form of (1), or with respect to the type of process giving rise to (1), or with respect to deterministic, stochastic, or adaptive features, and so on. For the purposes of computational study, it is convenient initially to pay attention to the dimension of the state vector p.

In Chapter I, in order to introduce the reader to both the basic ideas of dynamic programming and the routine techniques of the computational method we shall repeatedly employ, we consider some simple processes which give rise to sequences of functions of one variable.

In Chapter II, with the preliminaries disposed of, we consider some interesting problems giving rise to sequences of functions of two variables. After a discussion of the dimensionality difficulties that begin to loom large on the horizon, we show how they may be subdued in a number of cases by the use of a Lagrange multiplier.

In Chapter III, we group our efforts according to subject matter and present some analytic and computational solutions to various classes of smoothing and scheduling processes.

Chapter IV is devoted to the study of dynamic-programming problems that arise in the course of the computational solution of dynamic-programming problems. As will be noted, the equation in (1) requires the determination of the maximum over q. Since we do not wish to employ calculus, for a range of reasons described in the text, we must use a search process to obtain the maximizing q. In some cases, we can endure a straightforward process of enumeration; in other cases, it is essential to use a sequential method. This chapter is an introduction to this very difficult and entertaining problem area.

So far we have considered discrete processes over time. In Chapter V, we show how the theory of dynamic programming may be used to provide a very simple treatment of the theory of variational problems involving functions of one independent variable. The principle of optimality yields a nonlinear partial differential equation from which all of the classical results are quickly obtained.

In Chapter VI, we turn to one of the most interesting current applications of dynamic programming, the determination of optimal trajectories. Specific problems are discussed and their numerical solutions are given.

The next chapter, VII, is a brief foray into the domain of mathematical economics. Employing the type of input-output model made famous by the work of Leontieff, we consider the optimal utilization of a complex of interdependent industries.

In Chapters VIII and IX we discuss different aspects of the flowering theory of control processes. The first chapter is devoted to the formulation of various types of deterministic, stochastic, and adaptive processes; the second, following the work of Masanao Aoki, is devoted to some computational results.

Chapter X is a brief introduction to a very interesting and rewarding study of optimization processes with linear equations and quadratic criteria. The results are not only of importance in themselves, but also in connection with the use of successive approximations.

Following this, we discuss in some detail Markovian decision processes and give a number of applications. Some significant parts of this chapter are based on the work of R. Howard.

The final chapter is devoted to some preliminary results on the accuracy and stability of dynamic-programming techniques. This field of study is relatively uncultivated and many important problems remain to be investigated.

At the end of the text will be found four appendices containing some more detailed results, as well as some more recent results, due to O. Gross and M. Freimer and W. Karush in collaboration with several of the authors. A fifth appendix contains a description of the computer used during our researches, the RAND Johnniac.

As far as possible, we have tried to make this book self-contained. The reader desiring a broader background in dynamic programming may wish to consult R. Bellman, *Dynamic Programming*, Princeton University Press, 1957; a detailed discussion of the modern theory of control processes will be found in R. Bellman, *Adaptive Control Processes: A Guided Tour*, Princeton University Press, 1961. Numerous references to applications and original research papers will be found at the ends of the chapters. For those who wish a comprehensive bibliography, we recommend V. Riley and S. Gass, *Linear Programming and Associated Techniques*, Operations Research Office, Johns Hopkins Press, 1958.

A number of the results that follow were derived in collaboration with other mathematicians, or are based on their individual efforts. For the use of this research, we should like particularly to thank M. Aoki, T. Cartaino, M. Freimer, O. Gross, R. Howard, S. Johnson, R. Kalaba, and W. Karush.

The results presented in this volume were obtained in the course of mathematical research carried out at The RAND Corporation under a broad research program sponsored by the United States Air Force. We should like to express our appreciation for the opportunities thus afforded us.

Richard Bellman
Stuart Dreyfus

The RAND Corporation
Santa Monica, July 1961

Contents

CHAPTER I

ONE-DIMENSIONAL ALLOCATION PROCESSES

CHAPTER II

MULTIDIMENSIONAL ALLOCATION PROCESSES

CHAPTER III

ONE-DIMENSIONAL SMOOTHING AND SCHEDULING PROCESSES

CHAPTER IV

OPTIMAL SEARCH TECHNIQUES

CHAPTER V

DYNAMIC PROGRAMMING AND THE CALCULUS
OF VARIATIONS

CHAPTER VI
OPTIMAL TRAJECTORIES

CHAPTER VII
MULTISTAGE PRODUCTION PROCESSES UTILIZING
COMPLEXES OF INDUSTRIES

CHAPTER VIII

FEEDBACK CONTROL PROCESSES

CHAPTER IX

COMPUTATIONAL RESULTS FOR FEEDBACK CONTROL PROCESSES

CHAPTER X

LINEAR EQUATIONS AND QUADRATIC CRITERIA

CHAPTER XI

MARKOVIAN DECISION PROCESSES

CHAPTER XII

NUMERICAL ANALYSIS

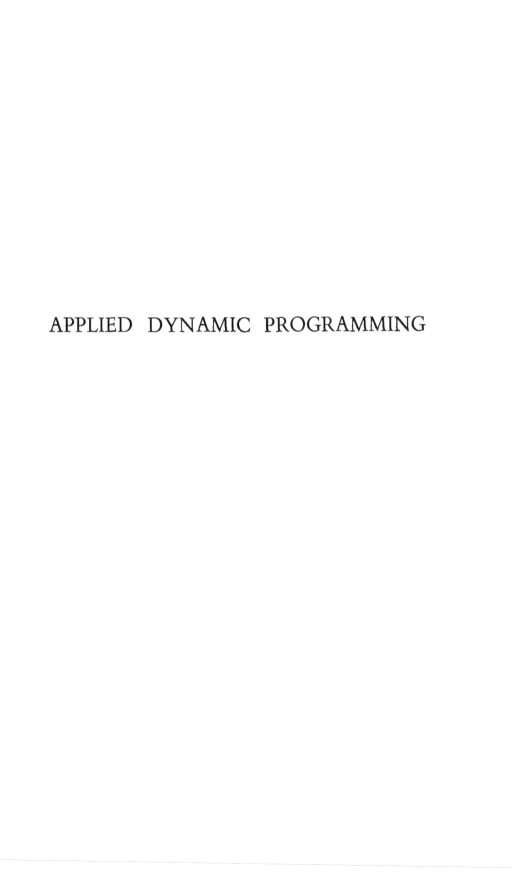

APPLIED DYNAMIC PROGRAMMING

CHAPTER I

One-dimensional Allocation Processes

1. Introduction

We shall begin our discussion with an investigation of a simple class of allocation processes arising in mathematical economics and operations research. The basic question is that of using resources of various types in efficient ways. In order to permit the reader to assimilate the techniques we shall employ throughout, we initially shall consider some rudimentary models involving a minimum of mathematical difficulties.

The simplicity of these preliminary problems permits us to examine and analyze methods which will be applied in later pages to study more realistic and complex matters. As we shall see, processes of significance in applications possess a number of simultaneous features of difficulty. Generally speaking, these require a variety of methods applied in unison, and often some amount of ingenuity. All our efforts will be directed towards the primary goal of obtaining numerical answers to numerical questions.

The first computation we perform is directed towards the determination of the maximum of the function of N variables

$$(1) \qquad R(x_1, x_2, \ldots, x_N) = g_1(x_1) + g_2(x_2) + \cdots + g_N(x_N)$$

taken over the region of values determined by the relations

$$(2) \quad (a) \qquad x_1 + x_2 + \cdots + x_N = x,$$

$$(b) \qquad x_i \geq 0.$$

There are many difficulties encountered in treating this apparently simple and straightforward problem. In the course of a careful and detailed examination of these obstacles, we shall generate sufficient motivation to present a new approach—the functional equation technique of dynamic programming.

The allocation process giving rise to the foregoing optimization will be used to introduce the basic ideas of dynamic programming and to illustrate the computational aspects in detail. In this discussion, and throughout, we shall provide the reader with basic information concerning coding times, running times, accuracy, stability, and flow charts.

3

Two further problems leading to analytic questions of the type appearing above will be treated, one arising from cargo-loading and the other connected with the reliability of a multicomponent device.

2. Verbal Description of an Allocation Process

Before any analytic formulation, let us present in purely verbal terms the category of processes we wish to study. Suppose that we have available a certain quantity of an economic *resource*. This abstract term may represent men, money, machines, fissionable material for nuclear reactors, water for agricultural and industrial purposes or for the generation of hydroelectric power, fuel for a space ship, and so on. A conflict of interests arises from the fact that a resource can be used in a number of different ways. Each such possible application we call an *activity*.

As a result of using all or part of this resource in any single activity, a certain *return* is derived. The return may be expressible in terms of the resource itself, i.e., money may beget more money, machines may produce more machines, or it may be measured in entirely different units, i.e., fuel produces velocity, money produces reliability, and so on. The magnitude of the return depends both upon the magnitude of resource allocated and upon the particular activity.

Our basic assumptions will be:

(1) (a) The returns from different activities can be measured in a common unit.
   (b) The return from any activity is independent of the allocations to the other activities.
   (c) The total return can be obtained as the sum of the individual returns.

In economic terms, the utility of the entire allocation process can be calculated by adding together the utilities of the individual activities.

The fundamental problem is that of dividing our resources so as to maximize the total return. This simple mathematical model of an allocation process furnishes useful information in a number of situations.

3. Construction of a Mathematical Model

Let us now formulate the foregoing optimization problem as a precise mathematical question. The number of different activities will be designated by N and enumerated in a fixed order, 1, 2, . . . , N. When we say that there are two activities under consideration, we shall mean that activities 1 and 2 are available; when five activities are designated, we shall mean activities 1, 2, 3, 4, 5, and so on. The way in which the activities are enumerated is unimportant, but once decided, must be adhered to thereafter.

4

Associated with each activity is a *utility function*. This function measures the dependence of the return from this activity upon the quantity of the resource allocated. If x_i denotes the quantity of resources assigned to the ith activity, we let $g_i(x_i)$ denote the return from the ith activity. The utility function $g_i(x_i)$ is shown in Fig. 1. The shape of this curve is a consequence of two important economic conditions. The first is that small allocations lead to essentially zero returns and the second is the saturation

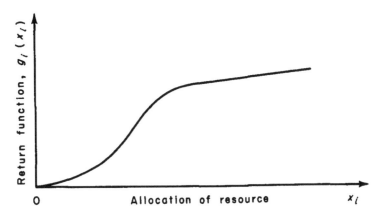

Figure 1

effect of large allocations, the "law of diminishing returns." As mentioned above, x_i and $g_i(x_i)$ will often be in different units.

The assumptions concerning independence of the activities and additivity of the associated utilities leads to the expression

(1) $$R(x_1, x_2, \ldots, x_N) = g_1(x_1) + g_2(x_2) + \cdots + g_N(x_N)$$

for the total utility of the allocation process.

The maximization problem arises from the fact that we have only a limited quantity of resources available. Calling this quantity x, we are led to a *constraint* of the form

(2) $$x_1 + x_2 + \cdots + x_N = x,$$

with $x_i \geq 0$. We wish then to maximize the function $R(x_1, x_2, \ldots, x_N)$ over all x_i subject to the foregoing constraints.

4. Discussion

Let us point out in passing that one of the major difficulties encountered in any study of economic, industrial, or military processes is that of determining the individual and collective utility functions. In many situations we neither know the precise form of the functions involved, nor even precisely what quantities should be maximized. This is particularly the case in processes involving human beings.

In many investigations of this nature, simulation processes play useful roles.

5. Calculus

Calculus can frequently be used to solve optimization problems of this type. Using a Lagrange multiplier,[1] λ, we form the auxiliary function

$$(1) \qquad S(x_1, x_2, \ldots, x_N) = g_1(x_1) + g_2(x_2) + \cdots + g_N(x_N) \\ - \lambda(x_1 + x_2 + \cdots + x_N),$$

and set the partial derivatives equal to zero. We obtain in this way the equations

$$(2) \qquad g_i'(x_i) - \lambda = 0, \quad i = 1, 2, \ldots, N.$$

Solving for x_i in terms of λ, say $x_i = h_i(\lambda)$, we determine λ by means of the constraint relation of (3.2),

$$(3) \qquad h_1(\lambda) + h_2(\lambda) + \cdots + h_N(\lambda) = x.$$

This is the usual pattern for determining the maximum of R.

For example, if we wish to minimize the function

$$(4) \qquad R = a_1 x_1{}^2 + a_2 x_2{}^2 + \cdots + a_N x_N{}^2, \quad a_i > 0,$$

over non-negative x_i satisfying (3.2), the relations of (2) become

$$(5) \qquad x_i = \frac{\lambda}{2a_i}.$$

The equation of (3) then reads

$$(6) \qquad \sum_{i=1}^{N} \frac{\lambda}{2a_i} = x,$$

whence

$$(7) \qquad \lambda = \frac{x}{\left[\sum_{i=1}^{N} \frac{1}{2a_i} \right]},$$

$$x_i = \frac{(x/2a_i)}{\left[\sum_{i=1}^{N} \frac{1}{2a_i} \right]}.$$

The minimum value is thus

$$(8) \qquad \frac{x^2}{\left[\sum_{i=1}^{N} \frac{1}{a_i} \right]}.$$

[1] Considerable attention will be given to Lagrange multipliers in Chapter II, §13 et seq. where we shall combine this classical technique with dynamic programming.

This is the type of problem and solution appearing in the textbooks on advanced calculus. Unfortunately, the problems that arise in applications of any significance are usually less amenable to routine techniques and require more sophisticated analysis.

It is rather amusing to point out that most of the examples used to illustrate the power of calculus, such as that given above, do not require calculus at all and may, more efficiently and more rigorously, be resolved by means of the much more elementary theory of inequalities.

6. Difficulties

Let us now examine in some detail the principal difficulties that arise when we attempt to apply the foregoing method to the allocation problem described in §2 and §3.

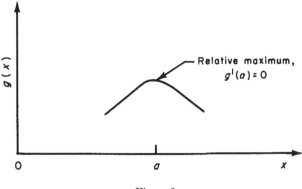

Figure 2

A. Relative Extrema. The observation that the slope of the tangent to a curve is equal to zero at a relative maximum or a relative minimum permits us to use calculus in the solution of optimization problems (see Fig. 2).

A corresponding result holds for functions of several variables, replacing the phrase "tangent to a curve" by "tangent plane to a surface."

Unfortunately the vanishing of the derivative is a necessary but not sufficient condition for an internal extremum. Not only is the derivative equal to zero at relative maxima and relative minima, but it also can be zero at points which are not relative extrema, such as horizontal points of inflection.

Consider, for example, the curve appearing in Fig. 3. The derivative, $g'(x)$, will vanish at the points b_1 and b_2, relative maxima, at the points a_1 and a_2, relative minima, and at point c_1 which is a horizontal point of inflection.

7

This difficulty, which is in the nuisance class in dealing with functions of one variable, becomes an almost insuperable barrier to the successful use of calculus in multidimensional maximization problems. This is particularly the case when the number of independent variables is large.

Consider, for example, the problem of maximizing the function $S(x_1, x_2, \ldots, x_N)$, appearing in (5.1), when each function $g_i(x)$ has the form given in Fig. 1. In this case, each of the equations of (5.2) can have two roots. Since it is not clear a priori which root corresponds to the

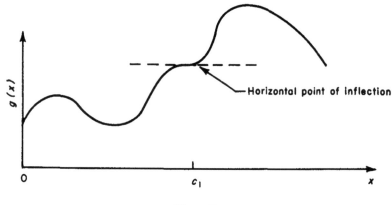

Figure 3

absolute maximum, we must try all combinations of values. This procedure requires an evaluation of 2^N cases. If $N = 10$, this number is 1024, a not unreasonable quantity; if $N = 20$, this number is slightly in excess of 10^6, a number which commands a certain respect.

With utility functions of still more complex nature, far larger sets of possibilities will occur. This is not only a theoretical embarrassment, but what is worse, a computational roadblock.

B. Constraints. In what has preceded we have applied the method of calculus in a routine fashion without paying attention to the fact that in many situations we actually seek a maximum over a finite region. Setting derivatives equal to zero yields internal extrema, as noted above, but it in general does not indicate extrema which are situated on the boundary of the region of variation. Consider, for example, a function of one variable $g(x)$ which has the form of Fig. 4. The derivative $g'(x)$ is equal to zero at a_1 and b_1, relative minima and maxima respectively, but not at $x = 0$, the point at which $g(x)$ assumes its absolute maximum over $[0, x_0]$.

This phenomenon is distressingly common in the study of economic and engineering control processes in which constraints such as

(1) $$a_i \leq x_i \leq b_i$$

8

are natural and sensible. In problems involving the maximization of functions of many variables, a combination of all of the possibilities resulting from relative extrema, stationary points of more complex nature and end-point values results in a prohibitive enumeration of cases.

It is important to realize that in optimization problems that reduce to combinatorial problems requiring a search over a number of cases, the number of cases usually increases in an exponential fashion, or worse, with the increase in dimension. If, for example, the total number of cases is 2^N,

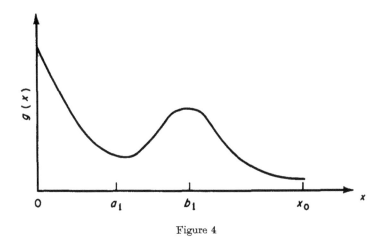

Figure 4

we do not double the time required when we go from N to $2N$, rather we completely change the order of magnitude. We discuss this in detail in §15.

Again, this multiplication of times may be merely a nuisance. To spend 100 minutes in calculation rather than 10 minutes is a matter of no consequence if the answer is of any importance. To be required, however, to devote 100 hours to a computational solution rather than 10 hours, may mean the difference between continuing a significant line of research or giving it up in favor of a more feasible investigation. Today, more than ever before in the history of science, theoretical formulation goes hand-in-hand with computational feasibility.

C. Maximization over Discrete Sets. The tool of calculus is directed at the optimization problem which involves continuous variation of the independent variables. Generally it is reasonable to take this type of variation as an approximation to the actual situation. In some cases, however, the accuracy of the solution is seriously affected by this smoothing. An extreme case is that where each variable takes only two distinct values, 0 or 1.

In a number of cases, by means of one artifice or another, continuous variation can be introduced. In the main, optimization over discrete sets of values requires new tools. At the present time, many significant classes of problems are far outside our reach.

D. *Nondifferentiable Functions.* We know that there exist continuous functions defined over an interval which possess no derivative at any point of the interval. We do not, of course, expect to encounter any functions of this nature in the course of a physical investigation. Whenever we appear to conjure up these frightening apparitions, a closer study generally reveals

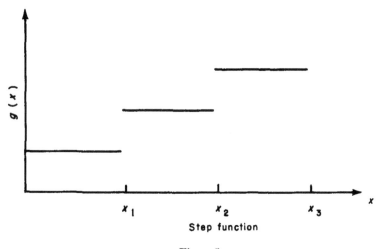

Step function

Figure 5

that certain unphysical assumptions have introduced these "pathological" functions.

We can, however, expect to meet functions possessing various minor inconveniences and handicaps, such as discontinuities at a finite set of points, or one-sided derivatives. Step functions are the simplest example of functions of this nature, serving as such useful approximations of smoother but far more complicated functions; see Fig. 5.

Another interesting and helpful class of functions is the set of polygonal functions generated by expressions of the following form (see Fig. 6):

(2) $$g(x) = \max (a_1x + b_1, a_2x + b_2, \ldots, a_kx + b_k).$$

In dealing with functions of this type, we can take derivatives, provided that we know the interval of interest. If this fact is unknown, we encounter many of the unpleasant features of the combinatorial search problem already mentioned. Quite often the position of the singularities is an essential part of the solution.

E. *Linearity.* At the opposite end of the difficulty spectrum are the problems in which all the functions appearing are linear. All derivatives exist in this case and yield little information, since we know a priori that the extrema are situated at boundary points of the region of variation. The theory of linear inequalities, with its offshoot, linear programming, is specifically designed to treat the question of maximizing a linear form

$$(3) \qquad\qquad L_N = \sum_{i=1}^{N} c_i x_i,$$

over all x_i subject to the constraints $x_i \geq 0$ and

$$(4) \qquad\qquad \sum_{j=1}^{N} a_{ij} x_j \leq b_i, \qquad i = 1, 2, \ldots, M.$$

It is, however, an all-purpose tool, which pays little attention to the underlying structure of the process under investigation. We can expect

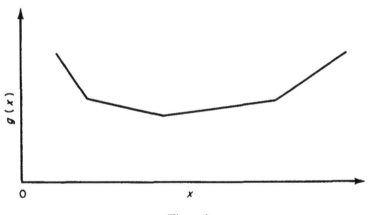

Figure 6

then in specific situations to devise much more efficient techniques for the solutions of the associated optimization problems, and this is indeed the case.

F. Stability. As we have pointed out above, calculus is based upon continuous variation of the independent variables. It follows that the results obtained in this way are very sensitive to local variations and therefore to small errors.

Consider two functions $g(x)$ and $h(x)$ shown in Figs. 7 and 8; the first is an idealized mathematical function and the second a "physical" function. The meaning of Fig. 8 is the following. If $h(x)$ is determined as a result of measurement or calculation, its value at any particular point x is not a number $h(x)$; rather, it has a distribution of values.

Consequently, although we may be willing to assign a value to $h(x)$ with a high probability of accuracy, we should be quite reluctant to assign a direction at any particular point. It follows that we do not wish to rely upon optimization techniques which require differentiation.

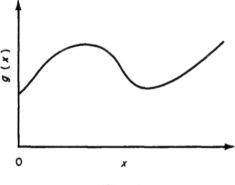

Figure 7

More specifically we wish to use a technique which guarantees that the error in the answer is no worse than the errors in the initial data. This is what we mean by *stability*.

The study of the stability of computational algorithms is one of the fundamental activities of the modern theory of numerical analysis. It is a

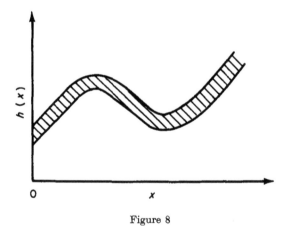

Figure 8

very difficult area, made more difficult by the fact that it is not generally realized as yet that the computational stability is intimately bound up with the original mathematical formulation of the physical process. Consequently, many numerical investigations are extraordinarily complicated by physically insignificant details of the original mathematical model.

7. Conclusion

The foregoing discussion leads us to the conclusion that powerful and versatile as calculus is, it is not uniformly successful in the treatment of optimization problems. In some cases it is completely inapplicable, and in other cases its uncritical use can lead to incorrect results. If we wish to guarantee a numerical solution to the simple allocation problem posed above, we must introduce some new mathematical methods.

8. Sensitivity Analysis

How should we measure the utility of a computational scheme? One approach is the following. If we are required to perform the same type of calculation repeatedly for different values of the basic parameters, can we use the information gained from one computation to aid in the following computation, or must we start each computation over again from the ground up? If an entirely new computation must be made for each set of parameters, it becomes extremely expensive to obtain all the desired information.

All of this is intimately related to the concept of a *sensitivity analysis*. It is generally true that in an investigation of a physical system, we are not content with the determination of the optimal behavior of the system for any single set of parameter values. Rather, we wish to allow the parameters to vary over a critical range of values, and then to observe how the optimal policy is affected by these changes. It is by observing the change in the structure of these policies as the parameters change that we gain the most vital information.

This idea holds uniformly in the intellectual realm and accounts for the success of Comparative Anatomy, Comparative Philology, Comparative Religion, and so on.

9. Dynamic Programming

These ideas are made explicit in the theory of dynamic programming. We shall start with a discussion of some simple problems in order to illustrate both the conceptual and computational aspects as clearly as possible.

As will be demonstrated, the functional equation technique overcomes all of the difficulties cited above—at least as far as one-dimensional allocation processes are concerned. Why difficulties arise in the treatment of more complicated processes, what these difficulties are, and what can be done to circumvent them will be the concern of subsequent chapters.

We may as well encourage the reader now with the frank admission that we by no means completely overcome or circumvent all the difficulties that arise and that there are thus ample opportunities for research in the application of these new techniques.

10. Functional Equations

To treat the particular problem of maximizing the function

$$(1) \qquad R(x_1, x_2, \ldots, x_N) = g_1(x_1) + g_2(x_2) + \cdots + g_N(x_N)$$

over the region $x_i \geq 0$, $\sum_{i=1}^{N} x_i = x$, we imbed it within a family of allocation processes. In place of considering a particular quantity of resources and a fixed number of activities, we consider the entire family of such problems in which x may assume any positive value and N may assume any integer value.

What seems at first sight to be a static process we artificially imbue with a time-like property by permitting, and indeed requiring, the allocations to be made one at a time. First a quantity of resources is assigned to the Nth activity, then to the $(N-1)$th activity, and so on. Viewed in this fashion, we have a *dynamic* allocation process.

Now to the analytic treatment! Since the maximum of $R(x_1, x_2, \ldots, x_N)$ over the designated region depends upon x and N, we make this dependence specific by introducing the sequence of functions $\{f_N(x)\}$ defined for $N = 1, 2, \ldots, x \geq 0$, as follows:

$$(2) \qquad f_N(x) = \max_{\{x_i\}} R(x_1, x_2, \ldots, x_N),$$

where $x_i \geq 0$, $\sum_{i=1}^{N} x_i = x$, as above.

The function $f_N(x)$ is then the optimal return from an allocation of the quantity of resources x to N activities. In two particular cases, the elements of the sequence $\{f_N(x)\}$ assume particularly simple values. It is clear that

$$(3) \qquad f_N(0) = 0, \quad N = 1, 2, \ldots,$$

provided that $g_i(0) = 0$ for each i, a sensible assumption, and also clear that

$$(4) \qquad f_1(x) = g_1(x),$$

for $x \geq 0$.

To obtain a recurrence relation connecting $f_N(x)$ and $f_{N-1}(x)$ for arbitrary N and x, we proceed as follows. Let x_N, $0 \leq x_N \leq x$, be the allocation made to the Nth activity. Then, regardless of the precise value of x_N, we know that the remaining quantity of resources, $x - x_N$, will be used to obtain a maximum return from the remaining $(N-1)$ activities.

Since this optimal return for $N-1$ activities starting with quantity $x - x_N$ is, by definition, $f_{N-1}(x - x_N)$, we see that the initial allocation of x_N to the Nth activity results in a total return of

$$(5) \qquad g_N(x_N) + f_{N-1}(x - x_N)$$

from the N-activity process,

An optimal choice of x_N is obviously one which maximizes this function. We thus obtain the basic functional equation

(6) $$f_N(x) = \max_{0 \le x_N \le x} [g_N(x_N) + f_{N-1}(x - x_N)],$$

for $N = 2, 3, \ldots,$ $x \ge 0$, with $f_1(x)$ determined by (4).

11. The Principle of Optimality

We have applied a very general technique in deriving the foregoing relation. It is called:

The Principle of Optimality. An optimal policy has the property that whatever the initial state and initial decision are, the remaining decisions must constitute an optimal policy with regard to the state resulting from the first decision.

All of our subsequent work will be based upon the application of this simple property of multistage decision processes. In this particular case, the property is readily established by a combination of induction and proof by contradiction.

12. A Direct Derivation

For those who may at this stage mistrust the optimality principle, let us present the following derivation of (10.6). Observing that

(1) $$\max_{\substack{x_1 + x_2 + \cdots + x_N = x \\ x_i \ge 0}} = \max_{0 \le x_N \le x} \left[\max_{\substack{x_1 + x_2 + \cdots + x_{N-1} = x - x_N \\ x_i \ge 0}} \right],$$

we can write

(2) $$f_N(x) = \max_{\substack{x_1 + x_2 + \cdots + x_N = x \\ x_i \ge 0}} [g_N(x_N) + g_{N-1}(x_{N-1}) + \cdots + g_1(x_1)]$$

$$= \max_{0 \le x_N \le x} \left[\max_{\substack{x_1 + x_2 + \cdots + x_{N-1} = x - x_N \\ x_i \ge 0}} (g_N(x_N) + g_{N-1}(x_{N-1}) + \cdots + g_1(x_1)) \right]$$

$$= \max_{0 \le x_N \le x} \left[g_N(x_N) + \max_{\substack{x_1 + x_2 + \cdots + x_{N-1} = x - x_N \\ x_i \ge 0}} (g_{N-1}(x_{N-1}) + \cdots + g_1(x_1)) \right]$$

$$= \max_{0 \le x_N \le x} [g_N(x_N) + f_{N-1}(x - x_N)],$$

the desired result.

13. Discussion

The recurrence relation of (10.6) yields a theoretical method for obtaining the sequence $\{f_N(x)\}$ inductively, once $f_1(x)$ is known. We see that $f_1(x)$ determines $f_2(x)$, that $f_2(x)$ leads to an evaluation of $f_3(x)$, and so on. The major problem we must face squarely is that of assessing the feasibility of new method; then we must ascertain whether or not it overcomes the difficulties encountered by the traditional techniques.

As we shall demonstrate, the method is quick and efficient. By means of examples we shall illustrate its efficacy. We can thus assert on the basis of some experience that the technique of dynamic programming yields a simple, quick and accurate solution to the general problem posed in §3.

14. Computational Scheme

Let us now examine carefully the way in which the recurrence relation of (10.6) can be used to determine the sequence $\{f_N(x)\}$ computationally. Although initially we shall discuss quite naive and direct techniques, subsequently we shall present some more sophisticated techniques.

Since we have renounced calculus and thus, in effect, analytic representations, we must first clearly understand what is meant by the statements that we are given the functions $g_i(x)$, $i = 1, 2, \ldots$, and that we are computing the elements of the sequence $\{f_N(x)\}$.

By a function defined over $x \geq 0$, such as $g_i(x)$ or $f_i(x)$, we shall mean the set of values assumed as x assumes all non-negative values—the usual definition. It is clearly impossible to tabulate *all* values of a function, or even any very large finite set of values. Consequently, we must use some type of interpolation scheme which permits us to recreate a general value from a few carefully chosen values.

There is very little sophistication involved in the choice of the values which we will tabulate to represent the function. Experience, memory requirements, accuracy requirements, and cost in time play major roles in the selection of the method used. Initially, we shall consider a simple and direct idea. Subsequently, we shall discuss a more advanced method.

To represent the entire set of values of $f_N(x)$ in the interval $[0, x_0]$, let us use the values assumed at the finite grid of values

$$(1) \qquad x = 0, \Delta, 2\Delta, \ldots, R\Delta = x_0.$$

It is agreed then that each element of the sequence $\{f_N(x)\}$ will be evaluated and tabulated at each of these points and only at these points.

Values of $f_N(x)$ for x-values distinct from these grid points will be obtained by *interpolation*. The type of interpolation used will depend upon the accuracy required and upon the time required to furnish this accuracy. If

$$(2) \qquad k\Delta < x < (k + 1)\Delta,$$

the simplest approximate value of $f_N(x)$ is obtained by setting

$$(3) \qquad f_N(x) = f_N(k\Delta).$$

The next simplest approximation is furnished by a linear interpolation formula

(4) $\qquad f_N(x) = f_N(k\Delta) + (x - k\Delta)[f_N((k + 1)\Delta) - f_N(k\Delta)]/\Delta.$

If we wish, we can use more accurate interpolation formulas based upon polynomials of higher degree.

In the allocation problem posed above, it is particularly convenient to allow the allocation variable x_N to range over precisely the same set of grid points as that prescribed for x. Hence in the maximization process, x_N can assume only the values given in (1).

The maximization in (10.6) is performed by a direct enumeration of cases, and comparison of values with no dependence upon calculus. In subsequent chapters we shall discuss techniques which in some cases permit an enormous simplification in the search procedure and thus a great saving in computing time. At the moment we shall consider the general case in which the functions considered possess no special structure which can be utilized to facilitate the search.

Let us now discuss the steps in greater detail. When $N = 1$, the function $f_1(x)$ is determined immediately by the relation

(5) $\qquad\qquad\qquad f_1(x) = g_1(x).$

The set of values $\{f_1(k\Delta)\}$, $k = 0, 1, \ldots, R$, is at this point stored in the memory of the computer.[2] We are now ready to compute $f_2(x)$ by means of the relation of (10.6) for $N = 2$, namely

(6) $\qquad\qquad f_2(x) = \max_{0 \leq x_2 \leq x} [g_2(x_2) + f_1(x - x_2)],$

where x assumes only the values $0, \Delta, 2\Delta, \ldots, R\Delta$. Since no enumerative process can yield maximization over a continuous range of values, we must replace the interval $[0, x]$ by a discrete set of values. Consequently, the relation in (6) is replaced by the approximating relation

(7) $\qquad\qquad f_2(x) = \max_{[k=0, 1, \ldots, R]} [g_2(k\Delta) + f_1(x - k\Delta)].$

The function $g_2(x)$, in the form of the sequence $\{g_2(k\Delta)\}$, has been stored in the memory of the computer. To begin the maximization process, the computer evaluates $g_2(0) + f_1(x)$ and $g_2(\Delta) + f_1(x - \Delta)$ and then compares them, keeping the larger quantity. The value $g_2(2\Delta) + f_1(x - 2\Delta)$ is then computed and compared with the previously obtained larger quantity, with the larger of these quantities retained. This process now continues until k has traversed all of the allowable values. This process yields $f_2(x)$ for a particular value of x.

---

[2] Unless otherwise specified, "memory" will be synonymous with "fast memory."

In the course of this search process, the computer determines not only the value of $f_2(x)$ at the x-values $0, \Delta, \ldots, R\Delta$, but also the value, or values, of x_2 at which the maximum is obtained in (6). Let us for the moment assume that the absolute maximum is attained at only a single x-value. We shall discuss the general case below.

Since this unique value will depend upon x, let us denote it by the function $x_2(x)$. For each value of x, the computer will store $x_2(x)$ and $f_2(x)$.

The result is that after two stages of this process, we can exhibit a table of values that looks like Fig. 9.

x	$f_1(x)$	$x_1(x)$	$f_2(x)$	$x_2(x)$
0	—	—	—	—
Δ	—	—	—	—
2Δ	—	—	—	—
.				
.				
.				
$R\Delta$	—	—	—	—

Figure 9

In this case, $f_1(x) = g_1(x)$ and $x_1(x) = x$.

This table yields the solution to the two-stage maximization problem in the following sense. Given a particular value of x, we scan the table of values of $x_2(x)$ until we find the corresponding value of x_2. Once this value has been determined, we are reduced to the problem of determining the optimal allocation in a one-stage process with resources $x - x_2(x)$, for which the solution is trivial.

This search operation can, of course, be done by the computer itself. Continuing this process for N stages, the result is that we can obtain the solution either in the form of the foregoing table, or in the form of the choices of $x_N, x_{N-1}, \ldots, x_2, x_1$ associated with each value of x.

15. Nonuniqueness of Maximum

Numbers stored in the computer's memory are usually correct to ten or more significant decimal figures, depending upon what is desired. Consequently, it is extremely unlikely that two values of x_2 will ever yield exactly the same maximum value. Nevertheless, the actual decision process may possess several alternative optimal policies. In some cases, we want merely the maximum return and a particular optimal policy; in other cases, we very much want all optimal policies and we may prize these more highly than the maximum return itself.

18

Furthermore, approximate optimal policies which yield returns to within some such figure as one percent of the actual maximum may be as important as the solution and even be more important in furnishing simple approximations for more complex situations. These near-optimal policies may be readily obtained by requiring the computer to retain not only the maximum value and the value of the x_i's which yield it, but also the value of the x_i's which yield values within a certain neighborhood of the maximum. This increases the memory requirements, and the time involved, but generally not in any prohibitive fashion.

16. Dynamic Programming versus Direct Enumeration

Once the original continuous variational problem has been replaced by a discrete variational problem, we can think in terms of determining the maximum value by a sheer enumeration of cases. There is no particular elegance or appeal in such a method, but it may work where more sophisticated approaches fail. As far as hand computation is concerned, time and accuracy considerations usually rule out this method. Once a digital computer with its miraculous speed is available, enumerative methods assume a certain feasibility.

Let us consider some simple allocation processes and see what would be involved in a straightforward examination of all possibilities. To begin, consider a simple situation where each of the independent variables x_i can run over ten different values. The N-variables maximization process will then involve 10^N different sets of choices.

In this process, the total number of possibilities is actually considerably less, since a choice of x_N immediately restricts the possible ranges of the other x_i. Let us ignore this point for the moment. As we shall see, it will not change some of the basic conclusions.

For a ten-stage process, we will then have 10^{10} cases to examine. This may not seem to be a very large quantity, but a small amount of calculation gives some idea of its true magnitude. At the rate of examination of one set of x_i-values per millisecond, 10^7 seconds would be required. This is something more than 10^5 hours, and thus of the order of magnitude of ten years. This is an unreasonable amount of time to spend on the numerical solution of a problem which represents reality as crudely as the one we have posed.

Suppose that we wish to consider a slightly more complex problem in which there are twenty different activities. Arguing loosely, as above, assume that this involves 10^{20} different possibilities. Since this quantity is 10^{10} times as large as 10^{10}, we see that no matter how much we reduce the time of the search process, this exponential growth in the number of possibilities as the dimension of the process increases renders enumeration of cases impossible.

We see then why we can argue so freely about the total number of cases. If we allow 100 or 1000 choices for each variable, a change in the order of magnitude of the number of possibilities for a ten-stage allocation process by a factor of 10^{10} does not materially affect the validity of our argument.

So much for naive approaches to optimization problems. It must be realized that large-scale processes will require both electronic and mathematical resources for their solution.

How is it, nonetheless, that the technique of dynamic programming enables one to easily and quickly resolve problems of far more complex nature than the type described above? From the estimates given, we see that the answer must reside in the fact that application of the functional equation technique is equivalent to using a search process that is far more efficient than the brute force examination of all cases.

It is the *principle of optimality* that furnishes the key. This principle tells us that having chosen some initial x_N, we do not then examine *all* policies involving that particular choice of x_N, but rather only those policies which are optimal for an $N - 1$ stage process with resources $x - x_N$. In this magical way, we keep operations essentially additive rather than multiplicative. The time required for a twenty-stage process is now almost precisely twice the time required for a ten-stage process.

17. What Difficulties Have We Overcome?

In §6, we discussed the major difficulties in the path of the application of calculus methods to maximization problems. Let us now see to what extent the technique of dynamic programming removes these obstacles.

In the first place, it is clear by a simple inductive argument that the method always yields the absolute maximum, rather than relative maxima. Secondly, observe that constraints of the type we have so far introduced greatly simplify the problem rather than complicate it. Any restriction such as $a_i \leq x_i \leq b_i$ which restricts the number of possibilities at each stage simplifies the search process and so reduces the computing effort. In other words, the fewer available policies at each stage, the quicker the calculation.

Precisely the same comment applies to maximization problems over discrete sets. The smaller the number of allowable choices, the simpler the computation. The simplest problems will be those where each x_i can assume only a few values such as 0 or 1.

Since we are using only tabulated values of the functions involved, their precise analytic structure is of no interest to us. This means that peculiarities of derivatives of any order need not concern us at all, and linearity is not a handicap. Let us again, however, point out that when certain structural features such as convexity, concavity, monotonicity, and so on are present, they may be used very effectively to simplify the search process. Matters of this nature will be discussed variously in subsequent chapters.

Finally, we come to the question of *sensitivity analysis* raised in §8. Two essential parameters in allocation processes of the type we have been discussing are the quantity of resources available and the number of activities in which we can engage. Our solution, expressed by the two functions $f_N(x)$ and $x_N(x)$, is obtained directly as a function of these basic parameters.

Questions that naturally arise in the course of formulation and solution of allocation problems of the type we have been discussing are:

(a) How do the return and policy depend upon initial conditions?
(b) Using an optimal policy, what is the value of changing the initial state?
(c) What is the advantage of adding one more activity, or of carrying on the process for one more stage?

Unless one possesses a very simple explicit analytic solution, information of this type is quite difficult to obtain from the conventional formulation.

The dynamic programming formulation, however, automatically imbeds the original problem within a family of analogous problems in which the basic parameters x and N assume sets of values which permit us to respond to these fundamental questions. In the allocation process, for example, solutions are found for activities ranging in number from 1 to N, and for quantities of resources from 0 to x. Consequently, after the computational solution for an N-stage process has been obtained, we are in a position to determine the trade-off between the state variable, x, and number of stages, N, for an immense variety of sub-problems. Since the optimal return is given as a function of the fundamental parameters x and N, a sensitivity analysis automatically accompanies the solution.

It therefore follows that the method we have presented overcomes all of the obstacles we have described. Why it is that with all these advantages we do not have a routine solution to all types of allocation processes will be discussed below. It can safely be said that there is still great need for ingenuity, and that much fascinating research remains to be done before a large number of significant processes can be treated effectively.

In this chapter, we wish to consider some simple problems in detail so that by the time we attack the more difficult problems there will be no questions remaining as to the basic ideas.

18. Flow Chart for General Allocation Process

In the discussion of the reduction of problems from mathematical formulation to computer code, which will occupy a large portion of our subsequent attention, we shall make frequent reference to "flow charts."

These are diagrams resolving a computational process into its component parts and exhibiting these sections in sufficient detail to be easily programmed by someone who is not necessarily familiar with the original mathematical problem or technique. By following one of these charts one can deduce exactly how the problem is to be solved numerically; see Fig. 10.

Since the present example is introductory, we shall now explain the rationale of the various steps in considerable detail. Later flow charts will follow a similar pattern and will be assumed to be self-explanatory.

Step 1. The basic code will use the recurrence relation (10.6) to compute a tabular function $f_k(x)$ using $f_{k-1}(x)$. In order to include the initial step of the calculation—Equation (10.4) which yields $f_1(x)$ within the general procedure—we define $f_0(x)$ to be identically zero. We thereby avoid writing a separate routine for the determination of $f_1(x)$. In practice, the storing of zeros is accomplished by merely setting all memory to zero prior to loading the program deck. Then the region designated as $f_0(x)$ is automatically zero. We can now have the computer determine $f_1(x)$ using $f_0(x)$ in the same manner as it determines $f_k(x)$ from $f_{k-1}(x)$. While $f_1(x)$ could be computed more quickly using Equation (10.4) directly, the savings in space and programming time obtained in this way easily offset this consideration. The intuitive justification of $f_0(x)$ being zero is that there can be no return from no activities, regardless of the quantity of initial resources, x. In some other processes unallocated resources will have a value, and this value will be taken as $f_0(x)$.

Step 2. The index k will denote the number of activities that we are considering, as discussed above. Initially we shall consider a problem involving only one activity. The index k will be increased as the calculation progresses (see Step 16).

Step 3. We shall compute a table of values representing the function $f_1(x)$ at discrete points. The initial argument for which we compute $f_1(x)$ is $x = 0$. After computing and storing $f_1(0)$, we compute $f_1(\Delta)$, and then $f_1(2\Delta)$, and so on until the table is complete.

Step 4. The internal working location β will contain the "best return so far" as we test various policies seeking that which maximizes. Setting this cell initially to a large negative number (denoted by $-\infty$, but, of course, not actually infinite) we guarantee that the first policy decision tested will be accepted as the "best so far." As in Step 1, this is an artificial device introduced to avoid treating the first step of a process as a special case.

Step 5. We use $x_k(x)$ to denote our allocation decision given a quantity of initial resource x at stage k. Since, to begin with, $k = 1$ and $x = 0$, we test 0 as the initial candidate for $x_1(0)$.

Step 6. This is the body of the calculation. We have now specified the stage k; the resource x; and the allocation $x_k(x)$. Using the return function $g_k(x_k)$ and optimal $(k-1)$-stage return, $f_{k-1}(x - x_k)$, we compute the total

22

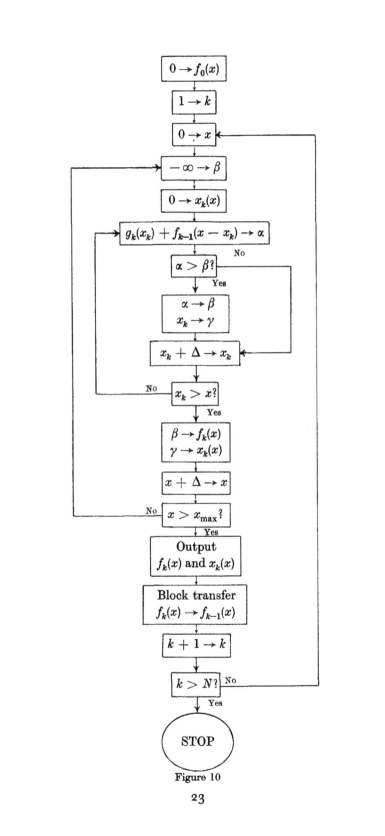

Figure 10

23

return associated with the given decision in the given state and store this number in location α.

Step 7. Compare this number with the number in cell β, the best return from all previously tested policies for this particular state and stage. If the current decision yields a smaller return than for some previous one, go on to Step 9. If this is the best allocation decision tested thus far, perform Step 8.

Step 8. Replace the contents of cell β by the greater return that has just been stored in cell α. (Where the meaning is obvious we shall not attempt to distinguish notationally between the name of a cell and its contents.) Cell γ is to contain the "best policy so far," hence we place x_k in cell γ.

Step 9. Having examined the effect of the allocation of quantity x_k to the kth activity, we now prepare to test the larger allocation $x_k + \Delta$.

Step 10. Is this allocation greater than our initial resource, x? If so, this decision is not permissible and we go on to Step 11. If $x_k + \Delta$ is an admissible decision, return to Step 6 to evaluate this decision, and to compare it with the previous decisions.

Step 11. We have now compared all decisions for a specific initial resource x. Store the maximum attainable return, $f_k(x)$, and the decision yielding this return, $x_k(x)$.

Step 12. Increase the initial resource by amount Δ. We now have a new problem involving the same number of activities but with a slightly greater initial resource.

Step 13. If the new problem involves a resource greater than that with which we began the N-activity problem, we clearly cannot reach the k-activity problem with that large a resource and we need not compute this result. We have thus completed the computation of the table of values of $f_k(x)$ and go on to Step 14. If this new x is admissible, we begin the entire maximization process over again by returning to Step 4.

Step 14. "Output" the results of the current step. These results, and in particular the policy decision as a function of resource, will be used later to determine the actual optimal policy and should therefore be stored on tape or punched into cards.

Step 15. The code refers to certain memory locations wherein it expects to find $f_{k-1}(x)$ and other locations where it stores the new table, $f_k(x)$. At this point in the code, we have completed the use of the old table to compute the new. From this point on, we shall use the newer table, $f_k(x)$, to compute $f_{k+1}(x)$. Since $f_k(x)$ is now to play the role of the "old" table, it is much easier and more efficient to relocate it in memory than to modify the addresses of all references to it in the code. This relocation of a whole section of memory is called a "block transfer" and is accomplished in a fraction of a second.

Step 16. We now proceed to the next activity and prepare to solve a family of problems involving $(k + 1)$ rather than k activities.

Step 17. If we have just computed $f_N(x)$, then $k = N$ and $k + 1 = N + 1$ is greater than N. We then stop and declare the calculation complete. If the new k is less than or equal to N, we return to Step 3.

This completes our analysis of the actual operations within the computer.

We shall often, throughout the text, refer to computing statistics based on our experience with the RAND Johnniac computer. Appendix 5 contains a description of the machine.

19. Numerical Results

In the preceding section we have described the actual steps of a computational solution of a general allocation problem. In the course of the solution, we have generated a series of N tables, each of which furnishes the total return and initial policy decision of a fixed number of activities for a range of initial resources.

The use of these tables to determine the solution of a particular problem (i.e., a specific number of activities and a given initial supply) constitutes a second and different phase of the calculation.

This technique is mentioned briefly in the latter part of §14. Here we wish to discuss the method in further detail and incidentally to provide a flow chart for the calculation.

The basic observation which guides us is the fact that the *last* table generates the optimal *initial* allocation for a process involving N activities, which in turn determines the initial supply for problems involving $(N - 1)$ activities. The next-to-last table then determines the optimal second decision.

In this manner, all output policy tables are processed in the reverse of the order in which they were calculated. The only information used at this stage is the set of policy tables $\{x_k(x)\}$. The return tables, $\{f_k(x)\}$, were vital to the generation of the sequence of results but are not necessary in this second phase of the computation.

A detailed explanation of the flow chart (Fig. 11) for this second phase of the solution of the allocation problem follows.

Step 1. We begin by considering a problem involving N activities with initial resource x_0. The cell k contains the variable denoting the number of activities, and x denotes the magnitude of the resource.

Step 2. Determine the policy associated with the above situation. This involves a table look-up using the $x_k(x)$-table generated in phase 1. The sequence $\{x_k(x)\}$ of these policy tables, generated in phase 1, is usually stored on tape or punched cards, and hence must be read into high-speed storage as needed. The appropriate policy is stored in cell α.

25

Step 3. The number of the activity considered and the policy are printed. This is one line of the final result table.

Step 4. The quantity of available resource is reduced by the amount allocated, α, and the number of activities under consideration is reduced by 1.

Step 5. If any activities are left, return to Step 2. This will involve reading a new policy table into memory. If no activities are left, stop.

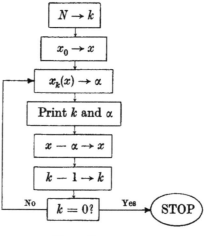

Figure 11

This completes the analysis of how a solution for a particular value of x and a particular value of N is obtained from the dynamic programming solution.

20. A Useful Device

Note that in the foregoing the results of phase 1 are processed in the opposite order from their generation. If tape storage is available, this is easily accomplished by the "read backwards" instructions.

For machines with limited secondary storage, stage-by-stage results must be punched onto cards. The following programming device, used successfully on the Johnniac, is then recommended.

Choose, or construct, a card format that can be inserted upside-down (i.e., face up, 12's edge first on most computers) without affecting the data read from the card. An example of such a card, part of a standard Johnniac input system, is shown in Fig. 12. When the card is turned over (with the address still on the left half of the card), the top rather than the bottom row is read first. However, after all twelve rows are read, the same data appears in the same cell as it would originally have appeared in if the card had been inserted conventionally. This allows us to place the entire output of phase 1 in the read unit, last card first (i.e., face up), achieving the desired inversion of ordering for phase 2.

If card storage is required, each of the N output tables of phase 1 should be preceded (i.e., followed when the order is reversed) by a transfer card, to be recognized as an end-of-table indicator in the course of phase 2 of the calculation.

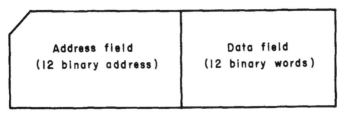

Figure 12

21. Stability

A number of very interesting mathematical questions arise in connection with the type of approximate technique we have employed. Not only are they of interest to the analyst, but they are of prime importance in connection with the successful application of these numerical methods. They are all related to the concept of *stability*.

We have taken an equation and replaced it by a related equation in which the maximization is performed over a smaller, finite range of values, and in which the functions involved are evaluated only at a finite set of points. Since both of these operations in general introduce inaccuracies, the question immediately arises as to the magnitude of the errors at each stage, and as to how these errors grow as the number of stages increases.

Problems of this general nature have been extensively investigated for ordinary and partial differential equations, but very little has been done as far as the functional equations of dynamic programming are concerned. We shall return briefly to this problem in Chapter XII.

22. A Cargo-loading Process

As a first illustration of the general techniques discussed in the preceding pages, let us consider a simple prototype of problems such as often arise in cargo-loading and packing.

Let us suppose that we are engaged in loading a vessel with a cargo composed of different types of items. Since these different items have various weights and values, the problem arises as to how to load a ship of limited capacity with the most valuable cargo. The reader, by means of a simple transformation of situations, will be able to conceive many questions of similar nature.

23. Mathematical Formulation

Let us assume that we have a vessel whose maximum capacity is z, and whose cargo is to consist of different quantities of N different items. Let

(1) v_i = the value of the ith type of item,
        w_i = the weight of the ith type of item,
        x_i = the number of items of type i which are taken.

Then the problem of determining the most valuable cargo is that of maximizing the linear form

$$(2) \qquad L_N(x) = \sum_{i=1}^{N} x_i v_i$$

subject to the constraints

$$(3) \quad (a) \qquad \sum_{i=1}^{N} x_i w_i \leq z,$$

$$(b) \qquad x_i = 0, 1, 2, \ldots .$$

The values $\{v_i, w_i\}$ are naturally taken to be positive.

24. Discussion

Were the constraint in (23.3b) merely that of $x_i \geq 0$, the problem would be a very simple one whose solution could be determined in the following way. Consider the ratios, v_i/w_i, $i = 1, 2, \ldots, N$, and let a be an index for which the ratio assumes its maximum value. Then, choose only items of type a, with the result that the maximum value of the cargo will be given by

$$(1) \qquad V_N = \frac{z v_a}{w_a} .$$

It is easy to show that in the presence of the constraint of (23.3b), which allows only a discrete set of values, the preceding solution is no longer generally valid. At the present time there exists no exact solution to the foregoing problem which has a simple analytic form.

Rounding of the solution for continuous variation to the nearest integer can be far from optimal. As an example, consider the following problem involving three items:

$$(2) \qquad z = \text{maximum capacity} = 100,$$
$$w_1 = 49, \qquad v_1 = 20,$$
$$w_2 = 50, \qquad v_2 = 75,$$
$$w_3 = 51, \qquad v_3 = 102.$$

Were it not for the integer constraint, we would load $100/51 \approx 1.96$ of item 3 with a value of $100 \cdot 102/51 = 200$. Since this is not allowed because of the integer constraint, we may be tempted to round 1.96 down to 1 and take one of item 1 to fill the remaining 49 lbs. The value of this policy is

122. Yet the true optimum, easily determined by a quick enumeration, is 150, and is obtained by loading two units of item 2.

In view of the obscure nature of the precise analytic solution, it is of interest to present a simple algorithm, based upon the previous treatment of general allocation processes, which rapidly yields the solution.

25. Recurrence Relations

Let us define, for $x \geq 0$ and $N = 1, 2, \ldots$, the function

$$(1) \qquad f_N(z) = \max_{\{x_i\}} L_N(x),$$

where the maximization is over the set of x_i-values determined by (23.3).

Then

$$(2) \qquad f_1(z) = \left[\frac{z}{w_1} \right] v_1,$$

where $[w]$ denotes the greatest integer less than or equal to w.

Proceeding as in §10, where the general recurrence relation may be found, we obtain the simple relation

$$(3) \qquad f_N(z) = \max_{x_N} \{ x_N v_N + f_{N-1}(z - x_N w_N) \},$$

with the maximization with respect to x_N is over the set of values

$$(4) \qquad x_N = 0, 1, 2, \ldots, \left[\frac{z}{w_N} \right].$$

In the next section, we shall present the actual routine used to compute both the sequence $\{ f_N(z) \}$ and the optimal choice of the x_i.

26. Discussion of Computational Procedure

The basic computation can be accomplished in about 25 instructions. Since this small section of code is traversed thousands of times, it might well be said that a millisecond saved is a second earned. In fact, except for the input-output times, the entire calculation time is essentially achieved by these 25 orders. They accomplish:

(1) The evaluation $v_i x_i$ of a choice to load x_i items of the ith type.
(2) Table look-up for the optimal return $f_{i-1}(z - w_i x_i)$ obtainable from items of the $(i - 1)$ previous types, with remaining capacity $(z - w_i x_i)$.
(3) The maximization of (1) + (2) over all x, where x is integral, non-negative, and not greater than the greatest integer in z/w_i.

The computation time depends on the distribution of the weights w_i. However, the following is a good estimate:

If

$N =$ number of types of items,

$z =$ maximum cargo weight allowable,

$\bar{w} =$ average w_i,

$.005 =$ time used in evaluating $x_i v_i + f_{n-1}(z - x_i w_i)$ for given values of x_i, v_i, w_i, z and f_{n-1},

then

$$\text{computing time} = .005 \left(\frac{z}{2\bar{w}}\right) zN \text{ seconds.}$$

Input-output time is a function of the quantity of information desired. Printing takes about one minute per item, while punching requires a similar amount of time. However, no printing except the final optimal policy is necessary, and the data punched can be stored on drum in a negligible time.

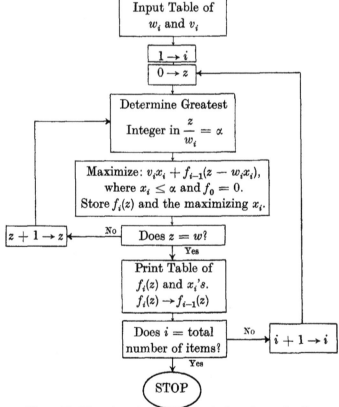

Figure 13. Flow chart for numerical solution of cargo-loading problem.

The flow chart used for the computer program is presented in Fig. 13. The numerical data for a small hypothetical problem involving eight types of items and a vessel of capacity 100 appears as Table 1. Table 2 then

TABLE 1

Type Number	Wt.	Value
1	20	72
2	18	60
3	14	40
4	12	27
5	10	20
6	16	50
7	22	85
8	24	96

TABLE 2

z	$f(z)$	No. of items of ith type loaded		
100	384	$x_8 = 4$		
95	373	$x_7 = 1$	$x_8 = 3$	
91	351	$x_7 = 3$	$x_8 = 1$	
89	340	$x_7 = 4$		
87	328	$x_3 = 1$	$x_8 = 3$	
85	317	$x_3 = 1$	$x_7 = 1$	$x_8 = 2$
83	308	$x_5 = 1$	$x_8 = 3$	
81	297	$x_5 = 1$	$x_7 = 1$	$x_8 = 2$

gives the optimal solution to this problem. In Fig. 14a we see how the optimal return depends upon the capacity of the vessel. Figure 14b shows how irregular the optimal policy may be when viewed as a function of the capacity variable. This is a result of the restriction to integer solutions.

Because improvements are being made so rapidly, the specific times given above will naturally appear rather "horse and buggyish" by the time this book appears in print. The reader familiar with the properties of the latest digital computer can readily make the necessary changes.

27. Reliability of Multicomponent Devices

Let us now turn to the discussion of a problem from an entirely different field. We choose this problem to illustrate an allocation process in which the criterion function is not additive.

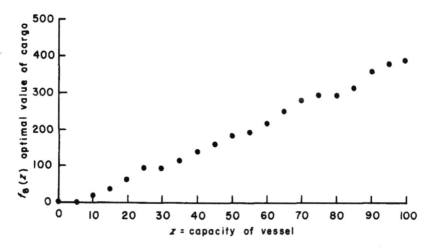

Figure 14a

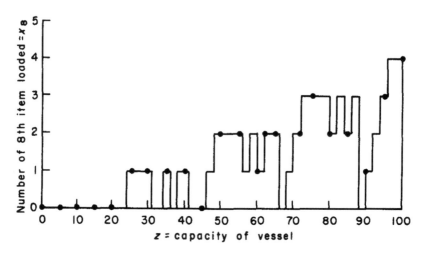

Figure 14b. Numerical solution of a small hypothetical cargo-loading
problem involving 8 types of items of given weights and values
and a vessel of capacity 100

One of the basic problems confronting the designer of any piece of
complex equipment is that of reliability. The situation is particularly
serious in connection with the manufacture of devices such as digital
computers. One malfunction in any of thousands of vacuum tubes,[3] one

---

[3] This rather antiquated and clumsy element by the standards of current trans-
istors and solid-state devices was used for want of better by the pioneers in the field
of digital computers.

mistake in any of millions of operations, and the entire calculation is useless.

In many cases, the problem can be posed as one involving the construction of a reliable device from less reliable components. A standard way of handling the problem is by means of duplication of components. For certain types of simple circuits, the resulting mathematical problem can be treated by means of dynamic programming techniques, as we shall see.

28. Reliability via Component Duplication

Let us suppose that the device we wish to construct can be considered to consist of a number of stages in series, as in the Fig. 15. The *reliability* of

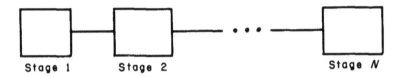

Figure 15

the device will be defined as the probability that it will operate successfully Considering the series arrangement, this overall probability can be taken to be the product of the probabilities of successful operation of the individual stages.

If the reliability is too small for efficient utilization, we can remedy the situation by putting duplicate components in parallel at each stage. The result is that the block diagram of the device looks like Fig. 16.

We assume that the units in each stage are supplied with switching circuits which have the property of shunting a new component into the circuit when the old one fails. The reliability of an individual stage now depends in a somewhat complicated way upon the number of components in parallel and the type of switching circuit employed.

Practical constraints of cost, weight, and size, and perhaps the additional errors introduced by switching circuits, prevent us from using an arbitrarily large number of duplicate components at each stage, and thus obtaining arbitrarily accurate operation.

The problem that we wish to consider here is that of determining the most efficient design utilizing duplication, taking into account constraints of the foregoing type.

We shall consider only a simple version at this time. A more complicated model will be considered in Chapter II in connection with two-dimensional allocation processes.

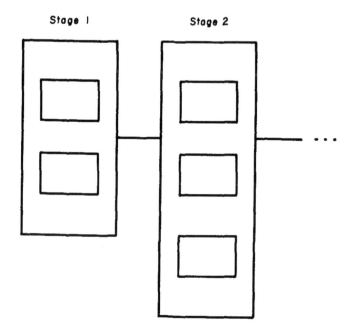

Figure 16

29. A Mathematical Model

For $j = 1, 2, \ldots, N$, let

(1) $\quad 1 + m_j =$ the number of duplicate components used at the jth stage,

where $m_j = 0, 1, 2, \ldots$, and

(2) $\quad \phi_j(m_j) =$ the probability of successful operation of the jth stage when $1 + m_j$ components are used at the jth stage.

We shall suppose that the functions $\phi_j(m_j)$ have been given to us and not concern ourselves with their specific forms.

The reliability of the N-stage device is then given by the expression

(3)
$$p_N = \prod_{j=1}^{N} \phi_j(m_j).$$

Let

(4) $\qquad c_j =$ the cost of a single component at the jth stage.

34

Agreeing to ignore the cost of the switching systems, the problem we wish to resolve is that of maximizing p_N subject to the constraints

(5) (a)
$$\sum_{j=1}^{N} m_j c_j \le c,$$

(b)
$$m_j = 0, 1, \ldots.$$

In writing the constraint equation immediately above, let us suppose that we have already taken account of the fact that at least one component must be used at each stage.

Let us denote by $f_N(c)$ the value of p_N, as defined in (3), obtained using an optimal policy. Then, for $N \ge 2$,

(6)
$$f_N(c) = \max_{m_N} \left[\phi_N(m_N) f_{N-1}(c - m_N c_N) \right],$$

where m_N is constrained by the relations

(7) (a)
$$m_N = 0, 1, \ldots,$$
(b)
$$m_N c_N \le c.$$

For $N = 1$, we have

(8)
$$f_1(c) = \phi([c/m_1]).$$

There will be a detailed discussion in §27 of Chapter II of the numerical solution of the case in which weight restrictions are also taken into account.

30. Parallel Operations

If two digital computers are available, or if one of the more modern computers allowing parallel operations to be performed simultaneously is obtainable, we can materially improve upon the foregoing procedures. Suppose that we wish to maximize the function

(1)
$$R_{2N} = g_1(x_1) + g_2(x_2) + \cdots + g_{2N}(x_{2N})$$

over the region

(2)
$$x_1 + x_2 + \cdots + x_N + x_{N+1} + \cdots + x_{2N} = x,$$

with $x_i \ge 0$. Set

(3)
$$x_1 + x_2 + \cdots + x_N = y_1,$$
$$x_{N+1} + x_{N+2} + \cdots + x_{2N} = y_2,$$

and

(4)
$$f_N(y_1) = \max_{x_1 + x_2 + \cdots + x_N = y_1} \left[g_1(x_1) + g_2(x_2) + \cdots + g_N(x_N) \right],$$

$$h_N(y_2) = \max_{x_{N+1} + \cdots + x_{2N} = y_2} \left[g_{N+1}(x_{N+1}) + \cdots + g_{2N}(x_{2N}) \right].$$

35

The functions $f_N(y_1)$ and $h_N(y_2)$ can be computed recursively by means of the algorithm discussed above. Once this has been done, we may determine the solution to the original maximization problem by maximizing $f_N(y_1) + h_N(y_2)$ over the set of values $y_1 + y_2 = x$, $y_1, y_2 \geq 0$.

The point is that $f_N(y_1)$ and $h_N(y_2)$ can be calculated simultaneously. This process can, of course, be continued further, dependent upon the parallel facilities available, memory capacity, and so on.

If we know in advance that the optimal choices of y_1 and y_2 will be in the neighborhood of $x/2$, we can reduce the memory requirements by approximately one-half, and also the total time required. This is an important point in connection with our later work where the problem of memory capacity becomes acute.

If the $g_i(x)$ are all identical, an enormous reduction in computing time can be effected if only the solutions of particular problems are desired. Thus, to calculate $f_{1024}(x)$, we would write

$$(5) \qquad f_{1024}(x) = \max_{0 \leq y \leq x} \left[f_{512}(y) + f_{512}(x - y) \right],$$

$$f_{512}(x) = \max_{0 \leq y \leq x} \left[f_{256}(y) + f_{256}(x - y) \right],$$

and so on. The function $f_{1024}(x)$ can thus be calculated in ten steps.

31. Conclusion

The purpose of this chapter has been to introduce the reader to the methodology of dynamic programming, including both computational and theoretical aspects. In order to acquaint the reader with the steps followed in the numerical treatment of optimization problems using the functional equation technique, we have considered two particular problems in detail—a general allocation problem and then a specific cargo-loading process.

The conclusion we can draw from this analysis is that the problem of determining the maximum of the function

$$(1) \qquad R(x_1, x_2, \ldots, x_N) = g_1(x_1) + g_2(x_2) + \cdots + g_N(x_N)$$

over the set of x_i-values determined by the relations

$$(2) \quad \text{(a)} \qquad \sum_{i=1}^{N} x_i = x, \qquad x_i \geq 0,$$

$$\text{(b)} \qquad a_i \leq x_i \leq b_i,$$

$$\text{(c)} \qquad x_i = x_{i0}, x_{i1}, \ldots, x_{ik},$$

is a routine problem readily and quickly resolved by means of the algorithm furnished by means of dynamic programming.

The computing time required is essentially directly proportional to N. For most problems of this type, the time for each stage will be of the order of seconds.

Comments and Bibliography

§1. For a detailed discussion of the foundations of the theory of dynamic programming, we refer the reader to

R. Bellman, *Dynamic Programming*, Princeton University Press, Princeton, New Jersey, 1957.

For a discussion of the connection between the ideas we employ here and classical ideas of iteration and continuous groups of transformations, see

R. Bellman, *Adaptive Control Processes: A Guided Tour*, Princeton University Press, Princeton, New Jersey, 1961.

For the economic and operations research background of the problems we treat in the first three chapters, we refer the reader to such books as

K. J. Arrow, S. Karlin, and H. Scarf, *Studies in the Mathematical Theory of Inventory and Production*, Stanford University Press, Stanford, California, 1958.

R. Dorfman, P. A. Samuelson and R. Solow, *Linear Programming and Economic Analysis*, McGraw-Hill Book Co., Inc., New York, 1958.

D. Gale, *The Theory of Linear Economic Models*, McGraw-Hill Book Co., Inc., New York, 1960.

C. C. Holt, F. Modigliani, J. Muth, H. Simon, *Planning Production, Inventories, and Work Force*, Prentice Hall, Inc., Englewood Cliffs, New Jersey, 1960.

R. A. Howard, *Dynamic Programming and Markov Processes*, John Wiley and Sons, New York, 1960.

S. Karlin, *Mathematical Methods and Theory in Games, Programming and Economics*, Addison-Wesley Publishing Co., Reading, Massachusetts, 1959.

A. Kaufman, *Méthodes et Modèles de la Recherche Opérationnelle*, Dunod, Paris, 1959.

P. Rosentiehl and A. Ghouila-Houri, *Les choix économiques, décisions séquentielles et simulation*, Dunod, Paris, 1960.

P. A. Samuelson, *Foundations of Economic Analysis*, Harvard University Press, Cambridge, Massachusetts, 1947.

§4. For some further discussion of the difficulties of model-building, see

R. Bellman, C. Clark, C. Craft, D. Malcolm, and F. Ricciardi, "On the construction of a multi-person, multi-stage business game," *Operations Research*, vol. 5, 1957, pp. 469–503.

R. Bellman and P. Brock, "On the concepts of a problem and problem-solving," *Amer. Math. Monthly*, vol. 67, 1960, pp. 119–134.

§10. For an analytic approach to this problem, see Appendix IV where some work of Bellman and Karush is discussed briefly. References to other work by Karush will be found there.

§14. This work on the computational solution of the functional equations obtained from the principle of optimality was begun by the authors in 1956 and continued in a series of in the main unpublished papers. A few, to which we shall refer occasionally, were published. The first of these was

R. Bellman and S. Dreyfus, "On the computational solution of dynamic programming processes—I: on a tactical air warfare model of Mengel," *Operations Research*, vol. 6, 1958, pp. 65–78.

§27. These results were given in

R. Bellman and S. Dreyfus, "Dynamic programming and the reliability of multicomponent devices," *Operations Research*, vol. 6, 1958, pp. 200–206.

For some further results and extensive references, see

A. J. Mayne, "Some reliability models of production lines with special reference to computer operation and scheduling," *Operations Research Quarterly*, vol. 11, 1960, pp. 16–30.

D. S. Stoller, *RAND Publications on Reliability*, The RAND Corporation Research Memorandum RM–2613, 1960.

A. A. Mullin, "The present theory of switching and some of its future trends," *Industrial Math. Jour.*, vol. 10, 1959–60, pp. 23–44.

S. K. Stein, "The mathematician as an explorer," *Scientific American*, May 1961, p. 148 ff.

The problems discussed in §22 and §27 can be regarded as linear and nonlinear programming problems with integral constraints. Although some work has been done in the direction of tackling these problems by means of the simplex technique by Gomory and others, many major problems remain. See

G. B. Dantzig, "On the significance of solving linear programming problems with some integer variables," *Econometrica*, vol. 28, 1960, pp. 30–44.

Other references may be found there.

Some other applications of the dynamic programming techniques which are of interest are

W. A. Hall and N. Buras, "The dynamic programming approach to water resources development," *Jour. Geophysical Research*, vol. 66, 1961, pp 517–520.

J. de Guenin, "Optimum distribution of effort: an extension of the Koopman basic theory," *Operations Research*, vol. 9, 1961, pp. 1–7.

The pages of *Management Science, Journal of the Society for Industrial and Applied Mathematics, Operations Research Quarterly, Journal of the Operations Research Society of America* and *Revue Française de Recherche Opérationnelle*, as well as the journals of the operations research societies of other countries, contain numerous other applications of dynamic programming.

For an interesting account of an allocation process using sophisticated mathematical tools, see

L. E. Dubins and E. H. Spanier, "How to cut a cake fairly," *Amer. Math. Monthly*, vol. 68, 1961 pp. 1–17.

CHAPTER II

Multidimensional Allocation Processes

1. Introduction

In the previous chapter, we computed the optimal policies for some allocation processes in which only one type of resource was available and where only one constraint was imposed upon the use of this resource. In this chapter we wish to consider a variety of more complex problems arising from more realistic descriptions of economic processes.

As we shall see, the basic formalism of dynamic programming carries over without a change. Nevertheless, formidable and challenging difficulties bar the way to the type of routine solution obtained in Chapter I. To overcome these difficulties, wholly or in part, we shall invoke a number of powerful and sophisticated mathematical devices.

One of the most powerful of these devices is the Lagrange multiplier. Although the multiplier is usually considered to be tightly bound to the calculus, we shall show that this is not necessarily its fundamental aspect. A synthesis of the functional equation technique of dynamic programming and the Lagrange multiplier yields a decomposition of complex processes into simpler parts. This decomposition enables us to resolve general classes of optimization problems.

We shall also use various forms of the method of successive approximations. One of the assets of the theory of dynamic programming is the fact that successive approximation techniques can be applied directly to the functional equations which arise, and also to the determination of optimal policies. The latter use is called "approximation in policy space." It always yields monotone approximation, if not monotone convergence. The classical application of successive approximations is to the functional equations, and does not necessarily involve monotone approximation.

As in the first chapter, we shall present many numerical results. Much of the work in this chapter is experimental, and thus in no sense to be considered final or optimal. As the reader will realize there is both room and need for considerable research in these areas.

2. Allocation Processes Involving Two Types of Resources

A straightforward extension of the simple allocation process described in §2 of Chapter I is a process requiring the allocation of two different types of resources into portions designated for a number of independent activities.

Let the two types of resources be present in quantities x and y respectively, and let x_i and y_i be respectively the quantities of these resources allocated to the ith activity. As before, we postulate the existence of a utility function

(1) $g_i(x_i, y_i) =$ the return from the ith activity due to respective allocations of x_i and y_i.

The mathematical problem that confronts us in the choice of a most efficient utilization of our resources is that of maximizing the function of $2N$ variables

(2) $$R(x_1, x_2, \ldots, x_N; \ y_1, y_2, \ldots, y_N) = \sum_{i=1}^{N} g_i(x_i, y_i)$$

subject to the constraints

(3) (a) $$\sum_{i=1}^{N} x_i = x, \qquad x_i \geq 0,$$

(b) $$\sum_{i=1}^{N} y_i = y, \qquad y_i \geq 0.$$

We call this a two-dimensional allocation process, regardless of the value of N, due to the fact that there are two different types of resources. As will be shown, the computational solution will be based on the calculation of sequences of functions of two variables.

3. Recurrence Relations

Following the same approach as in the previous chapter, we introduce the sequence of functions $\{f_N(x, y)\}$ defined by the relation

(1) $$f_N(x, y) = \max_{\{x, y\}} R_N(x_1, x_2, \ldots, x_N; y_1, y_2, \ldots, y_N),$$

where the maximization is over the region of x_i and y_i values defined by (2.3). The integer N takes the values $1, 2, \ldots$, while x and y assume all non-negative values.

For $N = 1$, we have

(2) $$f_1(x, y) = g_1(x, y),$$

and for $N \geq 2$, we have the recurrence relation

(3) $$f_N(x, y) = \max_{0 \leq x_N \leq x} \ \max_{0 \leq y_N \leq y} [g_N(x_N, y_N) + f_{N-1}(x - x_N, y - y_N)],$$

an immediate consequence of the principle of optimality. Before an investigation of the computational feasibility of this algorithm, let us discuss another way in which functions of two variables arise.

4. Allocation Processes Involving Two Types of Constraints

In many situations we encounter the problem of allocating one type of resource subject to two sets of constraints. The cargo-loading problem with both weight and size restrictions is an example of this. This type of problem may be considered to be a special case of the foregoing in which x_i and y_i are connected by a relation of the form $y_i = h_i(x_i)$.

The analytic problem that arises is then that of maximizing the function

$$(1) \qquad R(x_1, x_2, \ldots, x_N) = g_1(x_1) + g_2(x_2) + \cdots + g_N(x_N)$$

subject to the constraints

$$(2) \quad (a) \qquad\qquad x_i \geq 0,$$

$$(b) \qquad\qquad \sum_{i=1}^{N} a_i(x_i) \leq x,$$

$$(c) \qquad\qquad \sum_{i=1}^{N} b_i(x_i) \leq y.$$

Assuming that the $a_i(x_i)$ and $b_i(x_i)$ are monotone increasing functions of the x_i which approach ∞ as $x_i \to \infty$, we could, if we so desired, make a change of variable which replaces $a_i(x_i)$ by x_i, provided that the x_i are allowed to vary continuously. If x_i is restricted to discrete values such as $0, 1, 2, \ldots$, this change of variable is not possible.

Observe that we have replaced the equality constraints of (2.3) by inequalities. As far as both the process and the computational solution are concerned, this inessential change eliminates some delicate mathematical questions.

5. Recurrence Relations

Following the approach of §3, we set

$$(1) \qquad f_N(x, y) = \max_{\{x\}} [g_1(x_1) + g_2(x_2) + \cdots + g_N(x_N)],$$

where the variation is over the set of x_i determined by (4.2a, b, c). We have

$$(2) \qquad\qquad f_1(x, y) = \max_{\substack{a_1(x_1) \leq x \\ b_1(x_1) \leq y}} g_1(x_1),$$

and the general recurrence relation

$$(3) \qquad f_N(x, y) = \max_{\substack{a_N(x_N) \leq x \\ b_N(x_N) \leq y}} [g_N(x_N) + f_{N-1}(x - a_N(x_N), y - b_N(x_N))].$$

6. Computational Aspects

The recurrence relations we have derived in the preceding sections may be used to obtain the computational solution in very much the same way as described in Chapter I. Although *qualitatively* there is absolutely no difference in technique, we encounter startling *quantitative* differences, when we examine the operation from the standpoint of memory requirements, i.e., storage of data, and computing time. This theory furnishes a nice example of the classic precept that a major difference in magnitude can engender a significant difference in type.

In the computations discussed in Chapter I, we were required to store the values of a function of one variable, $f_N(x)$, at a set of grid-points $\{k\Delta\}$. Let us now approach (5.3) in the same spirit. To determine $f_N(x, y)$ in a region such as $0 \leq x \leq M$, $0 \leq y \leq M$, we agree as before to ask only for the values of the function at a set of lattice points, say the points $x = k\Delta$, $y = \ell\Delta$, $k, \ell = 0, 1, \ldots, M$.

Observe that whereas previously to specify $f_{N-1}(x)$ we needed a storage capacity of only $(M + 1)$ points, we now require a storage capacity of $(M + 1)^2$ values in order to retain knowledge of $f_{N-1}(x, y)$. If $0 \leq x \leq 1$, $0 \leq y \leq 1$ is our fundamental domain, and we take intervals of .01 in x and y; this means a change from about 10^2 points to essentially 10^4 points. Actually, the requirements are at least three times this, since we must simultaneously retain the function $f_{N-1}(x, y)$ and compute the new functions, the return function, $f_N(x, y)$ and the policy function $x_N = x_N(x, y)$.

7. Discussion

It is clear from the foregoing discussion that as we increase the number of resources and the number of constraints, we increase the number of independent variables appearing in the return function. Any attempt to tabulate these functions of many variables in a straightforward way is barred by the huge memory requirements which far outstrip contemporary machines, and, in some cases, any contemplated for the forseeable future.

Before describing various ways in which mathematical ingenuity can be used to resolve this dilemma of dimensionality—in carefully chosen cases—we shall present a routine application of the foregoing technique.

The problem treated below will also furnish an illustration of how processes involving random effects can be treated mathematically.

8. The Flyaway-kit Problem

Let us assume that we are about to dispatch a transport plane to an overseas base with a cargo which is to consist of replacement parts for airplanes. Suppose that there are N types of replaceable parts, and that each has associated with it a cost that is incurred if that part is needed at the base, but not available. Let us further assume that the demand for each part can be described by a known Poisson distribution. As constrained by the weight capacity W and space availability S of the cargo vehicle, how many items of each type shall be loaded so as to minimize the expected cost due to shortages at the base?

This problem is typical of many that are met in the study of inventory and equipment replacement processes.

9. Stochastic Aspects

Observe that for the first time we are treating a problem with stochastic features. As we shall see, once we have decided to minimize some *average* cost, the formulation along dynamic programming lines, and the computational solution follows the same path as before.

This is one of the great advantages of the techniques of dynamic programming—the fact that deterministic and stochastic processes can be treated by means of a unified approach.

10. Dynamic Programming Approach

Let w_i denote the weight of an item of the ith type, s_i its volume, λ_i the mean value of the Poisson distribution representing the demand for items of the ith type, and c_i the cost per item incurred in not fulfilling the demand. Finally, let us assume that we wish to determine the loading which minimizes the total expected cost, subject to the weight and volume restrictions.

If x_i is the number of items of the ith type which are loaded, and $P(z)$ represents the probability of a demand for z items, the expected cost due to unfulfilled demand will be

$$(1) \qquad c_1 \sum_{z=x_i+1}^{\infty} (z - x_i)P(z).$$

This expression is valid regardless of the form of the demand distribution. We carried out the calculation for a Poisson distribution since this type of distribution is frequently an excellent approximation to the observed distribution and its parameter, λ, can be estimated with comparative ease.

If $P(z, \lambda_i)$ denotes the Poisson distribution for the ith item, the total expected cost takes the form

$$(2) \qquad E_N = \sum_{i=1}^{N} c_i \left[\sum_{z=x_i+1}^{\infty} (z - x_i)P(z, \lambda_i) \right].$$

The mathematical problem is that of minimizing E_N over all x_i satisfying the three constraints

$$(3) \quad (a) \qquad x = 0, 1, 2, \ldots,$$

$$(b) \qquad \sum_{i=1}^{N} x_i w_i \leq w,$$

$$(c) \qquad \sum_{i=1}^{N} x_i s_i \leq s.$$

43

We now define $f_k(w', s')$ as the cost associated with an optimal choice of items of the first k types, where the cargo-vehicle weight restriction is w' and its space limitation is s', for w' and s' ranging over $0 \le w' \le w$ and $0 \le s' \le s$, respectively.

Our basic recurrence relation is then

(4)
$$f_k(w', s') = \min_{x_k} \left[c_k \sum_{z=x_k+1}^{\infty} (z - x_k)P(z, \lambda_k) \right.$$
$$\left. + f_{k-1}(w' - x_k w_k, s' - x_k s_k) \right],$$

where x_k is taken over the region

(5)
$$0 \le x_k \le \min \left\{ \left[\frac{w'}{w_k} \right], \left[\frac{s'}{s_k} \right] \right\}.$$

As before, $[x]$ denotes the greatest integer less than or equal to x.

In the next section we shall discuss the solution of equation (4) subject to the Restriction (3).

11. Computational Procedure

As each type of item is considered, the initial step is the computation of the expected cost of including 0, 1, 2, ... items of that type in the kit. The assumption of a Poisson distribution plus the knowledge of the mean number required and the cost per unit of shortage determines this table. As different policies are considered, the immediate or present cost of each choice is then determined by referring to the table. This cost is added to the expected cost associated with the remaining types of items in order to determine the total cost of the policy. The minimizing policy is then chosen on this basis.

Both a one-dimensional and a two-dimensional formulation were coded. In the first case, only a weight constraint was considered. Computation consumed about one minute per item when the total weight capacity was 1000 pounds and item weights were taken as small integers. In the two-dimensional formulation, both weight and size constraints were imposed. An upper limit of 30 on both weight and size resulted in a grid of 900 points and again consumed about one minute per item. The restriction to 30 values in each dimension means that small items must be grouped into larger units (as they generally are in practice) in order to make the computation meaningful. The bound of 30 could be increased to 100 with present memory capacity, with the result that the computation would take about ten times as long. The number "ten" is derived from the ratio $100^2/30^2$.

12. Example

In this section some typical results are displayed. They concern the optimal loading of ten types of items. Each type has four items as its expected demand, and an item of any type has 3 as its cost-of-shortage penalty value. The weight and size categories are shown in Table 1.

Sections of the table of values of the two-dimensional function $f_{10}(w, s)$, which represents the minimum cost associated with a kit of weight

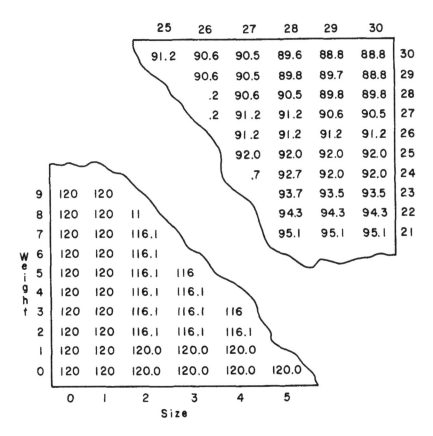

Figure 17. Sections of the table of values of the function $f_{10}(w, s)$, representing the minimum cost associated with a kit of weight w and size s in which 10 types of items are considered.

capacity w and size capacity s when all ten types of items are considered, are shown in Fig. 17.

Figure 18 displays the policy associated with the entries in Fig. 17. Each entry in Fig. 18 is the optimal number of items of type 10 loaded subject to weight and size restrictions (w, s).

Table 2 is a reproduction of the final printout resulting from phase 2 of the calculation (see §19 of Chapter I) and represents the solution of the problem.

45

TABLE 1

Weight and Size Categories

Item	Weight	Size
1	3	5
2	5	4
3	2	7
4	5	4
5	6	6
6	2	2
7	4	5
8	7	7
9	5	3
10	3	4

TABLE 2

Solution of Problem

Type of Item	Weight	Size	Number to Load	Cost	Cumulative Cost	Weight Left	Size Left
10	3	4	2	5.0	5.0	24	22
9	5	3	1	8.1	13.1	19	19
8	7	7	0	12.0	25.1	19	19
7	4	5	0	12.0	37.1	19	19
6	2	2	3	2.6	39.7	13	13
5	6	6	0	12.0	51.7	13	13
4	5	4	1	18.1	59.8	8	9
3	2	7	0	12.0	71.8	8	9
2	5	4	1	8.1	79.9	3	5
1	3	5	1	8.1	88.0	0	0

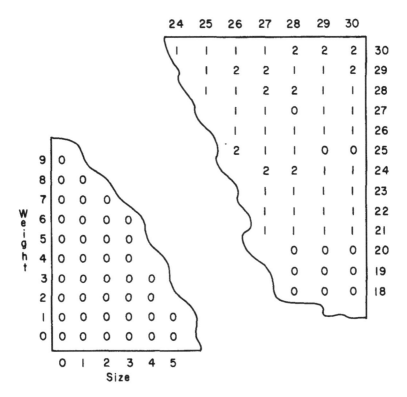

Figure 18. Sections of the table of values of the function $x_{10}(w, s)$, representing the optimal number of items of type 10 to be loaded subject to weight and size restrictions (w, s).

13. The Lagrange Multiplier

Let us begin our discussion of the Lagrange multiplier by describing the way in which it occurs in the treatment along the lines of calculus of maximization of a function of several variables subject to constraints. As we shall see subsequently, the technique has a simple geometric origin and thus is of much wider scope.

In order to keep the algebraic, analytic, and geometric details to a minimum, we shall consider the problem of maximizing the function of two variables, $F(x, y)$, over all x and y lying on the curve $G(x, y) = 0$. Proceeding formally, let (x_0, y_0) be an extremum point and set

$$(1) \qquad x = x_0 + \epsilon s, \qquad y = y_0 + \epsilon t,$$

where s and t are real parameters and ϵ is an infinitesimal. Then the condition that (x_0, y_0) be an extremum yields in the usual way the relation

$$(2) \qquad s\frac{\partial F}{\partial x_0} + t\frac{\partial F}{\partial y_0} = 0,$$

while the condition that (x, y) lie on $G(x, y) = 0$ similarly yields the relation

$$(3) \qquad s\frac{\partial G}{\partial x_0} + t\frac{\partial G}{\partial y_0} = 0.$$

Since these two equations are to hold for all s and t, we must have the determinantal relation

$$(4) \qquad \begin{vmatrix} \dfrac{\partial F}{\partial x_0} & \dfrac{\partial F}{\partial y_0} \\[2mm] \dfrac{\partial G}{\partial x_0} & \dfrac{\partial G}{\partial y_0} \end{vmatrix} = 0.$$

From this, it follows that there exists a quantity λ such that the two simultaneous equations

$$(5) \qquad \begin{aligned} \frac{\partial F}{\partial x_0} + \lambda\frac{\partial G}{\partial x_0} &= 0, \\[2mm] \frac{\partial F}{\partial y_0} + \lambda\frac{\partial G}{\partial y_0} &= 0 \end{aligned}$$

are valid.

These, however, are precisely the variational equations we would obtain if we looked for the extremum points of the new function

$$(6) \qquad H(x, y) = F(x, y) + \lambda G(x, y),$$

without regard to the constraint $G(x, y) = 0$. The parameter λ is the *Lagrange parameter*.

To determine λ, we can proceed as follows.[1] Using (5), we solve for x_0 and y_0 in terms of λ, and then use the relation $G(x, y) = 0$ to determine λ. In carefully chosen cases, this method works well. In general, we encounter many points of difficulty.

It is easy to see that the same method can be used to treat the problem of maximizing $F(x_1, x_2, \ldots, x_N)$ subject to a set of constraints $G_i(x_1, x_2, \ldots, x_N) = 0$, $i = 1, 2, \ldots, k$.

14. Geometric Origin

In the foregoing section, we have briefly sketched how the Lagrange multiplier arises in the study of variational problems involving continuous variation of the independent variables when the techniques of calculus are

---

[1] Compare the discussion of a specific example in §5 of Chapter I.

employed. Since we wish to treat more general variational questions, it is essential that we provide a broader setting for the Lagrange multiplier.

Consider the problem of determining the maximum of the function $F(x_1, x_2, \ldots, x_N)$ over all sets of x_i belonging to a set S and subject to a relation of the form $G(x_1, x_2, \ldots, x_N) \leq 1$. As the x_i range over all elements of S, let us compute the values of the quantities

(1)
$$y_1 = F(x_1, x_2, \ldots, x_N),$$
$$y_2 = G(x_1, x_2, \ldots, x_N).$$

This provides a *mapping* from a subset of the N-dimensional x_i-space to a part of the two-dimensional y_i-space. This region of the y_i-space is often

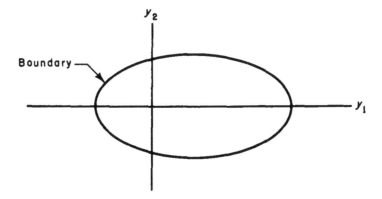

Figure 19

called a *moment space* for reasons which would take us too far afield to elaborate.

In order to motivate the simple geometric method we shall employ, let us assume that the set of points (y_1, y_2) traced out as $(x_1, x_2, \ldots, x_N)$ ranges over S constitute a convex set of points in the y_i-plane. We may think of this set as the interior of an oval, together with its boundary.

To solve the original maximization problem, requiring the extreme value of y_1 when y_2 has a fixed value (or is constrained above and below), we must determine points on the boundary of the oval (Fig. 19). Consequently, the original maximization problem is equivalent to the task of determining the boundary of the oval.

This boundary can be determined geometrically in the following fashion. Take a line in the (y_1, y_2)-plane, say

(2)
$$ay_1 + by_2 = k,$$

and move it parallel to itself until it is tangent to the oval. This geometric operation is clearly equivalent to the analytic operation of letting k vary over an interval of values.

The points of tangency are precisely the boundary points of the oval, as indicated in the Fig. 20.

If we repeat this operation with different values of a and b, which is to say, take lines in all directions, we sweep out the boundary. Observe that we are exploiting the basic *duality* of two-dimensional figures—the fact that a locus of points can be regarded as an envelope of tangents.

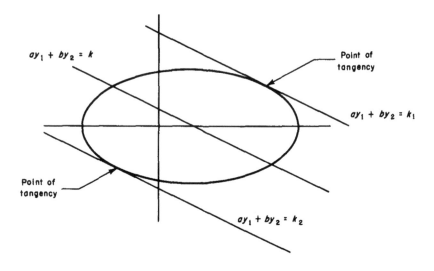

Figure 20

In order to use these ideas constructively to obtain specific analytic results, we note that the points of tangency are determined by the condition that the distance of the line $ay_1 + by_2 = k$ from the origin has an extreme value, a maximum or a minimum. For fixed a and b, the distance from the origin is proportional to k. Thus, maximization or minimization of the quantity k, which is given by

(3) $$ay_1 + by_2 = aF(x_1, x_2, \ldots, x_N) + bG(x_1, x_2, \ldots, x_N)$$

yields boundary points.

If a is not equal to zero, we can divide through and consider the equivalent problem of determining extreme values of the expression

(4) $$F(x_1, x_2, \ldots, x_N) + \lambda G(x_1, x_2, \ldots, x_N),$$

where we have set $b/a = \lambda$. We see then the true origin of the Lagrange multiplier, and how to extend these ideas to handle cases where several constraints occur.

Although the ideas are quite simple, some of the rigorous details rely upon a quite advanced concept, namely that of *convexity*. Consequently, we shall continue along our formal, intuitive road and refer the reader who is interested in proofs and extensions of these ideas to several references.

15. The Lagrange Multiplier as a Price

If we think of $F(x_1, x_2, \ldots, x_N)$ as representing our "return" due to an "allocation" $(x_1, x_2, \ldots, x_N)$ and $G(x_1, x_2, \ldots, x_N)$ as representing the "cost" of this allocation, then λ, or its negative, has the significance of a *price*. This intuitive concept can be made quite precise and is of fundamental import in mathematical economics in general and the theory of linear programming in particular.

In Appendix II at the end of the book, these ideas are discussed in some detail.

16. Use of the Lagrange Multiplier—I

Let us now return to the maximization problem discussed in §2 and see how we would treat it using a Lagrange multiplier. In place of the problem of maximizing

(1)

$$R(x_1, \ldots, x_N; \; y_1, \ldots, y_N) = g_1(x_1, y_1) + g_2(x_2, y_2) + \cdots + g_N(x_N, y_N)$$

subject to the constraints

(2) (a) $\qquad x_1 + x_2 + \cdots + x_N = x, \qquad x_i \geq 0,$

    (b) $\qquad y_1 + y_2 + \cdots + y_N = y, \qquad y_i \geq 0,$

we consider the problem of maximizing the modified function

(3) $\quad g_1(x_1, y_1) + g_2(x_2, y_2) + \cdots + g_N(x_N, y_N) - \lambda[y_1 + y_2 + \cdots + y_N]$

subject to the constraints

(4) (a) $\qquad x_1 + x_2 + \cdots + x_N = x, \qquad x_i \geq 0,$

    (b) $\qquad y_i \geq 0,$

where λ is for the moment a fixed parameter.

The maximization over y_i can be done independently of the maximization over the x_i. Let us then write

(5) $\qquad\qquad h_i(x_i, \lambda) = h_i(x_i) = \underset{y_i \geq 0}{\text{Max}} \; [g_i(x_i, y_i) - \lambda y_i].$

In order that this definition be meaningful, we want to assume that

(6) $\qquad\qquad g_i(x_i, y_i)/y_i \to 0 \quad \text{as} \quad y_i \to \infty.$

If this is not the case, this method fails. Since in applications this result is a consequence of the "law of diminishing returns," we shall continue on the assumption that it is valid.

The problem that remains is that of maximizing the function

$$(7) \qquad h_1(x_1) + h_2(x_2) + \cdots + h_N(x_N)$$

subject to the constraint of (4a). This problem is readily attacked by means of the functional equation technique presented in Chapter I.

The solution, $x_i(\lambda; x)$, $i = 1, 2, \ldots, N$, to this optimization problem will naturally depend upon λ, and the values of $y_i = y_i(\lambda)$ which will yield $h_i(x_i)$, following (5), will also depend upon λ. Let us then vary λ until the restriction

$$(8) \qquad \sum_{i=1}^{N} y_i(\lambda) = y$$

is met. We shall, several sections below, examine the validity and feasibility of this approach. Meanwhile, let us continue our discussion of the formal procedure.

17. Use of the Lagrange Multiplier—II

In the same general fashion, we consider the problem of maximizing the function

$$(1) \qquad g_1(x_1) + g_2(x_2) + \cdots + g_N(x_N)$$

subject to the constraints

$$(2) \quad \text{(a)} \qquad a_1 x_1 + a_2 x_2 + \cdots + a_N x_N \leq x,$$
$$\quad \text{(b)} \qquad b_1 x_1 + b_2 x_2 + \cdots + b_N x_N \leq y, \qquad x_i \geq 0.$$

Form the new function

$$(3) \quad g_1(x_1) + g_2(x_2) + \cdots + g_N(x_N) - \lambda[b_1 x_1 + b_2 x_2 + \cdots + b_N x_N]$$

and consider the problem of maximizing it over the region determined by (2a).

The associated recurrence relation has the form

$$(4) \qquad f_N(x) = \max_{0 \leq x_N \leq x/a_N} [g_N(x_N) - \lambda b_N x_N + f_{N-1}(x - a_N x_N)].$$

The solution, $x_i = x_i(\lambda; x)$, depends upon λ, as well as the return functions, $f_N(x)$.

The quantity λ is now varied until the constraint of (2b) is met.

18. Reduction in Dimensionality

Before proceeding to theoretical justification, and then some applications, let us emphasize the reduction in dimensionality that the method permits. Given the problem of determining the maximum of a function

(1) $$g_1(x_1) + g_2(x_2) + \cdots + g_N(x_N)$$

over the set of x_i-values determined by

(2) $$\sum_{j=1}^{N} a_{ij}x_j \le c_i, \quad i = 1, 2, \ldots, M,$$

and possibly by other relations such as

(3) (a) $\qquad\qquad x_i = 0, 1, 2, \ldots,$

(b) $\qquad\qquad a_i \le x_i \le b_i, \qquad i = 1, 2, \ldots, N,$

we can transform it into the problem of determining a sequence of functions of the M variables $c_1, c_2, \ldots, c_M$, $\{f_N(c_1, c_2, \ldots, c_M)\}$, by means of what should be by now a familiar algorithm.

Introducing k Lagrange multipliers, we can pose the new problem of maximizing

(4) $$\sum_{j=1}^{N} g_j(x_j) - \sum_{i=1}^{k} \lambda_i \left(\sum_{j=1}^{N} a_{ij}x_j \right)$$

subject to the $M - k$ constraints

(5) $$\sum_{j=1}^{N} a_{ij}x_j \le c_i, \qquad i = k+1, k+2, \ldots, M.$$

In this way, the problem is reduced to that of determining a sequence of functions of $M - k$ variables, together with a search over the k-dimensional λ-space. Since the restriction on the memory capacity of computers is such that it is preferable to carry out a large number of one-dimensional problems rather than one multidimensional problem, this procedure very often permits us to treat problems which would otherwise escape us.

Furthermore, it may turn out in many cases that a parametric representation of the solution in terms of the λ_i (the "prices") is just as valuable as one in terms of the resources, c_i.

What choice of k is made depends upon the individual problem, the type of computer available, and the time available for computation.

19. Equivalence of Variational Problems

We now wish to examine the connection between the variational problem in its original form and the problem arising from the use of the Lagrange multiplier. It is sufficient to consider a particular problem to indicate the type of result which can be obtained.

Consider the problem of maximizing

(1) $R(x_1, x_2, \ldots, x_N; y_1, y_2, \ldots, y_N) = g_1(x_1, y_1) + g_2(x_2, y_2) + \cdots$
$$+ g_N(x_N, y_N) - \lambda(y_1 + y_2 + \cdots + y_N)$$

subject to the constraints

(2) (a) $x_1 + x_2 + \cdots + x_N = x,$ $x_i \geq 0,$

   (b) $y_i \geq 0.$

Let $\bar{x}_i(\lambda),\ \bar{y}_i(\lambda),\ i = 1, 2, \ldots, N$ be a set of maximizing values in the foregoing problem. Then we wish to show that these values yield the maximum of the function

(3) $g_1(x_1, y_1) + g_2(x_2, y_2) + \cdots + g_N(x_N, y_N)$

subject to the constraints

(4) (a) $x_1 + x_2 + \cdots + x_N = x,$

   (b) $y_1 + y_2 + \cdots + y_N = y,$

where $y = \sum_{i=1}^{N} \bar{y}_i(\lambda).$

The point of this result is that no calculation is wasted. Every time that the problem in (1) is solved for a particular value of λ, we solve the original variational problem for a corresponding value of y.

The proof is by contradiction. Suppose there is a point $\{x_i,\ y_i\}$ satisfying the constraints of (4) such that

(5) $$\sum_{i=1}^{N} g_i(x_i, y_i) > \sum_{i=1}^{N} g_i(\bar{x}_i, \bar{y}_i).$$

Then, since

(6) $$\sum_{i=1}^{N} y_i = \sum_{i=1}^{N} \bar{y}_i = y,$$

we have

(7) $$\sum_{i=1}^{N} g_i(x_i, y_i) - \lambda \sum_{i=1}^{N} y_i > \sum_{i=1}^{N} g_i(\bar{x}_i, \bar{y}_i) - \lambda \sum_{i=1}^{N} \bar{y}_i.$$

This, however, contradicts the assumption that

$$[\bar{x}_1, \bar{x}_2, \ldots, \bar{x}_N;\ \bar{y}_1, \bar{y}_2, \ldots, \bar{y}_N]$$

is a maximizing set for the function in (1), subject to the constraints in (2).

20. Monotonicity in λ

What is to be expected in all applications is that as λ traverses the interval $[0, \infty]$, y will do likewise. To prove this rigorously, however, requires a certain amount of effort, and a number of assumptions concerning the functions $g_i(x, y)$.

Let us show quite simply that as λ increases from 0 to ∞, the quantity $\sum_{i=1}^{N} \bar{y}_i(\lambda)$ decreases monotonically. This is what we would expect from the fact that λ may be regarded as a *price*. Since, however, we are imposing very slight restrictions on the set of values that the x_i and y_i run over, we cannot expect to establish *strict* monotonicity of $\sum_{i=1}^{N} \bar{y}_i(\lambda)$, or continuity of this function as a function of λ.

Write

(1)
$$u_\lambda = \sum_{i=1}^{N} g_i(\bar{x}_i(\lambda), \bar{y}_i(\lambda)),$$

$$v_\lambda = \sum_{i=1}^{N} \bar{y}_i(\lambda).$$

Then, if $0 < \lambda < \mu$, by virtue of the maximization properties we have

(2)   (a)
$$u_\lambda - \lambda v_\lambda \geq u_\mu - \lambda v_\mu,$$

(b)
$$u_\mu - \mu v_\mu \geq u_\lambda - \mu v_\lambda.$$

Hence, using both sides of (2a) and (2b), we have

(3)
$$u_\lambda - \lambda v_\lambda \geq u_\mu - \mu v_\mu + (\mu - \lambda)v_\mu$$

$$\geq u_\lambda - \mu v_\lambda + (\mu - \lambda)v_\mu.$$

Thus,

(4)
$$(\mu - \lambda)v_\lambda \geq (\mu - \lambda)v_\mu.$$

Since $\mu - \lambda > 0$, we obtain the desired result,

(5)
$$v_\lambda \geq v_\mu.$$

Combining this result and (2a), we have

(6)
$$u_\lambda - \lambda v_\lambda \geq u_\mu - \lambda v_\mu,$$
$$\lambda v_\lambda \geq \qquad \lambda v_\mu,$$

whence

(7)
$$u_\lambda \geq u_\mu.$$

This monotonicity greatly simplifies the determination of a λ-value which yields a given y-value. The search techniques discussed in Chapter IV, or simpler methods, can now be used to reduce the time required to solve a specific problem.

21. Application of Lagrange Multiplier Technique— Advertising Campaign

Let us consider a situation in which an organization's production facilities are to be shared by a number of different product-divisions. Each of these divisions has submitted its estimate of potential earnings as a function of the manufacture of its particular item. In these circumstances, one might expect to encounter individual return curves having the familiar s-shape appearing in Fig. 21.

55

Let us use the equation

$$(1) \qquad r_i(x) = v_i[1 - (1 - e^{-a_i/x})^x]$$

to generate a utility function of the required shape.

Here, v_i represents the maximum potential profit that can be realized from the market, and a_i the level of competition for the market. A small allocation then yields little prospect for success, while a large allocation of production facilities produces a state of market saturation. A general discussion of the computation involved in the solution of such a problem, and numerical results, will be contained in a later section.

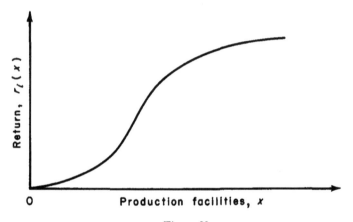

Figure 21

We have seen how a maximization problem involving one resource and N activities can be transformed into a sequence of one-dimensional maximization problems. Suppose, however, that it is required to allocate several resources, which means that the total payoff is now a function of several variables. We must then deal with a sequence of functions of several variables and face all the associated computational difficulties which come from this venture into the more realistic world.

As an example of such a process, let us suppose that the foregoing company with limited productive facilities also has limitations on its advertising budget. The return from a particular product-division is then taken to be

$$(2) \qquad r_i(x, y) = v_i[1 - (1 - e^{-a_i/(x+y)})^x],$$

where x is the production budget and y is the advertisement budget. This equation has the property that without production no profit can be realized regardless of advertising allocation, but in conjunction with production, the greater the advertising, the greater the return. Our problem is to choose x_i and y_i, $i = 1, 2, \ldots, N$, so as to maximize

$$(3) \qquad R_N = \sum_{i=1}^{N} r_i(x_i, y_i)$$

over all x_i and y_i, subject to the relations

$$(4) \qquad \sum_{i=1}^{N} x_i \leq x,$$

$$\sum_{i=1}^{N} y_i \leq y,$$

$$x_i, y_i \geq 0.$$

Setting $f_N(x, y)$ equal to the maximum of R_N over this region, the functional equation obtained in the usual way is

$$(5) \qquad f_N(x, y) = \max_{\substack{0 \leq x_N \leq x \\ 0 \leq y_N \leq y}} [r_N(x_N, y_N) + f_{N-1}(x - x_N, y - y_N)].$$

22. Lagrange Multiplier Technique

As we know, problems of large dimension easily exhaust computer memory facilities and consume excessive time. While the dynamic programming approach has the merit of effecting a considerable reduction in dimension, we have seen that we may still be overwhelmed by the difficulties attendant upon multidimensional functions. The use of Lagrange multipliers reduces these problems to a manageable size in many cases.

Let us assume that we have an infinite advertising budget, but that each dollar spent for publicity results in λ dollars being subtracted from our overall return. Clearly if λ is zero, we will advertise in an unlimited fashion, while if λ is large, we will not advertise at all. Each choice of λ will result in some value for $\sum_{i=1}^{N} \bar{y}_i$ between 0 and ∞ where $\bar{y}_i = \bar{y}_i(\lambda)$ is a maximizing choice of y_i. If we choose λ so that $\Sigma \bar{y}_i = y$, as indicated above, we have solved the original two-constraint problem without explicitly introducing the second constraint. Our functional equation associated with the problem of maximizing the function $\sum_{i=1}^{N} r_i(x_i, y_i) - \lambda \sum_{i=1}^{N} y_i$ is now

$$(1) \qquad f_N(x) = \max_{\substack{0 \leq x_N \leq x \\ 0 \leq y_N < \infty}} [r_N(x_N, y_N) - \lambda y_N + f_{N-1}(x - x_N)].$$

The original problem is solved by fixing λ, solving a one-dimensional problem, examining the resulting $\Sigma \bar{y}_i$, adjusting λ to make $\Sigma \bar{y}_i$ approximately equal to y, and resolving the problem for the new λ. We repeat this cycle until the λ yielding $\Sigma \bar{y}_i = \bar{y}$ is found. Usually three or four iterations suffice, depending on the effort expended in determining the new λ at each iteration. This iterative procedure will be discussed in some detail in a following section.

One two-dimensional calculation would yield the returns and optimal policies for all combinations of x and y less than or equal to their upper bounds. In the course of solution of this nature we calculate a function of two variables over a *region* of the (x, y) plane. Using the Lagrange multiplier approach we calculate a space curve giving the returns and policies over a *curve* in the (x, y) plane for each particular λ. Several values of λ result in several such curves in space. From these curves, one can deduce the general form of the complete function of two variables. This technique will be illustrated in the following section.

23. Computational Results

Consider first the one resource process discussed in §21—the simplest type of dynamic programming process. The coding of such a problem, for a high-speed digital computer such as the Johnniac or the IBM-709, can be accomplished in a couple of days using Fortran. The flow chart for this problem is shown in Fig. 22. To allocate 100 production units to 20 activities in an optimal fashion would require about ten minutes of computing time. Where activities 1 through 20 have values (potential markets) of 1 through 20 and competition is proportional to market values $(a_N = v_N = N)$, there results the allocation shown in Fig. 23. Figure 24 shows that though the individual return functions are highly nonlinear, the optimal return function for 20 activities is an almost linear function of total production.

Consider now the production-advertisement model of §§21–22. Using the Lagrange multipler technique, we have a one-dimensional problem for each fixed λ. We find that for $0 \leq x \leq 200$ the computation takes about two minutes per activity. Rewriting equation (22.1) as follows,

$$(1) \quad f_N(x) = \max_{0 \leq x_N \leq x} \left[\max_{0 \leq y_N < \infty} (r_N(x_N, y_N) - \lambda y_N) + f_{N-1}(x - x_N) \right]$$

$$= \max_{0 \leq x_N \leq x} [Q_N(x_N) + f_{N-1}(x - x_N)],$$

we see that we can first calculate the return as a function of x_N and then maximize over the x_N. We shall elaborate upon this idea in a following section. Computing time is greatly reduced by proving that if $\bar{y}_N > 0$ maximizes $r_N - \lambda y_N$ for $x = \bar{x}_N$, then for $x > \bar{x}_N$ the maximizing y_N will be less than $\bar{y}_N$.[2]

Figure 25 shows the function $r_N(x_N, y_N) - \lambda y_N$ as a function of y_N for two fixed values of x_N when $x_N^{(1)} > x_N^{(2)}$.

---

[2] This is a consequence of a knowledge of the structure of the function appearing in (21.2). See Appendix I by O. Gross.

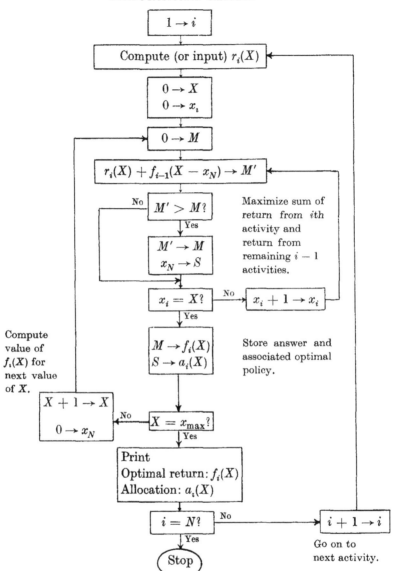

Figure 22. Flow Chart for 1-Dimensional Allocation Problem.

Activity	1 thru 9	10	11	12	13	14	15	16	17	18	19	20
Allocation	0	7	7	8	8	9	9	10	10	10	11	11

Figure 23. Optimal Allocation of 100 Units of Production to 20

Activities Where $R_i(X) = i[1 - (1 - e^{\frac{i}{x}})^x]$.

59

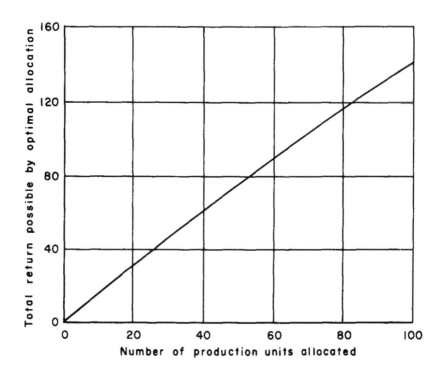

Figure 24. Total Return as Function of Production Units Where
Optimal Policy Is Used.

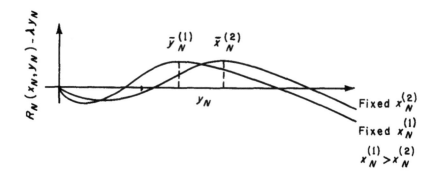

Figure 25. For Fixed λ, Optimal Allocation to Advertising, $\bar{y}_N$,
Decreases as Allocation to Production, x_N, Increases.

In Fig. 26 we see how the resulting sum Σy_i for optimal choice of y_i varies as x varies for fixed λ. The discontinuities result from the fact that, for small x, an increase in x results in the optimal allocation including an additional activity at nonzero level, and a jump in advertising.

Corresponding to each point of the curve in the (x, y) plane of the type shown in Fig. 26, the calculation also yields a return associated with the

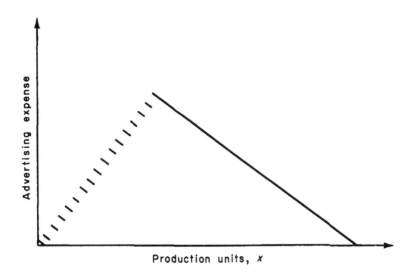

Figure 26. Amount Spent for Advertising, if Optimal Policy Is Used, for Fixed λ.

optimal allocation of x units to production and y to advertisement. After obtaining several such space curves using various values of λ, we can draw the contours of the two-dimensional return function (see Fig. 27).

We have analyzed a two-dimensional process. The straightforward two-dimensional dynamic programming approach for such an analysis would involve function tables of $200 \times 600 = 120,000$ values, and, consequently, hundreds of hours of computing time. The introduction of the Lagrange multiplier approach enables us to obtain equivalent results using 1000 memory cells in about three hours.

24. Calculation of the Lagrange Multiplier

If the Lagrange multiplier can be reasonably interpreted as a price, and if dollars are the dimension of both the objective function and the restricted variable, then the approximate value of the dimensionless multiplier can often be ascertained by cost analysis techniques prior to the digital computation.

In most cases, however, the multiplier, while still a "price," measures the trade-off between seemingly incommensurate quantities. For example, in a flyaway-kit problem with a size and weight restriction, elimination of the volume constraint via a Lagrange multiplier results in the multiplier having the unintuitive dimensions "outage cost/cubic foot." To determine

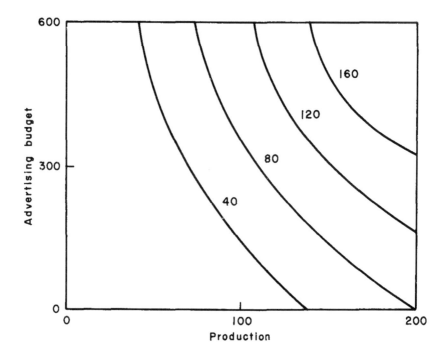

Figure 27. Total Return Obtained by Optimal Allocation of Various Combinations of Initial Resources.

a priori the numerical value of the multiplier, we would need to know how much an additional unit of volume would save in expected shortage cost using an optimal policy. Obviously, to know this would be to possess the answer to the original problem.

Our way out of this dilemma is an iterative one. We successively guess values of the multiplier until the correct one is found. The correct value is that price leading to an optimal solution exactly satisfying the constraint in question.

Let us consider the problem of actually carrying out this multiplier-guessing. Since each guess entails the complete solution of a dynamic programming problem, some effort can profitably be spent on an a priori analysis of this operation.

To give concreteness to our discussion, let us suppose that we wish to solve the problem of maximizing the function

(1) $$\sum_{i=1}^{N} g_i(x_i)$$

over all x_i subject to

(2)   (a) $$\sum_{i=1}^{N} x_i = x,$$

(b) $$\sum_{i=1}^{N} h_i(x_i) = h.$$

Suppose further that we have replaced the obvious two-dimensional formulation

(3) $$f_N(x, h) = \max_{x_N} [g(x_N) + f_{N-1}(x - x_N, h - h(x_N))],$$

where $0 \leq x_N \leq x$ and $h_N(x_N) \leq h$ by the one-dimensional version

(4) $$f_N(x) = \max_{x_N} [g_N(x_N) - \lambda h_N(x_N) + f_{N-1}(x - x_N)],$$

where λ is the Lagrange multiplier, to be determined such that

(5) $$\sum_{i=1}^{N} h_i(x_i) = h,$$

for the maximizing x_i.

No precise prescription exists for the first choice of λ. An intelligent guess must be made based on the individual problem.

In many cases, however, there does exist an efficient scheme for determining the third and subsequent guesses. This is based on an interpolation scheme. If two values of λ have been tried, one can calculate two sets of values for the following table:

(6)

λ	$f_N(x)$	Optimal Policy $\{x_i\}$	$\sum h(x_i)$

Then, knowing λ_0, λ_1, and the associated values of $\sum h(x_i)$, one can fit this data linearly to estimate λ_2 so that $\sum_i h_i(x_i)$ will equal h. The formula, denoting the values of $\sum_i h_i(x_i)$ by h_0 and h_1 respectively, is

(7) $$\lambda_2 = \frac{\lambda_1 - \lambda_0}{h_1 - h_0} (h - h_0) + \lambda_0.$$

If more than two values of λ have been evaluated, the two most recent can be used, or one can use a more accurate interpolation formula.

Since it is usually possible to determine a priori the result of choosing $\lambda = 0$, this information can be used without the time and expense of an actual computation. If this approach fails, it may be necessary to start the computation with two arbitrarily chosen values.

After using a linear fit to determine λ_2, it may be preferable to use all three results λ_0, λ_1, and λ_2 to determine λ_3 by fitting a cubic equation. Whether the additional programming required for this more sophisticated interpolation is warranted should be determined by the size of the problem.

Finally, it has been found to be efficient not to store policy information during the preliminary calculations designed to determine the correct value of the multiplier. After the correct multiplier has been determined, the calculation is redone, storing on tape or punched cards the optimal policy tables. Since output, even onto tape, slows a computer tremendously, the need for repeating one calculation does not render this scheme inefficient. During a calculation for a fixed λ, a table giving the optimal value of $\sum_{i=1}^{k} h_i(x_i) = H_k(x)$ is constructed as well as the usual $f_k(x)$ table. This table is a cumulative one and is updated at each stage by means of the relation

$$(8) \qquad\qquad H_k(x) = h_k(x_k) + H_{k-1}(x - x_k)$$

where the x_k is, as usual, the maximizing policy associated with the recurrence relation

$$(9) \qquad\qquad f_k(x) = \max_{x_k} \left[g_k(x_k) + f_{k-1}(x - x_k) \right].$$

It is important to observe that the $H_k(x)$ table is *one* continually updated table, similar to $f_k(x)$, not a set of tables such as the policy tables. In this way, it can always be stored in high-speed memory. The number $H_N(x)$ is the value of $\sum_{i=1}^{N} h_i(x_i)$ used to determine the next λ value. The quantity $f_N(x) + \lambda H_N(x)$ is the actual return from a policy optimal with respect to the Lagrange multiplier λ.

25. Pyramided Problems

The problem we have just discussed illustrates an interesting aspect of the formulation of dynamic programming problems. Due to the essential dependence of the difficulty of solution upon the number of state variables, some problems that appear extremely difficult from the conventional viewpoint are in fact simple from the dynamic programming standpoint, and conversely.

Two levels of policy decision problems are encountered in the above analysis. The apparently more simple problem is the optimal allocation of fixed production and advertising budgets to profit making. What would seem more difficult would be the problem of optimally dividing a fixed capital resource between production and advertising in such a way that the optimal use of the budgeted amounts maximizes profit. Yet this is not the case.

The first formulation leads to a two-dimensional problem. This problem was solved by the reduction to a sequence of one-dimensional problems by means of a Lagrange multiplier. Each one-dimensional problem solved was actually one of the second type above. By choosing the multiplier $\lambda = 0$ and maximizing over the range

$$(1) \qquad\qquad 0 \leq x_N + y_N \leq x,$$

we can attain a solution of the two-level allocation problem. The one-dimensional formulation would take the form

$$(2) \qquad f_N(x) = \max_{0 \leq x_N + y_N \leq x} [r_N(x_N, y_N) + f_{N-1}(x - x_N - y_N)].$$

This observation holds true for a wide range of *pyramided* problems. Later in this chapter we shall discuss transportation problems involving the optimal shipment from a few sources to many demand points. The reasoning we have applied above shows that the problem of optimal shipment from one manufacturing source to a few storage depots, and then to the demand points, leads to a problem which is of no greater difficulty.

26. Multidimensional Policy Space

In the advertising model we wished to maximize a function over two variables. In §23 we mentioned the fact that the equation

$$(1) \qquad f_N(x) = \max_{\substack{0 \leq x_N \leq x \\ 0 \leq y_N < \infty}} [r_N(x_N, y_N) - \lambda y_N + f_{N-1}(x - x_N)]$$

could be replaced by

$$(2) \qquad f_N(x) = \max_{0 \leq x_N \leq x} [Q_N(x_N) + f_{N-1}(x - x_N)],$$

where

$$(3) \qquad Q_N(x_N) = \max_{0 \leq y_N < \infty} (r_N(x_N, y_N) - \lambda y_N).$$

This viewpoint is of more than passing interest. If Equation (1) were programmed directly, for each value of x, all admissible pairs (x_N, y_N) would be evaluated, and as a result $r_N(x_N, y_N) - \lambda y_N$ would be *re-evaluated* for the same x_N and y_N many times. By first evaluating the function $Q_N(x_N)$, we avoid this needless duplication of effort.

This simplification comes about because the variable y_N appears only in the objective function and not in the argument of the function $f_{N-1}(x)$.

We will see this device used many times. It is of analytic as well as computational value in the warehousing problem of Chapter III.

27. The Reliability Problem

Let us now consider in more detail the reliability problem we have already discussed in §§27–28 of Chapter I. We shall suppose that if $1 + m_j$

components are used at the jth stage, then the probability of successful performance of this stage is given by the quantity $\phi_j(m_j)$, a known function.

We shall further suppose that we have two types of constraints, *cost* and *weight*. Let c_j be the cost of a single component at the jth stage, and w_j be its weight. The total weight and cost are then given by the expressions

(1)
$$C_N = \sum_{j=1}^{N} c_j m_j,$$

$$W_N = \sum_{j=1}^{N} w_j m_j.$$

The problem which we wish to investigate is that of maximizing the overall reliability

(2)
$$R_N = \prod_{j=1}^{N} \phi_j(m_j),$$

over all m_j subject to the constraints

(3) (a)
$$m_j = 0, 1, \ldots,$$

(b)
$$\sum_{j=1}^{N} c_j m_j \leq c,$$

(c)
$$\sum_{j=1}^{N} w_j m_j \leq w.$$

28. Introduction of Lagrange Multiplier

In order to avoid dealing with sequences of functions of two variables, we shall introduce a Lagrange multiplier. Consider the new problem of maximizing the expression

(1)
$$\left[\prod_{j=1}^{N} \phi_j(m_j) \right] e^{-\lambda \sum_{j=1}^{N} m_j w_j},$$

over all m_j satisfying only the first two constraints of (27.3). Setting $f_N(c)$ equal to this maximum value, where c is as in (27.3b), we have the recurrence relation

(2)
$$f_N(c) = \max_{0 \leq m_N \leq [c/c_N]} [\phi_N(m_N) e^{-\lambda m_N w_N} f_{N-1}(c - m_N c_N)],$$

$N = 2, 3, \ldots$, with

(3)
$$f_1(c) = \max_{0 \leq m_1 \leq [c/c_1]} [\phi_1(m_1) e^{-\lambda m_1 w_1}].$$

Once again, let us note that each m_i is constrained to assume only the values $0, 1, 2, \ldots$.

29. A Numerical Example

A numerical solution of problems of the foregoing species can be obtained quite easily. (A flow chart is given in §30.)

For illustrative purposes, consider a device containing five types of components whose costs, weights, and probabilities of successful operation are tabulated below:

Component Type	Cost	Weight	Probability of Success
1	5	8	0.90
2	4	9	0.75
3	9	6	0.65
4	7	7	0.80
5	7	8	0.85

We assume, as before, that one of each of these five types of components must be used. Furthermore, if m_j additional components of the jth type are used, the probability of successful operation of the jth stage is given by

$$(1) \qquad \phi_j(m_j) = 1 - (1 - p_j)^{m_j+1}.$$

With a total quantity of 100 units of cost and 104 units of weight, we wish to determine the number of components of each type that will maximize the overall probability of successful operation, given as above, by the expression

$$(2) \qquad \prod_{j=1}^{j=5} \phi_j(m_j).$$

Beginning with the equation

$$(3) \qquad f_1(c) = \max_{0 \le m_1 \le [c/c_1]} \phi_1(m_1)e^{-\lambda m_1 w_1},$$

we continue with the general relation

$$(4) \qquad f_i(c) = \max_{\{m_i\}} [\phi_i(m_i)e^{-\lambda m_i w_i} f_{i-1}(c - m_i c_i)],$$

for $i = 2, 3, \ldots$, where

$$(5) \qquad 0 \le m_i \le [c/c_i].$$

The quantity λ is to be determined so that $\sum_{i=1}^{i=5} m_i w_i = 104$.
    Starting with $\lambda = 0.001$, we obtain

$$(6) \qquad f_5(100) = \prod_{i=1}^{i=5} \phi_i(m_i) \exp(-\lambda m_i w_i) = 0.8882,$$

and the values $m_1 = 2$, $m_2 = 3$, $m_3 = 4$, $m_4 = 2$, $m_5 = 2$, with a total weight of $\sum_{i=1}^{i=5} m_i w_i = 97$. The probability of successful operation is $0.8882e^{97\lambda} = 0.977$.

We now decrease λ to .0008 so as to increase the total weight used. The results are

(7)
$$f_5(100) = 0.9063,$$

$$m_1 = 2, \quad m_2 = 3, \quad m_3 = 4, \quad m_4 = 3, \quad m_5 = 2,$$

$$\sum_{i=1}^{i=5} m_i w_i = 104.$$

The probability of successful operation is $(0.9063)e^{104\lambda} = 0.984$. This is the solution to the problem. The computer time consumed in the calculation was five minutes. It should be stressed that the same problem involving fifty types of items would require approximately fifty minutes, since the time required to solve the problem in this way is essentially proportional to the number of component types. The reason we do not say "directly proportional" lies in the search for the correct value of λ.

30. Flow Chart (See p. 69).

31. An Extension

Let us now consider a realistic variant of the foregoing problem. In place of assuming that our only freedom of action lies in the duplication of components, let us suppose that we have a choice of types of components to be used at each stage, say between those of type A and those of type B. Let $c_i(A)$, $w_i(A)$ denote the unit cost and weight for an A-type component at the ith stage, and $c_i(B)$, $w_i(B)$ the corresponding quantities for a B-type component. We could, if we so wished, allow combinations of types of items at each stage, without affecting the validity of the following treatment.

Given the overall restrictions on weight and cost, we wish as before to determine which type of component to use at each stage and in what quantity, so as to maximize the reliability of the device. Let

$$\phi_i(m_i; A), \quad \phi_i(m_i; B)$$

denote the reliability of the ith stage when m_i components of types A and B respectively are used in parallel.

As above, consider the sequence of functions $\{f_N(c, w)\}$ defined as the maximum reliability of an N-stage device subject to a cost constraint of c and a weight restraint of w. Then

(1)
$$f_1(c, w) = \max \left[\max_{m_1} \phi_1(m_1; A), \ \max_{m_1} \phi_1(m_1; B) \right]$$

where in the first expression we allow a range of choices

$$1 \le m_1 \le \min \{[c/c_1(A)], [w/w_1(A)]\},$$

and in the second a range

$$1 \le m_1 \le \min \{[c/c_1(B)], [w/w_1(B)]\}.$$

68

30. Flow Chart

Numerical Inputs:

c_{max} = initial amount of money
λ = Lagrange multiplier
N_{max} = number of items

Outputs: N tables:

   table of optimal probabilities
   table of optimal number of items
   table of cumulative weight

Input tables:

   Probabilities for each item
   cost of each item
   weight of each item
   maximum number of each item

$$1 \to f_0(c) \text{ for all } c$$

$$1 \to N$$

$$c_N \to c'$$
$$w_N \to w'$$
$$\bar{m}_N \to \bar{m}'$$

$$0 \to c$$

$$-\infty \to \beta$$

$$\min\left\{\bar{m}', \left[\frac{c}{c'}\right]\right\} \to m'$$

$$0 \to m$$

$$\phi_N(m)e^{-\lambda m w'}f_{N-1}(c - mc') \to \alpha$$

$\alpha > \beta$?   no

yes

$$\alpha \to \beta$$
$$m \to \gamma$$

$$m + 1 \to m$$

$m > m'$?   no

yes

$$\beta \to f_N(c)$$
$$\gamma \to m_N(c)$$

$$mw' + w_{N-1}(c - mc') \to w_N(c)$$

$$c + 1 \to c$$ no

$c > c_{max}$?   yes

Print Block Tr. f and w

$$N + 1 \to N$$

$N > N_{max}$?   no

yes

STOP

69

As in our previous discussion, m_1 can only assume the values 1, 2, ...

For general N we have the recurrence relation

(2)

$$f_N(c, w) = \max \left\{ \max_{m_N} \phi_N(m_N; \; A) f_{N-1}[c - c_N(A)m_N, \; w - w_N(A)m_N]; \right.$$

$$\left. \max_{m_N} \phi(m_N; \; B) f_{N-1}[c - c_N(B)m_N, \; w - w_N(B)m_N] \right\},$$

where, in the first expression,

(3) $$1 \leq m_N \leq \min \{[c/c_N(A)], [w/w_N(A)]\},$$

and in the second,

(4) $$1 \leq m_N \leq \min \{[c/c_N(B)], [w/w_N(B)]\}.$$

In both cases, m_N can assume only the integer values 1, 2, ...

Having seen how to formulate the two-dimensional version of the problem, we can now introduce a Lagrange multiplier and proceed as above to obtain a one-dimensional version.

32. The Hitchcock-Koopmans Transportation Problem

A problem of great significance in the field of mathematical economics is that of moving resources from one location to another in an efficient manner. This is one particular version of the general problem of determining the structure of an optimal network (where, of course, the notion of "optimality" depends upon the use to which the network will be put). Problems of this nature arise constantly in the economic, industrial, organizational, communication, electronic, and computing fields. Relatively few of these fascinating topological problems have been investigated in any detail, and none of them yield to simple analysis.

The model we shall discuss at some length is called the Hitchcock-Koopmans transportation model, although it was independently studied by Kantorovich and Aronszajn.

This particular problem has been extensively examined and analyzed with the result that there are now available a number of powerful and ingenious techniques due to Dantzig, Flood, Ford, and Fulkerson for treating some important special cases; references will be found at the end of the chapter. We shall consider here a different special case of the more general problem; a case which is particularly susceptible to the functional equation technique. With the restrictions we impose, we are able to treat more realistic processes which cannot be handled by the methods developed to treat linear models.

We shall show that the Hitchcock-Koopmans transportation problem can be conceived of as an allocation process to which functional equation techniques can be applied, directly and in conjunction with the Lagrange multiplier. From the pedagogical point of view, this process affords us an opportunity to introduce another powerful mathematical technique, the *method of successive approximations*. We shall discuss these matters in great detail below, together with the results of some numerical experimentation. Combining these two factota of analysis—functional equations and successive approximations—we can hope to tackle quite complex problems.

33. A Mathematical Model of a Transportation Process

Let us call the sites where the resources are located the *depots*, and the sites where the demands for these resources exist the *demand points*. Occasionally, and more picturesquely, these are called, respectively, *sources* and *sinks*.

We can envisage these as located in the following way:

Depots	Demand Points
$i = 1 : D_1$	$j = 1 : P_1$
$2 : D_2$	$2 : P_2$
.	.
.	.
.	.
$M : D_M$	$N : P_N$

although, of course, such neat arrangement is neither necessary, nor to be expected.

Although we shall formulate the process in general terms, we will be interested in treating only the case where either the number of depots or demand points is small. As long as one of these is small, the other number can be arbitrarily large without affecting the feasibility of solution. We shall further suppose that there is only one type of resource, and introduce the following data:

(1) x_i = the supply of this resource available at the ith depot,
     $i = 1, \ldots, M,$

  r_j = the demand for this resource at the jth demand point,
     $j = 1, \ldots, N.$

Assuming that the total supply is equal to the total demand, so that the problem is only one of distribution, we have the relation

(2)
$$\sum_i x_i = \sum_j r_j.$$

Although, as we shall see, the more general problem where supply exceeds demand can be treated by means of the same techniques, an important simplification results in this case of equality. This will be discussed in §37.

Let

(3) x_{ij} = the quantity of the resource sent from the ith depot to the jth demand point,

and let

(4) $g_{ij}(x_{ij})$ = the cost incurred by this operation.

The quantities x_{ij} are subject to three constraints:

(5) (a) *Non-negativity.*

(b) *Supply:* the total quantity shipped from any depot must equal the supply there.

(c) *Demand:* the total quantity shipped to any demand point must equal the demand at this site.

Observe that we are not allowing any *transshipment*, which is to say, we cannot ship from one depot to another and then to a demand point, or from one depot to a demand point and then to another demand point.

The foregoing verbal constraints yield the relations

(6) (a) $$x_{ij} \geq 0,$$

(b) $$\sum_{j=1}^{N} x_{ij} = x_i, \quad i = 1, 2, \ldots, M,$$

(c) $$\sum_{i=1}^{M} x_{ij} = r_j, \quad j = 1, 2, \ldots, N.$$

The problem that faces us is that of determining the quantities x_{ij} subject to the preceding constraints so as to minimize the total cost of transporting the resources

(7) $$C_{MN} = \sum_{i,j} g_{ij}(x_{ij}).$$

34. Discussion

This problem is obviously of great complexity unless we impose some further restrictions upon the form of the functions $g_{ij}(x)$, and even then, it is complicated if M and N are large. A case of particular interest, in itself and as a starting point for further investigations, is that in which the cost of shipping from any depot to any demand point is directly proportional to the quantity shipped, i.e.,

(1) $$g_{ij} = d_{ij} x_{ij}.$$

The coefficient d_{ij} may then be interpreted as a *distance*.

The minimization problem is then one within the domain of *linear programming*, and, as noted above, many elegant and rapid algorithms exist for its solution by hand and by digital computer.

These methods are, however, inapplicable if the cost functions are nonlinear, unless the functions $g_{ij}(x)$ possess certain simple structural properties which permit linear approximations to be made in one way or another, in an efficient manner.

35. Dynamic Programming Approach

Let us begin with a discussion of the case where there are two depots and an arbitrary number of demand points:

Depots	Demand Points
$D_1 : x_1$	$P_1 \quad : r_1$
	$P_2 \quad : r_2$
	.
$D_2 : x_2$	.
	.
	$P_{N-1} : r_{N-1}$
	$P_N \quad : r_N$

The key observation is that we can satisfy the demands one at a time beginning with the demand at P_N, following with the demand at P_{N-1}, and so on. As usual, we convert a static process into a dynamic process in order to apply the functional equation technique.

Let us then introduce the functions $f_N(x_1, x_2)$, defined for $N = 1, 2, \ldots$, $x_1, x_2 \geq 0$, by the description

(1) $f_N(x_1, x_2) =$ the cost incurred using an optimal policy starting with quantities x_1 and x_2 at the two depots, D_1 and D_2 respectively, and fixed requirements $r_1, r_2, \ldots, r_N$ at the N demand points, $P_1, P_2, \ldots, P_N$ respectively.

Supplying the demand at the Nth demand point first, we incur a cost of

(2) $$g_{1N}(x_{1N}) + g_{2N}(x_{2N}),$$

and reduce the stocks of resources to $x_1 - x_{1N}$ and $x_2 - x_{2N}$ at the two depots, D_1 and D_2. Using the principle of optimality, we obtain the recurrence relation

(3) $$f_N(x_1, x_2) = \min_{\{R_N\}} [g_{1N}(x_{1N}) + g_{2N}(x_{2N})$$
$$+ f_{N-1}(x_1 - x_{1N}, x_2 - x_{2N})],$$

73

for $N \geq 2$, where R_N is the two-dimensional region determined by the relations

(4)   (a) $$x_{1N} + x_{2N} = r_N,$$
     (b) $$0 \leq x_{1N} \leq x_1,$$
     (c) $$0 \leq x_{2N} \leq x_2.$$

For $N = 1$, we have

(5) $$f_1(x_1, x_2) = g_{11}(x_1) + g_{21}(x_2).$$

36. Discussion

It is clear that the same technique may be applied to handle the analogous problem involving any number of depots. However, as far as the computational solution is concerned, we encounter the usual dimensionality difficulties if $M \geq 3$.

In the following sections, we shall discuss a number of techniques which can be used to overcome this obstacle.

37. Reduction in Dimensionality

So far we have not used the additional bit of information that supply is equal to demand, which is to say that

(1) $$x_1 + x_2 = \sum_{i=1}^{N} r_i.$$

It follows that for a fixed set of requirements, the quantity x_2 is determined whenever x_1 is known. Consequently, we see that we may eliminate the state variable x_2 and write quite simply

(2) $$f_N(x_1, x_2) \equiv f_N(x_1).$$

The relation in (35.3) becomes

(3) $$f_N(x_1) = \min_{x_{1N}} [g_{1N}(x_{1N}) + g_{2N}(r_N - x_{1N}) + f_{N-1}(x_1 - x_{1N})],$$

where x_{1N} is constrained by the relations

(4)   (a) $$0 \leq x_1 - x_{1N},$$
     (b) $$0 \leq r_N - x_{1N} \leq \sum_{i=1}^{N} r_i - x_1.$$

The range of the variable x_1 in $f_N(x_1)$ is $[0, \sum_{i=1}^{N} r_i]$.

In the same fashion, the general problem involving M depots can be reduced to the computation of a sequence of functions of $M - 1$ variables. Hence, problems involving two depots are quite simple and those involving three depots still directly approachable; those involving four or more are dependent upon the use of special devices.

38. Increase in Grid Size

In connection with the foregoing remarks, let us note that one way to circumvent the dimensionality problem is to increase the grid size. In a problem involving two state variables, we can tolerate a range of one hundred different values for each variable, since this means a total of 10^4 grid points. Current machines (*circa* 1960) can treat problems with memory requirements of this order. It should be recalled that the effective dynamic programming memory is about one-third of the memory capacity of the computer due to the fact that we are simultaneously dealing with the "old" return function, $f_{N-1}(p)$, the "new" return function, $f_N(p)$, and the new policy function, $x_N(p)$. If there are several policy functions, the factor one-third must be further reduced.

On the other hand, if three state variables are present, a similar range for each variable would require a memory capable of handling 10^6 values, which is beyond present day capabilities. If, however, in place of one hundred different values of each variable, we employ twenty different values, involving only 8×10^3 values, then we have a problem still within our grasp. Hence we can always handle functions of more variables if we allow a smaller and cruder range for each variable.

Of course, we pay a price for this in the form of reduced accuracy. Subsequently, we shall discuss ways of overcoming this reduction in accuracy by using this approach in conjunction with the method of successive approximations.

39. Three Depots and a Lagrange Multiplier

As we have already observed, if there are three depots, we can treat the problem computationally in terms of sequences of functions of two variables. If, however, we introduce a Lagrange multiplier, we can further reduce the problem to that of computing a sequence of functions of one variable. Let us now examine the details.

Consider a three-depot problem in which there is a quantity x_1 at the first, and unlimited quantities at the second and third.

$$
\begin{array}{ll}
D_1 : x_1 & \qquad P_1 \quad : r_1 \\
D_2 : \infty & \qquad P_2 \quad : r_2 \\
D_3 : \infty & \qquad \cdot \\
& \qquad \cdot \\
& \qquad \cdot \\
& \qquad P_{N-1} : r_{N-1} \\
& \qquad P_N \quad : r_N
\end{array}
$$

We assume that shipping costs for the three sources to the various depots are as before, and that, in addition, for every unit shipped from D_2 we pay a quantity λ, and for every unit shipped from D_3 we pay a quantity 1.

In these circumstances, the total cost is given by the expression

$$
(1) \qquad \sum_{i=1}^{3} \sum_{j=1}^{N} g_{ij}(x_{ij}) + \lambda \sum_{j=1}^{N} x_{2j} + \sum_{j=1}^{N} x_{3j}.
$$

75

At first thought, the reader might imagine that two Lagrange multipliers should be used. The following argument shows that this is not necessary. Suppose that λ is varied until at the minimizing values of the x_{ij} we have $\sum_{j=1}^{N} x_{2j} = x_2$. Then, automatically we will have

$$(2) \qquad \sum_{j=1}^{N} x_{3j} = x_1 + x_2 - \sum_{j=1}^{N} r_j,$$

a fixed quantity, since supply is equal to demand. Hence, we could if we wished, eliminate the third term in (1) completely.

Let us set $f_N(x_1)$ equal to the minimum value of the function in (1), where the minimization is over the region

$$(3) \quad (a) \qquad \sum_{j=1}^{N} x_{1j} = x_1,$$

$$\quad (b) \qquad x_{1j}, x_{2j}, x_{3j} \geq 0.$$

To obtain a recurrence relation for f_N, we, as before, satisfy the demand at the Nth demand point first.

We then obtain the equation

$$(4) \qquad f_N(x_1) = \min_{R_N} [g_{1N}(x_{1N}) + g_{2N}(x_{2N}) + g_{3N}(x_{3N})$$
$$+ \lambda x_{2N} + x_{3N} + f_{N-1}(x_1 - x_{1N})],$$

where the R_N is the region determined by the relations

$$(5) \quad (a) \qquad x_{1N} + x_{2N} + x_{3N} = r_N,$$

$$\quad (b) \qquad 0 \leq x_{1N} \leq x_1,$$

$$\quad (c) \qquad x_{2N}, x_{3N} \geq 0.$$

The minimization over the variables x_{2N} and x_{3N} can be carried out explicitly, or computationally, in advance. Let

$$(6) \qquad g_N(x_{1N}; \lambda) = \min_{S_N} [g_{2N}(x_{2N}) + g_{3N}(x_{3N}) + \lambda x_{2N} + x_{3N}],$$

where S_N is the new region determined by

$$(7) \quad (a) \qquad x_{2N} + x_{3N} = r_N - x_{1N},$$

$$\quad (b) \qquad x_{2N}, x_{3N} \geq 0.$$

Then the recurrence relation of (4) becomes

$$(8) \quad f_N(x_1) = \min_{0 \leq x_{1N} \leq r_N} [g_{1N}(x_{1N}; \lambda) + g_N(x_{1N}; \lambda) + f_{N-1}(x_1 - x_{1N})].$$

The parameter λ is then varied between $-\infty$ and ∞ until the total quantity shipped from D_2 is x_2, the original resource level at D_2. The quantity taken from D_3 will then automatically be $x_3 = \sum_{j=1}^{N} r_j - x_1 - x_2$.

40. Example I—Two Depots, Ten Demand Points

As a first numerical example, let us assume quadratic costs plus a "set-up" cost for shipment from the two sources to the ten sinks. By a

EXAMPLE I—TWO DEPOTS, TEN DEMAND POINTS

"set-up" cost, we mean a cost which is independent of the quantity shipped, but which is not incurred if nothing is sent. The hypothetical cost and demand tables are shown below.

To Sink	From Depot 1			From Depot 2			Demand
	Set-up	x	x^2	Set-up	x	x^2	
1		1.0		2	3.1		10
2	1	2.0			4.1		25
3		3.0	.01		2.1		45
4		1.5			1.1	.1	15
5		2.5			2.6		5
6	10	5.0	—.01		3.0		15
7		3.0		5	1.0	.2	20
8		6.0			2.0		15
9	8	6.0	—.05		2.0		10
10		6.0			5.0	.01	20

This chart is to be interpreted in the following way. Each function $g_{ij}(x)$ has the form

$$(1) \qquad g_{ij}(x) = a_{ij}x + b_{ij}x^2 + c_{ij}(x),$$

where $c_{ij}(x)$ is what is often called a "set-up" cost, or "fixed charge," equal to zero if $x = 0$, and to a constant c_{ij} for $x > 0$.

The coefficient of x is found in the column under x, that of x^2 in the column under x^2, and the set-up coefficient under Set-up.

Thus, the cost of sending x from Depot 1 to Sink 3 is $.3x + .01x^2$; from Depot 1 to Sink 2, $1 + 2x$ if $x > 0$, 0 if $x = 0$.

Suppose that 100 units are to be shipped from Depot 1 and 80 from Depot 2. The optimal solution is shown below.

To Sink	From Depot 1	From Depot 2	Cost	Cum. Cost
1	10	0	10.00	10.00
2	25	0	51.00	61.00
3	5	40	99.25	160.25
4	15	0	22.50	182.75
5	5	0	12.50	195.25
6	0	15	45.00	240.25
7	20	0	60.00	300.25
8	0	15	30.00	330.25
9	0	10	20.00	350.25
10	20	0	120.00	470.25

This calculation consumed two minutes computing time and four minutes output time on the RAND Johnniac computer.

41. Flow Chart, Two Depots (See p. 79).

42. Example II—Three Depots, Ten Demand Points

To Example I, we add a third depot with the following shipment cost characteristics.

To Sink	Set-up	From Depot 3 x	x^2	Demand
1		7		25
2		3		40
3		9		60
4		1		30
5		1		20
6	5	2		30
7		4		35
8	6	3		30
9		5		25
10		6		40

155 additional units are placed at Depot 3 and the demands are increased to those shown above. Using the Lagrange multiplier technique, a choice of $\lambda = 2.0$ yields the desired result. The optimal solution follows.

To Sink	Depot 1	Depot 2	Depot 3	Cost	Cum. Cost
1	25	0	0	25.00	25.00
2	40	0	0	81.00	106.00
3	5	55	0	130.75	236.75
4	0	0	30	30.00	266.75
5	0	0	20	20.00	286.75
6	0	0	30	65.00	351.75
7	30	0	5	110.00	461.75
8	0	0	30	96.00	557.75
9	0	25	0	50.00	607.75
10	0	0	40	240.00	847.75

The calculation took seven minutes for each value of λ.

43. Successive Approximations

One way to overcome the dimensionality difficulties that beset us on every side is to invoke the aid of the most powerful of all tools of analysis, the method of successive approximations.

41. Flow Chart, Two Depots

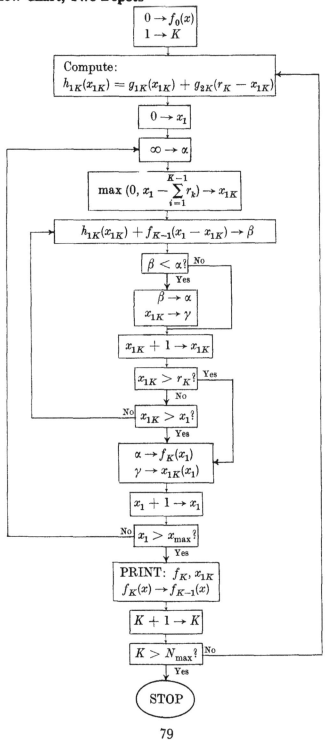

79

Abstractly, the method has the following outline. Given a functional equation, we guess a solution. If the initial guess is not the actual solution, we apply a correction, determined by the functional equation itself, and obtain in this way what we hope is a better guess at the solution. The process is continued until we either attain a solution, or come within prescribed limits of accuracy.

One way to employ this approach is the following. Let the given equation we wish to solve have the form

$$(1) \qquad T(u) = 0,$$

and let the equation $S(u) = v$ be easier to solve. Write the original equation in the form

$$(2) \qquad S(u) = S(u) - T(u),$$

and let our initial guess, u_0, be a solution of $S(u) = 0$. Let the next approximation, u_1, be determined by the equation

$$(3) \qquad S(u_1) = S(u_0) - T(u_0),$$

and generally, the $(n + 1)$-th approximation obtained from the nth approximation by means of the equation

$$(4) \qquad S(u_{n+1}) = S(u_n) - T(u_n).$$

If $S(u)$ is carefully chosen, and $T(u)$ possesses appropriate properties, the sequence $\{u_n\}$ will converge to a solution of $T(u) = 0$.

A great deal of work has been done in the application of this method to the study of differential equations, both ordinary and partial, and some preliminary effort in the direction of the functional equations of dynamic programming has been made. References to results and methods will be found at the end of the chapter.

Consistent with our general program, however, we shall proceed in a formal manner, merely indicating various approaches. The results of some numerical work will be given in order to illustrate an actual application of the method.

There are many different ways in which the basic ideas can be applied, and the field is virtually unexplored.

44. Approximation in Policy Space

A prototype equation for dynamic programming is, in abstract form,

$$(1) \qquad f(p) = \max_q \, [g(p, q) + f(T(p, q))].$$

Here p is the state variable and q the decision variable. The classical way to approach this equation in the usual situation in which an explicit analytic solution cannot be found is to guess an initial function, $f_0(p)$, and then determine a sequence of functions by means of the recurrence relation

$$(2) \qquad f_{n+1}(p) = \max_q \: [g(p, q) + f_n(T(p, q))], \quad n = 0, 1, \ldots .$$

In general, it is not difficult to establish the convergence of this sequence to a solution of (1), and usually the conditions which guarantee convergence also ensure uniqueness of solution.

Observe that there are really *two* unknown functions appearing in (1), the *return function*, $f(p)$, and the *policy function*, $q(p)$. They are, of course, not independent, since one determines the other. Given the return function, $f(p)$, the policy function is determined by the maximization operation on the right side of (1); given the policy function $q(p)$, the function $f(p)$ is determined as the solution of

$$(3) \qquad f(p) = g(p, q) + f(T(p, q)),$$

where $q = q(p)$. This equation is usually resolved by direct iteration.

The recognition of the parity of the two functions, $f(p)$ and $q(p)$, enables us greatly to increase the scope of the method of successive approximations. In addition to the type of approximation presented above, in (2), we can envisage a new type of approximation, peculiar to the theory of multistage decision processes, *approximation in policy space*.

In place of starting with an initial guess as to the form of $f(p)$, we start with an initial guess concerning the form of $q(p)$.

The corresponding return function, $f_0(p)$, is determined as the solution of

$$(4) \qquad f_0(p) = g(p, q_0) + f_0(T(p, q_0)),$$

where $q_0 = q_0(p)$. To obtain a better approximation, we determine $q_1 = q_1(p)$ as a function maximizing the function

$$(5) \qquad g(p, q) + f_0(T(p, q)),$$

and then determine $f_1(p)$ by means of the relation

$$(6) \qquad f_1(p) = g(p, q_1) + f_1(T(p, q_1)).$$

We continue in this way, obtaining thereby two sequences $\{q_n(p)\}$ and $\{f_n(p)\}$. In many cases, it is easy to demonstrate monotone convergence,

$$(7) \qquad f_0(p) \leq f_1(p) \leq \cdots .$$

In general, approximation in policy space, in one guise or another, will yield monotone approximation. What is interesting about this concept of approximation is that it can be applied to many equations not at all connected with decision processes. In this form, it constitutes the backbone of a technique called *quasilinearization*.

In the following pages we will discuss some examples of approximation in policy space, with numerical results.

45. Successive Approximations—II

Let us now return to the allocation process described above in §2. We wish to maximize the function

$$(1) \qquad f_N(x, y) = \sum_{i=1}^{N} g_i(x_i, y_i)$$

subject to the conditions

$$(2) \quad (a) \qquad \sum_{i=1}^{N} x_i = x, \quad x_i \geq 0,$$

$$(b) \qquad \sum_{i=1}^{N} y_i = y, \quad y_i \geq 0.$$

Let $x^0 = \{x_i^0\}$ be an initial guess as to the set of x_i values. This is a guess in "policy space." Then, determine the maximum of

$$(3) \qquad R_N(x, y) = \sum_{i=1}^{N} g_i(x_i^0, y_i)$$

over all y_i satisfying (2b), using the usual one-dimensional recurrence relation

$$(4) \qquad f_N(y) = \max_{0 \leq y_N \leq y} [g_N(x_N^0, y_N) + f_{N-1}(y - y_N)],$$

$N = 2, 3, \ldots,$ with

$$(5) \qquad f_1(y) = g_1(x_1^0, y).$$

This process yields, for each value of y, a set of y_i, $y^0 = \{y_i^0\}$. Using these values of the y_i which we call y_i^0, we consider the problem of maximizing the function

$$(6) \qquad \sum_{i=1}^{N} g_i(x_i, y_i^0),$$

over all values of the x_i satisfying (2a). This problem is solved using a recurrence relation similar to (4).

In this way, we obtain a set of x_i-values $x^1 = \{x_i^1\}$. We now repeat this process, obtaining in this way a pair of sequences $\{x^n\}, \{y^n\}, n = 1, 2, \ldots$. It is clear that the sequence of values $\{R_N(x^n, y^n)\}$ is monotone increasing. But it is not necessarily true that this sequence converges to the absolute maximum.

To see why this is so, consider, for example, a function of two variables, $z = g(x, y)$, represented by a surface such as is shown in Fig. 28.

Although the absolute maximum is at (x_0, y_0), if we make an initial guess $x = 0$, we become "stuck" (upon using the foregoing process involving maximization first over x and then over y, then over x, and so on), at the point $(0, 0)$, a relative maximum. An example of this will be given in §51.

82

On the other hand, if we start close enough to the point (x_0, y_0), then the foregoing method will converge to the desired point (x_0, y_0).

In any case, the method can always be used to test whether or not a particular choice of x_i and y_i yields a *relative maximum*, and if not, to converge upon the nearest relative maximum. By starting with initial vectors $\{x^0, y^0\}$, sufficiently distant from each other, we can expect to determine a number of relative maxima in this way, and, hopefully, the absolute maximum.

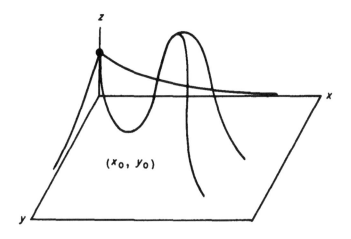

Figure 28

The problem of distinguishing an absolute maximum from relative maxima is one that plagues the optimization field. It cannot be expected that it will ever be overcome at one blow. What we can hope to accomplish is to add class after class of problems to our zoo of tame specimens.

46. Successive Approximations—III

Let us now discuss another use of successive approximations in which we exploit the continuity of the location of the value which yields the maximum.

Consider the problem described in §2, and note the dependence of the location of the maximizing point upon x and y. This dependence need not be uniformly continuous as simple examples can show. Take the one-dimensional case to illustrate this. Suppose that we have a function of x_1 and x_2, $g(x_1, x_2)$, which we wish to maximize over the region $x_1 + x_2 = x$, $x_1, x_2 \geq 0$. Write $f(x_1) = g(x_1, x - x_1)$ and consider its graph (Fig. 29) over $0 \leq x_1 \leq x$. Here the function possesses two relative maxima, one of which is an absolute maximum.

83

As x changes, if g is continuous in x_1 and $\dot{x}_2$, the location of x_m, the point yielding the absolute maximum, will change with x in a continuous fashion until we hit a value of x where the graph has the form of Fig. 30.

For this value of x, the relative maxima are equal in value.

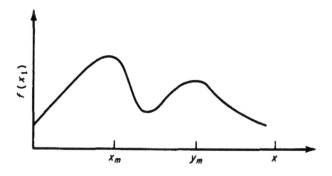

Figure 29

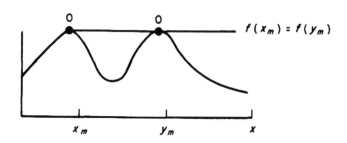

Figure 30

Now suppose that for a neighboring value of x, $f(y_m)$ is greater than $f(x_m)$. The result is that the location of the absolute maximum shifts abruptly from the neighborhood of x_m to the neighborhood of y_m. Hence, x_m considered as a function of x can possess points of discontinuity.

An interesting example of this phenomenon appears in connection with the equation

(1) $$f(x) = \max_{0 \le y \le x} [g(y) + h(x - y) + f(ay + b(x - y))].$$

If

(2) $$g(y) = e^{-10/y},$$

$$h(y) = e^{-15/y},$$

84

the function $f(x)$ has the smooth form of Fig. 31, while the policy function $y(x)$ has the form of Fig. 32. For certain values of x, there is an abrupt transition in the nature of the optimal policy.

We have delved into the minutiae in order that the reader may be properly forewarned of the difficulties contained in the method we shall now present. Our aim is to combine the method of successive approximations described above and the *method of continuity*, another of the fundamental tools of the analyst.

For $x = 0$, the only possible choice of the x_i is $x_i = 0$, $i = 1, 2, \ldots, N$. Hence, the problem of maximizing over the y_i is that of determining the maximum of

$$(5) \qquad R_N(0, y) = \sum_{i=1}^{N} g_i(0, y_i),$$

a problem we solve by means of sequences of functions of one variable. Suppose, for the moment, that this has a unique solution, $y^0 = \{y_i^0\}$. Then to solve the problem in which the constraints are now

$$(6) \qquad \sum_{i=1}^{N} x_i = \Delta, \quad x_i \geq 0,$$

$$\sum_{i=1}^{N} y_i = y,$$

where Δ is "small," we start with the initial approximation $y^0 = \{y_i^0\}$ and proceed to maximize over the x_i, as described in the foregoing sections. Obtaining the solution in this way, we repeat the steps for the problem in which the constraints are

$$(7) \qquad \sum_{i=1}^{N} x_i = 2\Delta,$$

$$\sum_{i=1}^{N} y_i = y.$$

Our initial y-approximation in this problem is the y-solution to (6).

If we feel that this method may take too long to get started in this fashion, we can use the straightforward technique to solve

$$(8) \qquad \sum_{i=1}^{N} x_i = x_0,$$

$$\sum_{i=1}^{N} y_i = y,$$

for some larger x_0, and a range of values of y, $0 \leq y \leq y_0$, and begin from this point.

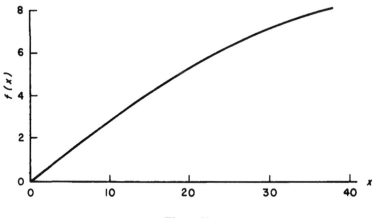

Figure 31

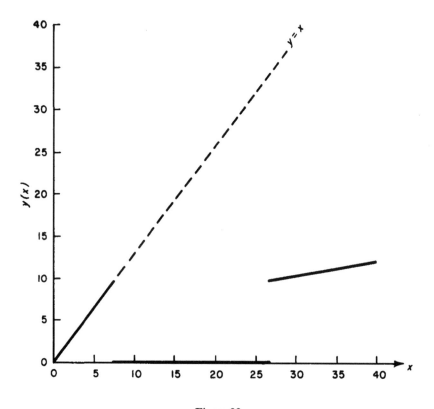

Figure 32

47. Coupling Coefficients

Sometimes we can apply the method of successive approximations in a different fashion. Suppose that we wish to maximize a function of the form

$$(1) \qquad \sum_{i=1}^{N} g_i(x_i) + \sum_{i=1}^{N} h_i(y_i) + t \sum_{i=1}^{N} k_i(x_i, y_i)$$

subject to the constraints

$$(2) \qquad \sum_{i=1}^{N} x_i = x, \quad \sum_{i=1}^{N} y_i = y, \quad x_i, y_i \geq 0.$$

Here t is a parameter which we allow to assume all non-negative values. If $t = 0$, we can solve the problem readily in terms of two sequences of functions of one variable.

Consequently, to solve the problem for small t, say $t = \Delta$, we use as an initial approximation the solution $\{x_i^0, y_i^0\}$ obtained for $t = 0$. Taking $x^0 = \{x_i^0\}$, we can simplify the search problem by restricting our attention to the neighborhood of $y = \{y_i^0\}$. Having obtained the solution corresponding to $t = \Delta$, we use this for the initial approximation to $t = 2\Delta$, and so on.

This idea of *decoupling* by means of a suitable approximation can be used in many ways, and affords many opportunities for ingenuity and special techniques.

48. Coarse Grid

Another way to approximate to the solution of the maximization problem is to use a coarse grid initially. Suppose that we wish to maximize the function

$$(1) \qquad g_1(x_1) + g_2(x_2) + \cdots + g_N(x_N),$$

subject to the constraint

$$(2) \qquad x_1 + x_2 + \cdots + x_N = x.$$

Let us begin by allowing x to assume a set of values $0, \delta, 2\delta, \ldots$, where δ is large compared to our usual grid size. Similarly, we allow the x_i to assume the same set of values—although some other set of values would do as well. The result is that the computation of the solution is speeded up in two ways. There are fewer values of $f_N(x)$ to tabulate and the search process for maximizing x_N at each stage is shorter.

We obtain in this way a set of functions $\{x_i(x)\}$, $i = 1, 2, \ldots, N$, the maximizing values, tabulated at the points $x = 0, \delta, 2\delta, \ldots$.

The risk one faces in using a coarse grid is that one may miss a very sharp absolute maximum and obtain instead a flat relative maximum. Consider, for example, a function of the type shown in Fig. 33.

A search at the values $0, \delta, 2\delta, \ldots$ will pick up the relative maximum at 2δ, but not the absolute maximum between 4δ and 5δ. Examples as drastic as this are, of course, unlikely. Nonetheless, we must always keep such possibilities in mind.

Let us suppose that we have actually determined the location of the actual $x_i = x_i(x) = x_i(x; \delta)$ to within $\pm\delta$, of the maximum position. Then,

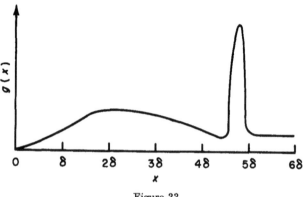

Figure 33

when using the finer grid, say $0, \Delta, 2\Delta, \ldots$, where $\delta = 10\Delta$ or 100Δ, we add the constraints

$$(3) \qquad x_i(x; \delta) - \delta \leq x_i(x) \leq x_i(x; \delta) + \delta, \qquad i = 1, 2, \ldots, N,$$

where $x_i(x; \delta)$ are the functions determined initially by use of the coarser grid.

Restrictions of this type cut down on the memory requirements and greatly reduce the time required in the determination of the maximum via a search process. An application of this idea will be referred to in §11 of Chapter III.

49. Successive Approximations in the Hitchcock-Koopmans Problem

Let us now return to the Hitchcock-Koopmans problem equipped with these new methods. We have seen that a process involving M depots can be treated directly in terms of functions of $(M - 1)$ variables, and by means of Lagrange multipliers in terms of functions of $M - k$ variables.

We shall now indicate how successive approximations can be used to treat the problem in terms of sequences of functions of one variable.

In order to attain this reduction, we shall proceed in the following fashion. To begin with, the supplies at the depots $D_3, D_4, \ldots, D_M$ are allocated to meet part of the requirements at the demand points in any

EXAMPLE I—RELATIVE MINIMUM

way whatsoever. The remaining supplies at D_1 and D_2 are then allocated to meet the remaining requirements at minimum cost.

This requires, as we know, only sequences of functions of one variable, and thus may be considered to be a routine operation. This represents the first step in the method of successive approximations. To continue, we use the same allocations from $D_4, \ldots, D_M$ as before, the allocation from D_1 determined by the minimization procedure, and determine the allocations from D_2 and D_3 to meet the remaining demands by means of a minimization procedure.

This represents the second step. To continue, we fix the allocations from $D_5, \ldots, D_M, D_1$, as before, use the allocation from D_2 determined by the previous minimization, and then solve the new problem of the minimization of shipping costs from D_3 and D_4. The process now continues in this way.

50. Convergence

It is clear to begin with that the minimum cost function must converge, since the cost is nonincreasing at each stage of the computation. It is, however, not clear to what the process converges, and as a matter of fact it is not difficult to construct examples in which the minimum is *not* attained in this way.

Our technique in both of the following examples is to fix initially the x_{3j} column subject only to the conditions that $\sum_j x_{3j} = x_3$ and no $x_{3j} > r_j$. In Example 1, we have distributed the supply at Depot 3 rather equally to the demand points. In Example 2, we successively fill the demands of each sink until we exhaust the supply at Depot 3. We then deduct this preassigned shipment from the demands at the various sinks and solve the remaining two-source problem. We use this solution to determine the x_{1j} for the second iteration. This solution determines the x_{2j} for iteration 3, after which we repeat the cycle by fixing x_{3j}. We continue this process until we obtain a stable allocation under all three types of sub-problems.

We consider three depots and ten demand points in the examples that follow.

51. Example 1—Relative Minimum

We consider the case where each function $g_{ij}(x)$ has the form

$$(1) \qquad g_{ij}(x) = a_{ij}x + b_{ij}x^2 + c_{ij}(x),$$

where $c_{ij}(x)$ is a "set-up" cost, or fixed charge, equal to zero if $x = 0$, and to the constant c_{ij} if $x > 0$.

The a_{ij} appear in the column under x, and the b_{ij} under x^2 in the following chart.

EXAMPLE 1

Sink	Source 1			Source 2			Source 3			Demand
	Set-up	x	x^2	Set-up	x	x^2	Set-up	x	x^2	
1		+1.0		+2.0	+3.1			+7.0		25
2	+1.0	+2.0			+4.1			+3.0		40
3		+3.0	+.01		+2.1			+9.0		60
4		+1.5			+1.1	+.10		+1.0		30
5		+2.5			+2.6			+1.0		20
6	+10.0	+5.0	−.01		+3.0		+5.0	+2.0		30
7		+3.0		+5.0	+1.0	+.20		+4.0		35
8		+6.0			+2.0		+6.0	+3.0		30
9	+8.0	+6.0	−.05		+2.0			+5.0		25
10		+6.0			+5.0	+.01		+6.0		40
										335

$$x_1 = \text{supply at Depot } 1 = 100$$
$$x_2 = \text{supply at Depot } 2 = 80$$
$$x_3 = \text{supply at Depot } 3 = 155$$

The results of the successive approximations are given below.

	Policy 1			Policy 2			Policy 3		
1	10	0	15	10	15	0	10	15	0
2	25	0	15	25	0	15	40	0	0
3	5	40	15	5	55	0	5	55	0
4	15	0	15	15	0	15	0	0	30
5	5	0	15	5	0	15	0	0	20
6	0	15	15	0	0	30	0	0	30
7	20	0	15	20	0	15	35	0	0
8	0	15	15	0	0	30	0	0	30
9	0	10	15	0	10	15	0	10	15
10	20	0	20	20	0	20	10	0	30
	cost = 1126.25			cost = 966.00			cost = 921.25		

EXAMPLE I—RELATIVE MINIMUM

	Policy 4			Policy 5			Policy 6		
1	25	0	0	25	0	0	25	0	0
2	40	0	0	40	0	0	40	0	0
3	0	60	0	0	60	0	0	60	0
4	0	0	30	0	0	30	0	0	30
5	0	0	20	0	0	20	0	0	20
6	0	0	30	0	0	30	0	0	30
7	35	0	0	35	0	0	35	0	0
8	0	0	30	0	0	30	0	0	30
9	0	10	15	0	20	5	0	20	5
10	0	10	30	0	0	40	0	0	40
	cost = 874.00			cost = 853.00			cost = 853.00		

	Policy 7			Actual Solution		
1	25	0	0	25	0	0
2	40	0	0	40	0	0
3	0	60	0	5	55	0
4	0	0	30	0	0	30
5	0	0	20	0	0	20
6	0	0	30	0	0	30
7	35	0	0	30	0	5
8	0	0	30	0	0	30
9	0	20	5	0	25	0
10	0	0	40	0	0	40
	cost = 853.00			cost = 847.75		

52. Example 2—Absolute Minimum

Let us now consider the case where each $g_{ij}(x)$ is convex and of the form $a_{ij}(x) + b_{ij}x^2$. The numbers are:

EXAMPLE 2

Sink	Source 1			Source 2			Source 3			Demand
	Set-up	x	x^2	Set-up	x	x^2	Set-up	x	x^2	
1		1.0	.20		3.1	.10		7.0		25
2		2.0	.06		4.1			3.0	.04	40
3		3.0	.01		2.1			9.0		60
4		1.5			1.1	.10		1.0		30
5		2.5	.05		2.6			1.0	.20	20
6		5.0	.01		3.0			2.0		30
7		3.0			1.0	.20		4.0		35
8		6.0			2.0			3.0	.10	30
9		6.0	.05		2.0			5.0		25
10		6.0			5.0	.01		6.0		40

$$x_1 = \text{supply at Depot 1} = 100$$
$$x_2 = \text{supply at Depot 2} = 97$$
$$x_3 = \text{supply at Depot 3} = 138$$

The results of the iterations follow.

	Policy 1			Policy 2			Policy 3		
1	0	0	25	0	4	21	15	4	6
2	0	0	40	0	0	40	21	0	19
3	0	0	60	0	60	0	0	60	0
4	17	0	13	17	0	13	0	0	30
5	11	9	0	11	0	9	13	0	7
6	0	30	0	0	0	30	0	0	30
7	32	3	0	32	0	3	35	0	0
8	0	30	0	0	20	10	0	20	10
9	0	25	0	0	13	12	0	13	12
10	40	0	0	40	0	0	16	0	24
	cost = 1535.249			cost = 1141.25			cost = 1040.55		

EXAMPLE 2—ABSOLUTE MINIMUM

	Policy 4				Policy 5				Policy 6		
1	12	7	6		12	4	9		15	4	6
2	21	0	19		21	0	19		21	0	19
3	7	53	0		7	53	0		7	53	0
4	0	0	30		0	0	30		0	0	30
5	11	2	7		11	0	9		13	0	7
6	0	0	30		0	0	30		0	0	30
7	33	2	0		33	0	2		35	0	0
8	0	20	10		0	20	10		0	20	10
9	0	13	12		0	20	5		0	20	5
10	16	0	24		16	0	24		9	0	31
	cost = 1035.439				cost = 1031.24				cost = 1026.44		

	Policy 7				Policy 8				Policy 9		
1	12	7	6		12	4	9		15	4	6
2	21	0	19		21	0	19		21	0	19
3	12	48	0		12	48	0		12	48	0
4	0	0	30		0	0	30		0	0	30
5	13	0	7		13	0	7		13	0	7
6	0	0	30		0	0	30		0	0	30
7	33	2	0		33	0	2		35	0	0
8	0	20	10		0	20	10		0	20	10
9	0	20	5		0	25	0		0	25	0
10	9	0	31		9	0	31		4	0	36
	cost = 1022.089				cost = 1020.69				cost = 1016.89		

	Policy 10				Policy 11				Policy 12		
1	12	7	6		12	6	7		15	6	4
2	21	0	19		21	0	19		21	0	19
3	17	43	0		17	43	0		17	43	0
4	0	0	30		0	0	30		0	0	30
5	13	0	7		13	0	7		13	0	7
6	0	0	30		0	0	30		0	0	30
7	33	2	0		33	1	1		34	1	0
8	0	20	10		0	22	8		0	22	8
9	0	25	0		0	25	0		0	25	0
10	4	0	36		4	0	36		0	0	40
	cost = 1013.04				cost = 1012.44				cost = 1009.64		

	Policy 13			Policy 14			Policy 15		
1	13	8	4	13	7	5	14	7	4
2	21	0	19	21	0	19	20	0	20
3	20	40	0	20	40	0	20	40	0
4	0	0	30	0	0	30	0	0	30
5	13	0	7	13	0	7	13	0	7
6	0	0	30	0	0	30	0	0	30
7	33	2	0	33	2	0	33	2	0
8	0	22	8	0	23	7	0	23	7
9	0	25	0	0	25	0	0	25	0
10	0	0	40	0	0	40	0	0	40
	cost = 1007.85			cost = 1007.75			cost = 1007.25		

	Policy 16			Policy 17			Policy 18		
1	13	8	4	13	8	4	14	8	3
2	20	0	20	20	0	20	20	0	20
3	21	39	0	21	39	0	21	39	0
4	0	0	30	0	0	30	0	0	30
5	13	0	7	13	0	7	12	0	8
6	0	0	30	0	0	30	0	0	30
7	33	2	0	33	2	0	33	2	0
8	0	23	7	0	23	7	0	23	7
9	0	25	0	0	25	0	0	25	0
10	0	0	40	0	0	40	0	0	40
	cost = 1006.76			cost = 1006.76			cost = 1006.41		

	Policy 19			Policy 20			Policy 21		
1	13	9	3	13	8	4	14	8	3
2	20	0	20	20	0	20	19	0	21
3	22	38	0	22	38	0	22	38	0
4	0	0	30	0	0	30	0	0	30
5	12	0	8	12	0	8	12	0	8
6	0	0	30	0	0	30	0	0	30
7	33	2	0	33	2	0	33	2	0
8	0	23	7	0	24	6	0	24	6
9	0	25	0	0	25	0	0	25	0
10	0	0	40	0	0	40	0	0	40
	cost = 1006.14			cost = 1006.04			cost = 1005.74		

EXAMPLE 2—ABSOLUTE MINIMUM

	Policy 22				Policy 23				Policy 24		
1	13	9	3		13	9	3		14	9	2
2	19	0	21		19	0	21		18	0	22
3	23	37	0		23	37	0		23	37	0
4	0	0	30		0	0	30		0	0	30
5	12	0	8		12	0	8		12	0	8
6	0	0	30		0	0	30		0	0	30
7	33	2	0		33	2	0		33	2	0
8	0	24	6		0	24	6		0	24	6
9	0	25	0		0	25	0		0	25	0
10	0	0	40		0	0	40		0	0	40
	cost = 1005.49				cost = 1005.49				cost = 1005.39		

	Policy 25				Policy 26				Policy 27		
1	13	10	2		13	9	3		13	9	3
2	18	0	22		18	0	22		18	0	22
3	24	36	0		24	36	0		24	36	0
4	0	0	30		0	0	30		0	0	30
5	12	0	8		12	0	8		12	0	8
6	0	0	30		0	0	30		0	0	30
7	33	2	0		33	2	0		33	2	0
8	0	24	6		0	25	5		0	25	5
9	0	25	0		0	25	0		0	25	0
10	0	0	40		0	0	40		0	0	40
	cost = 1005.36				cost = 1005.26				cost = 1005.26		

	Policy 28		
1	13	9	3
2	18	0	22
3	24	36	0
4	0	0	30
5	12	0	8
6	0	0	30
7	33	2	0
8	0	25	5
9	0	25	0
10	0	0	40
	cost = 1005.26		

It is rather interesting to observe that although accuracy to within 4 per cent was attained on the third iteration, twenty-eight iterations were required to obtain the absolute minimum. Furthermore, upon referring to the twenty-second and twenty-third steps, we see an example of no improvement when the allocation from the first depot was fixed, but, nevertheless, an improvement when the allocation from the second depot was fixed.

53. Stochastic Iteration

Instead of proceeding in the clockwise predetermined fashion described above, in which we choose the depots (D_1, D_2), (D_2, D_3), and so on, which makes it easy to construct examples in which we are led to corners and relative minima, it may be better to choose the two depots at random at each stage.

In the more general case where there are many depots, it will be necessary to test all possible combinations of two depots in order to guarantee that we have arrived at the absolute minimum. Even then, it is possible to contemplate situations in higher dimensional spaces in which even this type of subminimization will not be sufficient to ensure absolute minimization.

54. Conclusions

Our aim in the preceding pages has been to discuss the new problems posed by multidimensionality. In some cases, we can pursue a routine approach provided we have a modern machine and are willing to expend the required time and effort. In other cases, the memory requirements far exceed the capacity of the biggest of contemporary computers.

In order to handle the multidimensional problems posed by more realistic descriptions of economic allocation processes, we must invoke some more powerful techniques of classical analysis, the method of successive approximations and the method of continuity.

We have given some examples and some discussion to show that these methods can be employed and in some cases will yield satisfactory results. We shall come to discuss additional techniques that can be used, separately or in conjunction with those already presented. It is to be expected that significant complex processes will require all of these tools in unison, together with calculus, linear and nonlinear programming, and so on.

In treating these processes, we will face a metaprogramming problem, in which one of the basic difficulties will be that of determining which mathematical techniques to use and in what order. All of this is intimately connected with the concept of adaptive control processes, to which we shall refer again in Chapter VIII.

55. "Difficult Crossing" Problems

As a continuation of the analysis of §32, where the Hitchcock-Koopmans transportation problem was considered, let us discuss a type of mathematical puzzle that appears frequently in books on mathematical recreations.

A typical poser is the following:

"A group consisting of three cannibals and three missionaries seeks to cross a river. A boat is available which will hold two people, and which can be navigated by any combination of cannibals and missionaries involving one or two people. If the missionaries on either side of the river, or in the boat, are outnumbered at any time by cannibals, the cannibals will indulge in their anthropophagic tendencies and do away with the missionaries. What schedule of crossings can be devised to permit the entire group of cannibals and missionaries to cross the river safely?"

In the next section we shall formulate the problem in more general terms and then resolve it by means of the functional equation technique.

56. General Problem

Let us now consider the more general situation in which we start with m_1 cannibals and n_1 missionaries on one side of the river and m_2 cannibals and n_2 missionaries on the other. Let the rule be that on one bank we have a constraint $R_1(m_1, n_1) \geq 0$ to prevent the missionaries from being devoured, a similar constraint $R_2(m_2, n_2) \geq 0$ on the other, and a constraint $R_3(m, n) \geq 0$ in the boat, capable of carrying at most k people.

Given the integers m_1, n_1, m_2, n_2, it is not at all clear when it is possible to schedule a safe crossing. Consequently, we shall begin by treating the following problem. Starting with the given initial data, what is the maximum number of people that can be transported from one bank, say bank one, to the other, without permitting cannibalism?

57. Functional Equations

Since the total number of cannibals and of missionaries stays constant throughout the process, the state of the system at any time is specified by the numbers m_1 and n_1 defined above.

Let us then introduce the function

(1) $f_N(m_1, n_1) =$ the maximum number of people on the second bank at the end of N stages, starting with m_1 cannibals and n_1 missionaries on the first bank and quantities m_2 and n_2 respectively on the second bank.

We shall suppose that it is permissible at any stage to send no people back to the first bank from the second bank if everybody is already on the second bank.

One stage of the process consists of sending x_1 cannibals and y_1 missionaries from the first bank to the second bank and then of sending x_2 cannibals and y_2 missionaries back to the first bank.

Using the principle of optimality, we obtain the recurrence relation

$$(2) \qquad f_N(m_1, n_1) = \max_{x,y} f_{N-1}(m_1 - x_1 + x_2, n_1 - y_1 + y_2),$$

for $N \geq 2$, where the variables x_1, x_2, y_1, y_2 are subject to the constraints

$$
\begin{aligned}
&(3) \quad (\mathrm{a}) && 0 \leq x_1 \leq m_1, \quad 0 \leq y_1 \leq n_1, \\
&\qquad (\mathrm{b}) && 0 \leq x_2 \leq m_2 + x_1, \quad 0 \leq y_2 \leq n_2 + y_1, \\
&\qquad (\mathrm{c}) && x_1 + y_1 \leq k, \quad x_2 + y_2 \leq k, \\
&\qquad (\mathrm{d}) && R_3(x_1, y_1) \geq 0, \quad R_3(x_2, y_2) \geq 0, \\
&\qquad (\mathrm{e}) && R_1(m_1 - x_1, n_1 - y_1) \geq 0, \\
&\qquad (\mathrm{f}) && R_1(m_1 - x_1 + x_2, n_1 - y_1 + y_2) \geq 0, \\
&\qquad (\mathrm{g}) && R_2(m_2 + x_1, n_2 + y_1) \geq 0, \\
&\qquad (\mathrm{h}) && R_2(m_2 + x_1 - x_2, n_2 + y_1 - y_2) \geq 0.
\end{aligned}
$$

There are sets of x_1, x_2, y_1, y_2 satisfying these constraints, since by assumption $x_1 = x_2 = y_1 = y_2 = 0$ satisfies them.

For $N = 1$, we have

$$(4) \qquad f_1(m_1, n_1) = \max_{x,y} [(m_2 + x_1) + (n_2 + y_1)],$$

where x_1, y_1 are subject to the foregoing constraints.

58. Discussion

For small values of N and of m_1, m_2, n_1, n_2, the values of $f_N(m_1, n_1)$ can readily be computed by hand. In many cases, the constraints will be of such restrictive type that there will be a unique feasible policy, which automatically will be the optimal policy.

In the foregoing manner we simultaneously determine the minimum number of crossings necessary for the transference of all the people from one side of the bank to the other, whenever this is possible. To obtain this minimum number, we continue the process until a value of N is obtained for which $f_N = m_1 + m_2 + n_1 + n_2$.

59. Numerical Solution

We illustrate the above algorithm by solving the problem stated in §55.

We first recognize that only certain initial states for the N stage process are possible. All others lead to immediate cannibalism. If we let (i, j) be the state of i missionaries and j cannibals being on the starting bank of the river and $3 - i$ missionaries and $3 - j$ cannibals on the second bank, then only the states $(0, 1)$, $(1, 1)$, $(3, 1)$, $(0, 2)$, $(2, 2)$, $(3, 2)$, $(0, 3)$ and $(3, 3)$ are possible. We use the algorithm of §57 to compute

$$f_1(0, 1) = 6, \; f_1(1, 1) = 6, \; f_1(3, 1) = 2, \; f_1(0, 2) = 6,$$
$$f_1(2, 2) = 3, \; f_1(3, 2) = 2, \; f_1(0, 3) = 4, \; f_1(3, 3) = 1.$$

Observing that if $f_k(i, j) = 6, f_{k+l}(i, j) = 6$ for $l = 1, 2, \ldots$, we iterate the recurrence relation for all non-six values and get

$$f_2(3, 1) = 3, \; f_2(2, 2) = 4, f_2(3, 2) = 2, f_2(0, 3) = 6, f_2(3, 3) = 2.$$

Continuing the process,

$$f_3(3, 1) = 4, \; f_3(2, 2) = 6, \; f_3(3, 2) = 3, \; f_3(3, 3) = 2, \; f_4(3, 1) = 6,$$
$$f_4(3, 2) = 4, \; f_4(3, 3) = 3, f_5(3, 2) = 6, f_5(3, 3) = 4, f_6(3, 3) = 6.$$

Therefore the required number of crossings, starting with 3 cannibals and 3 missionaries on bank one, is 6. The optimal policy is easily determined if the maximizing decision is recorded at each stage.

Comments and Bibliography

The problem of the maximization or minimization of a function of N variables is one of the major questions of analysis and, quite naturally, an enormous amount of effort has been devoted to it. Since we are interested only in functions of quite special form, we have paid no attention to any of the general techniques that exist. For a discussion of the classical method of "steepest descent," see

P. C. Rosenbloom, "The method of steepest descent," *Numerical Analysis, Proceedings of the Sixth Symposium in Applied Mathematics*, McGraw-Hill Book Co., Inc., New York, 1956.

Many references will be found there. See also

J. Todd, "Motivation for working in numerical analysis," *Comm. Pure Appl. Math.*, vol. 13, 1955, pp. 97–116.

§14. For rigorous discussions of the fundamental notion of convexity, see

T. Bonessen and W. Fenchel, *Theorie der Konvexen Korper*, Ergebnisse der Math., vol. 3, 1934.

H. G. Eggleston, *Convexity*, Cambridge Tracts No. 47, Cambridge University Press, Cambridge, 1958.

For some analytic applications of the techniques of this section, see

E. F. Beckenbach and R. Bellman, *Inequalities*, Ergebnisse der Math., Springer, Berlin, 1961.

We use the duality of Euclidean geometry to provide a further decomposition of processes. This property will be utilized again in the study of the calculus of variations.

§15. For the interpretation of the Lagrange multiplier as a "price," see the book by P. Samuelson referred to at the end of Chapter I, and Appendix II by S. Dreyfus and M. Freimer.

§16. The use of the Lagrange multiplier in dynamic programming was first sketched in

R. Bellman, "Dynamic programming and Lagrange multipliers," *Proc. Nat. Acad. Sci. USA*, vol. 42, 1956, pp. 767–769.

§20. The reasoning here is borrowed from

R. Bellman, I. Glicksberg, and O. Gross, *Some Aspects of the Mathematical Theory of Control Processes*, The RAND Corporation, Report R–313, 1958, pp. 49–50.

§21. These results were presented in

S. Dreyfus, *Dynamic Programming Solution of Allocation Problems*, The RAND Corporation, Paper P-1083, May 9, 1957.

§27. These results were given in

R. Bellman and S. Dreyfus, "Dynamic programming and the reliability of multicomponent devices," *Operations Research*, vol. 6, 1958, pp. 200–206.

§32. An enormous amount of work has been done on the Hitchcock-Koopmans transportation problem. The first sophisticated mathematical study of transportation problems and the general linear programming problem was made by Kantorovich in 1939. A recent translation of this paper is

L. V. Kantorovich, "Mathematical methods of organizing and planning production," *Management Science*, vol. 6, 1960, pp. 366–422.

See also

F. L. Hitchcock, "The distribution of a product from several sources to numerous localities," *J. Math. Physics*. vol. 20, 1941, pp. 224–230.

R. Dorfman, P. A. Samuelson, and R. Solow, *Linear Programming and Economic Analysis*, McGraw-Hill Book Co., Inc., New York, 1960, Chapter 5.

G. B. Dantzig, "Applications of the simplex method to a transportation problem," *Activity Analysis of Production and Allocation*, J. Wiley and Sons, New York, 1951, Chapter 23.

T. S. Motzkin, "The assignment problem," *Proc. Sixth Symposium in Applied Mathematics*, vol. 6, 1953.

T. C. Koopmans and S. Reiter, "A model of transportation," ibid., Chapter 14.

M. M. Flood, "On the Hitchcock distribution problem," *Pacific J. Math.*, vol. 3, 1953, pp. 369–396.

L. Ford and D. R. Fulkerson, "Maximal flow through a network," *Canadian J. Math.*, vol. 8, 1956, pp. 399–404.

T. Fukao, "A computational method for dynamic linear programming," *J. Operations Research Soc. Japan*, vol. 2, 1960, pp. 98–113.

F. C. Toscano, *An Engineering Analysis of Cargo-handling—IX*, Department of Engineering, University of California at Los Angeles, 1960.

W. Szwarc, "The initial solution of the transportation problem," *Operations Research*, vol. 8, 1960, pp. 727–729.

The foregoing papers use linear programming methods or iterative techniques devised for this particular process. The analytic discussion in the text was presented in

R. Bellman, "Notes on the theory of dynamic programming: transportation models," *Management Science*, vol. 4, 1958, pp. 191–195.

The computational results were obtained subsequently, both because of the intrinsic interest of the problem and as indications of the power of the method of successive approximations.

§43. For a systematic discussion of successive approximations see

R. Bellman, "Functional equations and successive approximations in linear and nonlinear programming," *Naval Research Logs. Q.*, vol. 7, 1960, pp. 63–83.

For some other aspects of successive approximations, see

R. Kalaba, "On nonlinear differential equations, the maximum operation and monotone convergence," *J. Math. and Mech.*, vol. 8, 1959, pp. 519–573.

Here the technique of quasilinearization, a method whose origins lie in the work of Caplygin, is systematically used.

§44. For further discussions of approximation in policy space, see

R. Bellman, *Dynamic Programming*, Princeton University Press, Princeton, New Jersey, 1957.

————, *Adaptive Control Processes: A Guided Tour*, Princeton University Press, Princeton, New Jersey, 1961.

§46. The original version of Fig. 32, as it appears on p. 25 of *Dynamic Programming*, is incorrect. We wish to thank A. E. Bryson for discovering this.

§48. The technique of dynamic programming can be profitably combined with the gradient technique, or with Newton's method for solving systems of nonlinear equations, to provide quick and accurate numerical solution.

The success of gradient techniques, Newton's method, and other iterative techniques, usually depends upon starting sufficiently close to the extremum. This can often be guaranteed by using the functional equation technique with a coarse grid.

Alternatively, we can refine the grid when close enough to the extremum. This method works quite well in the study of some problems arising in statistical mechanics.

See

R. Kikuchi and J. W. Cahn, *Theory of Domain Walls in Ordered Structures— II. Pair Approximations for Nonzero Temperatures*, Hughes Research Laboratories, Research Report No. 177, 1961.

For some mathematical formulations of organization theory with the framework of decision processes, see

J. Marschak, "Towards an economic theory of organization and information," Chap. 14 in *Decision Processes*, Thrall, Davis, and Coombs, eds., John Wiley and Sons, New York, 1954.

————, "Elements for a theory of teams," *Management Science*, vol. 1, no. 2, 1954, pp. 127–137.

R. Radner, "The linear team: an example of linear programming under uncertainty," *Proc. Second Symposium in Linear Programming*, National Bureau of Standards, Washington, 1955.

——————, "The application of linear programming to team decision problems," *Management Science*, vol. 5, no. 2, 1959, pp. 143–150.

C. B. McGuire, "Some team models of a sales organization," *Management Science*, vol. 7, 1961, pp. 101–130.

For discussions of the construction of mathematical models, see

R. Bellman, C. Clark, C. Craft, D. Malcolm, and F. M. Ricciardi, "On the construction of a multi-stage, multi-person business game," *Operations Research*, vol. 5, 1957, pp. 469–503.

R. Bellman and P. Brock, "On the concepts of a problem and problem-solving," *Amer. Math. Monthly*, vol. 67, 1960, pp. 119–134.

For some discussions of the general allocation problem, see

K. J. Arrow and L. Hurwicz, "Decentralization and computation in resource allocation," *Essays in Economics and Econometrics*, University of North Carolina Press, pp. 34–104.

H. F. Karreman, "Programming the supply of a strategic material Part I. A nonstochastic model," *Naval Research Logs. Q.*, vol. 7, 1960, pp. 261–279.

A. Nomoto, "Exploration sequentielle," *Stogiaire de Cooperation Technique du Governement Francais de la Societe d'Electronique et d'Automatisme*, 1961.

§55–§58. An approach to "difficult crossing" problems was given by B. Schwartz in

B. Schwartz, "An analytic method for 'difficult crossing' puzzles," *Math. Mag.*, vol. 34, 1961, pp. 187–193,

based upon graph theory and topological considerations. The results given here appeared in

R. Bellman, "Dynamic programming and 'difficult crossing' puzzles," *Math. Mag.*, vol. 35, 1962.

Similar problems involving the pouring of different types of liquids from one type of jug to another so as to obtain a mixture of the desired type can also be treated by dynamic programming techniques, see p. 99, problem 38, of *Dynamic Programming*.

CHAPTER III

One-dimensional Smoothing and Scheduling Processes

1. Introduction

In the two previous chapters, we have shown that a variety of static allocation processes could be viewed as dynamic processes and thus be treated by means of the functional equation technique of dynamic programming. In this part, continuing the same approach, we wish to study some processes in the field of scheduling which arise naturally in dynamic form.

As well as obtaining algorithms suitable for computational solution along the lines previously indicated, in a number of cases we shall derive analytic descriptions of the optimal policy and analytic representations of the return function. Results of this type are interesting not only because of intrinsic elegance, but, as in the theory of differential equations, because exact results for simpler processes can be used to obtain approximate solutions to more complicated processes. Here, however, we have far greater flexibility since approximations can be made either in function space or policy space.

An important point to make, and one which we shall illustrate repeatedly throughout the remainder of the volume, is that the functional equation technique can be applied in different ways, in combination with classical techniques and separately, with different objectives in mind.

The difference between what we call an explicit analytic solution and what we call a computational solution is less of kind than of degree. Both are algorithms for obtaining numbers. In many cases, an "explicit" solution is useless for numerical purposes. The simplest example of this phenomenon occurs in the solution of linear systems of equations where the solution of Cramer, involving the quotient of two determinants, must be discarded in favor of iterative techniques as soon as the dimension becomes large. Many other examples occur in the field of differential equations.

2. Smoothing Processes

Consider a situation in which we want a system to operate in a specified state, and where we incur a cost dependent upon the deviation from this state. If we attempt to transform the system into the desired state, we incur additional costs dependent upon the effort devoted to effect this change.

Processes in which it is expedient to pursue a middle path, balancing one type of cost against another so as to maximize the utility of the overall operation, are called *smoothing processes*. In what follows we shall consider some decision processes of this type arising in economic activity. Subsequently, in Chapters VIII and IX, we shall treat questions of similar mathematical type arising in the field of engineering.

3. A Particular Smoothing Process

Let us begin our study with a simple process which arises frequently in the analysis of economic, industrial, and military operations. A supply depot is required at a preassigned set of times (such as every day or every week) to meet a set of known demands for services or supplies. If the demand is not met, a penalty is incurred. On the other hand, if the organization is overstaffed or overstocked, another type of penalty is levelled.

Were this the complete picture, the optimal control policy would be self-evident. Let us, however, introduce a cost for changing the level of services or supplies. This is quite realistic in many situations.

Given a set of demands which fluctuate greatly over time, it is now a nontrivial problem to determine how to adjust the service level, or stock level, so as to minimize the total cost of the process, compounded of penalty costs and costs of restocking.

4. Mathematical Formulation

Let $r_1, r_2, \ldots, r_N$ be a preassigned sequence of demands, where r_k is the demand at the kth stage. Let

(1) $x_k =$ the capability of the system at the kth stage,

$k = 1, 2, \ldots, N$, where $x_0 = c$ is a fixed initial level.

In this example, let us assume that it is required that

(2) $x_k \geq r_k, \qquad k = 1, 2, \ldots, N.$

In other words, we insist that the demand always be met.

Let us then introduce two cost functions

(3) $\phi_k(x_k - r_k) =$ the cost incurred at the kth stage if $x_k > r_k$,

     $\psi_k(x_k - x_{k-1}) =$ the cost incurred at the kth stage if $x_k \neq x_{k-1}$.

This latter function measures the cost involved in changing supply or service level.

The total cost incurred due to a choice of levels $x_1, x_2, \ldots, x_N$ is given by

$$(4) \qquad C(x_1, x_2, \ldots, x_N) = \sum_{k=1}^{N} [\phi_k(x_k - r_k) + \psi_k(x_k - x_{k-1})].$$

Our objective is to choose the x_k, $k = 1, 2, \ldots, N$, subject to the condition $x_k \geq r_k$, so as to minimize this function.

5. Functional Equations

In order to treat this minimization problem by means of functional equation techniques, we imbed this problem within the family of problems requiring the minimization of the function

$$(1) \qquad C_R = \sum_{k=R}^{N} [\phi_k(x_k - r_k) + \psi_k(x_k - x_{k-1})],$$

over the region defined by $x_k \geq r_k$, $k = R, R + 1, \ldots, N$, with $x_{R-1} = c$, for $R = 1, 2, \ldots, N$.

Let us define

$$(2) \qquad f_R(c) = \min_{\{x_k\}} C_R, \quad R = 1, 2, \ldots, N,$$

where the minimum is taken over the x_k-region defined above.

Then

$$(3) \qquad f_N(c) = \min_{x_N \geq r_N} [\phi(x_N - r_N) + \psi(x_N - c)],$$

a readily determined function.

The usual argument yields the recurrence relation

$$(4) \qquad f_R(c) = \min_{x_R \geq r_R} [\phi_R(x_R - r_R) + \psi_R(x_R - c) + f_{R+1}(x_R)],$$

for $R = 1, 2, \ldots, N - 1$. We thus have a simple algorithm for obtaining the computational solution of the optimization problem.

6. Discussion

For various classes of functions, $\{\phi_R(x)\}$, $\{\psi_R(x)\}$, and constraints of one type or another, the nature of the optimal policy can be determined explicitly. References to a number of results which have been obtained will be found in the bibliography at the end of this chapter.

7. Computational Aspects

Here, as in the cargo-loading process, discussed in §22 of Chapter I, we have a one-dimensional process with integral constraints. Furthermore, extrema are easy to locate by direct comparison, and, if grid points are chosen to be integers, no interpolation is required. The range of the quantity c is automatically limited and known in advance.

As a result, we have a short and straightforward fixed-point program with practically no difficulties as far as time or space are concerned. In fact, for the examples so far attempted, all computing was accomplished while the printer paper was being ejected.

In most dynamic programming processes, the variable under consideration can take on values which allow the argument of the function on the right-hand side to assume a wide range of values. For example, in the cargo-loading process, §22 of Chapter I, the number of units of type N to be loaded on a vessel of capacity w is permitted to assume any integer value between 0 and $[w/w_N]$. The remaining capacity $w - w_N x_N$ thus can take any value between 0 and w. As a result, $f_{N-1}(z)$ must be calculated in advance for values of z between 0 and w, before we can compute $f_N(w)$.

In the present process, however, we can determine in advance precisely which values of $f_{R+1}(x_R)$ will be needed to determine $f_R(c)$. Much time is saved by taking this fact into account.

To see this, observe that x_R is bounded below by the requirement r_R, and from above by the fact that it is never necessary to choose x_R to be greater than the quantity $\max_R r_R$. Hence, $f_{R+1}(x_R)$ need only be determined for the range $r_R \leq x_R \leq \max_R r_R$.

It follows that when $f_{R+1}(c)$ is computed from the relation

(1) $$f_{R+1}(c) = \min_{x_{R+1}} [\phi_R(x_R - r_R) + \psi_R(x_R - c) + f_{R+2}(x_{R+1})],$$

only the values satisfying the two constraints

(2) (a) $$r_R \leq c \leq \max_R r_R,$$

(b) $$r_{R+1} \leq x_{R+1} \leq \max_R r_R$$

are considered.

Although we view the problem as a stage-by-stage process to reduce the dimensionality of the maximization problem, we use our actual knowledge of future requirements to reduce the computational effort even further.

8. Results

In obtaining numerical results, three different criteria were used. In one case, the cost of surplus function $\phi_R(x_R - r_R)$ was taken to be simply $x_R - r_R$. In the second case, we set

(1) $$\phi_R(x_R - r_R) = x_R - r_R, \quad \text{for} \quad 0 \leq x_R - r_R \leq M,$$
$$\phi_R(x_R - r_R) = M, \quad \text{for} \quad x_R - r_R > M.$$

The third case involved rapidly increasing cost whenever the surplus exceeds M:

(2) $$\phi_R(x_R - r_R) = x_R - r_R, \quad 0 \leq x_R - r_R \leq M,$$
$$\phi_R(x_R - r_R) = x_R - r_R + \tfrac{1}{2}(x_R - r_R - M)^2, \quad x_R - r_R \geq M.$$

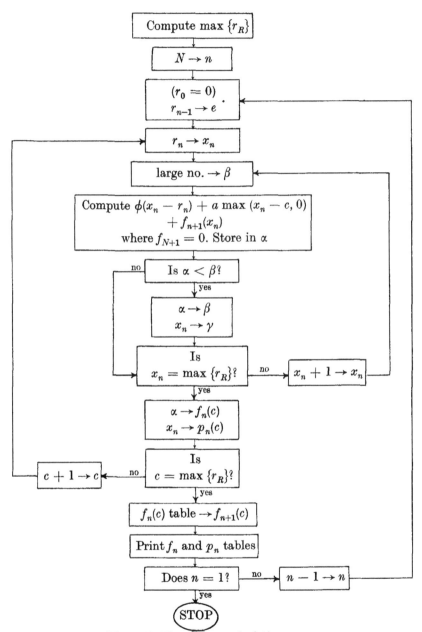

Figure 34. Flow diagram of solution.

The cost of increasing capability was taken to be directly proportional to the increase,

$$(3) \qquad \psi(x_R - x_{R-1}) = a \max (x_R - x_{R-1}, 0),$$

and there was no cost for decreasing capability. In all three cases, the costs were taken to be independent of the stage.

The following 27-period requirement schedule

$$(4) \quad [18, 13, 9, 6, 3, 5, 8, 3, 1, 9, 18, 11, 4, 3, 2, 4, 5, 9, 12, 13, 12,$$
$$11, 13, 7, 1, 8, 14]$$

was used with $a = 2$ or 4 and $M = 2$ or 4, for each of the three possible cost criteria. In each case, the starting level is taken to be zero. It should be noted that in many cases, the optimal policy is not unique. The one shown in the graphs, by means of heavy lines, is the result of an arbitrary decision regarding which of two minimizing values to use.

9. Flow Chart (see p. 107).

10. Some Graphical Results (Figs. 35–45)

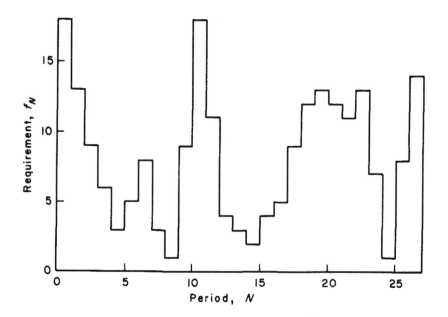

Figure 35. Requirement graph.

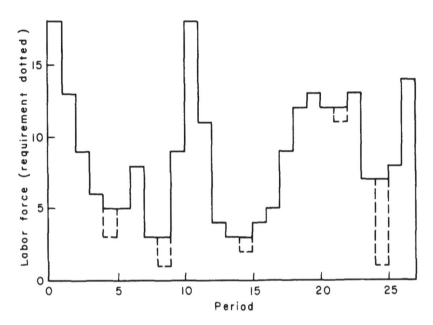

Figure 36. Optimal labor force under criterion 1, with $a = 2$; cost $= 120$.

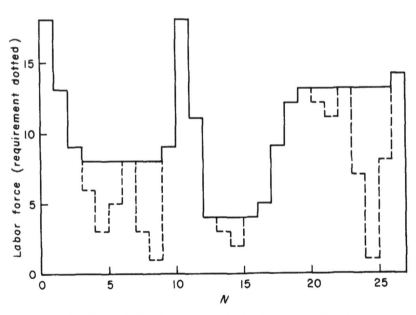

Figure 37. Optimal labor force under criterion 1, with $a = 4$; cost $= 203$.

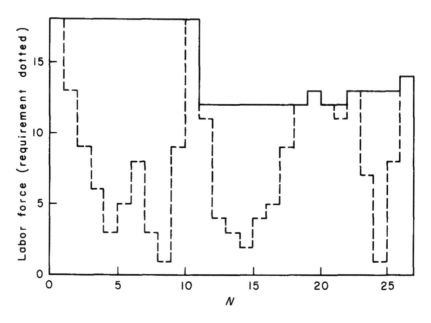

Figure 38. Optimal labor force under criterion 2, with $a = 2$, $m = 2$; cost = 80.

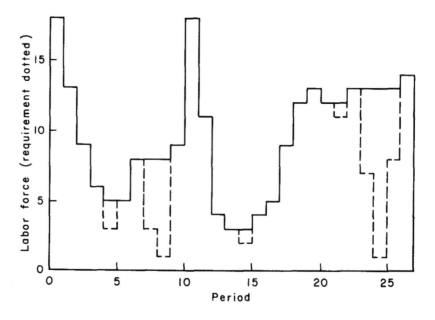

Figure 39. Optimal labor force under criterion 2, with $a = 2$, $M = 4$; cost = 110.

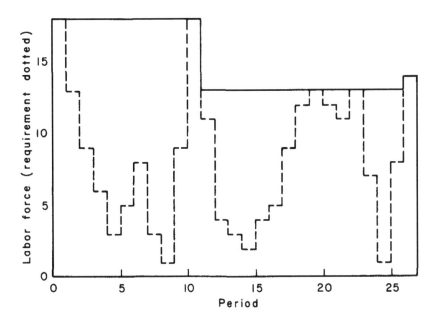

Figure 40. Optimal labor force under criterion 2, with $a = 4$, $M = 2$;
cost $= 118$.

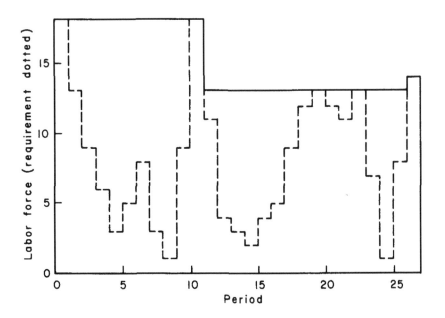

Figure 41. Optimal labor force under criterion 2, with $a = 4$, $m = 4$;
cost $= 154$.

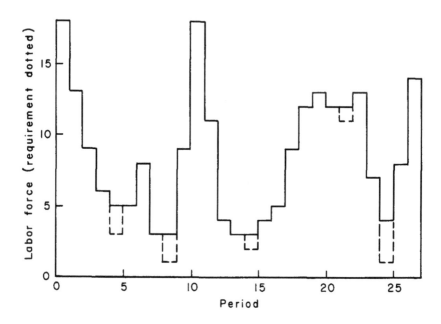

Figure 42. Optimal labor force under criterion 3, with $a = 2$, $m = 2$; cost $= 123.5$.

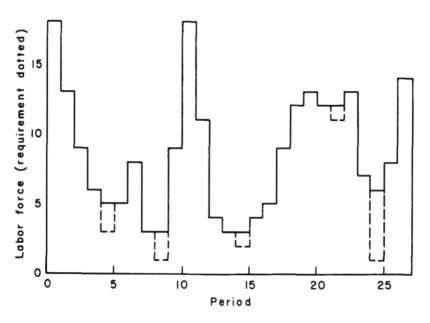

Figure 43. Optimal labor force under criterion 3, with $a = 2$, $m = 4$; cost $= 121.5$.

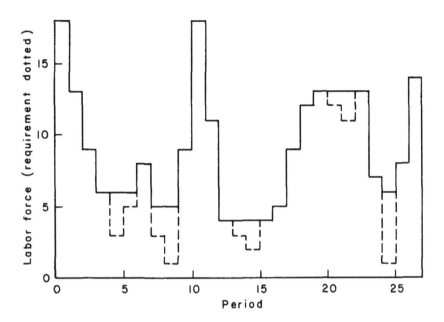

Figure 44. Optimal labor force under criterion 3, with $a = 4$, $m = 2$; cost $= 228$.

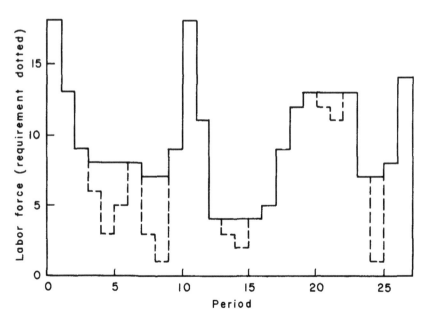

Figure 45. Optimal labor force under criterion 3, with $a = 4$, $m = 4$; cost $= 216.5$.

11. "Nearest Neighbor" Problems

Consider a set of points, p_i, along a line as indicated below,

|———|———|———|——————|———|
p_0 p_1 p_2 p_{N-1} p_N

and suppose that there is interaction only between neighboring points. If the quantities x_i measure the position of the point p_i, the total interaction is taken to be a specified function

$$(1) \qquad g_1(x_1 - x_0) + g_2(x_2 - x_1) + \cdots + g_N(x_N - x_{N-1}).$$

Fixing the values x_0 and x_N, the actual physical state of the system will be the values of $x_1, x_2, \ldots, x_{N-1}$ which minimize this function. The computational solution of this problem is readily obtained using the foregoing technique.

Problems of this type arise in statistical mechanics. References to treatments of this problem along classical lines, and by means of dynamic programming techniques will be found at the end of the chapter.

12. Equipment Replacement

One of the basic problems of our industrial society is that of the replacement of old machinery by new, of obsolete tools by modern devices. As equipment deteriorates with age, either actually, or relative to the performance of more recent inventions and improvements, there comes a time when the large initial outlay for new equipment, the loss due to the stoppage of work, and the cost of training new skills are all compensated for by the increase in productivity and decrease in operating costs.

We wish to determine optimal repair and replacement policies under various assumptions concerning present costs and operating characteristics—and future developments. Since decisions of this type must be made every year or so, depending upon the fundamental time period for the type of process we are discussing, it is clear that we face a multistage decision process.

Vital to any study of this type are the assumptions that are made concerning the future. We shall here consider only the relatively simple case where we are given a set of predictions for the future. How these predictions should be made and how they should be modified on the basis of experience are more sophisticated problems (also of dynamic programming type) which we shall not consider in this volume.

13. The Physical Process

To simplify the discussion of this introductory section, we shall suppose that we possess only a single machine which yields a certain revenue each year, requires a certain amount of care, and can be traded on a new machine at any time. The revenue, the upkeep cost, and the rebate on trade-in are all taken to depend upon the age of the machine in known fashions.

Given this information (Figs. 46, 47, 48) we wish to determine an optimal trade-in policy.

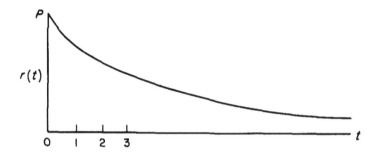

Figure 46. $r(t)$ = the yearly return of a machine of age t.

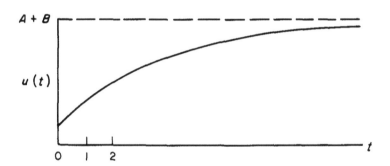

Figure 47. $u(t)$ = the yearly upkeep of a machine of age t.

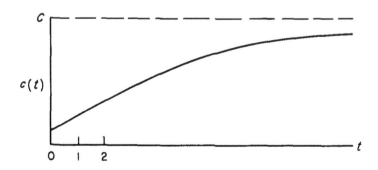

Figure 48. $c(t)$ = the cost of replacing a machine of age t.

14. Dynamic Programming Formulation

We shall suppose that decisions are made only at the times $t = 0, 1, 2, \ldots$, and that at each such time we have a choice of either keeping the old machine which we shall designate by a K for "keep," or buying a new one which is indicated by a P for "purchase." Introduce the function

(1) $f(t) = $ the total return over the time required starting with a machine of age t and using an optimal policy.

In order to keep the total return finite, we introduce a discount factor a. A unit of return one stage hence is considered to be worth a units at the present stage. This is a familiar device in mathematical economics.

Then we obtain, along familiar lines, the functional equation

(2) $$f(t) = \max \begin{bmatrix} P: & r(0) - u(0) - c(t) + af(1) \\ K: & r(t) - u(t) + af(t+1) \end{bmatrix}.$$

This is the first infinite process considered, and the first one in which we have used the functional notation $f(t)$ rather than a subscript notation f_t. As the reader will see, this simplifies our subsequent notation in which other subscripts occur.

15. Analytic Solution

It is clear that an optimal policy has the form: keep a new machine until it is T years old and then replace it by a new machine. Writing

(1) $$n(t) = r(t) - u(t),$$

we are led to the following system of equations:

(2) $$\begin{aligned} f(0) &= n(0) + af(1), \\ f(1) &= n(1) + af(2), \end{aligned}$$

$$\begin{aligned} f(T-1) &= n(T-1) + af(T), \\ f(T) &= -c(T) + n(0) + af(1). \end{aligned}$$

Solving this system of linear equations for $f(1)$, we obtain the relation

(3) $$f(1) = \frac{[n(1) + an(2) + \cdots + a^{T-2}n(T-1) + n(0)a^{T-1}] - a^{T-1}c(T)}{1 - a^T}.$$

The unknown quantity T is now chosen to maximize this expression for $f(1)$, since maximizing $f(1)$ clearly maximizes $f(0)$. The reader can convince himself, either analytically on the basis of the foregoing equations, or directly from the process, that starting with a machine of any age less than T, the optimal policy is to keep the machine until it is T years old and then replace it by a new one. What to do with a machine of age greater than T is not at all clear.

16. Technological Improvement

In §13, we assumed that revenue, upkeep cost, and replacement cost were functions of machine age alone. Typical data leads to the use of exponential curves such as are shown in Figs. 46, 47, and 48, where we may write

$$(1) \qquad \begin{aligned} r(t) &= Pe^{-st}, \\ u(t) &= A + B(1 - e^{-wt}), \\ c(t) &= C(1 - ke^{-dt}). \end{aligned}$$

Here P represents revenue from a new machine, A is the upkeep cost of a new machine, $A + B$ is the limiting upkeep cost as the machine ages, C is the cost of a new machine with no trade-in, k is the fraction of C remaining as trade-in value after purchase, and the exponents s, w, and d determine the rate at which the limiting values are approached.

Assume now that technological improvement occurs. As a result a machine produced during a future year N will have initial revenue greater than P and ultimately new machines will have initial revenue capacity $P + Q$. Let us assume that the improvement in initial performance is again an exponential function, this time of the year of manufacture rather than of age. Since the year of manufacture is determined by the absolute year N less the age of the machine t, we write

$$(2) \qquad r_N(t) = [P + Q(1 - e^{-g(N-t)})]e^{-st}.$$

If operating cost will tend to approach zero as technology improves, and if the increase in upkeep as the machine ages decreases by a factor u each year, we can write

$$(3) \qquad u_N(t) = Ae^{-z(N-t)} + B(1 - e^{-wt})u^{N-t}.$$

Cost of these new improved machines can be assumed to increase or decrease with time, or with no loss of generality we can assume it constant.

We have now defined a family of curves. For machines produced in any particular year, we have a curve of behavior as the machine ages. Figure 49 shows a typical family of such curves representing upkeep.

Although it is helpful for some purposes, and fairly realistic, to assume exponential technological change, the method of computational solution to be described in the next section does not make use of these special forms. In fact, straight tables of the various costs are actually as convenient to use as explicit analytic functions, and generally fit the facts better.

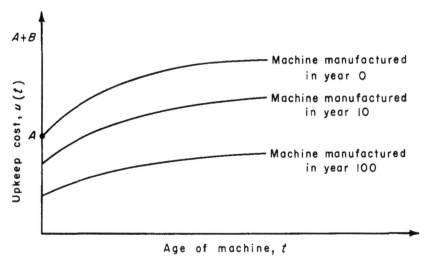

Figure 49

In most previous analyses of this problem, the exponentials were introduced to facilitate analytic solution.

17. Dynamic Programming Formulation

Let us introduce the functions

(1) $f_N(t) =$ the value at year N of the overall return from a machine which is t years old, where an optimal replacement policy is employed for the remainder of the process.

The future is discounted as before. However, we also assume that the process lasts N_0 stages, and then stops. Hence, $f_{N_0+1}(t) \equiv 0$.

Since the overall return associated with purchase at year N is

(2) $$f_N^{(P)}(t) = r_N(0) - u_N(0) - c_N(t) + af_{N+1}(1),$$

and the return from a decision to keep is

(3) $$f_N^{(K)}(t) = r_N(t) - u_N(t) + af_{N+1}(t + 1),$$

we obtain the equation

(4) $$f_N(t) = \max [f_N^{(P)}(t), f_N^{(K)}(t)],$$

or

(5) $$f_N(t) = \max \begin{bmatrix} P: & r_N(0) - u_N(0) - c_N(t) + af_{N+1}(1) \\ K: & r_N(t) - u_N(t) + af_{N+1}(t + 1) \end{bmatrix}.$$

The function $f_N(t)$ is taken to be zero for $N \geq N_0 + 1$.

Letting N assume the value N_0 in equation (5), we obtain an expression for $f_{N_0}(t)$ in terms of known functions. Hence, we can solve for $f_{N_0}(t)$, for all admissible t. Depending upon our as yet undetermined earlier decisions, we could have entered the last stage with anything from a one-year-old machine, bought in the previous period, to a very old machine, the one with which we started the process. Having constructed the function $f_{N_0}(t)$, we can use equation (5) to determine the function $f_{N_0-1}(t)$. Continuing this sequence, we obtain $f_1(t)$, the optimal return for a process starting in year 1. Recording the policy used in the maximization of equation (5), we have the replacement policy which yields the optimal return. This procedure constitutes a numerical solution of the problem.

18. Example

Let us solve the following simple example. We shall consider a ten-year process. Replacement, revenue, and upkeep costs for machines manufactured in each of the ten years are taken to be the following functions of machine age:

Machine made in year 1

Age of machine	0	1	2	3	4	5	6	7	8	9
Revenue	90	85	80	75	70	70	70	60	60	60
Upkeep	20	20	25	25	30	30	35	40	45	50
Replacement	200	220	240	250	255	260	265	270	270	270

Machine made in year 2

Age	0	1	2	3	4	5	6	7	8
Revenue	100	90	80	75	70	65	65	65	65
Upkeep	15	20	20	25	25	30	30	35	35
Replacement	200	220	240	250	255	260	265	270	270

Machine made in year 3

Age	0	1	2	3	4	5	6	7
Revenue	110	105	100	95	90	80	70	60
Upkeep	15	15	20	20	25	25	30	30
Replacement	200	220	240	250	255	260	265	270

Machine made in year 4

Age	0	1	2	3	4	5	6
Revenue	115	110	100	90	80	70	60
Upkeep	15	15	20	20	25	25	30
Replacement	210	215	220	225	230	235	240

Machine made in year 5

Age	0	1	2	3	4	5
Revenue	120	115	115	110	105	100
Upkeep	10	10	15	15	20	20
Replacement	210	215	220	225	230	235

Machine made in year 6

Age	0	1	2	3	4
Revenue	125	120	110	105	110
Upkeep	10	10	10	15	15
Replacement	210	220	230	240	250

Machine made in year 7

Age	0	1	2	3
Revenue	135	125	110	105
Upkeep	10	10	10	10
Replacement	210	220	230	240

Machine made in year 8

Age	0	1	2
Revenue	140	135	125
Upkeep	5	10	10
Replacement	220	230	240

Machine made in year 9

Age	0	1
Revenue	150	140
Upkeep	5	10
Replacement	220	225

Machine made in year 10

Age	0
Revenue	155
Upkeep	5
Replacement	220

Furthermore, we initiate the process with a machine, called the *incumbent machine,* of some age, say three years old, with the following future behavior:

Incumbent machine

Age	3	4	5	6	7	8	9	10	11	12
Revenue	60	60	50	50	50	40	40	40	30	30
Upkeep	55	55	55	60	60	60	60	65	65	70
Replacement	250	260	270	280	280	290	290	300	300	310

Let us now construct a table of $f_{10}(t)$. To compute $f_{10}(1)$, we compare the revenue minus upkeep for the old machine (a machine made in year 9 and now one year old) to the cost of replacing. Hence,

$$(1) \qquad f_{10}(1) = \max \begin{bmatrix} P: & 155 - 5 - 225 \\ K: & 140 - 10 \end{bmatrix} = 130,$$

and we keep the machine. One would hardly expect it to prove optimal to buy a new machine during the last stage of a process. Similarly,

$$(2) \qquad f_{10}(2) = \max \begin{bmatrix} P: & 155 - 5 - 240 \\ K: & 125 - 10 \end{bmatrix} = 115.$$

We complete the table of values of $f_{10}(t)$ as follows:

t	$f_{10}(t)$	Policy
1	130	K
2	115	K
3	95	K
4	85	K
5	80	K
6	30	K
7	30	K
8	30	K
9	10	K
12	−40	K

Let us compute the first two values of $f_9(t)$ and then present the complete set of tables constituting the solution. For computational convenience, we let $a = 1$, though in reality "a" should be taken small enough to reflect our uncertainty of the future as well as the discounted value of the dollar.

$$(3) \qquad f_9(1) = \max \begin{bmatrix} P: & 150 - 5 - 230 + 130 \\ K: & 135 - 10 + 115 \end{bmatrix} = 240,$$

$$f_9(2) = \max \begin{bmatrix} P: & 150 - 5 - 230 + 130 \\ K: & 110 - 10 + 95 \end{bmatrix} = 195.$$

Using equation (17.5) in this manner, we have, for our hypothetical machine, the following returns:

t	$f_9(t)$	Policy	t	$f_8(t)$	Policy	t	$f_7(t)$	Policy
1	240	K	1	310	K	1	385	K
2	195	K	2	275	K	2	360	K
3	175	K	3	260	K	3	215	K
4	165	K	4	145	P	4	190	K
5	75	K	5	125	K	5	175	P
6	70	K	6	110	P	6	170	P
7	60	K	7	105	P	9	145	P
8	25	K	10	75	P			
11	-25	P						

t	$f_6(t)$	Policy	t	$f_5(t)$	Policy	t	$f_4(t)$	Policy
1	465	K	1	390	K	1	435	K
2	295	K	2	345	K	2	385	K
3	265	K	3	325	P	3	370	K
4	245	P	4	320	P	6	285	K
5	240	P	7	295	P			
8	210	P						

t	$f_3(t)$	Policy	t	$f_2(t)$	Policy	t	$f_1(t)$	Policy
1	440	K	1	490	K	3	310	P
2	425	K	4	285	K			
5	280	K						

Let us review the derivation of the last number, $f_1(3) = 310$, for this represents the total return obtainable by using an optimal policy. We start year 1 with the incumbent machine, which we can replace or keep. If we replace the incumbent machine at a net cost of $250, the new machine (manufactured in year 1) will produce a net revenue of $70 for its first year plus the future profits ($490) derivable from a one-year-old machine beginning year 2. Therefore, the net gain is $310. If we keep the incumbent machine we accumulate a net revenue of $5 this year, and can earn $285 in all future years for a total profit of $290. Since $310 is greater than $290, we choose to purchase a new machine. Once we have decided to purchase, we see that we will start year 2 with a one-year-old machine, and the table says to keep it another year. We start year 3 with a two-year-old machine and again, following the table, we keep it. Retracing our steps in this manner, we see that the optimal policy is to purchase at year 1, keep until year 5, when we again purchase, and then keep this machine for the rest of the process. As a check on our work we can add up the gain from this policy, which is shown below:

Year	Policy	Profit
1	P	-180
2	K	65
3	K	55
4	K	50
5	P	-145
6	K	105
7	K	100
8	K	95
9	K	85
10	K	80
		310

As an interesting by-product of this analysis, we see that should we be forced to keep the incumbent machine during year 1, perhaps because of insufficient capital to replace, our optimal policy then says that we should keep the old machine until year 5, and then replace. This is the policy that results in a net profit of $290. Since the net gain of replacing now over that of keeping is $20, it is for management to decide if the initial outlay of $250 for a $20 net gain ís economical. One calculation of this sort, performed quite easily by hand in an hour or so, essentially tests all 2^{10} possible replacement schedules and chooses the best. In addition, it produces some additional worthwhile information. As a machine computation, a matter of seconds is required per stage.

19. Other Formulations

The technique of solution here described is sufficiently general to admit a wide variety of formulations of the equipment replacement problem. No unrealistic assumptions need be made in order to fit a restrictive mathematical model. For example, a third alternative policy, the purchase of a used machine, may be included if one can define a cost function, $g_N(t, x)$ which determines the cost of replacing a machine of age t by one of age x in year N. The recurrence relation in this case is

$$(1) \quad f_N(t) = \max \begin{bmatrix} \text{Purchase a new machine:} \\ \quad r_N(0) - u_N(0) - c_N(t) + af_{N+1}(1) \\ \\ \text{Purchase a machine of age } x: \\ \quad \max_x r_N(x) - u_N(x) - g_N(t, x) + af_{N+1}(x + 1) \\ \\ \text{Keep: } r_N(t) - u_N(t) + af_{N+1}(t + 1) \end{bmatrix}.$$

If we allow x to equal 0 and $c_N(t) = g_N(t, 0)$ we can include the purchase of a new machine as a special case of the purchase of a machine of age x. We may include the possibility of an overhaul in the same way if we are willing to agree that an overhauled machine of age t will have the characteristics of a machine of some smaller age t'. Here t' is a function of t and the effort devoted to overhaul.

To include overhaul in a completely general manner, we add a new dimension to the problem. Introduce the function

(2) $f_N(t_1, t_2) =$ value at year N of the overall return from a machine of age t_1, and last overhauled at age t_2, where an optimal replacement policy is employed for the remainder of the process.

We must now define our various costs in terms of both age, t_1, and age of the machine at its last overhaul, t_2. Having done this, we write a recurrence relation in a manner analogous to that given above, obtaining

(3)
$$f_N(t_1, t_2) = \max \begin{bmatrix} P: & r_N(0,0) - u_N(0,0) - c_N(t_1, t_2) + af_{N+1}(1,0) \\ K: & r_N(t_1, t_2) - u_N(t_1, t_2) + af_{N+1}(t_1 + 1, t_2) \\ 0: & r_N(t_1, t_1) - u_N(t_1, t_1) - 0_N(t_1, t_2) + af_{N+1}(t_1 + 1, t_1) \end{bmatrix},$$

where $0_N(t_1, t_2)$ is the cost of overhauling in year N a machine of age t_1 last overhauled at age t_2. The technique of numerical solution is analogous to that of §17, except we now compute a sequence of functions of two variables. Such a calculation for the range of values of t_1 and t_2 occurring here is still easily performed on a digital computer, regardless of the length of the process being analyzed.

Another formulation might make use of a stochastic model, with expected return being maximized. In such a model, probability of breakdown would be included as a function of year, age, utilization, and other factors, and a replacement policy maximizing some criteria of performance would be sought.

Problems of this type are particular examples of the Markovian decision processes discussed in Chapter IX. As we shall see, once we have established the existence of certain steady-state or asymptotic steady-state policies, using the functional equation approach, we can then discard the functional equations and use a number of different techniques to obtain approximate solutions. In this way we can often bypass the usual multi-dimensional worries.

The optimal inventory process we shall discuss below is an interesting combination of a smoothing and replacement problem.

20. A Warehousing Problem

Continuing our discussion of one-dimensional scheduling processes, let us focus upon a problem of the following nature:

"Given a warehouse with fixed capacity and an initial stock of a certain product which is subject to known seasonal price and cost variations, what is the optimal pattern of purchasing (or production), storage, and sales?"

Not only shall we obtain a simple computational approach by means of dynamic programming, but we shall derive by way of the basic functional equations an explicit analytic solution.

21. A Mathematical Model

Let us begin by introducing the following quantities:

(1) B = the storage capacity of the warehouse,

v = the stock on hand at any particular stage.

Consider a seasonal product to be bought (or produced), and then sold at each of N periods. When i periods, remain,

(2) c_i = cost per unit (bought or produced),

p_i = selling price per unit,

x_i = quantity bought (or produced),

y_i = quantity sold.

The following restrictions must be imposed upon possible policies:

(3) (a) *Buying constraints:* The stock on hand at the end of the ith period cannot exceed the warehouse capacity.

(b) *Selling constraints:* The amount sold in the ith period cannot exceed the amount available at the end of the $(i - 1)$-th period.

(c) *Nonnegativity constraints:* Amounts purchased or sold in any period are nonnegative.

As a consequence of these restrictions, the following inequalities must hold:

(4) *Buying constraints:*

$$v + \sum_{j=1}^{i} (x_j - y_j) \leq B, \quad i = 1, 2, \ldots, N,$$

Selling constraints:

$$y_i \leq v + \sum_{j=1}^{i-1} (x_j - y_j), \quad i = 2, 3, \ldots, N,$$

$$y_1 \leq v,$$

Nonnegativity constraints:

$$x_i, y_i \geq 0.$$

125

Subject to these constraints, we wish to maximize the total profit derived from the N-stage process, the function

(5) $$P_N = \sum_{j=1}^{N} (p_j y_j - c_j x_j).$$

22. Recurrence Relations

To treat this problem by means of dynamic programming techniques, let us introduce the sequence of functions $\{f_N(v)\}$ defined by the relation

(1) $$f_N(v) = \max_{\{y, x\}} P_N,$$

for the set of values $v \geq 0$, $N = 1, 2, \ldots$, where x_i and y_i are subject to the relations of (21.4).

For $N = 1$, we clearly have

(2) $$f_1(v) = \max (p_1 y_1 - c_1 x_1),$$

where the maximum is over the region defined by

(3) $$0 \leq y_1 \leq v, \quad x_1 \geq 0.$$

Hence,

(4) $$f_1(v) = p_1 v.$$

For $N \geq 2$, we obtain in the usual fashion the recurrence relation

(5) $$f_N(v) = \max_{x_N, y_N} [p_N y_N - c_N x_N + f_{N-1}(v + x_N - y_N)],$$

where the maximum is to be taken over the region

(6)　(a)　　　　　　　$0 \leq y_N \leq v,$

　　　(b)　　　　　　　$x_N \geq 0,$

　　　(c)　　　　　　　$v + x_N - y_N \leq B.$

23. Discussion

This is a simple recurrence relation which leads by not much more than a hand calculation to a rapid calculation of the maximum profit and the optimal policy. It so happens, however, that a great deal more can be obtained from the recurrence relations. We can obtain a simple explicit solution which unquestionably yields a hand calculation.

24. Preliminary Transformations

It turns out to be convenient to think in terms of the inventory level attained at the end of each period. Write

(1) $$v + x_N - y_N = u,$$

so that the maximization over the region determined in (22.6) can be written

(2)
$$\max_{0 \le u \le B} \left[\max_{0 \le y_N \le v, \, x_N \ge 0} \right].$$

Then the relation in (22.5) may be written

(3)
$$f_N(v) = \max_{0 \le u \le B} [\phi_N(u, v) + f_{N-1}(u)],$$

where

(4)
$$\phi_N(u, v) = \max_{x_N, y_N} (p_N y_N - c_N x_N),$$

and x_N, y_N are constrained by the inequalities

(5) (a) $\qquad\qquad\qquad v + x_N - y_N = u,$

(b) $\qquad\qquad\qquad y_N \le v,$

(c) $\qquad\qquad\qquad x_N, y_N \ge 0.$

In the determination of the function $\phi_N(u, v)$, we are faced with the maximization of a linear function over the points on a straight line, which means that we need only investigate the end points.

When $0 \le u \le v$, the two points under consideration are $x_N = 0$, $y_N = v - u$, and $x_N = u$, $y_N = v$. In this region,

(6)
$$\phi_N(u, v) = \max [p_N(v - u), \, p_N v - c_N u].$$

Arguing similarly, for $v \le u \le B$,

(7)
$$\phi_N(u, v) = \max [-c_N(u - v), \, p_N v - c_N u].$$

For fixed v, $0 \le v \le B$, the result can be shown geometrically in two cases which are illustrated in Figs. 50 and 51.

Having established the nature of the function $\phi_N(u, v)$, we shall proceed to a derivation of the analytic structure of the sequence $\{f_N(v)\}$.

25. Analytic Structure

The structure of the function, $f_N(v)$, defined in equation (24.3) is not immediately obvious. However, the following surprising property holds:

Theorem 1. The function $f_N(v)$ is linear in v, the coefficients being functions of $p_1, \ldots, p_N$ and $c_1, \ldots, c_N$, namely

(1)
$$f_N(v) = K_N(p_1, p_2, \ldots, p_N; c_1, c_2, \ldots, c_N)$$
$$+ L(p_1, p_2, \ldots, p_N; c_1, c_2, \ldots, c_N)v.$$

Furthermore, the optimal policy, u, is independent of v, the initial stock, and depends only upon the selling prices and costs.

Case 1: $c_N > p_N$

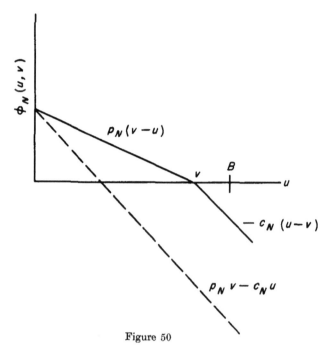

Figure 50

Case 2: $p_N > c_N$

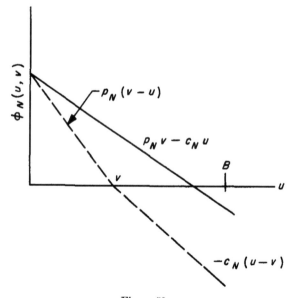

Figure 51

26. Proof of Theorem 1

The proof is by induction. Clearly $f_1(v) = p_1 v$ since the zero stage return, $f_0(u)$, is identically zero. Assume that $f_{N-1}(v) = K_{N-1} + L_{N-1}v$ where K_{N-1} and L_{N-1} are determined by the $(N-1)$ prices and costs, $\{p_i, c_i\}$, $i = 1, 2, \ldots, N-1$. We shall show that $f_N(v)$ has the same form where the coefficients now depend upon the sequence $\{p_i, c_i\}$, $i = 1, 2, \ldots, N$. As in Case 1, let c_N be greater than p_N. Due to our hypothesis concerning the linearity of $f_{N-1}(u)$, the maximum must occur at one of three points: $u = 0$, $u = v$, or $u = B$. Thus,

$$(1) \qquad f_N(v) = \max\,[\phi_N(0, v) + f_{N-1}(0),$$
$$\phi_N(v, v) + f_{N-1}(v),\ \phi_N(B, v) + f_{N-1}(B)],$$

or

$$(2) \qquad f_N(v) = \max\,[p_N v + K_{N-1},\ K_{N-1} + L_{N-1}v,$$
$$-\,c_N(B - v) + K_{N-1} + L_{N-1}B].$$

Since the third quantity in (2) is greater than the first two if and only if $c_N < L_{N-1}$, we have established the condition for a choice of $u = B$. The second quantity is maximum when $p_N < L_{N-1} < c_N$ and the first is largest when $L_{N-1} < p_N$. In all three cases it should be noted that the maximizing u is independent of v. If u is taken equal to B, then

$$(3) \qquad f_N(v) = (K_{N-1} + L_{N-1}B - c_N B) + c_N v.$$

Hence, $K_N = K_{N-1} + L_{N-1}B - c_N B$ and $L_N = c_N$. If $u = v$,

$$(4) \qquad f_N(v) = K_{N-1} + L_{N-1}v,$$

whence $K_N = K_{N-1}$ and $L_N = L_{N-1}$. Finally, $u = 0$ leads to

$$(5) \qquad f_N(v) = K_{N-1} + p_N v.$$

Hence, $K_N = K_{N-1}$, $L_N = p_N$. In each case, $f_N(v)$ is a linear function of v with the new coefficients depending upon $p_1, \ldots, p_N$ and $c_1, \ldots, c_N$.

The second case, $p_N > c_N$, remains to be considered. Since both $\phi_N(u, v)$ and $f_{N-1}(u)$ are linear, we must investigate only two points, $u = 0$ and $u = B$. Here,

$$(6) \qquad f_N(v) = \max\,[\phi_N(0, v) + f_{N-1}(0),\ \phi_N(B, v) + f_{N-1}(B)],$$

$$(7) \qquad f_N(v) = \max\,[p_N v + K_{N-1},\ p_N v - c_N B + K_{N-1} + L_{N-1}B].$$

We have a maximum at $u = 0$ if $L_{N-1} < c_N$ and at $u = B$ if the reverse inequality is true. In these cases,

$$(8) \qquad f_N(v) = K_{N-1} + p_N v,$$

if $u = 0$, with $K_N = K_{N-1}$, $L_N = p_N$. On the other hand,

$$(9) \qquad f_N(v) = (K_{N-1} + L_{N-1}B - c_N B) + p_N v$$

if $u = B$, with $K_N = K_{N-1} + L_{N-1}B - c_N B$, $L_N = p_N$. This completes the proof.

27. Discussion

Let us now consider the economic interpretation of the problem, and investigate our analytic results.

Apparently, if $c_N > p_N$, we have three alternatives, dependent upon other parameters. Equations (26.3)-(26.5) have the following significance: (26.3) represents a purchase of enough goods to fill the warehouse and the current cost of this decision, $\phi_N(B, v)$ is $c_N(B - v)$. On the other hand, equation (26.4) corresponds to doing nothing, with an associated current cost of zero. Finally, the equation in (26.5) arises from selling all v items with which the period was entered, with an immediate return of $p_N v$.

Turning to equation (26.8), where $p_N > c_N$, we have a slightly different interpretation. Here, a policy dictating a final level of B means the sale of v and purchase of B, with associated cost $p_N v - c_N B$. A choice of $u = 0$, as above, means the sale of the entire stock, v, and a return of $p_N v$. In all, we then have four distinct policies: sell; buy; sell and buy; do nothing.

In each case, the policy is pursued up to the constraint of warehouse capacity, or the stock on hand.

28. A Numerical Example

Recalling the definition of p_i and c_i to be costs when i periods remain, let us, to illustrate the solution, consider the following ten-period process.

i	1	2	3	4	5	6	7	8	9	10
c_i	3	5	2	3	3	4	3	2	8	8
p_i	2	3	1	5	5	4	1	7	6	3

We wish to compute K_{10}, L_{10}, and u_{10}, the return coefficients and the policy when ten periods remain, i.e., the decision made at the beginning of the process. Since $f_1(v) = p_1 v$, we conclude that $K_1 = 0$, $L_1 = p_1$, $u_1 = 0$, whence

$$(1) \qquad K_1 = 0, \quad L_1 = 2, \quad u_1 = 0.$$

We note now that $c_2 > p_2$ which means that we refer to equations (26.3)-(26.5). Since $L_1 < p_2$, equation (26.5) is applicable, yielding the values

$$(2) \qquad K_2 = 0, \quad L_2 = 3, \quad u_2 = 0.$$

For the third from last period, the relations $c_3 > p_3$ and $L_2 > c_3$ enable us to use (26.3). Hence,

$$(3) \qquad\qquad K_3 = B, \quad L_3 = 2, \quad u_3 = B.$$

Continuing this process,

$$(4) \qquad\qquad \begin{aligned} K_4 &= B, & L_4 &= 5, & u_4 &= 0, \\ K_5 &= 3B, & L_5 &= 5, & u_5 &= B, \\ K_6 &= 4B, & L_6 &= 4, & u_6 &= B, \\ K_7 &= 5B, & L_7 &= 3, & u_7 &= B, \\ K_8 &= 6B, & L_8 &= 7, & u_8 &= B, \\ K_9 &= 6B, & L_9 &= 7, & u_9 &= v, \\ K_{10} &= 6B, & L_{10} &= 7, & u_{10} &= v. \end{aligned}$$

For this numerical example, our conclusions are that an optimal policy leads to a profit of $6B + 7v$, where v is the stock at the beginning of the 10-stage process and B is the warehouse capacity. The optimal policy requires no action during the first two periods, sells v and buys B during period 3, keeps the warehouse full during the 4th and 5th periods, sells B and buys B during period 6, sells B during period 7, buys B during the 8th period, and finally sells out during period 9.

29. Conclusions

We have established the following results:

1. The optimal N-stage return is a linear function of initial stock with coefficients dependent upon the costs and selling prices.

2. The optimal policy at any stage is *independent* of initial stock at that stage.

3. The optimal policy will always have the following simple structure: Do no buying or selling for the first k stages (k may equal zero), and then oscillate between a full and empty warehouse condition for the remainder of the process.

30. The Caterer Problem

A problem of quite different origin, but of analogous analytic structure is the following:

"A caterer knows that in connection with the meals he has arranged to serve during the next n days, he will need r_j fresh napkins on the jth day, $j = 1, 2, \ldots, n$. There are two types of laundry service available. One type requires p days and costs b cents per napkin; a faster service requires q days, $q < p$, but costs c cents per napkin, $c > b$. Beginning with no usable napkins on hand or in the laundry, the caterer meets the demands by purchasing napkins at a cents per napkin. How does the caterer purchase and launder napkins so as to minimize the total cost for n days?"

This problem can be approached in several different ways, one which leads to functions of far too many variables, a second which permits a fairly explicit analytic solution and thus a quite simple computational solution, and a third which yields an immediate simple solution.

The second approach is based upon an important idea which can be used to simplify a number of analytic problems arising in variational theory. Consequently, we shall discuss it below, despite the existence of the trivial solution, since we can use the basic idea again in connection with bottleneck processes, and in our discussion of the use of successive approximations.

31. Dynamic Programming Approach—I

The first approach to the problem by means of dynamic programming proceeds as follows. The state of the process at any time may be specified by the stage, i.e., day, and by the number of napkins due back from the laundry in 1, 2, up to p days hence. On the basis of that information, we must make a decision as to how many napkins to purchase, and how to launder the accumulated dirty napkins.

It is not difficult to formulate the problem in this way, using the functional equation approach. Unfortunately, if p is large, we founder on the shoals of dimensionality.

As we shall see, the proper dimensionality of the problem is $p - q$, when formulated in a different manner. The fact that a particular process can be approached in several different ways is one of the essential facts we learn from this problem.

32. Dynamic Programming Approach—II

In place of the approach mentioned above, let us proceed with the equations defining the process in the usual way until an appropriate point at which we shall reintroduce the dynamic programming approach.

It is first of all clear from the above formulation of the problem that we may just as well purchase all the napkins at one time at the start of the process. Let us then begin by solving the simpler problem of determining the laundering process to employ given an initial stock of S napkins. Clearly,

(1) $$S \geq \max_k r_k.$$

Let us now make a simplifying observation that all the dirty napkins returned at the end of each day are sent out to the laundry, either to the fast service or to the slow service.

The process then continues as follows. At the end of the kth day, the caterer divides r_k, the quantity of dirty napkins on hand, into two parts,

$r_k = u_k + v_k$, with u_k sent to the q-day laundry, and v_k sent to the p-day laundry.

Continuing in this way, we see that the quantity, x_k, of clean napkins available at the beginning of the kth day is determined by the following recurrence relation,

$$(2) \qquad x_1 = S,$$

$$x_k = (x_{k-1} - r_{k-1}) + u_{k-q} + v_{k-p},$$

where $u_k = v_k = 0$ for $k \le 0$.

The cost incurred on the kth day is

$$(3) \qquad bv_k + cu_k, \quad k = 1, 2, \ldots, N - 1.$$

Hence, the total cost is

$$(4) \qquad C_N = b \sum_{k=1}^{N-1} v_k + c \sum_{k=1}^{N-1} u_k.$$

The problem is to minimize C_N subject to the constraints on the u_k

$$(5) \quad (a) \qquad 0 \le u_k \le r_k,$$

$$(b) \qquad x_k \ge r_k, \quad k = 1, 2, \ldots, N.$$

In order to illustrate the method, we shall consider two particular cases.

$$(6) \quad (a) \qquad q = 1, \quad p = 2,$$

$$(b) \qquad q = 1, \quad p = 3.$$

The general case will be discussed following this.

33. Analytic Solution for $q = 1$, $p = 2$

The equations in (32.2) assume the form

$$(1) \qquad x_1 = S,$$

$$x_2 = (x_1 - r_1) + u_1,$$

$$x_3 = (x_2 - r_2) + u_2 + v_1,$$

$$.$$
$$.$$
$$.$$

$$x_{n-1} = (x_{n-2} - r_{n-2}) + u_{n-2} + v_{n-3},$$

$$x_n = (x_{n-1} - r_{n-1}) + u_{n-1} + v_{n-2}.$$

Let us now solve for the x_k in terms of the u_k and v_k. This is the essential device which greatly reduces the dimensionality of the process. We shall meet this technique again below.

We have

(2) $x_1 = S,$

$$x_2 = (S - r_1) + u_1,$$

$$x_3 = (S - r_1 - r_2) + (u_1 + u_2) + v_1,$$

$$x_4 = (S - r_1 - r_2 - r_3) + (u_1 + u_2 + u_3) + v_1 + v_2,$$

.

.

.

$$x_{n-1} = (S - r_1 - r_2 - \cdots - r_{n-2}) + (u_1 + u_2 + u_3 + \cdots + u_{n-2}),$$
$$+ (v_1 + v_2 + \cdots + v_{n-3}),$$

$$x_n = (S - r_1 - r_2 - \cdots - r_{n-1}) + (u_1 + u_2 + u_3 + \cdots + u_{n-1}),$$
$$+ (v_1 + v_2 + \cdots + v_{n-2}).$$

Since $r_k = u_k + v_k$, this may be written

(3) $$x_k = S - v_{k-1}, \quad (v_0 = 0), \quad k = 1, 2, \ldots, n.$$

Turning to (32.4), we wish to minimize

(4) $$C_N = c \sum_{k=1}^{N-1} r_k + (b - c) \sum_{k=1}^{N-1} v_k,$$

over all v_k subject to the constraints

(5) (a) $$0 \le v_k \le r_k,$$

(b) $$S - v_{k-1} \ge r_k \quad \text{or} \quad S - r_k \ge v_{k-1}.$$

Since $(c - b) > 0$, we wish to choose v_k as large as possible. Hence,

(6) $$v_k = \min (r_k, S - r_{k+1}), \quad k = 1, 2, \ldots, N - 1.$$

This determines the structure of the optimal policy. Using this explicit form of the solution, it is not difficult to determine the minimizing value of S.

34. Analytic Solution for $q = k$, $p = k + 1$

It is readily seen upon writing down the equations that the case $q = k$, $p = k + 1$ leads to a system of equations of the same type as given above for $q = 1$, $p = 2$. This illustrates the fact that it is only the difference $p - q$ which determines the level of difficulty of the problem.

35. Analytic Solution for $q = 1$, $p = 3$ —I

In order to illustrate the method which is applicable to the general case, let us consider the case $q = 1$, $p = 3$.

The equations in (32.2) assume the form

(1)
$$x_1 = S,$$
$$x_2 = x_1 - r_1 + u_1,$$
$$x_3 = x_2 - r_2 + u_2,$$
$$x_4 = x_3 - r_3 + u_3 + v_1,$$
$$\cdot$$
$$\cdot$$
$$\cdot$$
$$x_n = x_{n-1} - r_{n-1} + u_{n-1} + v_{n-3}.$$

Thus,

(2)
$$x_1 = S,$$
$$x_2 = S - r_1 + u_1,$$
$$x_3 = (S - r_1 - r_2) + u_1 + u_2,$$
$$x_4 = (S - r_1 - r_2 - r_3) + u_1 + u_2 + u_3 + v_1,$$
$$\cdot$$
$$\cdot$$
$$\cdot$$
$$x_n = (S - r_1 - r_2 - r_3 - \cdots - r_{n-1})$$
$$+ u_1 + u_2 + u_3 + \cdots + u_{n-1} + v_1 + v_2 + \cdots + v_{n-3}.$$

Hence,

(3)
$$x_1 = S,$$
$$x_2 = S - v_1,$$
$$x_3 = S - v_1 - v_2,$$
$$x_4 = S - v_2 - v_3,$$
$$\cdot$$
$$\cdot$$
$$\cdot$$
$$x_n = S - v_{n-2} - v_{n-1}.$$

We wish to maximize $\sum_{k=1}^{N-1} v_k$ subject to the constraints

(4)
$$S - v_1 \geq r_1, \qquad\qquad S - r_1 \geq v_1,$$
$$S - v_1 - v_2 \geq r_2, \qquad \text{or} \qquad S - r_2 \geq v_1 + v_2,$$
$$\cdot \qquad\qquad\qquad\qquad \cdot$$
$$\cdot \qquad\qquad\qquad\qquad \cdot$$
$$\cdot \qquad\qquad\qquad\qquad \cdot$$
$$S - v_{n-2} - v_{n-1} \geq r_{n-1}, \qquad S - r_{n-1} \geq v_{n-2} + v_{n-1},$$

and

(5)
$$0 \leq v_i \leq r_i.$$

36. Analytic Solution for $q = 1$, $p = 3$ —II

Our problem reduces to that of maximizing the linear form

$$(1) \qquad L_N = \sum_{k=1}^{N} v_k,$$

subject to a set of constraints of the form

$$(2) \quad (a) \qquad b_1 \geq v_1,$$
$$b_2 \geq v_1 + v_2,$$
$$\cdot$$
$$\cdot$$
$$\cdot$$
$$b_N \geq v_N + v_{N-1},$$
$$(b) \qquad r_k \geq v_k \geq 0.$$

Having chosen v_1, it is clear that we have a problem of precisely the same type remaining for the other variables $v_2, v_3, \ldots, v_N$. Let us then define the sequence of functions $\{f_k(x)\}$, $k = 1, 2, \ldots, N - 1$, as follows:

$$(3) \qquad f_k(x) = \max_{R_k} \sum_{l=k}^{N} v_l,$$

where R_k is the region defined by

$$(4) \quad (a) \qquad x \geq v_k \geq 0,$$
$$b_{k+1} \geq v_k + v_{k+1},$$
$$\cdot$$
$$\cdot$$
$$\cdot$$
$$b_N \geq v_{N-1} + v_N,$$
$$(b) \qquad r_{k+1} \geq v_{k+1} \geq 0,$$
$$\cdot$$
$$\cdot$$
$$\cdot$$
$$r_N \geq v_N \geq 0.$$

We have

$$(5) \qquad f_{N-1}(x) = \max\,[v_{N-1} + v_N],$$

where

$$(6) \qquad x \geq v_{N-1} \geq 0,$$
$$b_N \geq v_{N-1} + v_N, \quad r_N \geq v_N \geq 0.$$

Hence,

$$(7) \qquad f_{N-1}(x) = \min\,[b_N, x + r_N].$$

136

Employing the principle of optimality, we see that

$$(8) \qquad f_k(x) = \max_{0 \le v_k \le v_k^*} [v_k + f_{k+1}(\min(r_{k+1}, b_{k+1} - v_k))],$$

where $v_k^* = \min[x, b_{k+1}]$, for $k = 1, 2, \ldots, N - 1$.

37. Analytic Solution

It can now be shown by a simple, but rather arithmetic, argument that

$$(1) \qquad f_k(x) = \min[P_k, x + Q_k],$$

where

$$(2) \qquad P_k = \min[P_{k+1} + b_{k+1}, Q_{k+1} + b_{k+1}], \quad P_{N-1} = b_N,$$

$$Q_k = \min[P_{k+1}, r_{k+1} + Q_{k+1}],$$

$k = 1, 2, \ldots, N - 1$. Furthermore, similar results hold for the general case where $p - q$ may be any integer.

We have engaged in this analysis in order to show that the functional equation technique can be used to obtain explicit analytic solutions of a number of scheduling problems which take the form of that posed in §36.

38. A Common-sense Solution

Let us now show that the original problem, given in §30, can be solved by some quite simple reasoning. Consider the case where $p = 2, q = 4$ first.

Adhering to the previous meaning of u_k, v_k, r_k, and x_k, the following two inequalities concerning the demands in these future periods that can be effected by the decision at time k must be satisfied for the choice of v_k:

$$(1) \qquad x_k - r_k - r_{k+1} + v_{k-2} + u_{k-1} + u_k \ge r_{k+2},$$

$$x_k - r_k - r_{k+1} - r_{k+2} + u_{k-1} + u_k + u_{k+1} + v_{k-3} + v_{k-2} + v_{k-1} \ge r_{k+3}.$$

Regrouping and transposing (recalling that $u_k + v_k = r_k$),

$$(2) \qquad v_k \le x_k - r_{k+1} - r_{k+2} + v_{k-2} + u_{k-1} = L_1,$$

$$v_k \le x_k - r_{k+1} - r_{k+2} - r_{k+3} + u_{k+1} + u_{k-1} + v_{k-3} + v_{k-2} + v_{k-1} = L_2.$$

Assuming proportional cost, which is independent of time, as above, we assert that u_{k+1} can be taken equal to r_{k+1}. This is because in examining the present with the aim of sending as many as possible to the slow laundry, one can assume that all future napkins are sent to the fast laundry. We now choose

$$(3) \qquad v_k = \min(L_1, L_2(u_{k+1} = r_{k+1}), r_k)$$

to obtain the solution.

A numerical example with $S = 20$, $p = 2$, $q = 4$, is shown in Fig. 52.

k	1	2	3	4	5	6	7	8	9
r_k	3	5	6	4	9	2	1	10	1
v_k	3	5	2	4	9	0	1	10	1
u_k	0	0	4	0	0	2	0	0	0
x_{k+1}	17	12	6	9	5	5	10	9	8

Figure 52

Consider now the general case. The inequalities to be satisfied are

$$(4) \quad S - v_{k-q+p+1} - v_{k-q+p+2} - \cdots - v_k - r_{k+1} - \cdots - r_{k+p-1} \geq r_{k+p},$$
$$S - v_{k-q+p+2} - v_{k-q+p+3} - \cdots - v_{k+1} - r_{k+2} - \cdots - r_{k+p} \geq r_{k+p+1},$$
$$\vdots$$
$$S - v_k - v_{k+1} - \cdots - v_{k+q-p-1} - r_{k+q+p} - \cdots - r_{k+q-2} \geq r_{k+q-1},$$

$q - p$ relations, and $v_k \leq r_k$.

Let us now use these inequalities to determine bounds on v_k. In order to allow v_k to be as large as possible, we take v_{k+i}, $i \geq 1$, equal to zero in the foregoing constraints. As before, this is permissible since an increase of v_k by 1 and a decrease of v_{k+1} by 1 do not affect the sum $\sum_{j=1}^{N} v_j$. Setting all $v_{k+i} = 0$, $i \geq 1$, in the foregoing inequalities, and transposing, we obtain the following restrictions:

$$(5) \qquad v_k \leq S - \sum_{i=k-q+p+1}^{k-1} v_i - \sum_{i=k+1}^{k+p} r_i,$$

$$v_k \leq S - \sum_{i=k-q+p+2}^{k-1} v_i - \sum_{i=k+2}^{k+p+1} r_i,$$

$$\vdots$$

$$v_k \leq S - \sum_{i=k+q-p}^{k+q-1} r_i,$$

$$v_k \leq r_k.$$

As an example, consider the case where $S = 20, q = 5, p = 2$ (see Fig. 53).

r_k	1	10	2	8	3	2	14	1
v_k	1	8	0	4*	0	1	14	1
u_k	0	2	2	4	3	1	0	0
x_{k+1}	19	9	9	3	5	14	1	4

Figure 53

The starred number, 4, is obtained as follows:

(6) $4 = \min (20 - 8 - 0 - 3 - 2, 20 - 0 - 2 - 14, 20 - 14 - 1, 8)$.

39. Inventory Problems

There are a large number of processes which involve ordering supplies at the present so as to anticipate an unknown demand in the future. We shall treat here only the simple case where the distribution of demand is assumed known.

Let us consider a process involving the stocking of a single item. We assume that orders for further supplies are made at each of a finite set of times, and immediately fulfilled. After the order has been made and filled, there is a demand made for the item. This demand is satisfied as far as possible, with any excess of demand over supply leading to a penalty cost.

We suppose that the following functions are known:

(1) (a) $\phi(s)ds =$ the probability that the demand will lie between s and $s + ds$.

(b) $k(z) =$ the cost of ordering z items to increase the stock level.

(c) $p(z) =$ the cost of ordering z items to meet an excess, z, of demand over supply, the *penalty cost*.

To simplify the situation, let us assume that these functions are independent of time. Our aim is to determine an ordering policy which minimizes the expected cost of carrying out an N-stage process. Let us then introduce the function

(2) $f_N(x) =$ the expected cost of an N stage, starting with a stock level x and using an optimal ordering policy.

Let us suppose that we order at the first stage a quantity $y - x$ to bring the level up to y. Then the expected cost is given by the function

$$(3) \qquad k(y - x) + \int_y^\infty p(s - y)\phi(s)\, ds.$$

Hence,

$$(4) \qquad f_1(x) = \min_{y \geq x}\left[k(y - x) + \int_y^\infty p(s - y)\phi(s)\, ds \right].$$

The usual argumentation yields the recurrence relation

$$(5) \qquad f_n(x) = \min_{y \geq x}\left[k(y - x) + \int_y^\infty p(s - y)\phi(s)\, ds \right.$$
$$\left. + f_{n-1}(0) \int_y^\infty \phi(s)\, ds + \int_0^y f_{n-1}(y - s)\phi(s)\, ds \right],$$
$$n \geq 2,$$

upon an enumeration of the various possibilities corresponding to the different cases of an excess of demand over supply, and supply over demand.

The reader should compare this problem to that of Chapter II, §10. There we dealt with an expected current cost of a decision with a known change of state; here we have a stochastic current cost of a decision and a new state which is also stochastic. Precisely the same formalism handles both cases.

40. Discussion

Computationally, we have a feasible algorithm for computing the sequence $\{f_N(x)\}$ and the optimal ordering policy, $\{y_N(x)\}$. We can, however, go much further under various reasonable assumptions concerning the functions $k(z)$, $p(z)$, and $\phi(s)$, and obtain simple characterizations of the optimal policy.

A case of particular interest is that where $k(z)$ and $p(z)$ are linear functions of z of the form

$$(1) \qquad \begin{aligned} k(z) &= kz, & k &> 0, \\ p(z) &= pz, & p &> 0. \end{aligned}$$

In this case, we can show that the optimal policy has a very simple and intuitive structure, to wit: for each N, there is an associated stock level, s_N, with the property that if $x > s_N$, we order nothing, while if $x < s_N$, we order $s_N - x$ to bring the stock level up to s_N.

At first sight, the functional equation given above looks quite different from the relations obtained in the equipment replacement problem and its extensions. If, however, we consider only discrete levels of stock and a discrete set of demands, we obtain an equation of the following form

$$(2) \quad f_n(i) = \min_{j \geq i} \left[k(j-i) + \sum_{r=j+1}^{\infty} p(r-j)\phi_r + f_{n-1}(0) \sum_{r=j}^{\infty} \phi_r \right. $$
$$\left. + \sum_{r=0}^{j} f_{n-1}(j-r)\phi_r \right],$$

for $i = 0, 1, 2, \ldots, M, \quad n = 1, 2, \ldots$.

We see then that the optimal inventory equation can also be considered as a special case of the general equation derived from Markovian decision processes, discussed in Chapter XI.

41. A Further Reduction

In some cases, a deterministic inventory problem can be reduced from a one-dimensional problem involving a sequence of functions of one variable (a simple enough task for a computer) to one of considerably simpler form that can easily be solved by hand computation.

For the ith period, $i = 1, \ldots, N$, define the following quantities:

(1) $d_i =$ the amount demanded,
      $i_i =$ the interest charge on inventory carried forward,
      $S_i =$ the ordering (or set-up) cost,
      $x_i =$ the amount ordered.

We require that all demands must be met, and wish to minimize the total cost. We consider that only a set-up cost is involved in ordering. We do not include the actual procurement cost of items since we assume that the procurement cost is linear and constant over time. Thence, except for set-up cost, the total cost of procurement is the same for any program matching the demand.

Letting I denote inventory entering a period, one can readily prove the following statements:

1. There exists an optimal program such that $Ix_i = 0$ for all i. That is to say, if we enter a period with a surplus we do not make any purchase.

2. There exists an optimal program such that for all i, $x_i = 0$ or $\sum_{j=1}^{k} d_j$ for some k, $i \leq k \leq N$. That is, we buy just enough to meet future demands through some future period k.

3. There exists an optimal program such that if d_{i*} is satisfied by some x_{i**}, $i** < i*$, then d_i, $i = i** + 1, \ldots, i* - 1$ is also satisfied by $i**$.

4. Given that $I = 0$ for period i, it is optimal to consider periods 1 through $i - 1$ independently of the remainder of the process.

Now, letting $F(i) =$ the minimum cost for periods 1 through i, we have

$$(2) \quad F(i) = \min \left[\begin{array}{l} \min_{1 \leq j < i} \left[S_j + \sum_{h=j}^{i-1} \sum_{k=h+1}^{i} i_h d_k + F(j-1) \right], \\ S_i + F(i-1) \end{array} \right],$$

where $F(1) = S_1$ and $F(0) = 0$.

Hence we compute recursively one function of one variable, rather than a sequence of functions of one variable.

42. Production Line Scheduling

The last problem we wish to consider is a very simple version of a significant class of problems that arise in production scheduling. Since so few of these problems are approachable by any means, and since the solution we obtain has such an elegant form, we feel that it is worth presenting. It can be used to furnish approximate solutions to the more complicated versions.

Consider N different articles which must pass through two processing stages, one after the other. Only one article can be processed at any stage at any time, and we assume that the order of the items cannot be changed once the processing has begun. Given the time required for each article to go through each stage, in what order should the articles be fed into the first stage in order to minimize the total time required to process all the items?

An explicit solution can be given for the two-machine process, and will be presented below. There seems to be no corresponding result for the case of three or more machines.

43. Mathematical Formulation

Let

(1) $a_i =$ the time required to process the ith item on the first machine,
  $b_i =$ the time required to process the ith item on the second machine.

The operation is taken to proceed as follows. The items are arranged in some order, which may as well be $1, 2, \ldots, N$. This is shown schematically in Fig. 54.

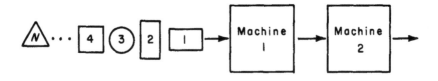

Figure 54

After the first item goes through Machine One, it is then sent through Machine Two. As soon as Machine One is finished with the first item, it begins its processing in Machine Two. However, Machine Two cannot begin on item two until it has completely processed the first item.

The problem then is that of arranging the times so as to minimize the total time that the second machine is inactive waiting for items from the first machine. The complexity of the problem is a consequence of the fact that different items require different times for processing by the two machines.

Let

(2) x_i = the inactive period of the second machine immediately before the ith item is fed into the second machine.

Then we have the following recurrence relations:

(3)
$$x_1 = a_1,$$
$$x_2 = \max (a_1 + a_2 - b_1 - x_1, 0),$$
$$x_1 + x_2 = \max (a_1 + a_2 - b_1, a_1),$$
$$x_3 = \max \left(\sum_{i=1}^{3} a_i - \sum_{i=1}^{2} b_i - \sum_{i=1}^{2} x_i, 0 \right),$$
$$x_1 + x_2 + x_3 = \max \left(\sum_{i=1}^{3} a_i - \sum_{i=1}^{2} b_i, \sum_{i=1}^{2} a_i - b_1, a_1 \right),$$

and, inductively,

(4)
$$\sum_{i=1}^{N} x_i = \max_{1 \le u \le N} K_u,$$

where

(5)
$$K_u = \sum_{i=1}^{u} a_i - \sum_{i=1}^{u-1} b_i.$$

We wish to determine a permutation of the items which minimize the expression in (4).

Although this can be done directly, using the explicit representation given above, it is instructive to use functional equation techniques as we shall do below.

44. Dynamic Programming Approach

Let us introduce the function

(1) $f(a_1, b_1, a_2, b_2, \ldots, a_N, b_N; t)$ = the time consumed processing the N items, when the second machine is committed t time units ahead, the processing times are a_i, b_i respectively, and an optimal scheduling policy is employed.

If the ith item is fed into the machines first, we see that we obtain the functional equation

(2)
$$f(a_1, b_1, a_2, b_2, \ldots, a_N, b_N; t)$$
$$= \min_{i} [a_i + f(a_1, b_1, a_2, b_2, \ldots, 0, 0, \ldots, a_N, b_N; b_i + \max (t - a_i, 0))]$$

where the $(0, 0)$ combination is now where (a_i, b_i) was before.

In order to use this relation to obtain the optimal ordering, we consider the effect of interchanging the order of two succeeding items. Then, feeding in first the ith and then the jth item, we have

(3) $\quad f(a_1, b_1, a_2, b_2, \ldots, a_N, b_N; t)$
$$= a_i + a_j + f(a_1, b_1, \ldots, 0, 0, \ldots, 0, 0, \ldots, a_N, b_N; t_{ij}),$$

where

(4) $\quad \begin{aligned}
t_{ij} &= b_j + \max[b_i + \max(t - a_i, 0) - a_j, 0] \\
&= b_j + b_i - a_j + \max[\max(t - a_i, 0), a_j - b_i] \\
&= b_j + b_i - a_j + \max[t - a_i, a_j - b_i, 0] \\
&= b_j + b_i - a_j - a_i + \max[t, a_i + a_j - b_i, a_i] \\
&= b_j + b_i - a_j - a_i + \max[t, \max[a_i + a_j - b_i, a_i]].
\end{aligned}$

We see then that if

(5) $\qquad \max[a_i + a_j - b_i, a_i] < \max[a_i + a_j - b_j, a_j],$

it pays to interchange the order, from (i, j) to (j, i).

This criterion can be written

(6) $\quad a_i + a_j + \max[-b_i, -a_j] < a_i + a_j + \max[-b_j, -a_i].$

Thus, we compare

(7) $\qquad \max[-b_i, -a_j] \quad \text{and} \quad \max[-b_j, -a_i].$

45. Determination of Optimal Ordering

In order to determine the optimal ordering according to the preceding result, we proceed as follows:

1. List the values of the a_i and b_i in two vertical columns.

i	a_i	b_i
1	a_1	b_1
2	a_2	b_2
.		
.		
.		
N	a_N	b_N

2. Scan all the time periods for the shortest one.
3. If it is an a_i value, place the corresponding item first.
4. If it is a b_i value, place the corresponding item last.
5. Cross off both times for that item.
6. Repeat the steps on the reduced set of $2n - 2$ time values.

7. In case of ties, for the sake of definiteness, choose the item with smaller subscript to be first. In case of a tie between a_i and b_i values, order the item according to the a-value first.

46. An Example

Consider the following example.

i	a_i	b_i
1	4	5
2	4	1
3	30	4
4	6	30
5	2	3

At the first step, we have

i	a_i	b_i
1	4	5
3	30	4
4	6	30
5	2	3
2	4	1

At the next step,

i	a_i	b_i
5	2	3
1	4	5
3	30	4
4	6	30
2	4	1

We see then that the optimal arrangement is (5, 1, 4, 3, 2).

47. Conclusions

Our aim in this chapter has been to show that a number of scheduling problems, some actually called scheduling problems and others masquerading under the names of "smoothing," "equipment replacement," and "inventory control," can be treated by means of dynamic programming techniques. Many of these problems reduce to very simple and quick machine calculations, while in a number of other cases, the functional equations can be used to provide explicit expressions for the optimal policies and return functions.

As we have mentioned above, one of the important reasons for considering these fairly simple models of economic processes lies in the fact that the solutions obtained can be used to furnish approximate policies for more complex and realistic models. Furthermore, the type of sensitivity analysis that these solutions yield will guide us in the construction of larger models.

Comments and Bibliography

§1. A great deal of work has been done in the field of smoothing and scheduling. The reader interested in these matters may refer to

R. Bellman, *Dynamic Programming*, Princeton University Press, Princeton, New Jersey, 1957.

————, "Mathematical aspects of scheduling theory," *J. Soc. Indust. Appl. Math.*, vol. 4, 1956, pp. 168–205.

K. J. Arrow, S. Karlin, and H. Scarf, *Studies in the Mathematical Theory of Inventory and Production*, Stanford University Press, Stanford, California, 1958.

In addition, a number of papers in this field, treating the mathematical problems in different ways, may be found in the issues of the *Journal of the Operations Research Society of America, Management Science, Naval Research Logistics Quarterly, Econometrica* and *Journal of the Society for Industrial and Applied Mathematics*.

§4. For a study of some continuous versions of smoothing processes, see Chapters 4, 5, and 6 of the book by Arrow, Karlin, and Scarf mentioned above. Some other papers in this field are

R. Bellman, I. Glicksberg, and O. Gross, "Some problems in the theory of dynamic programming—a smoothing problem," *J. Soc. Indust. Appl. Math.*, vol. 2, 1954, pp. 82–89.

E. H. Bowman, "Production scheduling by the transportation method for linear programming," *Operations Research*, vol. 4, 1956, pp. 100–103.

A. Charnes, W. W. Cooper, and B. Mellon, "Model for optimizing production by references to cost surrogates," *Econometrica*, vol. 23, 1955, pp. 307–323.

G. B. Dantzig and S. Johnson, *A Production Smoothing Problem*, The RAND Corporation, Research Memorandum RM–1432, 1955.

A. Hoffman and W. Jacobs, "Smooth patterns of production," *Management Science*, vol. 1, 1954, pp. 86–91.

S. M. Johnson, "Sequential production planning over time at minimum cost," *Management Science*, vol. 3, 1957, pp. 435–437.

W. Karush and A. Vazsonyi, "Mathematical programming and service scheduling," *Management Science*, vol. 3, 1957, pp. 140–148.

F. Modigliani and F. Hohn, "Production planning over time and the nature of the expectation and planning horizon," *Econometrica*, vol. 23, 1955, pp. 46–66.

F. Morin, "Note on an inventory problem," *Econometrica*, vol. 23, 1955, pp. 447–450.

§11. Problems of this nature arise in statistical mechanics. Theoretical and computational details may be found in

J. W. Cahn and R. Kikuchi, *Theory of Domain Walls in Ordered Structures— II. Pair Approximation for Nonzero Temperatures*, Hughes Research Laboratories, Research Report No. 177, 1961.

§12. A great deal of work has been done on the equipment replacement problem. For the conventional approaches and the industrial background, see

T. Whitin, *The Theory of Inventory Management*, Princeton University Press, Princeton, New Jersey, 1953.

For an approach by means of variational techniques using a continuous model, see

A. Alchian, *Economic Replacement Policy*, The RAND Corporation, Report R-224, April 12, 1952.

The method used here is presented in

R. Bellman, "Equipment replacement policy," *J. Soc. Indust. Appl. Math.*, vol. 3, 1955, pp. 133–136.

S. Dreyfus, "A generalized equipment study," *J. Soc. Indust. Appl. Math.*, vol. 8, 1960, pp. 425–435.

See also

B. J. Marks, *A Dynamic Approach to the Prediction of Demand for Replacement Parts*, 1960, unpublished.

D. W. Jorgenson, *Optimal Scheduling of Replacement and Checkout—IV. Computation by Successive Approximations*, 1960, unpublished.

D. W. Jorgenson and R. Radner, *Optimal Replacement and Inspection of Stochastically Failing Equipment*, The RAND Corporation, Paper P-2074, 1960.

T. Fukao, T. Yamazaki, and S. Kimura, "An application of dynamic programming to economic operation problem of a power system," *Electrotechnical J. of Japan*, vol. 5, no. 2, 1959, pp. 64–68.

T. Fukao and T. Yamazaki, "A computational method of economic operation of hydrothermal power systems including flow-interconnected hydropower plants (Dynamic linear programming method)," *Electrotechnical J. of Japan*, vol. 6, 1960, pp. 22–26.

T. Fukao, "Operation problems of flow-interconnected hydro-plants systems, II," *Bull. Electrotechnical Lab.*, vol. 24, no. 6, 1960; "III," no. 7.

A. J. Truelove, "Strategic reliability and preventive maintenance," *Operations Research*, vol. 9, 1961, pp. 22–29.

A. J. Rowe, *Application of Computer Simulation to Sequential Decision Rules in Production Scheduling*, System Development Corporation, SP-112, 1959.

————, *Towards a Theory of Scheduling*, System Development Corporation, SP-61, 1960.

Y. Fukuda, *Optimal Disposal Policies*, Planning Research Corporation, Los Angeles, PRC R-152, 1960.

A. Kaufmann, *Methodes et Modeles de la Recherche Operationelle*, DUNOD, Paris, 1959.

W. Sinden, "The replacement and expansion of durable equipment," *J. Soc. Indust. Appl. Math.*, vol. 8, 1960, pp. 466–480.

W. Szwarc, "Solution of the Akers-Friedman scheduling problem," *Operations Research*, vol. 8, 1960, pp. 782–788.

E. W. Barankin and J. Denny, *Examination of an Inventory Model Incorporating Probabilities of Obsolescence*, University of California Statistical Laboratory, 1960.

E. W. Barankin, *A Delivery-lag Inventory Model with an Emergency Provision*, University of California Statistical Laboratory, 1960.

R. E. Levitan, "The optimum reject allowance problem," *Management Science*, vol. 6, 1959, pp. 172–186.

R. McNaughton, "Scheduling with deadlines and loss functions," *Management Science*, vol. 6, 1959, pp. 1–12.

R. Radner, *Opportunistic Replacement of a Single Part in the Presence of Several Monitored Parts*, 1961, unpublished.

The more realistic situation where the rates of repair and obsolescence are not completely known in advance may also be treated by means of dynamic programming techniques. See

R. Bellman, *Adaptive Control Processes: A Guided Tour*, Princeton University Press, Princeton, New Jersey, 1961.

A very interesting type of repair and replacement problem has recently been studied by D. J. White. Here the problem is when to examine the system. The functional equations that arise have the form

$$f_n(x) = \max_{m \le n} T(m, x, f_m(x)).$$

§20. The problem was formulated in this fashion by A. S. Cahn,

A. S. Cahn, "The warehousing problem," *Bull. Amer. Math. Soc.*, vol. 54, 1948, p. 1073,

and generalized in

A. Charnes and W. W. Cooper, *Generalizations of the Warehousing Model*, ONR Research Memorandum No. 34, Graduate School of Industrial Administration, Carnegie Institute of Technology, 1955.

The present treatment is contained in

R. Bellman, "On the theory of dynamic programming—a warehousing problem," *Management Science*, vol. 2, 1956, pp. 272–276.

S. Dreyfus, "An analytic solution of the warehousing problem," *Management Science*, vol. 4, 1957, pp. 99–104.

The analytic solution is found in the second reference.

§30. The caterer problem has been discussed by linear programming and other techniques in a number of places. See

W. Jacobs, "The caterer problem," *Naval Research Logs. Q.*, vol. 1, 1954, pp. 154–165.

J. W. Gaddum, A. J. Hoffman, and D. Sokolowsky, "On the solution to the caterer problem," ibid.

W. Prager, *On the Caterer Problem*, LBM–13, Division of Applied Mathematics, Brown University, 1956.

The method given in §30–§37 is contained in

R. Bellman, "On a dynamic programming approach to the caterer problem—I," *Management Science*, vol. 3, 1957, pp. 270–278.

It was inspired by an analytic solution of the $q = 1$, $p = 2$ case obtained by O. Gross. The method is significant since it can be used in a number of situations where the "common sense" approach of the next section fails. Furthermore, the basic idea can be applied to many other situations. See §14 of Chapter VIII, and

R. Bellman, "Some new techniques in the dynamic programming solution of variational problems," *Q. Appl. Math.*, vol. 16, 1958, pp. 295–305.

R. Bellman and R. Kalaba, "Reduction of dimensionality, dynamic programming and control processes," *J. Basic Engineering*, March 1961, pp. 82–84.

§38. This solution is contained in some unpublished work of S. Dreyfus, and is equivalent to the solution of Beale contained in

E. M. Beale, Letter to the Editor, *Management Science*, vol. 4, 1957, p. 110.

§39. See the book by Arrow, Karlin and Scarf referred to above, and Chapter 5 of the book by Bellman, for an extensive list of references. The pioneering mathematical works in the field are

K. J. Arrow, T. E. Harris, and J. Marschak, "Optimal inventory policy," *Econometrica*, July 1951.

A. Dvoretsky, J. Kiefer, and J. Wolfowitz, "The inventory problem, I, II," *Econometrica*, vol. 20, 1952, pp. 187–222.

R. Bellman, I. Glicksberg, and O. Gross, "On the optimal inventory equation," *Management Science*, vol. 2, 1955, pp. 83–104.

The first sophisticated mathematical discussion of inventory problems is contained in the Arrow, Harris, Marschak paper, and the first treatment of existence and uniqueness theorems and of unknown distribution of demand given by Dvoretsky, Kiefer, and Wolfowitz. The first use of the functional equation to determine the structure of the optimal policy was made by Bellman, Glicksberg, and Gross, and this activity was extensively pursued by Arrow, Karlin, and Scarf in their book.

Some more recent results are given in the book by Arrow, Karlin, and Scarf, and in

B. Lefkowitz, et al., *The Development and Implementation of Advanced Inventory Control Procedures*, Stanford Research Institute, 1960.

G. Hadley and T. M. Whiten, *A Dynamic Model for Procurement*, Stanford Research Institute TM-13, 1961.

——————————————, *Optimal Procurement Policy under Conditions of Repetitive Demand Cycles*, Stanford Research Institute TM-14, 1961.

S. G. Allen, *A Redistribution Model with Set-up Charge*, Stanford Research Institute TM-17, 1961.

P. R. Winters, *Constrained Inventory Rules for Production Smoothing*, ONR Research Memorandum No. 79, Carnegie Institute of Technology, 1961.

W. Sadowski, *A Few Remarks on the Assortment Problem*, Cowles Foundation Discussion Paper No. 67, 1959.

H. Kasugai and T. Kasegai, "Note on minimax regret ordering policy," *J. Oper. Res. Japan*, vol. 3, 1961, pp. 155–169.

H. Scarf, *Optimal Policies for the Inventory Problem with Stochastic Lead Time*, Planning Research Corporation, Los Angeles, November 1960.

M. Beckmann, *An Inventory Model for Arbitrary Interval and Quantity Distributions of Demand*, Planning Research Corporation, Los Angeles, September 1960.

Y. Fukuda, *Bayes and Maximum Likelihood Policies for a Multi-echelon Inventory Problem*, Planning Research Corporation, Los Angeles, June 1960.

A. J. Gradwohl, *Case Studies on the Multi-echelon Inventory Problem*, Planning Research Corporation, Los Angeles, December 1959.

Y. Fukuda, *Optimal Disposal Policies*, Planning Research Corporation, Los Angeles, March 1960.

For a discussion of the mathematical theory of inventories from the purely descriptive standpoint, see

P. A. P. Moran, *The Theory of Storage*, Methuen and Co., 1959,
where numerous other references will be found.

Finally, let us mention the as yet unpublished work of D. Iglehart on the asymptotic behavior of the solutions of equations such as (39.5) as $n \to \infty$. Once it has been established that $f_n \sim nc$ as $n \to \infty$, the groundwork has been laid for the concept of a steady-state policy. Furthermore, this policy can be found by other techniques which circumvent the multidimensional miseries of dynamic programming.

§41. See

H. M. Wagner and T. M. Whitin, "Dynamic versions of economic lot size model," *Management Science*, vol. 5, 1958, pp. 89–96.

§42. The solution given here was first obtained by Johnson in a different fashion. See

S. Johnson, "Optimal two-and-three-stage production schedules with setup times included," *Naval Research Logs. Q.*, March 1954.

For further results and references, see

F. M. Tonge, *A Heuristic Program for Assembly Line Balancing*, The RAND Corporation, Paper P-1993, 1960.

R. Bellman, "Mathematical aspects of scheduling theory," *J. Soc. Indust. Appl. Math.*, vol. 4, 1956, pp. 168–205.

B. Giffler, *Mathematical Solution of Production Planning and Scheduling Problems*, IBM Technical Report, Advanced Systems Development Division, 1960.

I. Nabeshima, "The order of n items processed on m machines," *J. Oper. Res. Soc. Japan*, vol. 3, 1961, pp. 170–175.

For a discussion of stochastic decision processes, see

E. S. Phelps, *The Accumulation of Risky Capital: A Discrete-time Sequential Utility Analysis*, Cowles Discussion Paper, 1961.

M. Shubik, "Approaches to the study of decision-making relevant to the firm," *J. Business*, vol. 34, 1961, pp. 101–118.

CHAPTER IV

Optimal Search Techniques

1. Introduction

In the previous sections, we have repeatedly encountered equations of the form

$$(1) \qquad f_N(x) = \max_y g(x, y, f_{N-1}(y)),$$

where the maximization is to be accomplished by a direct examination of possibilities. If y can assume a number of different values, $y_1, y_2, \ldots, y_M$, this straightforward procedure envisages the calculation of the values $g(x, y_1, f_{N-1}(y_1))$, $g(x, y_2, f_{N-1}(y_2))$, and so forth, and a comparison of values. If M is large, a great deal of time can be consumed in the calculation of the values $g(x, y_i, f_{N-1}(y_i))$ and in the comparisons.

The question arises as to whether we can locate the maximum value in a more efficient fashion. This is a significant question, since the feasibility of solution of a problem by one technique or another depends upon the relative times required to obtain the solution. We may frequently wish to allow a large number of policy choices at each stage in order to ensure the accuracy of the solution. Consequently, it is important to study search processes in their own right.

We shall show that for one very important and often met case, there exist techniques which reduce the time in a phenomenal way. Following our discussion of the determination of the maximum of a function, we shall study the problem of determining the location of the zero of a monotone decreasing function.

These problems are particular cases of search problems—questions of extraordinary difficulty insofar as solution and even formulation are concerned. It is rather amusing to note that the computational solution of dynamic programming processes itself raises further dynamic programming problems.

The results and techniques of this chapter are due to O. Gross and S. Johnson.

2. Unimodal Function

Let us begin by introducing the concept of a *unimodal function*.

Definition. A function $f(x)$ is unimodal in an interval $[0, b]$ if there is a number x_0, $0 \leq x_0 \leq b$, such that $f(x)$ is either strictly increasing for

$x \leq x_0$, and strictly decreasing for $x > x_0$, or else strictly increasing for $x < x_0$, and strictly decreasing for $x \geq x_0$.

The most important example of functions of this nature are concave functions.

3. Optimal One-dimensional Maximization

It is clear that the unimodal property will never allow us to determine the maximum value of $f(x)$, but it will allow us to determine very accurately the location of x_0. We wish to prove

Theorem 1. Let $y = f(x)$ be a unimodal function on an interval $0 \leq x \leq L_n$. Suppose that L_n is a number with the property that the point at which $f(x)$ achieves its maximum can be located within an interval of unit length by calculating at most n values, and making comparisons.

Introduce the quantity

$$(1) \qquad\qquad F_n = \operatorname{Sup} L_n.$$

Then

$$(2) \qquad\qquad F_n = F_{n-1} + F_{n-2}, \qquad n \geq 2,$$

with $F_0 = F_1 = 1$.

The numbers F_n are the Fibonacci numbers, which occur in the most unexpected places. We shall discuss them below.

Proof. The proof will be inductive. Observe that $F_0 = 1$, and that $F_1 = 1$, since one value of a unimodal function gives essentially no more information about the location of the maximizing value than none.

Fix $n \geq 2$, and compute $y_1 = f(x_1)$, $y_2 = f(x_2)$, for x_1 and x_2 two values in $(0, L_n)$, to be determined subsequently with $x_1 < x_2$. If $y_1 > y_2$, the maximum value occurs in $[0, x_2]$, while if $y_2 > y_1$, the maximum is in $[x_1, L_n]$. If $y_1 = y_2$, we choose either of these intervals, even though we know the maximum occurs in $[x_1, x_2]$.

We are thus left with a sub-interval of $[0, L_n]$ and the value of $f(x)$ at an interior point.

For $n = 2$, $L_2 = 2 - \epsilon$, we take $x_1 = 1 - \epsilon$, $x_2 = 1$, where ϵ is small. This shows that $\operatorname{Sup} L_2 \geq 2$. On the other hand, the foregoing analysis shows that $\operatorname{Sup} L_2 < 2 + \delta$ for any $\delta > 0$. Hence,

$$(3) \qquad\qquad F_2 = 2 = F_1 + F_0.$$

Let us now proceed inductively. Assume that $F_k = F_{k-1} + F_{k-2}$ for $k = 2, \ldots, n - 1$. We wish to show, on this assumption, that

$$(4) \qquad\qquad F_n = F_{n-1} + F_{n-2}.$$

Suppose we calculate $f(x)$ at the two points x_1 and x_2 on $[0, L]$. Then we have the picture in Fig. 55. If $y_1 > y_2$, we are left with the situation in Fig. 56. It follows that $x_2 < F_{n-1}$, since we are allowed only $n - 2$ more choices, with x_1 a first choice for the case where $n - 1$ calculations are allowed. Furthermore, $x_1 < F_{n-2}$, since the maximum could occur on $(0, x_1)$, with only $n - 2$ choices left.

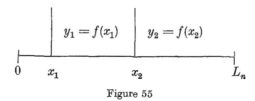

Figure 55

Similarly, if $y_2 > y_1$, we have $L_n - x_1 < F_{n-1}$. Thus,

$$(5) \qquad L_n < x_1 + F_{n-1} < F_{n-1} + F_{n-2},$$

whence

$$(6) \qquad F_n = \operatorname{Sup} L_n \leq F_{n-1} + F_{n-2}.$$

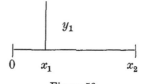

Figure 56

It remains to derive the reverse inequality. Choose

$$(7) \qquad L_n = \left(1 - \frac{\epsilon}{2}\right)(F_{n-1} + F_{n-2}), \quad x_1 = \left(1 - \frac{\epsilon}{2}\right)F_{n-2},$$

$$x_2 = \left(1 - \frac{\epsilon}{2}\right)F_{n-1}.$$

Since ϵ can be made arbitrarily small, this shows that $F_n \geq F_{n-1} + F_{n-2}$. The two inequalities yield the desired equality.

Furthermore, this yields an optimal testing procedure for any small ϵ. After comparing $f(x_1)$ and $f(x_2)$, we are left with an interval of length $L_{n-1} = (1 - \epsilon/2)F_{n-1}$, and with a value at an optimal first position for the smaller interval. Continuing in this way, we have $L_k = (1 - \epsilon/2)F_k$ for $2 \leq k \leq n$. Finally, $L_2 = (1 - \epsilon/2)F_2 = 2 - \epsilon$, so that the final interval is of unit length.

4. The Fibonacci Numbers

Although the sequence $\{F_n\}$ generated by the recurrence relation

$$(1) \qquad F_n = F_{n-1} + F_{n-2}, \quad F_0 = F_1 = 1$$

154

starts out slowly,

$$(2) \qquad 1, 1, 2, 3, 5, 8, 13, 21, 34, 55, \ldots,$$

we have $F_{20} > 10,000$. Thus the position of a maximum can always be located within 10^{-4} of the original interval length in at most 20 calculations.

To determine the analytic form of F_n, observe that r^n is a solution of (1), ignoring the boundary conditions, if

$$(3) \qquad r^2 = r + 1.$$

The two values of r are $(1 \ \sqrt{5})/2$.

Hence, if we set

$$(4) \qquad F_n = c_1\left(\frac{\sqrt{5}+1}{2}\right)^n + c_2\left(\frac{1-\sqrt{5}}{2}\right)^n,$$

we have the solution of (1) provided we fit the values at $n = 0$ and $n = 1$. Thus,

$$(5) \qquad 1 = c_1 + c_2,$$

$$1 = c_1\left(\frac{\sqrt{5}+1}{2}\right) + c_2\left(\frac{1-\sqrt{5}}{2}\right).$$

The values for c_1 and c_2 are

$$(6) \qquad c_1 = \frac{1+\sqrt{5}}{\sqrt{5}}, \quad c_2 = \frac{\sqrt{5}-1}{\sqrt{5}}.$$

Since $(\sqrt{5}+1)/2 > 1$ and $(\sqrt{5}-1)/2 < 1$, we see that for large n, F_n is very accurately given by $\left(\frac{1+\sqrt{5}}{\sqrt{5}}\right)\left(\frac{\sqrt{5}+1}{2}\right)^n$. It follows that one can obtain exponential increases in accuracy at a cost of a few additional computations.

The ratio F_n/F_{n-1} approaches $(\sqrt{5}+1)/2$ which is approximately 1.62. Hence, the first two values, x_1 and x_2, should be chosen at a distance $.62L$ from either end of the interval $[0, L]$. This uniform testing policy would be an excellent approximate policy for all except the last few stages, at which point it is of little import whether the best policy is used or not. This simple search policy is particularly applicable for use with digital computers.

5. The Golden Mean, an Aside

Take a line segment $[0, L]$ and divide it into two parts so that one part is $(\sqrt{5}+1)/2$ times the other. The rectangle formed by these sides was supposed by the Greeks to have the most pleasing proportions, and consequently was often used in their architecture.

6. The Discrete Case

Let us now consider the case where $f(x)$ is defined only over a discrete set of points. In this case, we can establish

Theorem 2. Let $y = f(x)$ be a unimodal function defined on a set of H_n discrete points. Let H_n be an integer with the property that the maximum value can always be identified by n observations and subsequent comparisons, and set

(1) $$K_n = \text{Max } H_n.$$

Then

(2) $$K_n = -1 + F_{n+1}, \quad n \geq 1.$$

Proof. Number the points in some order $1, 2, 3, \ldots, H_n$. To begin with, it is clear that $K_1 = 1, K_2 = 2, K_3 = 4$. Now take $n > 3$, and assume that $K_k = -1 + K_{k+1}$ for $k < n$.

Let us calculate $f(x)$ at x_1 and x_2. Arguments analogous to those given above, show that

(3) $$x_1 \leq K_{n-2} + 1, \qquad H_n - x_1 \leq K_{n-1},$$

whence

(4) $\quad H_n \leq K_{n-2} + 1 + K_{n-1} = (F_{n-1} - 1) + 1 + (F_n - 1) = F_{n+1} - 1.$

This maximum value is attained if $x_1 = F_{n-1}$ and $x_2 = F_n$. This establishes the desired result, and yields the optimal policy.

7. Zeros of Functions

It is interesting to see if the same ideas can be used to obtain a search technique for finding the zero of a function in an interval, given the information that the function is monotone decreasing. It turns out that further information is required in order to pose an interesting problem. We shall treat the following question:

"Let $f(x)$ be a continuous and convex function in $[0, L]$. Apart from this, $f(x)$ is unknown. However, any particular value of $f(x)$ can be computed, and we start initially with the information that $f(0) > 0, f(L) < 0$.

Given an integer $n > 0$, how do we proceed to locate the root of $f(x)$ in $[0, L]$ with maximum accuracy in n steps, where a step consists of calculating a value of $f(x)$ at any point we choose, and comparing it with previously obtained values?"

8. Functional Equations

To make the problem precise, we formulate it in terms of minimizing the maximum length of interval for which it can be asserted that it must include the desired zero, after n observations, taken sequentially.

Without loss of generality, we can always consider the diagram shown in

Fig. 57. Here $f(0) = 1$, $f(1) = -Y$, $Y > 0$. Since f is convex, the zero must lie on $[0, W]$, where $W = 1/(1 + Y)$. If we have just one more reading to make ($n = 1$), then we choose the point x on $(0, W)$ and calculate $f(x)$. The optimal choice of x will be derived below.

It can be shown by simple dominance arguments that no reading of f need ever be taken outside any interval on which the zero has been located.

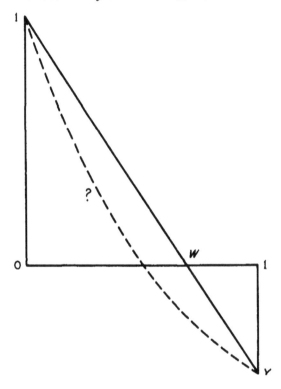

Figure 57

Having chosen x, and calculated $f(x)$, we encounter exactly one of the following cases (barring $f(x) = 0$, of course, the best possible case).

Case 1. If $f(x) = v > 0$, then by drawing straight lines joining known points on the graph of f, we have the picture shown in Fig. 58, with the root located on (S, W') as implied by the convexity of f.

Case 2. If $f(x) = -v' < 0$, the picture is as shown in Fig. 59, with the root located on $(\max(0, S'), W'')$ as indicated.

Let $S'' = \max(0, S')$. If x is the final point at which $f(x)$ is to be determined (i.e., $n = 1$), then it is chosen so as to minimize the maximum possible value of $\max(W' - S, W'' - S'')$, consistent with our choice.

Before going into the algebraic details of the solution for $n = 1$, let us consider the general n-stage process in which we have several more readings to make. In either of the two cases diagrammed above, all the essential data can be described by a basic triangle determined by a two-parameter system in the following way.

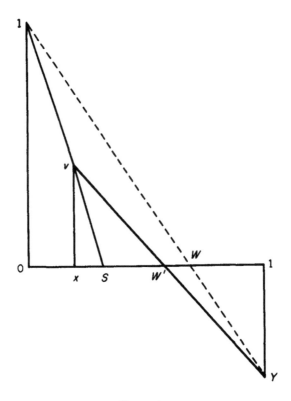

Figure 58

Referring to Fig. 58, we can conclude that the graph of f lies above the line segment vS, and below the segment $vW'Y$ (where the letters stand for both points and values in the obvious manner). If we now draw the line segment SY, it may or may not be crossed by the curve $y = f(x)$; but if it is crossed, at some point P, say, we can replace that portion of the curve lying below PY by PY without losing information. This device does not violate the convexity condition, and it includes the worst possible case. This can be shown by simple dominance arguments based on our knowledge of the function at any particular stage.

The essential data can thus be described by the triangle vSY. Since a vertical reduction in scale leaves the problem invariant, and a horizontal reduction leaves it relatively invariant, the triangle vSY can be replaced by a triangle of standard form described pictorially by two parameters, Y, S, as in Fig. 60.

Similarly, in the second case (Fig. 59), the graph of f lies above $S'v'$ and below $1W''v'$. Draw the line segment from 1 to S' and replace any portion

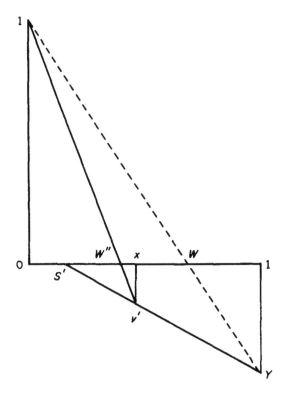

Figure 59

of the graph of f lying below this line by the line itself from 1 to the point of crossing. This does not effect the choice of subsequent x's, since they will all be chosen on minimal bracketing intervals. This again can be shown by simple dominance arguments. Thus, in the second case, by a similar suitable reduction to scale, we are led to another representation of Fig. 60.

Now define the function of two variables S and Y:

(1) $R_n(S, Y) =$ the minimum length of interval on which we can guarantee locating the zero in $[0, 1]$ of any convex function f, given that $f(0) = 1$, $f(1) = -Y < 0$, the information that the root is greater than S and the fact that we have n readings to make.

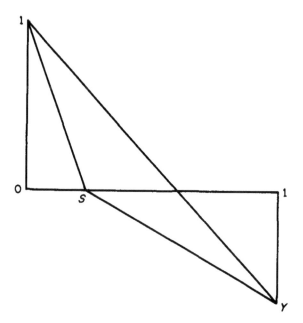

Figure 60

If $n = 0$, we have clearly,

$$(2) \qquad R_0(S, Y) = \frac{1}{1 + Y} - S.$$

Next, using the principle of optimality, and taking into account the scale factors, we obtain for $n > 0$ the following recurrence relation:

$$(3) \qquad R_n(S, Y) = \min_{S \le x \le \frac{1}{1+Y}} \max \left\{ \begin{array}{l} \displaystyle \max_{0 \le v' \le \frac{Y(x-s)}{1-S}} x R_{n-1}\left(\frac{xy - v'}{x(y - v')}, v'\right) \\ \displaystyle \max_{0 \le v \le 1 - x(1+Y)} (1 - x) R_{n-1}\left(\frac{x}{1 - x} \cdot \frac{v}{1 - v}, \frac{y}{v}\right) \end{array} \right\},$$

with the upper and lower expressions after the brace corresponding to the second and first cases, respectively. The scale factors are obtained in a completely elementary manner by means of similar triangles.

The ranges of the variables S, Y above are given by $Y \ge 0$, $0 \le S \le 1/(1 + Y)$. To render the expressions more amenable to computation on the Johnniac, the following changes of variable were made:

$$(4) \quad W = \frac{1}{1 + Y}, \quad \phi_n(S, W) = R_n(S, Y),$$

$$\text{whence } R_n(S, Y) = \phi_n\left(S, \frac{1}{1 + Y}\right).$$

An additional modification of the variables v, v' reduces the system to

(5) $\phi_0(S, W) = W - S$,

$$\phi_n(S, W) = \min_{S \leq x \leq W} \max \left\{ \begin{array}{l} x \max_{S \leq t \leq x} \phi_{n-1}\left(\dfrac{t}{x}, \dfrac{W(1 - t)}{W(1 - x) + x - t}\right) \\ (1 - x) \max_{x \leq t' \leq W} \phi_{n-1}\left(\dfrac{t' - x}{1 - x}, \dfrac{W(t' - x)}{t' - Wx}\right) \end{array} \right\},$$

where $0 \leq S \leq W \leq 1$.

The functions $\phi_n(S, W)$ were then computed for $n = 1, 2, 3, 4$ by means of a discrete approximation using various grid sizes and linear interpolation.

The minimizing x's were recorded since these form the basis of our optimal policy, i.e., $x^* = x_n^*(S, W)$ is the point at which we evaluate the unknown function f given the information that the root lies on (S, W) in our basic triangle and that there are n evaluations to be made. The point x_n^* is, of course, itself measured on the basic triangle. To take care of the general situation, we must, of course, relate our readings to the original scale. If we let $\rho_n(S, Y)$ denote the fraction of the distance between S and W occupied by x_n^*, we readily obtain

$$\rho_n(S, Y) = \frac{x_n^*(S, W) - S}{W - S},$$

where $W = 1/(1 + Y)$. It is now a relatively easy matter to relate x_n^* to the original scale, and thus to obtain the procedure cycle outlined below.

Graphs of the functions $R_n(0, Y)$ and $\rho_n(0, Y)$ for $n = 1, 2, 3, 4$ are included at the end of this Chapter.

9. The Special Case $n = 1$

We shall begin this section with a few remarks intended primarily to validate certain assumptions made, tacitly or otherwise, in the derivation of the foregoing functional equation. We shall close this section with a brief treatment of the special case $n = 1$, $S = 0$, which provided us with an excellent check on the validity of the data obtained from the Johnniac. The remarks are as follows:

1. Suppose we are at a certain stage in an optimal sequential minimax search, with several values of f computed, and ready to choose our next point of evaluation. Let a, b denote the closest evaluation points on the left and right respectively of the minimal interval (S, W) on which the root is known to lie. Then in an optimal procedure, x is chosen on (a, b). To see this, we need only state that since the unknown function f may indeed be piecewise linear (a possible contingency) outside (a, b), it is clear that any such subsequent reading would in such a case afford no information regarding the character of f within (a, b), pertinent to the location of its zero, not already implied by the quantities a, b, $f(a)$, $f(b)$, S, and W, or

indeed by any of the previous readings, for that matter. Similar, but slightly more involved arguments, can be given to show that the next reading should be taken on the interval (S, W).

2. In the treatment of Case 2, it was tacitly assumed that $Y_x < Y$, or, equivalently, that the SY line has a negative slope as shown in the figure. Again, it can be shown by dominance arguments that the worst situation occurs when f is monotone, and indeed when the graph of f lies above the line SY. It is this condition which determines the limits of the variable v in the upper line of the functional equation for R_n. It is precisely such dominance considerations as these which, though enabling us to express the functional equation in a relatively simple form and thus to obtain an optimal "policy" via its recursive computation, nonetheless, do not enable us to obtain an optimal "procedure" directly from the equation.

3. We now conjecture that the functional equation for R_n may be validly simplified by assuming that the maximum in the upper line of the equation is always taken on at the upper end-point of the range of v. This is true, for example, if $n = 1$. However, this assertion has not been established in general, and, consequently, the transformed equation for Φ_n was subsequently submitted to the Johnniac in its present form. It turns out that the resulting data supported the conjecture.

4. $R_n(S, Y)$ is separately decreasing in S and Y. To see this for the first variable, for example, upon recalling the definition of $R_n(S, Y)$, we observe that, other things being the same, the information that the root is greater than S *includes* the information that the root is greater than S' if $S' < S$. On the basis of the additional information, then, we can clearly *guarantee at least* as short a final bracketing interval with a larger S value if we are proceeding optimally, i.e., $R_n(S, Y) \le R_n(S', Y)$ if $S > S'$. An analogous argument applies for the second variable.

10. $n = 1$, $S = 0$

Let us now present a brief discussion of some results obtained for the case $n = 1$, $S = 0$. We shall spare the reader the elementary, albeit complicated, algebraic details involved and simply state that upon substituting the function

$$(1) \qquad\qquad R_0(S, Y) = \frac{1}{1 + Y} - S$$

in the right member of our functional equation and setting $S = 0$ in the result we obtain a relatively simple algebraic minimax problem for the determination of $R_1(0, Y)$.

The substitution $\rho = x(1 + Y)$ then yields, upon performing the minimax operation, the following equation relating the optimal ratio ρ and the variable Y:

(2)
$$(\rho^4 - 2\rho^3 - 5\rho^2 - 2\rho + 1)Y^2 + 2(2\rho^3 - \rho^2 - 3\rho + 1)Y$$
$$+ (2\rho - 1)^2 = 0,$$

with the restrictions $Y > 0$, $0 \le \rho \le 1$.

Since the discriminant of this quadratic expression in Y turns out to be precisely $8\rho^3$, we readily obtain the following simple rational parameterization of the (ρ, Y) curve:

(3)
$$\left. \begin{array}{l} \rho = \tfrac{1}{2}(1 - t)^2 \\[2mm] Y = \dfrac{4t^2}{1 - 4t - t^4} \end{array} \right\}, \quad 0 \le t \le t_0.$$

To determine the value of t_0 we note that the limiting form of the polynomial equation as $Y \to \infty$ is simply the coefficient of the leading term in Y set equal to zero:

(4)
$$\rho^4 - 2\rho^3 - 5\rho^2 - 2\rho + 1 = 0.$$

This equation has a unique root on the interval $(0, 1)$ and is given by

(5)
$$\rho_1^* = \frac{1 + 2\sqrt{2} - \sqrt{5 + 4\sqrt{2}}}{2} \approx .282.$$

It follows from the parametric representation of ρ that

$$t_0 = 1 - \sqrt{2\rho_1} \approx .250.$$

As a check on this, we note that this value of t_0 is the smallest positive root of the denominator in the parametric expression for Y.

The graphs of $R_1(0, Y)$, $\rho_1(Y)$ were plotted from manual computations using the preceding formulas and these compared quite favorably with the results from the Johnniac. Unfortunately, however, due presumably to the choice of insufficiently small grid sizes imposed by the Johnniac's limited memory, a cumulative error caused, in effect, a gradual upward creep in the tails of the ρ curves. These were smoothed out to agree with theory to obtain the included graphs. The R curves, fortunately, seemed quite insensitive to choice of grid size.

Let us also mention the fact that further checks on the computations were provided by the easily derived relationships:

$$\phi_n(W, W) = 0, \quad \phi_n(S, 1) = \frac{1 - S}{2^n},$$

and these were found to fit the Johnniac data exactly.

11. Description of the Computational Procedure

Let us now describe the procedure cycle. Suppose we are in the situation in which we know $f(a) = Y_a > 0$, $f(b) = -Y_b$, $Y_b > 0$, where $a < b$, and the root $> S$ and we have n more readings to make. Then we have bracketed the root on the interval (S, W), where

$$W = a + (b - a)\frac{Y_a}{Y_b + Y_b}.$$

If $n = 0$, the computation ceases and the values S, W are recorded.

If $n > 0$, calculate the value of $f(x)$ at $x = S + (W - S) \cdot \rho_n\left(\frac{Y_b}{Y_a}\right)$. Then,

if $f(x) = Y_x > 0$, set $a' = x$, $b' = b$, and $S' = x + (x - a)\frac{Y_x}{Y_a - Y_x}$. If, however, $f(x) = -Y_x < 0$, set $a' = a$, $b' = x$, and if $Y_x > Y_b$, set $S' = S$; otherwise set $S' = \max\left(S, x - (b - x)\frac{Y_x}{Y_b - Y_x}\right)$.

Finally, set $n' = n - 1$.

We are now in the situation in which we know that $f(a') = Y_{a'} > 0$, $f(b') = -Y_{b'}$, $Y_{b'} > 0$, where $a' < b'$, and the fact that the root is greater than S' with n' more readings to make. This completes the cycle. (As the problem is stated, $S = a$ initially.)

In the next section, we shall illustrate how this procedure works on a particular example.

Remark 1. The foregoing procedure is an *approximation* to the actual minimax procedure. The theoretically correct procedure would only involve replacing the expression $\rho_n\left(\frac{Y_b}{Y_a}\right)$ in the formula for x above by $\rho_n\left(\frac{S - a}{b - a}, \frac{Y_b}{Y_a}\right)$, where $\rho_n(S, Y)$ is as defined above. Since the objective function is relatively insensitive to S in our choice of $\rho_n(S, Y)$ in the vicinity of the minimax, we feel that the approximation

(1) $$\rho_n(0, Y) \approx \rho_n(S, Y)$$

is justified, and define $\rho_n(Y) \equiv \rho_n(0, Y)$. This approximation renders the procedure more adaptable to machine computation.

12. A Numerical Application—Comparing the Bisection Technique

Suppose we are desirous of bracketing in on the zero of a certain complicated function f defined over the interval $(0, 1)$. We know that f is continuous and convex and that, in fact, $f(0) = 1$, $f(1) = -1$. However, since the function requires one hour of machine time to evaluate a single point, we are ignorant of the fact that to all intents and purposes it is given by the relatively innocuous expression

$$f(x) = \max\left(-1, \left(x - \frac{1}{3}\right)\left(\frac{x}{2} - 3\right)\right).$$

We can afford to make three evaluations of the function ($n = 3$). Upon referring to the graph of $R_3(0, Y)$ with $Y = \dfrac{Y_0}{Y_1} = 1$, we see that we can guarantee locating the root on an interval of length .01 times the original interval, i.e., on an interval of length .01. However, since the graphs represent the worst that can happen to us, we expect to do much better, and indeed this turns out to be the case.

Let us proceed to calculate:

Cycle 1. $a = 0, b = 1, Y_a = 1, Y_b = 1, S = 0, n = 3$, whence by our formula, $W = .5$, and we have located the root on $(0, .5)$. Next, $x = 0 + (.5 - 0)\rho_3(1) = .5(.148) = .074$, and we find that $f(.074) = .76839 > 0$; so $a' = .074, b' = 1$, and $s' = .074 + \dfrac{.074(.76839)}{1 - .76839} = .31950$. Finally, $n' = 2$.

Cycle 2. (dropping primes on the new variables). $a = .074, b = 1, Y_a = .76839, Y_b = 1, S = .31950, n = 2$, whence by our formula, $W = .074 + \dfrac{.926(.76839)}{1.76839} = .47636$, and we have located the root on $(.31950, .47636)$ Next, $x = .31950 + .15686\rho_2\left(\dfrac{1}{.76839}\right) = .31950 + (.15686)(.198) = .35066$, and we find that $f(.35066) = -.04795 < 0$, so $a' = .074, b' = .35066$ and since $Y_x < Y_b$, $S' = \max\left(.31950, .35066 - \dfrac{(1 - .35066)(.04795)}{1 - .04795}\right) = .31950$. Finally, $n' = 1$.

Cycle 3. $a = .074, b = .35066, Y_a = .76839, Y_b = .04795, S = .31950, n = 1$, whence by our formula, $W = .074 + \dfrac{(.35066 - .074)(.76839)}{.76839 + .04795} = .33441$, and we have located the root on $(.31950, .33441)$. Next, $x = .31950 + (.33441 - .31950)\rho_1\left(\dfrac{.04795}{.76839}\right) = .31950 + (.01491)\rho_1(.624) = .32440$, and we find that $f(.32440) = .02535 > 0$, so $a' = .32440, b' = .35066$, and $S' = .32440 + \dfrac{(.32440 - .074)(.02535)}{.76839 - .02535} = .33294$.

Cycle 4. $a = .32440, b = .35066, Y_a = .02535, Y_b = .04795, S = .33294, n = 0$, whence by our formula,

$$W = .32440 + \dfrac{(.35066 - .32440)(.02535)}{.02535 + .04795} = .33348,$$

and we have located the root on $(.33294, .33348)$. $n = 0$, so the computation ceases and the interval $(.33294, .33348)$ is recorded.

13. Discussion

Since the bisection procedure does not take cognizance of the convexity of the function, one would obtain initially without any evaluation of f that the root lies on $(0, 1)$; with one evaluation, $(0, .5)$; with two evaluations, $(.25, .5)$; and finally, with three evaluations, $(.25, .375)$. The lengths of these bracketing intervals are, then, $1, .5, .25, .125$, respectively. Comparing

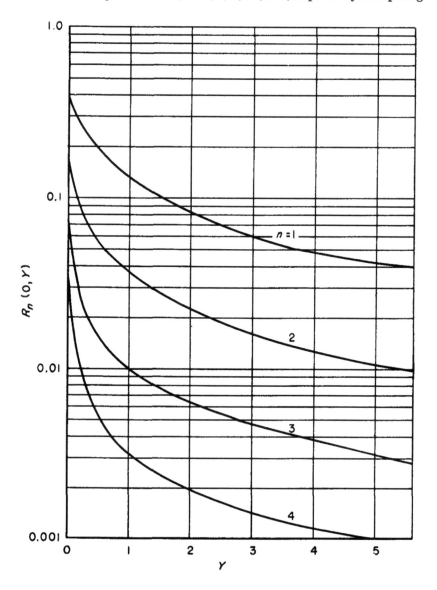

Figure 61

these with those obtained by the procedure above, namely .5, .15686, .01491, .00054, we see that our procedure does have a definite advantage in this instance. In fact, in any instance of a convex function with the same starting values as our example, we can guarantee in three evaluations, a bracketing interval of length less than or equal to .01, as was pointed out earlier. This value compares favorably with .125. (See Figs. 61 and 62.)

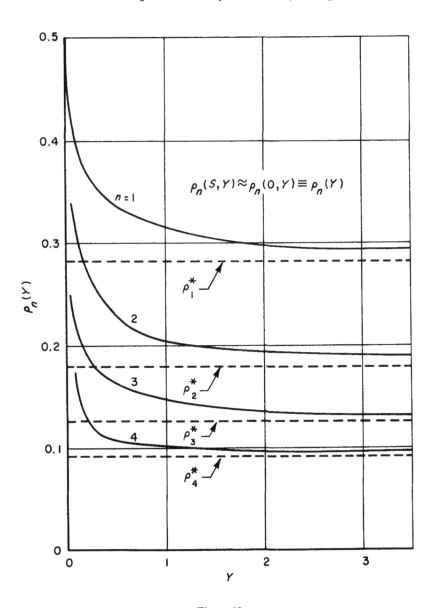

Figure 62

14. The Defective Coin Problem

The problem of ascertaining the minimum number of weighings which suffice to determine the defective coin in a set of N coins of the same appearance, given an equal arm balance and the information that there is precisely one defective coin present, is well known. A large number of ingenious solutions exist, some based upon sequential procedures and some not.

Oddly enough, the corresponding problem for more than one defective coin has attracted little attention. The problem is of significance because it represents one of the simplest examples of a sequential testing problem replete with the difficulties of combinatorial nature and with the difficulties inherent in the concept of "information."

A small amount of analysis discloses the enormous difference in complexity between the one-coin and two-coin problem. Starting with a set of N coins known to contain precisely one defective coin and an equal arm balance, the only permissible operation is that of weighing one group of k coins against another group of k coins chosen from the original set. If the two groups balance, we immediately conclude that the defective coin is in the remaining group of $N - 2k$ coins. If the two groups do not balance, we know that the defective coin is in one of the two sets of k coins. Taking the simple case where we know in advance that the defective coin is heavier than any of the other coins, we see that regardless of the outcome of the first test, we face a problem of exactly the same type as the original at the end of the test, and with a smaller number of coins. This invariance permits us to apply the theory of dynamic programming to this problem in a quite simple fashion.

The problem in the case where there are known to be two or more defective coins is far more complex because we cannot draw any such definite conclusions at the end of a single test. We shall analyze this in detail in the following section. The purpose of the following sections is to indicate a systematic way in which the theory of dynamic programming can be used to provide a computational solution to the determination of optimal and suboptimal testing policies. We shall illustrate this by means of some numerical results obtained using a digital computer.

15. The Two-coin Problem

Let us now consider the case where there are two defective coins in a set of N coins, and where these two coins are known to be heavier than the other coins in the set. Let us consider the possibilities attendant upon a single weighing involving two sets of k coins each.

(a) If the two sets balance, either they both possess one defective coin, with no defective coins remaining in the group of $N - 2k$ coins, or each group of k possesses no defective coins and the two defectives are in the remaining group of $N - 2k$ coins.

(b) If the two sets do not balance, either one set possesses one defective coin with at most one in the remaining $N - 2k$ coins, or one set of k coins possesses two defectives with none in the remaining $N - 2k$.

We see that the original information pattern has ramified. As the testing continues, this ramification increases at an alarming rate if we allow all possible testing programs. Observe that the set of possible tests has become very much larger than what it was in the simple case where there was known to be only one defective.

At the end of the first test, we can choose a subset from the first group of k coins, another subset from the second set of k coins, and a third subset from the group of $N - 2k$ coins, and then match this set of coins against a similar set. Although many of these tests are clearly inefficient and majorized by simpler policies, it is not easy to rule out all tests of this type without a good deal of difficult analysis. Furthermore, it is not clear a priori that some tests of this nature may not be useful.

In what follows, however, in order to simplify the analysis and speed up the calculations, we shall not allow any mixed tests of the type described above. We shall allow the information obtained from the testing of one group of coins to be used in the testing of any other group.

16. Analytic Formulation

From what has been said above, we see that regardless of the definite information we start with, and regardless of the outcome of a particular test, we end up in a situation in which we must face alternatives. Let us then assume from the very beginning that we are given an initial probability distribution $p = [p_0, p_1, p_2]$, where p_i is the probability that there are exactly i defective coins in the set of N coins, for $i \equiv 0, 1, 2$. Assuming that these defective coins are distributed in a uniform fashion among the N coins, we can immediately calculate the corresponding probability distribution for any set of k coins drawn from the original group of N.

We shall only consider policies of the following type. Given a set of N coins and an associated probability distribution $p = [p_0, p_1, p_2]$, we draw two groups of k coins each at random and balance them against one another. If they balance, which means that each group now has at most one defective, we search one of the groups. If this has no defectives, then the other batch of k coins has none, and we go on to examine the remaining group of $N - 2k$ coins. If the first batch has one defective, then the second batch has exactly one defective, and there is no need to examine the remaining $N - 2k$ coins.

If the two groups of k each unbalance, we proceed to isolate the defectives in the heavier batch. If this has one defective, then the other batch of k has no defective, and we proceed to find the remaining defective in the group of $N - 2k$ coins, if there is indeed one more. If the k-group has two defectives, we need not examine either of the other two groups of coins.

Prior to writing down the functional equation we shall use to determine the optimal choice of k, let us introduce the following quantities:

$f_N(p_0, p_1, p_2)$ = expected number of weighings required to determine all defectives, given p_0, p_1, p_2 and using a suboptimal procedure for N coins.

$q_N(p_0, p_1; k)$ = Prob(two k-batches balance).

$P_B(0)$ = Prob(no defectives in each k-batch, given that the arms balance).

$P_B(1)$ = Prob(one defective in each, given that the arms balance).

$P_U(1)$ = Prob(one defective in one k-batch and none in the other, given that the arms are unbalanced).

$P_U(2)$ = Prob(two defectives in one k-batch and none in the other, given that the arms are unbalanced).

$p(r; s; t)$ = Prob(r defectives in the first k-batch, s in the second k-batch, and t in the untested $N - 2k$ batch).

$$f_N(0, p_1, p_2) \equiv g_N(0, p_1, p_2) \equiv g_N(p_1, p_2) \equiv g_N(p_1).$$
$$f_N(p_0, p_1, 0) \equiv h_N(p_0, p_1, 0) \equiv h_N(p_0, p_1) \equiv h_N(p_0).$$
$$f_N(0, 1, 0) \equiv d_N(0, 1, 0) \equiv d_N.$$

17. Values of $p(r;s;t)$

In order to derive the basic recurrence equations, it will be of use to tabulate the various values of $p(r; s; t)$:

$$p(1; 1; 0) = \frac{2k^2}{N(N-1)} p_2;$$

$$p(1; 0; 1) = \frac{2k(N-2k)}{N(N-1)} p_2;$$

$$p(0; 1; 1) = \frac{1k(N-2k)}{N(N-1)} p_2;$$

$$p(2; 0; 0) = \frac{k(k-1)}{N(N-1)} p_2;$$

$$p(0; 2; 0) = \frac{k(k-1)}{N(N-1)} p_2;$$

(1)

$$p(0; 0; 2) = \frac{(N-2k)(N-2k-1)}{N(N-1)} p_o;$$

$$p(0; 1; 0) = \frac{k}{N} p_1;$$

$$p(1; 0; 0) = \frac{k}{N} p_1;$$

$$p(0; 0; 1) = \frac{N-2k}{N} p_0;$$

$$p(0;0; 0) = p_0.$$

18. The Basic Functional Equation

Applying the principle of optimality in the usual fashion, the basic equation from which the search policies are derived is readily seen to be

$$
\begin{aligned}
(1) \qquad f_N(p_0, p_1, p_2) = \min_k \{ & 1 + q_N(p_0, p_1; k)[h_k(p_0^{(1)}) \\
& + P_B(0) f_{N-2k}(p_0^{(2)}, p_1^{(2)}, p_2^{(2)}) + P_B(1) d_k] \\
& + (1 - q_N(p_0; p_1; k))[g_k(p_1^{(3)} + P_U(1) h_{N-2k}(p_0^{(4)})] \},
\end{aligned}
$$

where the $p_1^{(j)}$ are probabilities conditional upon the various possible results of the weighing of the two k-batches, and

$$
(2) \qquad \sum_i p_1^{(j)} = 1, \quad \text{all } j.
$$

The superscript (1) corresponds to balance of the two groups oi k. The superscript (2) corresponds to the case where the defectives are known to be in the remaining $N - 2k$ coins. The superscript (3) corresponds to unbalance of the original two groups of k, and the superscript (4) to the penultimate case described in Sec. 16.

The $p_1^{(j)}$ are given by

(3)

$$
p_0^{(1)} = \left[p_0 + p_2 \frac{(N-2k)(N-2k-1)}{N(N-1)} \right] \Big/ \left[p_0 + p_2 \left\{ \frac{(N-2k)(N-2k-1) + 2k^2}{N(N-1)} \right\} \right];
$$

$$
p_1^{(1)} = 1 - p_0^{(1)};
$$

$$
p_0^{(2)} = p_0 \Big/ \left[p_0 + p_1 \left(\frac{N-2k}{N} \right) + p_2 \frac{(N-2k)(N-2k-1)}{N(N-1)} \right];
$$

$$
p_1^{(2)} = p_1 \left(\frac{N-2k}{N} \right) \Big/ \left[p_0 + p_1 \left(\frac{N-2k}{N} \right) + p_2 \frac{(N-2k)(N-2k-1)}{N(N-1)} \right];
$$

$$
p_2^{(2)} = 1 - p_0^{(2)} - p_1^{(2)};
$$

$$
p_0^{(3)} = 0;
$$

$$
p_1^{(3)} = \left[p_1 \frac{2k}{N} + p_2 \frac{4k(N-2k)}{N(N-1)} \right] \Big/ \left[p_1 \frac{2k}{N} + p_2 \left(\frac{4k(N-2k) + 2k(k-1)}{N(N-1)} \right) \right];
$$

$$
p_2^{(3)} = p_2 \frac{2k(k-1)}{N(N-1)} \Big/ \left[p_1 \frac{2k}{N} + p_2 \left(\frac{4k(N-2k) + 2k(k-1)}{N(N-1)} \right) \right];
$$

$$
p_0^{(4)} = p_1 \frac{2k}{N} \Big/ \left[p_1 \frac{2k}{N} + p_2 \frac{4k(N-2k)}{N(N-1)} \right];
$$

$$
p_1^{(4)} = 1 - p_0^{(4)};
$$

$$
p_2^{(4)} = 0.
$$

Also

(4)

$$q_N(p_0, p_1; k) = p_0 + p_1 \frac{(N - 2k)}{N} + p_2 \left[\frac{(N - 2k)(N - 2k - 1) + 2k^2}{N(N - 1)} \right],$$

and

(5)
$$P_B(0) = p_0^{(1)};$$
$$P_B(1) = p_1^{(1)};$$
$$P_U(1) = p_1 \frac{2k}{N} + p_2 \frac{4k(N - 2k)}{N(N - 1)}.$$

The equations for d_N, $h_N(p_0)$, and $g_N(p_1)$ are special cases of equation (1), and reduce to:

(6)
$$d_N = \min_k \left[1 + \frac{N - 2k}{N} d_{N-2k} + \frac{2k}{N} d_k \right],$$

$$h_N(p_0) = \min_k \left[1 + q_N(p_0, 1 - p_0; k) h_{N-2k}(p_0^{(2)}) \atop + (1 - q_N(p_0, 1 - p_0; k)) d_k \right],$$

and

(7)
$$g_N(p_1) = \min_k \left[1 + q_N(0, p_1; k)[h_k(p_0^{(1)}) \atop + P_B(0)g_{N-2k}(p_1^{(2)}) + P_B(1)d_k] \atop + (1 - q_N(0, p_1; k))[g_k(p_1^{(3)}) \atop + P_U(1)h_{N-2k}(p_0^{(4)})]. \right.$$

19. Computational Procedures

Using Equations (18.1), (18.6), and (18.7), approximate values of f_N and the corresponding values of k which yield the minima were obtained for $N = 1, \ldots, 99$, for values of p, at increments of 0.1. These values of f_N and k were computed iteratively using a Univac 1105. Due to the storage size of computers existing today, to the dimensionality of the problem, and to the limited amount of computer time available, the method of computation was rather crude and hence the results give only an approximate idea as to the nature of the exact solution. However, some clues are obtained. It will be possible to obtain more accurate solutions using exactly the same techniques with smaller increments on the p_i when computers with larger memories become available.

The crudity of the results is due to the fact that the $p_i^{(j)}$ themselves take on values in the continuum $[0, 1]$ for the various values of p_0, p_1, p_2, k, and N. That is, the $p_i^{(j)}$ calculated from Equations (18.3) are not 0, 0, 1, 0.2, $\ldots$, 0.9, 1.0, but take on intermediary values whose corresponding functional values $f_r(p_0^{(j)}, p_1^{(j)}, p_2^{(j)})$ have to be approximated by interpolation on

172

previously obtained $f_r(p_0', p_1', p_2')$'s, where $p_0', p_1' p_2'$ have values $0, 0.1, \ldots, 0.9, 1.0$.

We shall call these eleven values the set P; also $\underline{p}_i^{(j)}$, $\bar{p}_i^{(j)}$ are those consecutive members of P that contain $p_i^{(j)}$.

For the cases in which $\bar{p}_0^{(j)} + \bar{p}_1^{(j)} \gg 1$, the interpolation on $f_r(p_0^{(j)}, p_1^{(j)})$, (where $p_2^{(j)}$ is redundant, since $p_0^{(j)} + p_1^{(j)} + p_2^{(j)} = 1$), is of the form

$$(1) \quad f_r(p_0, p_1) = .01(p_0 - \underline{p}_0) f_r(\bar{p}_0, \bar{p}_1) + (\bar{p}_0 - p_0) f_r(p_0, \bar{p}_1)(p_1 - \underline{p}_1)$$

$$+ .01(p_0 - \underline{p}_0) f_r(\bar{p}_0, p_1) + (\bar{p}_0 - p_0) f_r(p_0, p_1)(\bar{p}_1 - p_1).$$

When $\bar{p}_0^{(j)} + \bar{p}_1^{(j)} \equiv 1.1$, the interpolation has to be modified so that only $f_r(p_0, \bar{p}_1)$, $f_r(\bar{p}_0, p_1)$, and $f_r(p_0, p_1)$ occur in the expression. Obviously,

TABLE I

Values of k_N For $N = 80$

p_0 \ p_1	0	.1	.2	.3	.4	.5	.6	.7	.8	.9	1.0
0	7	7	7	8	8	8	18	18	40	40	27
.1	3	7	8	8	10	10	40	40	40	27	
.2	4	10	10	12	14	40	40	40	29		
.3	5	8	9	10	40	40	40	40			
.4	7	7	40	40	40	40	40				
.5	8	8	40	40	21	40					
.6	7	38	40	40	40						
.7	7	38	39	40							
.8	32	37	39								
.9	28	37									
1.0	—										

the incremental interval 0.1 is large and creates inexactness in the computations, but the fact that all $f_r(p_0, p_1)$, $r < N$, had to be stored to obtain f_N made a smaller interval impossible. Also, one would intuitively feel that the f's and their corresponding k's which minimize (which we shall define as k_N) might be discontinuous at the boundaries $p_0^{(j)} = 1$, $p_1^{(j)} = 1$, and $p_0^{(j)} + p_1^{(j)} = 1$, and this again is a drawback to the use of interpolation.

Since the number of values of $f_N(p_0, p_1)$ calculated is over 6000, limitations on space preclude printing all of them and their corresponding k_N's. However, as examples of the basic data obtained, Tables I to IV show these data for $N = 80$ and 90.

TABLE II

Values of f_N For $N = 80$

p_1 \ p_0	0	.1	.2	.3	.4	.5	.6	.7	.8	.9	1.0
0	6.447	6.512	6.539	6.535	6.497	6.416	6.283	6.072	5.748	5.143	4.000
.1	4.674	5.773	6.146	6.309	6.298	6.164	5.928	5.496	4.913	3.927	
.2	4.534	5.293	5.736	5.988	5.837	5.588	5.204	4.663	3.720		
.3	4.344	4.920	5.422	5.486	5.243	4.911	4.408	3.450			
.4	4.056	4.689	5.114	4.890	4.619	4.154	3.100				
.5	3.781	4.340	4.524	4.272	3.835	2.750					
.6	3.452	4.058	3.917	3.445	2.400						
.7	3.160	3.488	3.021	2.050							
.8	2.706	2.481	1.675								
.9	1.715	1.315									
1.0	—										

TABLE III

Values of k_N For $N = 90$

p_1 \ p_0	0	.1	.2	.3	.4	.5	.6	.7	.8	.9	1.0
0	7	8	8	9	10	10	10	22	45	45	27
.1	5	8	10	10	10	10	22	45	45	31	
.2	5	10	10	10	14	15	45	45	32		
.3	6	9	9	45	45	45	45	45			
.4	6	8	9	45	45	45	45				
.5	9	9	45	45	45	45					
.6	8	10	44	45	45						
.7	8	37	44	44							
.8	36	42	44								
.9	32	41									
1.0	—										

TABLE IV

Values of f_N For $N = 90$

p_1 \ p_0	0	.1	.2	.3	.4	.5	.6	.7	.8	.9	1.0
0	6.591	6.657	6.690	6.687	6.634	6.553	6.432	6.236	5.909	5.272	4.156
.1	4.770	5.895	6.269	6.437	6.436	6.321	6.103	5.656	5.030	4.068	
.2	4.664	5.409	5.819	6.085	5.943	5.694	5.343	4.765	3.849		
.3	4.450	5.034	5.508	5.654	5.396	5.033	4.501	3.520			
.4	4.153	4.767	5.208	5.004	4.733	4.238	3.160				
.5	3.867	4.422	4.607	4.371	3.913	2.800					
.6	3.523	4.134	3.988	3.513	2.440						
.7	3.217	3.541	3.061	2.053							
.8	2.747	2.527	1.702								
.9	1.748	1.320									
1.0	—										

From the $f_N(p_0, p_1, p_2)$ and their corresponding k_N's obtained, various properties of the process that suggest themselves are:

(2) (a) $f_N(0, 0, 1) = \log_2 N$,

(b) $f_N(0, 0, 1) = \max_{\{p_i\}} f_N(p_0, p_1, p_2)$,

(c) $\dfrac{f_N(p_0, p_1, p_2)}{\log_2 N}$ tends to a limit as $N \to \infty$, p_0, p_1, p_2 remaining fixed.

The validity of the last statement is suggested by a statistical analysis performed on the data for $N = 79 - 99$; it was decided to use these

TABLE V

N	$s_N(0, 0)$	$s_N(.2, .5)$	$s_N(.6, .3)$	$s_N(.8, .1)$
79	1.470	1.305	.784	.570
80	1.471	1.275	.786	.566
81	1.469	1.290	.779	.571
82	1.470	1.282	.788	.565
83	1.468	1.292	.781	.570
84	1.468	1.262	.785	.564
85	1.466	1.291	.778	.568
86	1.467	1.268	.786	.562
87	1.464	1.277	.778	.566
88	1.465	1.271	.779	.562
89	1.462	1.281	.772	.566
90	1.465	1.265	.781	.561
91	1.463	1.289	.774	.563
92	1.464	1.274	.777	.561
93	1.462	1.283	.770	.557
94	1.463	1.275	.779	.559
95	1.461	1.283	.773	.555
96	1.462	1.268	.773	.558
97	1.460	1.281	.767	.556
98	1.461	1.270	.776	.557
99	1.460	1.278	.770	.553

values of N to make things as asymptotic as possible while still retaining sufficient data to provide indications of trends. For these values of N, and for all $\{p_i\}$ in P, the statistics

$$r_N(p_0, p_1) = \frac{k_N(p_0, p_1)}{N}$$

and

$$S_N(p_0, p_1) = \frac{f_N(p_0, p_1)}{\log_2 N}$$

were computed. For fixed p_i, the $s_N(p_0, p_1)$ are amazingly constant over N, examples being given in Table V. Quadratic regressions on p_0 and p_1 were performed on the means of r_N and s_N (averaged over N); i.e., on the statistics

$$(3) \qquad r(p_0, p_1) = \frac{1}{21} \sum_{N=79}^{99} r_N(p_0, p_1),$$

$$s(p_0, p_1) = \frac{1}{21} \sum_{N=79}^{99} s_N(p_0, p_1).$$

The regressions are:

(4) (a) $r = -1.076 + 6.014p_0 - .594p_0{}^2 + 8.350p_1 - 3.431p_1{}^2,$
with $\sigma_r = .956$, and

(b) $s = 1.017 - .869p_0 + .013p_0{}^2 + .388p_1 - .764p_1{}^2,$
with $\sigma_s = .070.$

Equation (19.4b), with its low variance and its constant near unity, suggests that the regression is fairly accurate.

However, Equation (19.4a), with its high value of σ_r, is not too satisfactory. One reason for this result is that the k_N's are in some cases highly

TABLE VI

N	$r_N(.3, .3)$	$r_N(.6, .1)$	$r_N(.8, .1)$
79	.1392	.4810	.3544
80	.1250	.4750	.4625
81	.4938	.1111	.4691
82	.1341	.4756	.4634
83	.1325	.1084	.3614
84	.5000	.4762	.4643
85	.4941	.1059	.4706
86	.1279	.4767	4651
87	.1264	.4828	.3678
88	.5000	.4773	.4659
89	.4944	.1124	.3596
90	.5000	.1111	.4667
91	.1538	.1099	.3956
92	.5000	.4783	.4674
93	.4946	.1075	.4624
94	.5000	.4787	.4894
95	.1368	.4737	.4632
96	.5000	.4792	.3750
97	.4948	.4742	.4639
98	.1327	.1122	.4694
99	.1313	.1111	.4646

erratic through N for this fixed p_0, p_1. This is probably partly because (i) there might be some k's which produce almost the same value of f and the crudity of the computations does not prefer the best consistently, and (ii) the interpolations, as mentioned previously, might not give good results at the boundaries $p_0^{(j)} = 1$, $p_1^{(j)} = 1$, and $p_0^{(j)} + p_1^{(j)} = 1$. Reason (i) is backed up by the basic data in that, for many values of p_0, p_1, two highly different values of k recur consistently and one of them is probably the correct one. Examples from the basic data appear in Table VI.

20. Information Theory Considerations

Using information theory, a lower bound on f_N for a completely optimal policy may be derived. In one weighing there are three possible outcomes: balance and unbalance each way. In such a weighing it therefore follows that the expected value of information acquired is at most $\log_2 3 = 1$ unit.

If there is no defective coin, the knowledge of this is equivalent to $-\log_2 p_0$ units of information. If there is one defective coin, it may be any of the N, each with probability p_1/N; hence the amount of information corresponding to the determination of each one of these possibilities is $-\log_2(p_1/N)$, so that the expected amount of information corresponding to these N possibilities is

$$N\left(\frac{p_1}{N}\right)\left(-\log_2\frac{p_1}{N}\right) = -p_1\log_2\frac{p_1}{N}\text{ units.}$$

Similarly, the information corresponding to the case of two defectives is found to be

$$-p_2\log_2\frac{p_2}{N(N-1)/2}.$$

Hence the lower bound on f_N is the ratio of the expected amount of information to the unit of information $\log_2 3$:

(1) $$F = -\sum_{i=0}^{2} p_i\log_3 p_i + p_1\log_3 N + p_2\log_3\frac{N(N-1)}{2}.$$

A comparison of this with our data confirms statements (b) and (c) in Sec. 19, but suggests once again that the crudity of the interpolation procedure has somewhat underestimated the f_N's, at least for $p_0 + p_1 \leq 0.6$. For example, in Table IV the underlined values of f_N are below the bound F computed from Eq. (20.1). Nevertheless, we may take some comfort in the fact that the values of f_N obtained would suggest that our suboptimal policies are good, since the values are of the same order as F.

The following points may also be deduced from (20.1):

(2) $$\frac{F}{\log_2 N} \to (p_1 + 2p_2)\log_3 2,$$

which supports statement (c) of the last section. When $p_2 = 1$, this expression becomes $2 \log_3 3 = 1.26$, and hence the statement equivalent to (a) should be

(3) $$f_N(0, 0, 1) \to 1.26 \log_2 N,$$

for an optimal policy.

Finally, it may be shown that the minimum of F over $p_0 + p_1 + p_2 = 1$ occurs when

(4) $$p_0 = \frac{p_1}{N} = \frac{p_2}{N(N-1)/2},$$

the asymptotic solution to which is $p_2 = 1$, confirming statement (b).

Comments and Bibliography

The problem of determining optimal search procedures for locating the absolute maximum of a function of N variables is a very difficult problem. See, for example,

A. Gleason, "A search problem on the n-cube," *Proc. Symposia in Appl. Math.*, vol. 10, 1960, pp. 175–178.

P. Wolfe, *The RAND Symposium on Mathematical Programming, Linear Programming, and Recent Extensions*, The RAND Corporation, Report R-351, 1959.

Even in the case where it is known, a priori, that the function is unimodal, the problem has been resolved only for functions of one variable. The simplest discussion is to be found in § 22 of Chapter 1 of *Dynamic Programming*, following an unpublished paper by S. Johnson. A more complicated discussion may be found in

J. Kiefer, "Sequential minimax search for a maximum," *Proc. Amer. Math. Soc.*, vol., 4, 1953, pp. 502–506,

and further results in

J. Kiefer, "Optimum sequential search and approximation methods under minimum regularity assumptions," *J. Soc. Indust. Appl. Math.*, vol. 5, 1957, pp. 105–136.

The results pertaining to the location of the root of a monotone function follow

O. Gross and S. Johnson, "Sequential minimax search for a zero of a convex function," *Math. Tables and Other Aids to Computation*, vol. 13, 1959, pp. 44–51.

Some other pertinent papers are

M. Sandelius, "On an optimal search procedure," *Amer. Math. Monthly*, vol. 68, 1961, pp. 133–134.

H. Robbins, "Some aspects of the sequential design of experiments," *Bull. Amer. Math. Soc.*, vol. 58, 1952, pp. 527–536.

A. Dvoretzky, "On stochastic approximation," *Proc. Third Berkeley Symposium on Mathematical Statistics and Probability*, University of California Press, Berkeley, California, vol. 1, 1956, pp. 39–56.

G. E. P. Box, "Evolutionary operations, a method for increasing industrial productivity," *Appl. Stat.*, vol. 6, 1957, pp. 3–23.

D. J. Newman, "Locating the maximum point on a unimodal surface," *Notices of the Amer. Math. Soc.*, vol. 6, 1959, p. 799.

J. Kiefer and J. Wolfowitz, "Stochastic estimation of the maximum of a regression," *Ann. Math. Stat.*, vol. 23, pp. 462–466.

R. C. Norris, *A Method for Locating the Maximum of a Function of A Single Variable in the Presence of Noise*, Lincoln Laboratory, 22G-0035, 1960.

E. J. Magee, *An Empirical Investigation of Procedures for Locating the Maximum Peak of a Multiple-peak Regression Function*, Lincoln Laboratory, 22G-0046, 1960.

§5. See a detailed and entertaining discussion of such matters,

H. Weyl, *Symmetry*, Princeton University Press, Princeton, New Jersey, 1952.

A particularly important application of the general theory of search processes is to the problem of medical diagnosis and treatment. For recent work in this area and additional references, see

R. S. Ledley and L. B. Lusted, "Reasoning foundation of medical diagnosis," *Science*, vol. 130, 1959, pp. 9–21.

N. Mantel, "Principles of Chemotherapeutic screening," *Proc. Fourth Berkeley Symposium*, University of California Press, Berkeley, California, to appear, in 1962.

B. B. Winter, "Optimal diagnostic procedures," *IRE Trans. on Reliability and Quality Control*, vol. RQC-9, 1960, pp. 13–19.

§14–§20. The material of these sections is taken from

R. Bellman and B. Gluss, "On various versions of the defective coin problem," *Information and Control*, vol. 4, 1961, pp. 118–131.

CHAPTER V

Dynamic Programming and the Calculus of Variations

1. Introduction

We shall see in subsequent chapters that a number of significant processes arising in the study of trajectories, in the study of multistage production processes, and finally in the field of feedback control can be formulated as problems in the calculus of variations. Although the techniques of this theory play a vital role in the analytic treatment of many classes of variational questions, they have so far been of little use in the computational solution of the problems of contemporary science and engineering.

In order to explain this phenomenon, we shall present the very rudiments of the calculus of variations and then discuss in detail the difficulties that lie in the way of a computational solution along these lines. We shall present the dynamic programming approach to problems of this nature and indicate how some of these difficulties are by-passed or overcome.

Following this, we shall indicate briefly how the functional equation approach, based upon the principle of optimality, yields the fundamental classical results of the calculus of variations and the Hamilton-Jacobi theory as well.

The reader interested only in the computational solution of trajectory and feedback control processes can skip this chapter on a first reading. In each of the following chapters, devoted respectively to trajectories, multistage production processes (a particular class of feedback control processes of economic origin), and feedback control problems of engineering origin, the discussion will be self-contained. In Chapter XII, devoted to a discussion of numerical aspects, we shall present a solution of the brachistochrone problem along dynamic programming lines.

In an appendix, we discuss a new approach due to Bryson which appears quite promising as far as breaking the dimensionality barrier is concerned.

2. Functionals

The ordinary calculus deals with the problem of maximizing or minimizing a function of N variables

$$(1) \qquad F = F(x_1, x_2, \ldots, x_N).$$

In the calculus of variations, we consider problems involving functions of an infinite number of variables, or, equivalently, functions of functions. The term commonly used to describe a scalar value dependent upon a function is *functional*. Just as a function is a rule for assigning a number to a finite set of numbers, so a functional is a rule for assigning a number to a function, or set of functions.

The simplest and most important functional is the Riemann integral

$$(2) \qquad J(y) = \int_a^b y(x)\, dx$$

defined for all functions $y(x)$ which are continuous over $[a, b]$.

We shall concern ourselves in what follows with functionals of the form

$$(3) \qquad J(y) = \int_a^b g(y(x), y'(x), x)\, dx,$$

where, as customary, $y'(x)$ represents the derivative of $y(x)$. The function $y(x)$ will in general be subject to end-point conditions of the form

$$(4) \qquad y(a) = c_1, \quad h(y(b), y'(b)) = c_2.$$

The meaning of relations of this type will be discussed below.

Of wider scope is the problem of minimizing or maximizing a functional of the form

$$(5) \qquad J(y) = \int_a^b g(y(x), z(x), x)\, dx$$

where x, y, and z are connected by a differential equation

$$(6) \qquad \frac{dz}{dx} = H(z, y, x), \quad z(0) = c_1.$$

Still more general is the problem of maximizing or minimizing an expression

$$(7) \qquad J(y) = \int_a^b g(z(x), y(x), x)\, dx + h(z(b), y(b), b),$$

with x and y subject to (6), and possibly to side constraints.

This problem is called the *problem of Bolza*, while the problem of finding the extremum of a function of the end-point b,

$$(8) \qquad J(y) = h(z(b), y(b), b),$$

is called the *problem of Mayer* in the calculus of variations. We shall refer to this last problem as a *terminal control process*.

Both problems are particular cases of the optimization of a Riemann·Stieltjes integral

$$(9) \qquad J(y) = \int_a^b g(z(x), y(x), x)\, dG(x),$$

a problem which we shall not discuss. In most important applications, the functional $J(y)$ has the form given in (7), where either g or h is identically zero.

3. The Formalism of the Calculus of Variations

Let us now describe the basic approach of the calculus of variations and present some classical results. We do this in order to compare the two different techniques—those of the calculus of variations and those of dynamic programming. In subsequent discussion we will indicate advantages and disadvantages of each technique. It is most likely that a synthesis of the two methods will ultimately prove capable of handling the truly complex problems of optimal control and optimal trajectory. That the two methods are truly complementary will be a consequence of the geometric interpretations presented below.

In the calculus of variations, we seek to obtain an equation for the optimizing function. Proceeding purely formally, without regard for the many formidable questions of existence and uniqueness of solution which arise at the very outset, let us examine the problem of finding a function $y(x)$ which minimizes the functional

$$(1) \qquad \int_a^b F(y(x), y'(x), x) \, dx.$$

We shall employ a straightforward extension of the variational approach used for functions of a finite number of variables. As a matter of fact, the fundamental equation of the calculus of variations was derived by Euler by means of a passage to the limit from the finite to the infinite. As is to be expected from similar analysis in ordinary calculus, the conditions that we obtain will be necessary, and, in general, not sufficient.

Let $y(x)$ denote a minimizing function, which we may consider to furnish a relative minimum. If $z(x)$ is any "nearby" function, we must then have

$$(2) \qquad J(z) \geq J(y).$$

To represent the fact that $z(x)$ is a nearby function, let us write

$$(3) \qquad z(x) = y(x) + \epsilon g(x),$$

where $g(x)$ is an as yet unspecified function and ϵ is a small parameter. The function $z(x)$ is not the most general nearby function, but this is not important to us, since, as indicated above, we are concerned with obtaining *necessary* conditions. It is important to realize that in order to obtain necessary conditions, we can vary over any convenient class of nearby functions.

The inequality in (2) then becomes

$$(4) \qquad J(y + \epsilon g) \geq J(y)$$

182

for *all* ϵ and $g(x)$, or, in explicit terms,

$$(5) \qquad \int_a^b F(y + \epsilon g, y' + \epsilon g', x)\,dx \geq \int_a^b F(y, y', x)\,dx.$$

To derive a more useful result from this, we expand the left-hand side as a function of the parameter ϵ. It is sufficient to retain only the constant and linear term in this expansion since ϵ is assumed to be a small parameter. We thus obtain the relation

$$(6) \qquad J(y) + \epsilon \left[\int_a^b (F_y g + F_{y'} g')\,dx \right] + 0(\epsilon^2) \geq J(y).$$

For this inequality to be valid for both positive and negative values of the small parameter ϵ, we must have

$$(7) \qquad \int_a^b (F_y g + F_{y'} g')\,dx = 0.$$

Since $g(x)$ was arbitrary, this relation must be true for all functions $g(x)$ possessing derivatives in $[a, b]$.

It is useful to note that the equation in (7) could also be derived from the condition that $\partial J / \partial \epsilon$ must equal zero at $\epsilon = 0$.

In order to extract the most from this result, we integrate the second term in the integrand by parts, obtaining

$$(8) \qquad \int_a^b \left[g(x)F_y - g(x)\frac{d}{dx}(F_{y'}) \right] + \left[g(x)F_{y'} \right]_a^b = 0.$$

Since we are presently concerned with necessary conditions within the interval of interest, let us for the moment set

$$(9) \qquad g(a) = g(b) = 0.$$

This is equivalent to the statement that we keep the end-points of the optimizing curve fixed. We then have the result that

$$(10) \qquad \int_a^b g(x)\left[F_y - \frac{d}{dx}(F_{y'}) \right]dx = 0$$

for all admissible $g(x)$. Were this true for *all* $g(x)$, it would be trivial that the coefficient function must be zero, i.e.,

$$(11) \qquad F_y - \frac{d}{dx}F_{y'} = 0.$$

To establish this, we need only take $g(x) = F_y - dF_{y'}/dx$ itself. The integrand in the relation in (10) then becomes a perfect square whence (11) follows. However, as we have pointed out above, we are not really considering all possible $g(x)$, but only those which have derivatives, and indeed only those which have derivatives which are well enough behaved so that the preceding integrals make sense. Since we do not know the nature of the solution in advance, there is no guarantee that the function $F_y - dF_{y'}/dx$, is an admissible $g(x)$.

Nevertheless, one of the fundamental results of the calculus of variations (the "fundamental lemma of the calculus of variations") asserts that if (10) is satisfied by all admissible $g(x)$, then equation (11) does hold.

A rigorous formulation of these variational problems and detailed proofs of these results will be found in several of the standard texts referred to at the end of the chapter. We shall not pursue the matter any further here, since, as shall be seen below, we have various means of by-passing a number of the questions of rigor.

The equation in (11) when written out represents a second order equation which is, apart from easily determined cases, nonlinear. It is called the *Euler equation* of the variational problem, and is a necessary condition completely analogous to that derived in the finite dimensional case by setting the first partial derivatives equal to zero.

Only in rare cases is an explicit analytic solution of this equation obtainable in terms of the standard functions of analysis. The classic examples may be found in references given at the end of the chapter.

4. Necessary Conditions

As in the calculus case, the same variational equation is obtained for both minimizing and maximizing functions, as well as for functions yielding stationary points of more complex nature. Rules for distinguishing between the various contingencies are to some extent known, but the overall picture is quite cloudy.

Two of the most important conditions for a minimum are:

The Weierstrass Condition. Let $z(x)$ be a function distinct from the extremal function $y(x)$, and $z'(x)$ its derivative. Then we must have

$$(1) \qquad F(x, y, z') - F(x, y, y') - (z' - y')F_{y'}(x, y, y') \geq 0.$$

The left-hand side of this inequality is called the *Weierstrass E-function.*

The Legendre Condition. For $y(x)$ to be a minimizing arc, we must have

$$(2) \qquad\qquad F_{y'y'}(x, y, y') \geq 0.$$

This corresponds to the usual second derivative condition of the calculus.

These conditions, which are nonintuitive from the standpoint of the classical calculus of variations approach to optimization problems, will be shown to follow logically and simply from the dynamic programming approach, presented below.

5. Natural Boundary Conditions

Occasionally in variational processes the extremal function is constrained to satisfy end conditions of the form

$$(1) \qquad G(y(a), y'(a)) = 0, \quad H(y(b), y'(b)) = 0.$$

More frequently, the initial conditions yield a certain constraint, but the terminal conditions are imposed by the variational problem itself. Referring to equation (3.8), we see that if y must assume fixed values at a and b, then it is sensible to require that $g(x)$ vanish at these points. On the other hand, if $y(x)$ is determined only at b or not specified at all, then the variation of $g(x)$ at the point $x = a$ yields the further relation

$$(2) \qquad F_{y'} = 0 \quad \text{at} \quad x = a.$$

This last condition is called a *natural boundary condition*.

6. Isoperimetric Problems

Frequently, we encounter the problem of maximizing or minimizing the functional $J(y)$ subject to an integral constraint of the form

$$(1) \qquad \int_a^b G(y, y', x)\, dx = c_1.$$

In applications, this usually signifies the finiteness of some resource. Under various conditions, it can be shown that as in the ordinary calculus, we can employ a *Lagrange multiplier* and treat the new problem of finding the extremum of the functional

$$(2) \qquad \int_a^b [F(y, y', x) - \lambda G(y, y', x)]\, dx.$$

We thus obtain the modified Euler equation

$$(3) \qquad (F - \lambda G)_y - \frac{d}{dx}(F_{y'} - \lambda G_{y'}) = 0,$$

where λ is a constant which must be determined by use of the relation in (1).

As we shall show below, this result also follows from the functional equation approach of dynamic programming. As may be expected, it is not a simple matter to carry through the solution of a problem of this type to the very end.

7. Shortcomings of the Calculus of Variations

The difficulties that we enumerated in connection with the use of the calculus in the treatment of finite dimensional optimization problems are, as should be expected, present in these more complex variational problems over function spaces, and present in more complex forms.

After the initial development of the calculus of variations by Euler, Lagrange, Weierstrass, Hilbert, Bolza, Bliss, and others, the subject became, to a large extent, more fit for the textbook than the laboratory. Reasonably, one could hope for no more satisfactory description of the solution than that given by a differential equation, a result obtained by Euler. Consequently, the subsequent work was devoted to rigorizing the known formalism, resulting in the derivation of various necessary and sufficient conditions for various types of extrema, and in extending the class of functionals to which these techniques could be applied.

Little emphasis was placed on the problem of obtaining numerical results and the major emphasis was placed upon existence and uniqueness theorems.

The advent of the high-speed digital computer, however, has greatly affected mathematical thinking. With this powerful tool at our disposal, we now evaluate analytic techniques not only with regard to their elegance, but also in relation to their computational feasibility. The Euler equation, which rates so highly as far as its analytical aspects are concerned, must now be judged from the viewpoint of numerical solution. Unfortunately, it is most unsatisfactory from this standpoint.

There are actually several distinct types of difficulty associated with the classical formulation of variational questions. Some of these stem from the variational problem itself, and some stem from the Euler equation. Let us discuss first the numerical solution of the Euler equation.

As pointed out above, this is in the main a nonlinear equation. Furthermore, this is a nonlinear equation with a two-point boundary condition. In order to appreciate what this last statement means, let us briefly review what the computational solution of a differential equation entails.

Since there is a negligible probability of a usable explicit analytic solution, we must have recourse for the purposes of numerical computation to analogue devices, including the use of Monte Carlo methods, or to digital computers. In the majority of cases, it is the digital computer which must be used.

Since a digital computer employs only the usual operations of arithmetic, we must convert the equation under consideration into a form which requires only the use of these operations, and requires no transcendental operations such as differentiation or integration. This means that we must approximate to integrals by sums and to derivatives by differences. This approximation can be done in an unlimited number of ways, requiring a careful balancing of accuracy factors, stability factors, and time factors. All of this means, of course, that at the present time numerical computation is more of an art than a science.

Avoiding all the fine details which enter inevitably into any particular computation, let us present the general idea of digital computer solution of a differential equation. Given the equation

(1) $$y' = f(x, y), \quad y(x_0) = c_0,$$

an *initial value* problem, we replace the derivative by an approximate expression such as

(2) $$y'(x) \cong [y(x + \Delta) - y(x)]/\Delta$$

or

(3) $$y'(x) \cong [y(x + \Delta) - y(x - \Delta)]/2\Delta.$$

Using the first choice (in some ways, the worst possible choice), the differential equation in (1) is now replaced by the difference equation, say

(4) $$\frac{y(x + \Delta) - y(x)}{\Delta} = f(x, y), \quad y(x_0) = c,$$

and x is allowed to assume only the values x_0, $x_0 + \Delta$, $x_0 + 2\Delta$, $x_0 + 3\Delta$, and so on.

Given the initial value, $y(x_0)$, we evaluate $y(x_0 + \Delta)$ by means of the formula in (4). Using the new value $y(x_0 + \Delta)$, the formula is used again to determine the value of y at $x = x_0 + 2\Delta$, and so on. This type of operation, an iterative process, is ideally suited to a digital computer since it requires that the same type of operation be repeated over and over again. Consequently, one set of instructions suffices to carry out the entire process.

The choice of Δ depends upon the accuracy required and the time that one is willing to spend on the computation. Generally, the smaller the value of Δ, the more accurate the solution obtained in this way. On the other hand, the time required to determine the value of y at some point $x = x_1$ is clearly proportional to $1/\Delta$. Furthermore, stability considerations enter. For this reason, the second approximation, that given in (3), is greatly preferable to that given in (2).

We shall not enter any further into these important matters here, since little has been done in this direction in connection with the solution of variational problems. The reader interested in the results known for differential equations may refer to the references given at the end of the chapter.

The same method is employed to solve a system of differential equations of the form

(5) $$\frac{dy_i}{dx} = f_i(x, y_1, y_2, \ldots, y_N), \quad y_i(0) = c_i, \quad i = 1, 2, \ldots, N.$$

If we use vector notation,

(6) $$\frac{dy}{dx} = f(x, y), \quad y(0) = c,$$

the procedure is formally precisely as given above.

Since digital computers are ideally designed to solve differential equations with initial conditions, it is a completely routine effort to think in terms of the solution of one hundred or even one thousand simultaneous equations of the type appearing in (5).

8. Two-point Boundary Value Problems

The situation changes drastically when two-point boundary value problems are introduced. Consider a second order equation of the form

$$(1) \qquad y'' = g(x, y, y'), \quad x_0 \leq x \leq x_1,$$

where the solution is subject to the boundary conditions

$$(2) \qquad y(x_0) = c_1, \quad y(x_1) = c_2.$$

Using finite difference approximations, and setting

$$(3) \qquad \begin{aligned} y'(x) &= [y(x + \Delta) - y(x)]/\Delta, \\ y''(x) &= [y(x + 2\Delta) - 2y(x + \Delta) + y(x)]/\Delta^2, \end{aligned}$$

we see that, although $y(x_0)$ is given, we have no apparent way of determining $y(x_0 + \Delta)$, since $y'(x_0)$ has not been specified.

The standard escape from this cul-de-sac is to guess a value for $y'(x_0)$ and then use the methods described in §7 to obtain a value for $y(x_1)$. The initial guess for $y'(x_0)$ is then repeatedly modified until there is an acceptable fit between the prescribed value at x_1 and that obtained from the integration.

When the Euler equation is nonlinear, the technique for adjusting the initial choice of $y'(x_0)$ is completely catch-as-catch-can with no Marquess of Queensberry rules. In many cases, instability of both analytic and computational origin produces wild fluctuations in the value of $y(x_1)$ as a consequence of small changes in the value of $y'(x_0)$.

There is no practical way of predicting numerical instabilities for simultaneous nonlinear differential equations, but experience with the variational approach to trajectory problems indicates strongly that instability presents a very real and often insurmountable problem.

It is desirable then to have a way of obtaining the computational solution of the original variational problem which does not depend upon the solution of nonlinear differential equations with two-point boundary conditions.

9. Constraints

A far more serious difficulty from many points of view than that connected with the purely computational problem arising from the two-point boundary conditions arises from the presence of constraints on the nature of the optimizing function.

Consider, for example, the problem of minimizing the functional

(1)
$$J(y) = \int_a^b g(y, y', x)\, dx$$

subject to a constraint of the form

(2)
$$|y'| \le c_1.$$

Since the existence of the Euler equation is based upon the assumption that a free variation is permitted in the vicinity of an extremal, we must

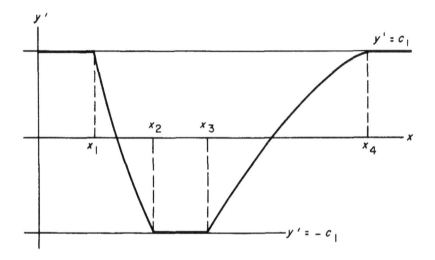

Figure 63

face the fact that there may be no Euler equation at all! The solution may consist of intervals in which $y' = c_1$, interlaced by intervals in which $y' = -c_1$. Or there may be intervals where $y' = c_1$ or $y' = -c_1$, together with intervals in which $|y'| < c_1$, which means that the Euler equation will be satisfied within these intervals where $|y'| < c_1$. The solution may then have the form of Fig. 63.

It is not difficult to construct examples where this oscillation can occur as often as is desired. Even simple versions of trajectory, control, and bottleneck processes can yield solutions with three or four alternations. The result of this complexity is that problems of this nature are extraordinarily difficult to attack. They require a combination of analytic techniques and ingenuity, and at the present time, there exist no known uniform methods for obtaining explicit solutions. References will be found to a number of particular problems which have been solved.

Whatever the difficulties present in the computational solution to the usual variational problem, they are mild compared to those encountered here. Not only must one guess initial values, but in some cases initial phases of solution and the persistence of these phases must be guessed as well. The problem above where $|y'| \leq c_1$, can be handled, with the aid of Lagrange multipliers and guesses as to initial conditions. The problem of minimizing subject to the constraint $|y| \leq c_2$ seemingly cannot be handled in this fashion.

As we shall see, the dynamic programming approach affords a way around these difficulties, and, in many cases, is actually aided in the computational solution by the presence of constraints.[1]

10. Linearity

The study of the optimal utilization of economic complexes, discussed in Chapter VII, leads to the analytic problem of maximizing the inner product

(1) $$J(y) = (x(T), a),$$

where x and y are connected by means of the vector-matrix equation

(2) $$\frac{dx}{dt} = Ax + By, \quad x(0) = c,$$

and the inequality constraint ·

(3) $$Cy \leq Dx.$$

Here the linearity completely precludes the classical variational approach. There is no Euler equation for this maximization problem.

11. The Formalism of Dynamic Programming

Let us now briefly sketch the dynamic programming approach to variational problems. As before, we shall proceed in a purely formal way.

Consider the problem of minimizing the functional

(1) $$J(y) = \int_a^b F(x, y, y') \, dx,$$

where the function y is subject to the initial condition $y(a) = c$. The minimum value will be a function of the initial x-value a, and the initial y-value c. Here c measures the initial state of the system and a the duration of the process.

Let us then introduce the function

(2) $$f(a, c) = \min_y J(y).$$

[1] Cf. the discussion in §17 of Chapter I.

What we have done is to imbed the particular problem posed above where a and c are constants within the family of problems generated by allowing a and c to be parameters with the range of variation $-\infty < a < b$ and $-\infty < c < \infty$.

We shall begin by obtaining an equation for the function $f(a, c)$, and then show how this equation yields the results we have previously noted in the sections on the calculus of variations, together with some further results.

Since the integral has the requisite additivity property

$$(3) \qquad \int_a^b = \int_a^{a+\Delta} + \int_{a+\Delta}^b,$$

the principle of optimality readily yields the functional equation

$$(4) \quad f(a, c) = \min_{y[a, a+\Delta]} \left[\int_a^{a+\Delta} F(x, y, y')\, dx + f(a + \Delta, c(y)) \right],$$

where the minimization is over all functions y defined over $a \leq x \leq a + \Delta$, with $y(a) = c$, and $c(y) = y(a + \Delta)$.

We shall make use of this relation in two ways, analytically by letting $\Delta \to 0$ and computationally by taking Δ small, but nonzero. We shall discuss this point in great detail below.

Throughout what follows we shall assume that the function $f(a, c)$ has continuous first and second partial derivatives.

12. The Basic Nonlinear Partial Differential Equation

Observe that a choice of $y(x)$ over $[a, a + \Delta]$, with $y(a)$ constrained to equal c, can be construed to be a choice of $y'(x)$ over $[a, a + \Delta]$. If Δ is small, the choice of $y'(x)$ over $[a, a + \Delta]$ is equivalent to a choice of $y'(a)$, assuming continuity of $y'(x)$. Thus, writing

$$(1) \qquad \int_a^{a+\Delta} F(x, y, y')\, dx = F(a, c, y'(a))\Delta + o(\Delta),$$

$$c(y) = a + y'(a)\Delta + o(\Delta),$$

and $v \equiv y'(a)$, we can express (11.4) in the following terms:

$$(2) \qquad f(a, c) = \min_v [F(a, c, v)\Delta + f(a + \Delta, c + v\Delta)] + o(\Delta).$$

Letting $\Delta \to 0$, this yields in the limit the nonlinear partial differential equation

$$(3) \qquad -\frac{\partial f}{\partial a} = \min_v \left[F(a, c, v) + v \frac{\partial f}{\partial c} \right].$$

The initial condition is $f(b, c) = 0$ for all c, and the equation in (3) is taken to hold for $a < b$.

13. The Euler Equation

In order to avoid constant translation of results, let us take the lower limit a to be x and let y' denote what we have called v above.

Proceeding formally, power series expansion of (12.2) yields the equation

$$(1) \quad f(x, y) = \min_{v'} \left[F(x, y, y')\Delta + f(x, y) + \frac{\partial f}{\partial x}\Delta + \frac{\partial f}{\partial y} y'\Delta + \cdots \right].$$

Letting $\Delta \to 0$, this leads to the nonlinear partial differential equation

$$(2) \qquad\qquad 0 = \min_{v'} \left[F(x, y, y') + \frac{\partial f}{\partial x} + y' \frac{\partial f}{\partial y} \right]$$

(the equation of (12.3)). This equation is equivalent to the two equations

$$(3) \qquad\qquad F_{y'} + \frac{\partial f}{\partial y} = 0,$$

obtained by taking the partial derivative with respect to y', and

$$(4) \qquad\qquad F + \frac{\partial f}{\partial x} + y' \frac{\partial f}{\partial y} = 0,$$

valid for x, y, and y' related by (3). Differentiating (3) with respect to x, we obtain

$$(5) \qquad\qquad \frac{d}{dx} F_{y'} + \frac{\partial^2 f}{\partial x\, \partial y} + \frac{\partial^2 f}{\partial y^2} y' = 0,$$

and partial differentiation with respect to y of (4) gives

$$(6) \qquad F_y + F_{y'} \frac{\partial y'}{\partial y} + \frac{\partial^2 f}{\partial x\, \partial y} + \frac{\partial^2 f}{\partial y^2} y' + \frac{\partial f}{\partial y} \frac{\partial y'}{\partial y} = 0.$$

These last two equations, combined with (3), yield the classical Euler equation

$$(7) \qquad\qquad \frac{d}{dx} F_{y'} - F_y = 0.$$

The usual derivation of this result from (2) relies upon the theory of characteristics.

14. The Legendre Condition

We have used the fact that the derivative of the function in (13.2) must equal zero at a minimum. The additional requirement that the second derivative of (13.2) with respect to y' must be positive, in order to yield a minimum, leads to the inequality

$$(1) \qquad\qquad F_{y'y'} > 0$$

which is the classical Legendre condition.

15. The Weierstrass Condition

The Legendre condition does not rule out the possibility of a relative minimum. For an absolute minimum to exist, we must have the inequality

$$(1) \qquad F(x, y, y') + \frac{\partial f}{\partial x} + y' \frac{\partial f}{\partial y} \leq F(x, y, Y') + \frac{\partial f}{\partial x} + Y' \frac{\partial f}{\partial y}$$

for all functions $Y' = Y'(x, y)$ or

$$(2) \qquad F(x, y, Y') - F(x, y, y') + (Y' - y') \frac{\partial f}{\partial y} \geq 0$$

which, using Equation (13.3), yields

$$(3) \qquad F(x, y, Y') - F(x, y, y') - (Y' - y')F_{y'} \geq 0,$$

the Weierstrass necessary condition for an absolute minimum.

16. Several Dependent Variables

The preceding method is readily carried over to treat the problem of minimizing the functional

$$(1) \quad J(y_1, y_2, \ldots, y_n) = \int_x^b F(y_1, y_2, \ldots, y_n; y_1', y_2', \ldots, y_n'; x_1) \, dx_1,$$

where

$$(2) \qquad y_1(x) = y_1, \qquad y_2(x) = y_2, \ldots, y_n(x) = y_n.$$

If higher derivatives occur, a change of variable can be used to reduce the problem to the foregoing. For example, if we wish to minimize

$$(3) \qquad J(y) = \int_x^b F(y, y', y'', x_1) \, dx_1$$

over all y satisfying the conditions

$$(4) \qquad y(x) = y_1, \qquad y'(x) = y_2,$$

we introduce the new variables

$$(5) \qquad \begin{aligned} y_1 &= y(x), \\ y_2 &= y'(x). \end{aligned}$$

Then the problem becomes that of minimizing

$$(6) \qquad J(y_1, y_2) = \int_x^b F(y_1, y_1', y_2', x) \, dx,$$

subject to the constraint

$$(7) \qquad y_1' = y_2, \qquad y_1(x) = c_1, \qquad y_2(x) = c_2.$$

For the sake of notational simplicity, let us consider only the simple case where there are no side differential equations.

Following the reasoning of §13, we obtain the equation

$$(8) \qquad 0 = \min_{y_1', \ldots, y_n'} \left[F + \frac{\partial f}{\partial x} + \sum_{j=1}^{n} y_j' \frac{\partial f}{\partial y_j} \right]$$

which yields the further equations

$$(9) \qquad F_{y_i'} + \frac{\partial f}{\partial y_i} = 0, \qquad i = 1, \ldots, n,$$

$$(10) \qquad F + \frac{\partial f}{\partial x} + \sum_{j=1}^{n} y_j' \frac{\partial f}{\partial y_j} = 0.$$

From these, as above, we derive the relations

$$(11) \qquad \frac{d}{dx} F_{y_i'} + \frac{\partial^2 f}{\partial y_i \partial x} + \sum_{j} \frac{\partial^2 f}{\partial y_i \partial y_j} y_j' = 0, \qquad i = 1, \ldots, n,$$

and, taking partial derivatives with respect to y_i,

$$(12) \qquad F_{y_i} + \sum_{j=1}^{n} \frac{\partial F}{\partial y_j'} \frac{\partial y_j}{\partial y_i} + \frac{\partial^2 f}{\partial x \partial y_i} + \sum_{j=1}^{n} y_j' \frac{\partial^2 f}{\partial y_i \partial y_j}$$
$$+ \sum_{j=1}^{n} \frac{\partial f}{\partial y_j} \frac{\partial y_j'}{\partial y_i} = 0,$$
$$i = 1, \ldots, n.$$

We thus obtain the set of Euler equations

$$(13) \qquad \frac{d}{dx} F_{y_i'} - F_{y_i} = 0, \qquad i = 1, \ldots, n.$$

17. An Isoperimetric Problem

Let us add the restriction that

$$(1) \qquad \int_x^b G(x_1, y, y') \, dx_1 = z,$$

where z is a given value. Our basic function, the value of the minimum, is now one of three variables, x, y, and z. In other words, z is an additional state variable. Hence we write

$$(2) \qquad f(x, y, z) = \min_{\{y\}} \int_x^b F(x_1, y, y') \, dx_1$$

subject to the restriction in (1).

The analogue of the equation in (12.2) is

$$(3) \quad f(x, y, z) = \min_{y'} [F(x, y, y')\Delta + f(x + \Delta, y + y'\Delta, z - G(x, y, y')\Delta)].$$

Proceeding as before, we derive the partial differential equation

$$(4) \qquad 0 = \min_{y'} \left[F(x, y, y') + \frac{\partial f}{\partial x} + y' \frac{\partial f}{\partial y} - G(x, y, y') \frac{\partial f}{\partial z} \right].$$

This yields, upon differentiation, the relation

$$(5) \qquad 0 = F_{y'} + \frac{\partial f}{\partial y} - G_y \frac{\partial f}{\partial z},$$

and the equation

$$(6) \qquad 0 = F + \frac{\partial f}{\partial x} + y' \frac{\partial f}{\partial y} - G \frac{\partial f}{\partial z}.$$

Differentiation of (5) with respect to x, and partial differentiation with respect to y of (6), combine to yield

$$(7) \qquad \frac{d}{dx} \frac{\partial}{\partial y'} \left(F - \frac{\partial f}{\partial z} G \right) - \frac{\partial}{\partial y} \left(F - \frac{\partial f}{\partial z} G \right) = 0.$$

Partial differentiation of (6) with respect to z yields the following results:

$$(8) \qquad 0 = \frac{\partial^2 f}{\partial x \partial z} + y' \frac{\partial^2 f}{\partial y \partial z} - G \frac{\partial^2 f}{\partial z^2},$$

$$(9) \qquad 0 = \frac{d}{dx} \left(\frac{\partial f}{\partial z} \right),$$

$$(10) \qquad \frac{\partial f}{\partial z} = \text{constant}.$$

18. Lagrange Multiplier

We have thus shown that $\partial f / \partial z$ plays the role of the Lagrange multiplier. Furthermore, we have established the well-known fact that it is constant, i.e., independent of x, in the isoperimetric problem. Equation (17.7) is the Euler equation for the discussion of the variational problem based upon a Lagrange multiplier λ, where the basic functional is taken to be

$$(1) \qquad \int_x^b [F(x_1, y, y') - \lambda G(x_1, y, y')] \, dx_1.$$

19. Natural Boundary Conditions

Suppose that $y(a)$ is not specified. Then the optimal initial y-value has the property that the change in the minimal value of the integral to the final point $(b, y(b))$ caused by a change in initial point $y(a)$ is zero. Otherwise, there would be a better starting point. Therefore

$$(1) \qquad \left. \frac{\partial f}{\partial y} \right|_{x=a} = 0,$$

which, together with (13.3), yields

$$(2) \qquad F_{y'} \Big|_{x=a} = 0.$$

This is the natural boundary condition associated with an unspecified boundary value.

20. A Transversality Condition

Let us now suppose that the y-curve sought must start somewhere on a given curve $y = g(x)$. To treat this problem, we reason as follows. For the optimal curve, the change in f as the initial point varies along the specified curve must be zero. This is equivalent to saying that at the initial point

$$(1) \qquad \frac{\partial f}{\partial x} + g' \frac{\partial f}{\partial y} = 0.$$

Referring to (13.4),

$$(2) \qquad F + y' \frac{\partial f}{\partial y} - g' \frac{\partial f}{\partial y} = 0,$$

and from (13.3),

$$(3) \qquad F + (g' - y')F_{y'} = 0.$$

This condition on the initial derivative y' in terms of the initial point (x, y) and the slope of $g(x)$ is a classical transversality condition.

21. The Erdmann Corner Conditions

We now ask under what conditions the optimal y' may be discontinuous. Examination of (13.3) and the continuity of $\partial f/\partial y$ show that $F_{y'}$ is a continuous function across the discontinuity, and (13.4) now tells us that

$$(1) \qquad F - y'F_{y'}$$

is a continuous function across the discontinuity. These are the Erdmann corner conditions.

22. Implicit Variational Problems

Let us now consider a very important class of variational problems in which no simple explicit expression exists for the functional to be minimized. As an example of a problem of this nature, let us suppose that we are given a set of differential equations

$$(1) \qquad \frac{dy_i}{dt} = g_i(y_1, y_2, \ldots, y_N; z; t), \quad y_i(0) = c_i, \quad i = 1, 2, \ldots, N,$$

and asked to determine the unknown function z so as to minimize the time required to transform the system into the state $(d_1, d_2, \ldots, d_N)$. Here the functional $T = T(z)$ is determined by the conditions

(2) $$y_i(T) = d_i, \qquad i = 1, 2, \ldots, N.$$

In other words, we wish to transform a system from an initial state into a desired state in minimum time. It is clear that many engineering and industrial control problems can be phrased in these terms.

To determine the structure of the solution, we introduce the function

(3) $f(y, t) =$ time required to transform the system in state y at time t into the desired final state.

Then the principle of optimality yields the equation

(4) $$f(y, t) = \min_{z(t)} \left[\Delta + f(y + g\Delta, t + \Delta) \right] + o(\Delta).$$

In place of (1), we use the notation $dy/dt = g$. Then passing to the limit as $\Delta \to 0$, we obtain, purely formally as before, the relation

(5) $$0 = \min_z \left[1 + \sum_{i=1}^{N} f_{y_i} g_i + f_t \right].$$

From this we derive two relations

(6) $$0 = \sum_{i=1}^{N} f_{y_i} \frac{\partial g_i}{\partial z}$$

$$0 = 1 + \sum_{i=1}^{N} f_{y_i} g_i + f_t.$$

We can now draw the following conclusions by examination of the relations in (6):

(7) (a) $f_t = 0$ at $t = T$ by the definition of $f(y, t)$.

(b) $\sum_{i=1}^{N} f_{y_i}(T) g_i(T) = -1$ at T, using (6) and the condition in (a).

(c) If the g's are not time dependent, $\sum_{i=1}^{N} f_{y_i} g_i = -1$ all along the optimal path (this is a first integral of the solution).

(d) It follows from the definition of $f(y, t)$ that for y's not prescribed at T, $f_{y_i}(T) = 0$.

In the classical literature, the f_{y_i} are called λ_i, the *multiplier functions*.

If the multipliers, the f_{y_j}, are known at a point, the above equations tell us how to determine the optimal decision, z, at that point. It remains to determine how the multipliers change as functions of time along the optimal path. We would like to be able to compute df_{y_j}/dt. Differentiation shows us that

(8) $$\frac{d}{dt} f_{y_j} = \sum_i \left(\frac{\partial}{\partial y_i} f_{y_j} \right) \frac{dy_i}{dt} = \sum_i \left(\frac{\partial}{\partial y_i} f_{y_j} \right) g_i$$

$$= \sum_i \left(\frac{\partial}{\partial y_j} f_{y_i} \right) g_i.$$

For the important case where the form of the differential equations is independent of time, partial differentiation of (6) with respect to y_j yields the relation

(9)
$$0 = \sum_i \left(\frac{\partial}{\partial y_j} f_{v_i} \right) g_i + \sum_i f_{v_i} \left(\frac{\partial g_i}{\partial y_j} + \frac{\partial g_i}{\partial z} \frac{\partial z}{\partial y_j} \right).$$

Combining these two results and those of (6), we obtain the Euler equations for the time derivative of the multipliers

(10)
$$\frac{d}{dt} f_{v_i} + \sum_{j=1}^{N} \frac{\partial g_j}{\partial y_i} f_{v_j} = 0, \qquad i = 1, \dots, N.$$

These N first order differential equations for the multiplier functions, together with the N original equations

(11)
$$\frac{dy_i}{dt} = g_i(y, z, t)$$

and Equation (6) constitute a set of $2N + 1$ equations which can be solved for the N multiplier functions, the N variables $y_1, y_2, \dots, y_N$, and the policy function. The $2N$ constants of integration are determined by the N initial y values, the specified final y values, and the conditions of (7d).

As in earlier sections, various other necessary conditions follow readily from the requirement that the value of z in (5) yields an absolute minimum.

The above problem is of a type called "the problem of Mayer." More generally, we can combine the Lagrange and Mayer problems and seek to minimize the integral of a function plus a function evaluated at the end-point, where the function evaluated at the endpoint contains some variables whose final values are unspecified in advance. The above formalism is applicable, and results are easily deduced. This very general problem is called the "problem of Bolza."

23. Inequality Constraints

In many recent applications , we have encountered problems where there are inequality constraints on the decision variables.

With reference to the problem posed in the foregoing section, let us now assume that the forcing function z is to be chosen subject to the inequality constraint

(1)
$$h(y, z) \leq 0.$$

At the boundary of this constraint region, the first equation in (22.6) is lacking. Thus, (22.10) becomes

(2)
$$\frac{d}{dt} \frac{\partial f}{\partial y_i} + \sum_{j=1}^{N} \frac{\partial g_j}{\partial y_i} \frac{\partial f}{\partial y_j} + \left(\sum_{j=1}^{N} \frac{\partial g_j}{\partial z} \frac{\partial f}{\partial y_j} \right) \frac{\partial z}{\partial y_i} = 0.$$

On the boundary of the constraint region, determined by $h(y, z) = 0$, we have

(3)
$$\frac{\partial h}{\partial y_i} + \frac{\partial h}{\partial z}\frac{\partial z}{\partial y_i} = 0.$$

Then (2) can be written as

(4)
$$\frac{d}{dt}\frac{\partial f}{\partial y_i} = -\sum_{j=1}^{N}\lambda_j\frac{\partial g_j}{\partial y_i} + \mu\frac{\partial h}{\partial y_i},$$

where

(5)
$$\lambda_j = \frac{\partial f}{\partial y_j}$$

and

(6)
$$\mu = \frac{\sum_{j=1}^{N}\frac{\partial g_j}{\partial z}\frac{\partial f}{\partial y_j}}{\frac{\partial h}{\partial z}}.$$

We see then that inequality constraints of the foregoing type can easily be included. In classical theory μ appears as an additional Lagrange multiplier introduced to incorporate the constraint.

24. The Hamilton-Jacobi Equation

Let us now show how the Hamilton-Jacobi equation of classical mechanics follows in a very simple fashion from the principle of optimality, in conjunction with the Hamilton principle that a particle moves so as to minimize the Lagrangian $\int L(q, \dot{q}, t)\, dt$.

Let q, a vector, describe the state of a system (i.e., q is a point in configuration space in the terminology of classical mechanics), and let $\dot{q} = dq/dt$ be the decision variable to be chosen optimally. The problem is to transform state Q given at time t_0 into q at time t in such a way as to minimize the functional $\int L(q, \dot{q}, t_1)\, dt_1$. We proceed as follows. Define

$$S(q, t; Q, t_0) = \text{the minimum value of the functional} \int_{t_0}^{t} L(q, \dot{q}, t_1)\, dt_1$$

subject to the preceding boundary conditions.

Then, regarding both ends of the interval as variable, we have the two relations

(1) $S(q, t; Q, t_0) = \min\limits_{\dot{Q}(t_0)} [L(Q, \dot{Q}, t_0)\Delta + S(q, t; Q + \dot{Q}\Delta, t_0 + \Delta)],$

(2) $S(q, t; Q, t_0) = \min\limits_{\dot{q}(t)} [L(q, \dot{q}, t)\Delta + S(q - \dot{q}\Delta, t - \Delta; Q, t_0)].$

These equations result from the application of the principle of optimality at each end of the interval.

At time t_0,

(3)
$$0 = \min_Q \left[L + Q \frac{\partial S}{\partial Q} + \frac{\partial S}{\partial t_0} \right]$$

which implies, upon defining $\partial L / \partial Q$ as momenta P,

(4)
$$\frac{\partial L}{\partial Q} = - \frac{\partial S}{\partial Q} = P.$$

At the general time t, expansion of (2) yields the two equations

(5)
$$0 = L - \dot{q} \frac{\partial S}{\partial q} - \frac{\partial S}{\partial t},$$

(6)
$$\frac{\partial L}{\partial \dot{q}} = \frac{\partial S}{\partial q} = p.$$

Defining the Hamiltonian function $H(q, p, t)$ as $p\dot{q} - L$, (5) becomes the Hamiltonian-Jacobi partial differential equation

(7)
$$0 = H\left(q, \frac{\partial S}{\partial q}, t \right) + \frac{\partial S}{\partial t}.$$

The initial condition that at time t_0 the configuration is Q determines the required constants of integration for the solution function $S(q, t; Q, t_0)$. Furthermore, if the initial momenta P are known, Equation (4) gives us $q = q(t; Q, P, t_0)$ and (6) yields $p = p(t; Q, P, t_0)$. Hence, solution of the Hamilton-Jacobi equation (7) tells us the position q and momenta p as functions of time and the initial conditions. Since methods for analytically determining the solution of (7) and finding the coordinates and momenta as functions of time are discussed in many texts, we shall not pursue the matter any further.

25. Discrete Approximations

If we wish to employ digital computers in the numerical solution of variational problems along the foregoing lines, it is necessary to convert the nonlinear partial differential equation of (12.3) into an equation requiring only arithmetic operations.

There are several ways of doing this. One class of methods depends upon a discrete approximation to the exact equation; the other depends upon deriving an exact equation for a discrete approximation to the original continuous process. The first is the conventional technique which is described and discussed in a number of easily available sources. Since we shall not employ it in this volume, let us proceed to discuss the second method which we shall use to treat trajectory processes, multistage production processes, and feedback control processes.

In place of allowing a choice of a function $y(x)$ over the interval $[a, b]$, let us suppose that we are allowed only to choose the values of $y(x)$ at the points $a = k\Delta, (k + 1)\Delta, \ldots, N\Delta = b$. In place of minimizing the integral

$$(1) \qquad J(y) = \int_a^b g(y, y', x)\, dx,$$

we seek to minimize the finite sum

$$(2) \qquad J_k(y) = \sum_{i=k}^{N-1} g(y_i, (y_{i+1} - y_i)/\Delta, i\Delta)\Delta,$$

where we write $y(i\Delta) = y_i$, and approximate to the derivative y' by the expression $(y_{i+1} - y_i)/\Delta$.

Generally, in place of minimizing

$$(3) \qquad J(y) = \int_a^b g(y, z, x)\, dx,$$

where

$$(4) \qquad \frac{dy}{dx} = h(y, z, x), \qquad y(a) = c,$$

we wish to minimize the sum

$$(5) \qquad J_k(y) = \sum_{i=k}^{N-1} g(y_i, z_i, i\Delta)\Delta,$$

where

$$(6) \qquad y_{i+1} = y_i + h(y_i, z_i, i\Delta)\Delta, \qquad y_k = c.$$

Writing

$$(7) \qquad f_k(c) = \min_{\{y_i\}} J_k(y),$$

the usual argument yields the nonlinear difference equation

$$(8) \qquad f_k(c) = \min_{z_k} [g(c, z_k, k\Delta)\Delta + f_{k+1}(c + h(y_k, z_k, k\Delta)\Delta)].$$

If z_k is subject to constraints, the minimization is taken over the constrained set.

In the limit as $\Delta \to 0$, we obtain, of course, the same nonlinear partial differential equation as before. It is this type of equation which we will use to obtain the computational solution of trajectory problems in the next chapter.

26. Discussion

The discrete variational problem described above is obtained by using the simplest approximation formula for the area under a curve. Use of the trapezoidal rule will result in a more complicated expression than that appearing in (25.5), while more accurate quadrature formulas such as, for example, that of Gauss, will lead to sums of the form

$$
\text{(1)} \qquad J_k(y) = \sum_{i=k}^{N-1} c_i g(y_i, z_i, x_i) \Delta,
$$

where the x_i are no longer regularly spaced. This idea will be developed further in Chapter XII. Since these variational problems can be treated by means of precisely the same functional equation technique, at the cost of slight additional effort, we can obtain a great increase in accuracy.

Similarly, (25.6) is derived from (25.4) by using the crude approximation

$$
\text{(2)} \qquad \int_{i\Delta}^{(i+1)\Delta} \frac{dy}{dx} \, dx = \int_{i\Delta}^{(i+1)\Delta} h(y, z, x) \, dx \simeq h(y_i, z_i, i\Delta)\Delta,
$$

or

$$
\text{(3)} \qquad y_{i+1} - y_i \simeq h(y_i, z_i, i\Delta)\Delta.
$$

Once again, a more accurate quadrature formula will yield a considerable increase in accuracy at small cost in computational effort.

In what follows, however, we shall employ only the simplest rectangular approximation, and deal with relations such as those appearing in (25.5) and (25.6), since these will be sufficient to indicate the techniques that can be used.

27. Two-point Boundary Value Problems

At first sight, it is rather surprising that the functional equation approach replaces two-point boundary value problems by initial value problems.

Consider the problem of minimizing the sum

$$
\text{(1)} \qquad J_k(y) = \sum_{i=k}^{N-1} g(y_i, z_i, i\Delta)\Delta,
$$

where

$$
\text{(2)} \quad \text{(a)} \qquad y_k = c,
$$
$$
\qquad \text{(b)} \qquad y_{i+1} = y_i + h(y_i, z_i, i\Delta)\Delta,
$$

and there is no restriction on the value of y_{N-1}. Then the recurrence relation of (25.8) holds for $k = 0, 1, 2, \ldots, N - 2$, with

$$
\text{(3)} \qquad f_{N-1}(c) = \min_{z_{N-1}} g(c, z_{N-1}, (N-1)\Delta)\Delta.
$$

We call this an initial value problem since $f_{N-1}(c)$ is known and leads by means of a simple iterative procedure, the relation of (25.8), to the determination of $f_0(c)$.

What happens when the value of y_N is prescribed in advance? Then $f_{N-1}(c)$ in place of being determined by (3) is determined by the expression

$$
\text{(4)} \qquad f_{N-1}(c) = g(c, \bar{z}_{N-1}, (N-1)\Delta)\Delta,
$$

where $\bar{z}_{N-1}$ is fixed by the relation

(5) $$y_N = c + h(c, \bar{z}_{N-1}, (N-1)\Delta)\Delta.$$

In other words, $\bar{z}_{N-1}$ is determined by the condition that we must go from the state c to the fixed state y_N.

Once the correct value of $f_{N-1}(c)$ is obtained in this way, the calculation proceeds as before, using (25.8).

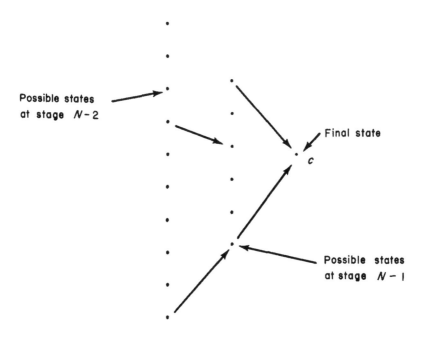

Figure 64

When there are constraints on z, it may not be possible to get to y_N at stage N from every state c at stage $N-1$. In that case, $f_{N-1}(c)$ is only defined for those c from which we get to y_N. Similarly, $f_{N-2}(c)$ is only defined for those c from which one can get to the possible states at stage $N-1$, and so on (see Fig. 64).

As usual, constraints simplify the numerical solution when the dynamic programming approach is followed.

28. Duality

Let us amplify the previous comment that the calculus of variations and dynamic programming are complementary theories. The calculus of variations considers the extremal curve to be a locus of points, and attempts to determine this curve by means of a differential equation. The theory of dynamic programming regards the extremal as an envelope of tangents, and attempts to determine the optimal direction at each point on an extremal.

The duality of Euclidean geometry asserts that a curve can equally be regarded as a locus of points or an envelope of tangents. Consequently, we see that the two approaches we have presented—that of the calculus of variations and that of dynamic programming—are dual to each other.

It is for this reason that we can expect that a combination of the two approaches will prove far more powerful than any single method by itself.

29. Conclusion

In this chapter we have introduced the reader to the fundamental problems of the calculus of variations, and the approaches to these problems along the lines of the classical methods and the theory of dynamic programming.

After presenting some of the basic results of the calculus of variations, we have shown how they can be derived in very simple steps from the functional equation obtained from the principle of optimality.

We have covered in some detail the difficulties encountered in attempting to use the Euler equation and then have shown how the functional equation technique eliminates these difficulties. In the succeeding chapters we will illustrate this statement with examples from the study of optimal trajectories, multistage production processes, and feedback control.

To keep the tale interesting, other difficulties arise, notably the "curse of dimensionality".

Comments and Bibliography

§1. The reader interested in the classical calculus of variations may wish to refer to

R. Courant and D. Hilbert, *Methods of Mathematical Physics*, Interscience Publishers, Inc., New York, 1958.

G. A. Bliss, *Lectures on the Calculus of Variations*, University of Chicago Press, Chicago, Illinois, 1946.

For a treatment of the variation of composite functionals of the form

$$F(y) = \int_a^b g(t, x, y, F_1(y), F_2(y), \ldots)\, dt,$$

where F_1, F_2 are integral functionals, see

R. S. Ingarden, "Composite variational problems," *Bull. de l'Academie Polonaise des Sciences*, Serie des sci. math., astr., et phys., vol. 7, 1959, pp. 687–689.

§7. For a discussion of the stability problems connected with differential equations, see

R. Bellman, *Stability Theory of Differential Equations*, McGraw-Hill Book Co., Inc., New York, 1954,

where many other references may be found.

§9. The reader interested in examining the solutions of particular classes of variational problems may wish to consult

R. Bellman, I. Glicksberg, and O. Gross, "On some variational problems occurring in the theory of dynamic programming," *Rend. Circ. Mate. Palermo*, serie 2, tomo 3, 1954, pp. 1–35.

————, "Some problems in the theory of dynamic programming—a smoothing problem," *Soc. Indust. Appl. Math.*, vol. 2, 1954, pp. 82–89.

R. Bellman, I. Glicksberg, and O. Gross, "On the 'bang-bang' control problem," *Q. Appl. Math.*, vol. 14, 1956, pp. 11–18.

————, "Some non-classical problems in the calculus of variations," *Proc. Amer. Math. Soc.*, vol. 7, 1956, pp. 87–94.

R. Bellman, W. H. Fleming, and D. V. Widder, "Variational problems with constraints," *Annali di Mate.*, vol. 41, 1956, pp. 301–323.

§11. The approach given here is contained in Chapter 9 of *Dynamic Programming*. It was presented first in some earlier papers:

R. Bellman, "Dynamic programming and a new formalism in the calculus of variations," *Proc. Nat. Acad. Sci. USA*, vol. 39, 1953, pp. 1077–1082.

————, "On the application of dynamic programming to variational problems arising in mathematical economics," *Proc. Symposium in Calculus of Variations and Applications*, McGraw-Hill Book Co., Inc., New York, 1956, pp. 115–138.

§12. For a rigorous derivation of the basic nonlinear partial differential equation of (12.3) from the standpoint of the classical theory, see

H. Osborn, "On the foundations of dynamic programming," *J. Math. and Mech.*, vol. 8, 1959, pp. 867–872.

§13. One derivation of the Euler equation using characteristic theory may be found in Chapter 7 of

R. Bellman, *Dynamic Programming of Continuous Processes*, The RAND Corporation, Report R-271, 1954.

The results are due to Osborn. Another derivation may be found in

S. Dreyfus, "Dynamic programming and the calculus of variations," *J. Math. Anal. and Appl.*, vol. 1, 1960, pp. 228–239,

where the remaining results of the chapter are presented.

§22. Interest in implicit variational problems has revived in recent years in connection with a type of feedback control called "bang-bang." See

J. P. LaSalle, "On time-optimal control systems," *Proc. Nat. Acad. Sci. USA*, vol. 45, 1959, pp. 573–577.

R. Bellman, I. Glicksberg, and O. Gross, "On the 'bang-bang' control problem," *Q. Appl. Math.*, vol. 14, 1956, pp. 11–18.

Extensive references to the "maximum principle" of Pontryagin and subsequent work by the Russian school may be found in

R. Bellman, *Adaptive Control Processes: A Guided Tour*, Princeton University Press, Princeton, New Jersey, 1961.

See also

J. P. LaSalle and S. Lefschetz, "Recent Soviet contributions to ordinary differential equations and nonlinear mechanics," *J. Math. Anal. and Appl.*, to appear in vol. 2, 1961.

C. A. Desoer, "The bang-bang servo problem treated by variational techniques,"_*Information and Control*, vol. 2, 1959, pp. 333–348.

————, "Pontrjagin's maximum principle and the principle of optimality," *J. Franklin Inst.*, vol. 271, 1961, pp. 361–368.

§24. The discussion contained here follows

S. Dreyfus, "Dynamic programming and the calculus of variations," *J. Math. Anal. and Appl.*, vol. 1, 1960, pp. 228–239.

For the classical approach, see

E. T. Whittaker, *A Treatise in the Analytic Dynamics of Particles and Rigid Bodies*, Cambridge University Press, Cambridge, 1944.

§25. For proofs of the convergence of the discrete variational problem to the continuous variational problem, see Chapter 9 of *Dynamic Programming*, where results of W. Fleming may be found.

R. Bellman, "Functional equations in the theory of dynamic programming —VI: a direct convergence proof," *Ann. Math.*, vol. 65, 1957, pp. 215–223.

H. Osborn, "The problem of continuous programs," *Pacific J. Math.*, vol. 6, 1956, pp. 721–731.

§27. For further discussion, see the book by Bellman cited above. For conventional approaches, see

L. Fox, *The Numerical Solution of Two-point Boundary Problems in Ordinary Differential Equations*, Oxford University Press, Oxford, 1957.

L. Collatz, *Numerische Behandlung von Differentialgleichungen*, Berlin-Gottingen-Heidelberg, second edition, 1955.

For a new approach based upon the idea of quasilinearization, see

R. Kalaba, "On nonlinear differential equations, the maximum operation, and monotone convergence," *J. Math. and Mech.*, vol. 8, 1959, pp. 519–574.

For an application to optics, see

R. Kalaba, "Dynamic Programming, Fermat's Principle and the Eikonal Equation," *Jour. Optical Soc. America*, vol. 51, 1961, pp. 1150–1151.

We have said little about the connections between stability and control. For an interesting discussion of these matters, see

T. Hacker, "Stability of partially controlled motions of an aircraft," *J. Aerospace Sci.*, vol. 28, 1961, pp. 15–26.

R. Bellman, "Directions of mathematical research in nonlinear circuit theory," *IRE Trans. of Professional Group on Circuit Theory*, vol. CT-7, 1960, pp. 542–553.

CHAPTER VI

Optimal Trajectories

1. Introduction

The commercial and military uses of aircraft, the scientific aspects of satellites, and the glamour of interplanetary travel have all combined to produce an enormous focussing of attention upon the determination of feasible and optimal trajectories.

As aircraft attain higher performance capabilities, the flight paths yielding minimum time and those yielding maximum range become progressively less intuitive. On the other hand, because of the increased significance of time in our modern society and the increased cost of fuel, the determination of efficient operation becomes progressively more essential.

With planes capable of either ground level or stratospheric flight at subsonic or supersonic speeds, the number of possible types of flight profile becomes vast, with a corresponding complexity of optimal policy.

The intricacies of the problem of ascertaining optimal trajectories become clear when one realizes that the attractive supersonic region of operation is separated from the subsonic region by a transition screen, the sonic barrier, which induces a very high drag. No simple policy based upon single-stage considerations can be expected to determine efficient flight paths which penetrate this barrier. Yet, change-of-state phenomena associated with high-performance craft strongly indicate the desirability of supersonic flight.

Turning to rockets and satellites, the fact that every pound of "payload" may necessitate thousands of pounds of fuel makes it equally essential that trajectories be carefully selected. Not only must guidance and control be painstakingly calculated, but the very kind of control that is exerted must be selected properly. We shall discuss this point in more detail below.

In the pages that follow we shall use dynamic programming in both expected and unexpected ways to study a variety of problems arising in aerodynamics and control processes. Although many of these problems can be posed in the terms of the calculus of variations, we shall, for reasons discussed in the previous chapter, use the functional equation approach to obtain numerical results.

2. A Simplified Trajectory Problem

Although the computational approach of dynamic programming is by now certainly familiar to the reader, we feel that it is nonetheless worthwhile to formulate and solve a simple optimal path problem. The applicability of the techniques we employ here will become apparent when we consider the minimum time-to-climb problem for airplanes.

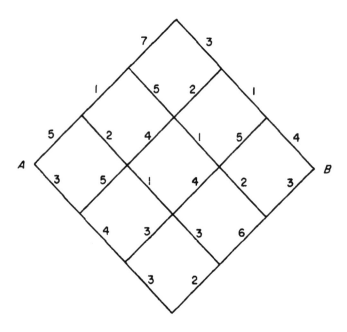

Figure 65

Suppose we wish to find that path, always moving to the right, which minimizes the sum of numbers encountered while going from A to B in the network shown in Fig. 65. Considering A as the origin, and B as the point (0, 6), we have the recurrence relation

$$f(x, y) = \min \begin{bmatrix} d(x, y; x + 1, y + 1) + f(x + 1, y + 1) \\ d(x, y; x + 1, y - 1) + f(x + 1, y - 1) \end{bmatrix},$$

where $d(x, y; x + 1, y + 1)$ represents the number on the link between the points (x, y) and $(x + 1, y + 1)$, a number which we consider to represent the distance between (x, y) and $(x + 1, y + 1)$. To solve, we first note that $f(5, 1) = 4$ and $f(5, -1) = 3$. Using these values for $f(5, y)$ we determine $f(4, y)$. Thus $f(4, 2) = 1 + 4 = 5$, $f(4, 0) = \min \begin{bmatrix} 5 + 4 \\ 2 + 3 \end{bmatrix} = 5$ and $f(4, -2) = 6 + 3 = 9$. We also note that from $f(4, 0)$ our optimal choice is to go diagonally down. In an analogous manner we compute $f(3, y), f(2, y)$, $f(1, y)$, and finally $f(0, 0)$. The solution, with arrows indicating the optimal direction, is summarized by the table of values appearing in Fig. 66.

3. A Dual Problem

In the preceding discussion we have defined $f(x, y)$ as the minimum sum *from the point* (x, y) *to the end point*. This resulted in an iterative technique working back from the termination point. However, we could just as well have defined a different function $g(x, y)$ as the minimum sum *from the initial point to* (x, y). This would result in a forward iteration yielding the solution shown in Fig. 67. Here the arrows must be interpreted as indicating the direction *from* which one arrives at a point. Both cases yield, as they must, identical results for the best path, and sum, from A to B. This duality of approaches should be kept in mind during subsequent discussions.

4. The Minimum Time-to-climb Problem

The following problem will be considered in detail: What flight path, in the altitude-velocity plane, minimizes the time required for an airplane to climb from initial altitude H and velocity V to a prescribed final altitude H_F and velocity V_F?

The equation of motion derived from quasi steady-state assumptions describing this problem is taken to be

(1)
$$\frac{dH}{dt} = \frac{\dfrac{V}{W}(T - D)}{1 + \dfrac{V}{g}\dfrac{dV}{dH}} = V \sin \Theta,$$

where the thrust, T, is a function only of altitude, H, and velocity, V, since we shall assume a fixed throttle setting. For simplicity in this example we assume that the drag, D, is likewise a function of H and V, thereby neglecting the drag due to flight path inclination and normal accelerations. We also limit ourselves here to those paths containing neither dives nor zooms. A more precise solution wherein drag is considered a function of H, V, climb angle Θ, and $\dot{\Theta}$ and with no artificial restrictions on admissible paths is also possible by means of dynamic programming and will be considered in §9.

5. Dynamic Programming Formulation

The fundamental equation of dynamic programming with respect to the minimum time-to-climb problem is

(1) $f(H, V) = \min_{\Theta} [t(H, \Delta H, V, \Theta) + f(H + \Delta H, V + \Delta V[H, \Delta H, V, \Theta])]$.

209

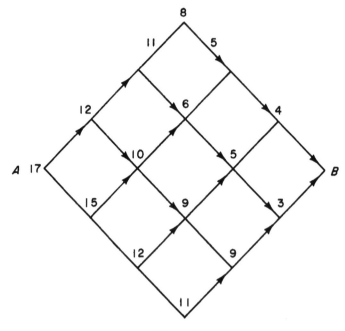

Figure 66

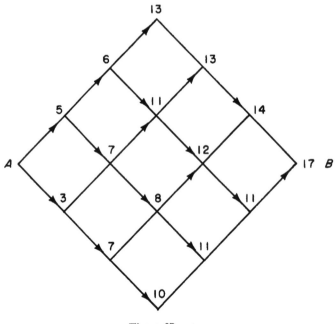

Figure 67

In this equation $f(H, V)$ represents the minimum time-to-climb from initial position (H, V) to the prescribed final altitude and velocity. The expression $t(H, \Delta H, V, \Theta)$ is the time consumed climbing to altitude $H + \Delta H$ at climb angle Θ. Equation (1) states the obvious fact that the total time to climb is the sum of:

(a) the time to climb at some angle Θ to a nearby altitude, and

(b) the minimum time to climb from that new position to the end point, minimized over all permissible angles Θ.

This equation will be the basis of our analytic and computational discussion.

6. Analytic Solution

Substituting the expressions from (4.1) into (5.1) we obtain the equation

$$(1) \quad f(H, V) = \min_{\Theta} \left[\frac{\Delta H}{V \sin \Theta} + f\left(H + \Delta H, V + \left[\frac{\frac{g}{W}(T - D)}{V \sin \Theta} - \frac{g}{V} \right] \Delta H \right) \right].$$

Expansion of the right-hand side in a power series about the point (H, V) yields the new equation

$$(2) \quad f(H, V)$$

$$= \min_{\Theta} \left[\frac{\Delta H}{V \sin \Theta} + f(H, V) + \Delta H \frac{\partial f}{\partial H} + \left[\frac{\frac{g}{W}(T - D)}{V \sin \Theta} - \frac{g}{V} \right] \Delta H \frac{\partial f}{\partial V} + o(\Delta H) \right]$$

where $o(\Delta H)$ represents higher order terms in ΔH. Cancelling $f(H, V)$, dividing by ΔH, and letting $\Delta H \to 0$, we see that

$$(3) \quad 0 = \min_{\Theta} \left[\frac{1}{V \sin \Theta} + \frac{\partial f}{\partial H} + \frac{\frac{g}{W}(T - D)}{V \sin \Theta} \frac{\partial f}{\partial V} - \frac{g}{V} \frac{\partial f}{\partial V} \right].$$

Examination of this equation leads to three cases:

(4) (a) If $\left[1 + \frac{g}{W}(T - D) \frac{\partial f}{\partial V} \right] > 0$, choose $\sin \Theta$ as large as possible.

(b) If $\left[1 + \frac{g}{W}(T - D) \frac{\partial f}{\partial V} \right] < 0$, choose $\sin \Theta = 0$.

(c) If $\left[1 + \frac{g}{W}(T - D) \frac{\partial f}{\partial V} \right] = 0$, $\quad \frac{\partial}{\partial V}(TV - DV) = \frac{V}{g} \frac{\partial}{\partial H}(TV - DV)$.

The equation in case (c) is derived by solving for $\partial f/\partial H$ and $\partial f/\partial V$, using the fact that (3) is valid. We next equate $\partial^2 f/\partial H \, \partial V$ and $\partial^2 f/\partial V \, \partial H$. The resulting equation defines a curve in the (H, V) plane.

We may now conclude that the optimal climb path consists of a basic curve independent of end points, together with transition paths of either level flight or steepest climb.

Direct solution of equations of the type appearing in (3) presents many difficulties. At the present time, only trial and error procedures yield the correct combination of Euler paths and transition curves in the general case. In certain special cases, analytic techniques can be employed.

7. Computational Procedure

Turning now to a consideration of the computational aspects of the minimum time-to-climb problem, suppose we wish to fly from point 1 to

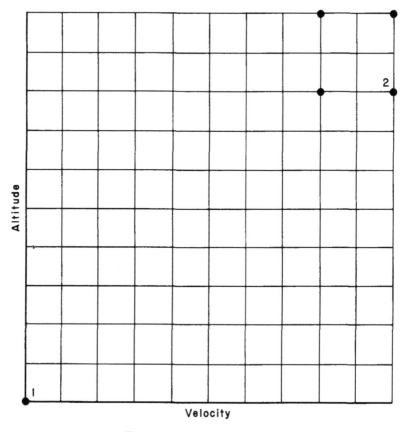

Figure 68. Altitude-velocity grid.

point 2 of Fig. 68 in minimum time. We can think of the H-V plane as a grid of elements of arbitrary size. Let us restrict ourselves to only horizontal and vertical moves in increments corresponding to the grid size. In the physical sense we are restricting the airplane motion to incremental climbs at constant velocity and incremental accelerations at constant altitude. The linearity of our "degenerate" quasi steady-state equations permits this.

We could now try the direct approach; this is, starting at point 1 try all possible paths and find the minimum-time path by elimination. This brute force approach is prohibitive timewise even with computing machinery; for example, a 10×10-element grid requires about 875,000 separate calculations to try all paths.

We use instead the method discussed in §2. We construct an auxiliary matrix with the following properties:

(1) The minimum-sum path from any point to the end point 2 is given by following the path as indicated by the arrows.

(2) The numerical value of the time for the minimum-sum path from any point is given by the numbers in the matrix.

Only a small number of calculations are required to construct this matrix. For example, a 10×10-element grid requires 180 separate calculations as compared with 875,000 calculations for the brute force approach.

8. A Sample Problem

In order to display some numerical results of the application of dynamic programming to the minimum time-to-climb problem, a hypothetical turbojet-powered interceptor airplane was selected capable of level flight at 60,000 ft. altitude and a Mach number of 2.0. We are assuming that the reader is familiar with the conventional terminology of aeronautical engineering. Assumption of a parabolic polar, and the equations of motion lead to the following expressions:

(1) $$C_D = C_{D_0} + KC_L{}^2,$$

(2) $$C_L = \frac{NW}{qS},$$

(3) $$N = \cos \Theta + \frac{V^2}{g} \Theta' \sin \Theta,$$

(4) $$q = 1481 \delta_{am} M^2 = 1481 \delta_{am} (V/V_S)^2.$$

For climb at $M = $ constant,

(5) $$\Delta t = \frac{\Delta H \left(1 + \dfrac{V}{g} \dfrac{\Delta V}{\Delta H}\right)}{\dfrac{V}{W}(T - D)}.$$

For acceleration at $H = $ constant,

(6) $$\Delta t = \frac{\dfrac{W}{g} \Delta V}{(T - D)}.$$

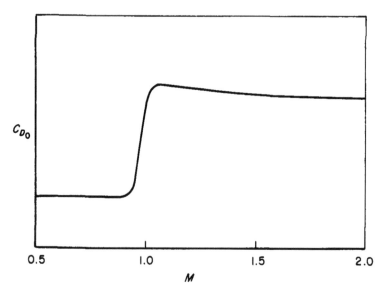

Figure 69. Zero-lift drag coefficient.

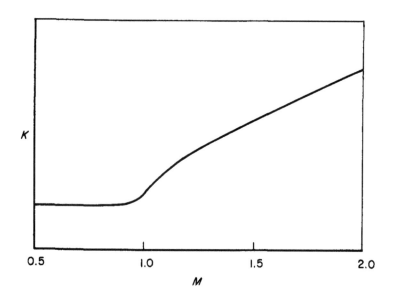

Figure 70. Drag-due-to-lift factor.

C_{D_c}, the zero-lift coefficient, and K, the drag-due-to-lift factor, are functions of Mach number as shown in Figs. 69 and 70. The available thrust is a function of altitude and speed if throttle setting is fixed, and is shown in Fig. 71.

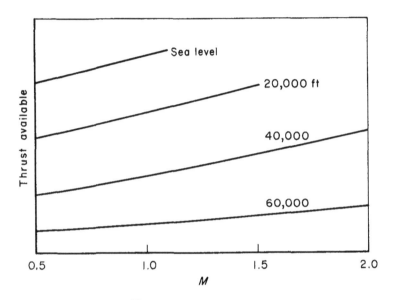

Figure 71. Thrust available.

We proceed by forming the (H, V) matrix for which we have chosen $\Delta H = 1000$ ft. and $\Delta M = .02$. A starting point of $(H = 0, M = .8)$ and a final point of $(H = 60,000, M = 2.0)$ result in a 61×61-element matrix. (The matrix in general need not be square.) A second matrix, analogous to that of the previous example, was developed by a high-speed digital computer and minimum-time paths were determined for several cases. The results are shown in Figs. 72–74.

Considering Fig. 72, the form of the general solution discussed previously can be recognized. The portions of the path GH and IJ are the Euler paths in two branches. The portion FG is the transition path from the starting point to the subsonic Euler path. The portion HI is the transition between the subsonic and supersonic branches of the Euler curves. The portion JK is the transition from the supersonic Euler path to the end point.

In Case A of Fig. 72, the gross weight of the airplane was held constant at 40,000 lb. and the load factor N was assumed to be unity. Time to climb along the optimal path is 277 sec.

In Case B, the effect of changing gross weight along the flight path was considered by introducing the specific fuel consumption as a function of altitude and speed. Since we move backwards in forming the second matrix, the technique employed is to start with several assumed values of final gross weight and calculate the increase as we move through the matrix. The interesting by-product is, of course, time-to-climb data for a variety of starting gross weights. For 40,000-lb. starting gross weight the time is 252 sec. and the fuel used is 3450 lb.

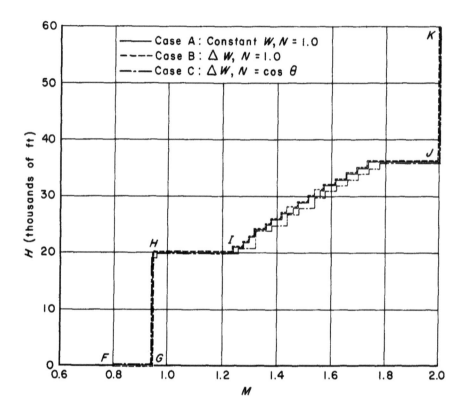

Figure 72. Altitude-Mach number trace of minimum-time paths.

For Case C, the effect of including the climb angle in the airplane drag was investigated. The effect of normal accelerations on drag was neglected. The technique employed is an iterative process similar to that employed for a gross-weight change. Time to climb for Case C is 251 sec. It is appreciated that the drag corrections due to normal accelerations are important, especially at the transition points such as the leveling off from the initial climb to horizontal acceleration, and a general solution including this effect can be obtained by an extension of the method described here (see §9).

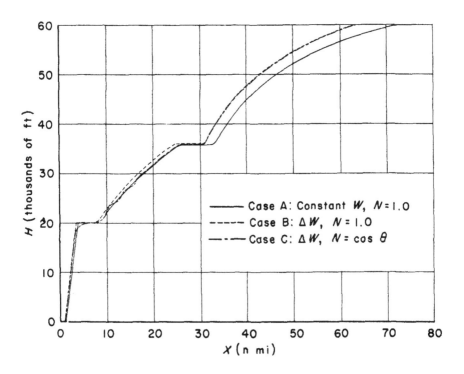

Figure 73. Altitude-horizontal distance profile of minimum-time paths.

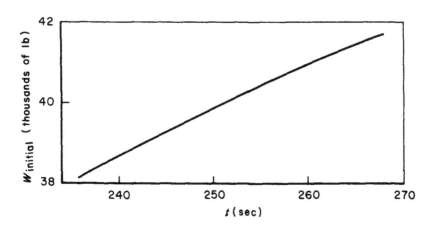

Figure 74. Effect of initial gross weight on minimum time-to-climb.

Figure 73 shows the altitude-horizontal distance profile for the three cases investigated, where the horizontal distance, for small Δt, is computed as the product of Δt and the average horizontal velocity component. Figure 74 shows the useful curve which is the result of the computational technique employed in Case B.

As for the practical application of the theoretical results, it may be optimistic to expect either human or autopilots to follow complicated altitude-velocity climb schedules such as those shown here.

Fortunately, a more practical path consisting of two constant-Mach number climbs and one constant-altitude acceleration can be found which will, timewise, approach closely the complicated path found in the numerical example. Consequently, the most useful purpose of the theoretical solution may well be to serve as a guide and criterion to establishing practical minimum-time paths.

9. A Generalized Climb Problem

The minimum time-to-climb problem discussed in the previous sections can be made to conform much more closely to reality if certain additional factors are included. In particular, it appears that:

(1) Drag due to path inclination and normal acceleration should be included.

(2) Allowable normal accelerations should be limited due to pilot and plane stress.

(3) Dives and zooms should be allowed.

(4) The flight range should be specifiable.

The inclusion of these factors is not beyond the limits of present computability. They do, however, lead to considerably more programming and computing effort. Ideally, both a fast and easy first approximation method such as that described above, and the more complete solution to be discussed below, should be available to design and performance engineers.

The inclusion of drag due to path inclination and normal accelerations is accomplished by the introduction of the path inclination angle Θ, and its derivative $\dot{\Theta}$ into the formulation. This leads to a two-dimensional problem. Acceleration limitations determine a bound on the variable $\dot{\Theta}$. Programming $\dot{\Theta}$ is equivalent to programming the angle of attack.

To include dives, gain of velocity at the expense of altitude, and zooms, gains of altitude and loss of velocity, a new monotonically varying quantity to play the role of stage must be found. This variable is *energy height*, defined as:

(1)
$$E = H + \frac{1}{2g} V^2.$$

For all reasonable trajectories, this variable will increase during powered flight, though altitude and velocity may individually fluctuate. Note that no additional quantity has been introduced, since knowledge of E and H determines V by means of (1).

Finally, range, S, can be specified by the introduction of a constant Lagrange multiplier, which can be experimentally determined by iterative solution.

With these additions, the recurrence relation takes the form

$$(2) \quad f_E(H, \Theta)$$
$$= \min_{a \leq \frac{d\Theta}{dE} \leq b} \left[\frac{dt}{dE} \Delta E + \lambda \frac{ds}{dE} \Delta E + f_{E+\Delta E}\left(H + \frac{dH}{dE} \Delta E, \Theta + \frac{d\Theta}{dE} \Delta E\right)\right],$$

where

$$(3) \qquad\qquad \frac{dE}{dt} = \frac{V}{W}(T - D),$$

$$\frac{ds}{dE} = \frac{W \cos \Theta}{T - D},$$

$$\frac{dH}{dE} = \frac{W \sin \Theta}{T - D},$$

and

$$(4) \qquad\qquad T = T(E, H),$$
$$D = D(E, H, \Theta, \dot{\Theta}),$$

and the stress limitations in Equation (2) are given by

$$(5) \qquad\qquad a = a(E, H, \Theta),$$
$$b = b(E, H, \Theta).$$

Numerical solution, as has often been discussed before, involves the successive computation of a sequence of tables of values of a function of two variables.

10. A Satellite Trajectory Problem

In the sections immediately following, we wish to study the problem of putting a satellite into orbit. Since the question is quite complex, we shall study a simplified version.

The problem is interesting from both analytic and computational points of view.

Analytically, this is a problem of the Mayer type with one of the state variables, the horizontal velocity, to be maximized at burnout, subject to certain constraints. If the thrust is preprogrammed or constant, the analysis of the previous chapter is applicable. If thrust magnitude which enters linearly is to be chosen optimally subject to certain constraints, an analytic treatment is difficult, but the computational algorithm of dynamic programming still applies.

11. The Simplified Problem

Our aim is to ascertain the thrust control policy and fuel consumption policy which will put a satellite into orbit at a specified altitude with a maximum horizontal component of velocity.

In order to keep the numerical effort within reasonable bounds, we take advantage of the essential simplifications that result from the neglect of various aerodynamic forces, and the assumption that the terrestrial gravitational field is plane-parallel.

The determination of paths of minimum fuel, maximum altitude, and so on, can be carried out along the lines indicated in the preceding discussion. Similarly, the more realistic processes corresponding to spherical gravitational field can be treated by means of the same techniques, at the expense of considering functions of two or more variables.

12. Mathematical Formulation

The equations of motion of a satellite traveling over a flat earth in a Cartesian coordinate system will be taken to be

(1)
$$\frac{du}{dt} = p \cos \phi,$$

$$\frac{dw}{dt} = p \sin \phi - g,$$

$$\frac{dy}{dt} = w,$$

$$\frac{dx}{dt} = u.$$

Here (see Fig. 75)

(2) (a) x and y are, as usual, the horizontal and vertical coordinates,
(b) u and w are the horizontal and vertical projections of velocity,
(c) p is the magnitude of acceleration due to reaction force,
(d) ϕ is the inclination of the thrust to the horizontal.

If we introduce the quantity V as the velocity available to the satellite in the idealized case of no gravitational force, we obtain the relation

(3)
$$\frac{dV}{dt} = -p.$$

The variable V will be a monotone function of the quantity of fuel. Since

(4)
$$p = \frac{gP}{M},$$

where P is the thrust, and

(5)
$$P = -\frac{c}{g}\frac{dM}{dt},$$

where M is the weight and c is the exit velocity of the gases, we can solve for M in terms of the "ideal available velocity," V, obtaining the equation

(6)
$$M = M_e e^{V/c},$$

where M_e is the weight of the empty rocket.

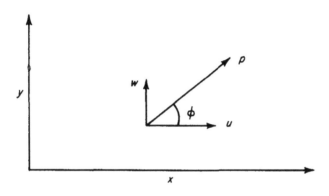

Figure 75

The equations of motion, (1), together with (6), which yields mass as a function of V, and (4), which furnishes the acceleration in terms of thrust and mass, enable us to determine optimal inclinations and optimal magnitude of thrust as functions of V.

13. Analytic Solution

If p is constant, then the method of the previous chapter yields the important conclusion that the optimal policy, ϕ, is characterized by the property that

(1)
$$\frac{d}{dt}\tan\phi = \lambda,$$

a *constant*.

14. Dynamic Programming Approach—I

Let us now see how we can employ the functional equation approach of dynamic programming to obtain a computational solution.

The state variables are altitude y, vertical component of velocity w, and available velocity V. Consequently, we introduce the function

(1) $f(V, w, y) =$ the additional horizontal velocity obtained starting at altitude y, vertical component of velocity w and ideal available velocity V, and using an optimal policy.

Referring to the defining equations of motion in §12, and using the principle of optimality, we obtain the functional equation

$$(2) \quad f(V, w, y) = \max_{\phi, P} \left[\cos \phi \Delta V + f\left(V - \Delta V, w + \frac{dw}{dV} \Delta V, y + \frac{dy}{dV} \Delta V\right) \right]$$

$$= \max_{\phi, P} \left[\cos \phi \Delta V + f\left(V - \Delta V, w + \left(\sin \phi - \frac{M_e e^{V/c}}{P}\right) \Delta V, \right.\right.$$

$$\left.\left. y + \frac{w M_e e^{V/c}}{gP} \Delta V\right) \right],$$

where ΔV is regarded as a small quantity.

Letting V assume only a finite set of values $0, \Delta V, 2\Delta V, \ldots, N\Delta V$, we see that the computation becomes that of determining a sequence of functions of two variables $f_N(w, y) \equiv f(N\Delta, w, y)$, using (2).

15. Dynamic Programming Approach—II

In order to simplify the computation, we use a Lagrange multiplier formalism, as discussed in Chapter II, §16, to reduce the problem to one of determining a sequence of functions of one variable.

In place of maximizing the final value of u, subject to the constraints on a final altitude and on w, we consider the problem of maximizing

$$(1) \qquad -\int_{V_0}^{0} \cos \phi \, dV + \lambda \int_{V_0}^{0} \frac{dy}{dV} \, dV,$$

subject to the constraints of the equations of motion. Here λ is the Lagrange parameter.

The new functional equation for the maximum value is

$$(2) \quad f(V, w)$$

$$= \max \left\{ \max_{\phi, P} \left[\cos \phi \, \Delta V + \frac{\lambda w M_e e^{V/c}}{gP} \Delta V \right] \right.$$

$$\left. + f\left(V - \Delta V, w + \left(\sin \phi - \frac{M_e e^{V/c}}{P}\right)\Delta V\right), \lambda w \Delta t + f(V, w - g\Delta t) \right\},$$

where the second alternative within the max $\{\ \}$ represents a decision to coast for a small time interval Δt.

The parameter λ is adjusted until the altitude constraint is met. By using the Lagrange parameter, we have partitioned a problem originally involving a sequence of functions of *two* variables into a set of problems involving functions of *one* variable. The gain in computing time and effort is considerable.

16. Computational Aspects

The numerical solution is obtained by iterating the recurrence equation (15.2) backwards from the known final values. The calculation is begun by observing that, if burnout occurs with a vertical component of velocity w, the additional altitude obtained during coasting will be $w^2/2g$ and the additional horizontal velocity will be zero. Hence $f(0, w) = \lambda w^2/2g$. A table containing $f(0, w)$ for a range of w values (we do not yet know to what burnout value of w the optimal policy will lead) is stored in the high-speed memory of the computer.

This tabular function is now used to determine a new function, $f(\Delta V, w)$, the total additional horizontal velocity plus λ times the altitude that can be attained starting with a small quantity ΔV of "available velocity (fuel)" and vertical velocity component w. This calculation is performed using equation (15.2). We actually evaluate the gain associated with choices of different ϕ's and P's and compare this with the return from a decision to coast. On this basis we pick the optimal decision. The return from this decision is recorded in the computer memory as the value of $f(\Delta V, w)$ for the particular value of w considered. A second table is constructed giving the optimal decision that yielded $f(\Delta V, w)$. A third table, $J(\Delta V, w)$, is maintained giving the total altitude gained when following an optimal path starting from $(\Delta V, w)$. Since we are flying so as to maximize horizontal velocity plus λ times altitude, this third table is just a convenient record that is not used in the calculation, but which, when the iteration of equation (15.2) is finished, yields immediately the total altitude (and hence the horizontal velocity, $f(V, 0) - \lambda J(V, 0)$), gained by following an optimal trajectory.

Once the technique described above for calculating $f(\Delta V, w)$ using the table of $f(0, w)$ has been programmed for a computer, it is a simple matter to have the same code calculate $f(2\Delta V, w)$ from $f(\Delta V, w)$ and, finally, $f(V, w)$ from $f(V - \Delta V, w)$. Notice that at each stage of this computation only one table of the function f is needed to compute the next table in the sequence. Once a table has been computed and used in the calculation of the next table it can be printed by the computer and destroyed in memory. Hence the computer memory capacity required is determined by the number of discrete points chosen for the w-table, and does not depend on the fineness of the ΔV grid. The total time for a calculation depends inversely on the size of ΔV.

At the completion of the backwards iteration of equation (15.2) one knows the horizontal velocity and altitude obtained by an optimal policy for the specified initial conditions. Also the initial decision for the starting point is determined by the nature of the calculation of $f(V, w)$. To reconstruct the optimal path in its entirety, one now determines the new value of w after using the prescribed decision for the first ΔV interval. In calculating $f(V - \Delta V, w)$ for this w-value, an optimal decision was determined and recorded (since the actual w may not be a point of the w-grid, interpolation may be necessary) and this decision is used during the interval $V - \Delta V$ to $V - 2\Delta V$. In this manner we use the output of the sequence of calculations, processing them in the opposite order from that in which they were computed.

The above operation may be performed easily by the computer as the final step of the calculation if the requisite tables are stored on tape or punched into cards.

Once the problem has been solved, one examines the final altitude to determine if the required height was attained. A new value of the Lagrange multiplier λ is then calculated based upon previous values and results, and the calculation is repeated.

One calculation yields the optimal path, in terms of horizontal velocity and λ (altitude), for a wide range of initial vertical components of velocity. This variety of results is of interest in problems where initial vertical velocity is not necessarily specified and the answers for a range of values are desired. Secondly, after several variations of λ, optimal trajectories to several different altitudes are known, yielding an interesting estimate of the trade-off between altitude and velocity along optimal trajectories.

17. Numerical Results

For all calculations, we have assumed a hypothetical rocket with the following characteristics:

Empty weight, $M_e = 5000$ lbs.
Exhaust velocity, $c = 11,000$ ft/sec.
Maximum thrust, $P_{max} = 300,000$ lbs.
Minimum thrust with engine on, $P_{min} = 50,000$ lbs.
Total ideal available velocity $= 30,000$ ft/sec.

These data imply a total weight at takeoff of 76,456 lbs.

A value of λ of .00142 yielded a final altitude of approximately 450 miles with a horizontal component of velocity at this altitude of 26,300 ft/sec.

Various parameters and grid-sizes required for numerical solution were chosen as follows:

(1) $\Delta V = 1000$. Therefore the recurrence relation was iterated 30 times.

(2) $\Delta w = 50$. Each table of $f(V, w)$ contained 281 numbers, since w was allowed to assume value from 0 to 14,000.

(3) $\Delta \phi = .01$ radian. Admissible thrust angles were 0, .01, .02, . . . , $\pi/2$ radians.

(4) Thrust could assume values 300,000, 250,000, 200,000, 150,000, 100,000, or 50,000.

These numbers were determined experimentally. They possess the property that a further refinement has little or no effect on the computed solution.

A condensed summary of the solution, as computed on the RAND Johnniac computer in 20 minutes, is shown below.

It should be noted that, although in this simplified study the rocket is revealed to be flown at maximum thrust until burnout and the thrust direction obeys a simple law, the computational scheme assumes neither of these results. It is therefore applicable to more general problems that are not amenable to conventional mathematical analysis.

V (ft/sec)	Mass (lb)	h (ft)	w (ft/sec)	u (ft/sec)	ϕ (rad.)	P (lbs)	Time (sec)
30,000	76,456	0	0	0	.560	300,000	0
25,000	48,529	16,045	1,514	4,279	.523	300,000	33.3
20,000	30,803	57,720	3,306	8,625	.501	300,000	54.4
15,000	19,552	106,344	5,259	13,020	.490	300,000	67.8
10,000	12,410	152,954	7,330	17,436	.480	300,000	76.3
5,000	7,877	192,848	9,464	21,871	.480	300,000	81.7
burnout	5,000	224,920	11,650	26,313	.472	300,000	85.1
end of coast	5,000	2,337,679	0	26,313	0	0	444.7

It is of interest to check the numerical accuracy of this calculation by comparing the variation of $\tan \phi$ to the linear rule derived. We fit $\tan \phi(t)$ above by a least square linear fit $\tan \bar{\phi}(t) = \alpha + \beta t$ where $\alpha = .623945$ and $\beta = -.001336$, and obtain the table:

t	$\phi(t)$	$\tan \phi(t)$	$\tan \bar{\phi}(t)$	$\lvert\tan \phi - \tan \bar{\phi}\rvert$
0	.560	.6269	.6239	.0030
33.3	.523	.5766	.5795	.0029
54.4	.501	.5476	.5513	.0037
67.8	.490	.5334	.5334	.0000
76.3	.480	.5206	.5220	.0014
81.7	.480	.5206	.5148	.0058
85.1	.472	.5093	.5103	.0010

18. Flow Chart (See p. 226)

The program is shown diagrammatically in Fig. 76.

19. A New Guidance Concept

The state-variable concept of dynamic programming gives rise quite naturally to a new approach to guidance and feedback control in general.

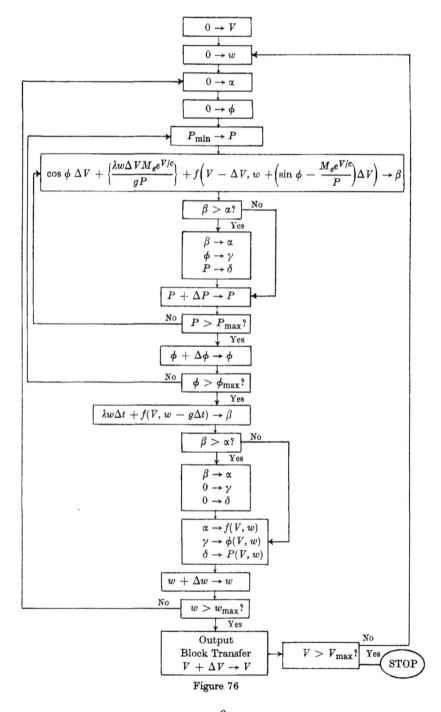

Figure 76

The older variational approach attempts to determine, for any given problem, the equation of the best trajectory. It is natural that this leads to a guidance philosophy based on the precalculation of a desired path, and the programming of the guidance computer to follow this path. If the missile should stray due to unexpected forces, or minute malfunctions, a feedback mechanism senses this deviation and attempts to return to the prescribed path. The use of such a device necessarily leads to stability difficulties with the ever present danger of increasing oscillations due to overcorrection.

All such difficulties are automatically avoided in the state-variable approach. Once the rocket has strayed, the optimal path is no longer the precalculated one, but a new one determined by the new state of the rocket. Any attempt to return to the old path is not only difficult, but is indeed nonoptimal, in general. It is precisely the information needed to accomplish this—the optimal decision as a function of all possible reasonable states—that is produced in a dynamic programming calculation. By building this information into the guidance system (an engineering problem as yet little investigated), easily flown and truly optimal paths can be generated.

20. Multistage Rockets

We shall discuss here an entirely different type of multistage problem, bred by the space age. As is indicated by the name itself, problems concerning the optimal configuration for multistage rockets are conveniently approached by way of dynamic programming. To illustrate the applicability of the technique, we have chosen the following problem.

21. The Optimal Staging Problem

We shall consider the problem, arising in rocket design, of the determination of the proper number and size of booster stages. As the reader of any daily paper these days is aware, current satellite carriers and space probe vehicles are constructed of several fuel carrying sections. After the propellant contained in a particular section has been expended, the casing of the stage is dropped in order to reduce the total weight. Ideally, one would prefer an infinite-stage rocket, the extra casing weight being dropped continuously as fuel is consumed. However, this leads to infinitely many timing and control devices and, consequently, a rather high probability of malfunction. Granting, then, that one is willing to use a reasonably small number of stages, the question of fuel allocation among the stages arises. It is a simplified version of this aspect of the problem that we shall discuss here. We shall seek to determine the amount of fuel to be stored in each stage of a k-stage rocket, in order to impart to the nose cone and payload a specified final velocity. We shall make the assignment so as to minimize the total fuel used, i.e., initial weight. We wish to solve this problem for a

k-stage rocket, where k takes on values $1, 2, 3, \ldots, N$. This whole range of problems can be solved in one dynamic programming computation. The choice of the optimal k can then be made on the basis of the trade-off between weight and reliability.

22. Formulation

We wish to minimize the weight necessary to achieve a specified velocity, and we shall assume that the trajectory is known. One variable necessary to describe the state of the missile at the beginning of a stage is the *velocity* attained, or, equivalently, the velocity left to be attained by subsequent booster stages. It is also necessary to know the *weight* of the rocket in order to compute its performance during a given stage. All other data necessary to the stage-performance computation is assumed known a priori, independent of the calculated configuration. Since the criterion function to be minimized is the weight necessary to attain the final velocity, and the optimal weight of the rocket at a given velocity is precisely that necessary to attain the final velocity, the value of the objective function (i.e., weight) at a given stage and the value of the state variable (i.e., velocity) determine the performance during the stage.

Analytically, let us define

(1) $f_k(v) =$ minimum weight of a k stage rocket achieving a final velocity v.

Now, if v_k is the as yet undetermined velocity to be added during stage k and the function $w(v_k, f_{k-1}(v - v_k))$ is the additional fuel and casing weight necessary to do this, we have, by the principle of optimality, the recurrence relation

(2) $$f_k(v) = \min_{v_k} \, [w(v_k, f_{k-1}(v - v_k)) + f_{k-1}(v - v_k)].$$

The nature of the function w is the unique aspect of this problem. Nowhere, to this point, have we encountered the situation of the $(k - 1)$-stage return function appearing in the single-stage portion of the recurrence relation. That this offers no additional computational difficulties can be easily verified by the reader upon checking the computational algorithm used so often in this book. Numerical results obtained in this fashion will be found in references given at the end of the chapter.

23. Higher Dimensional Problems

As the reader will note, the illustrative problems chosen in this chapter are all of low dimensionality as far as dynamic programming is concerned. The airplane minimum time-to-climb problem of §4 led to a quick and easily programmed way of roughly approximating the optimal path. Though this is a desirable result, one also would like to be able to calculate solutions to problems including many more realistic factors such as those included in the formulation of §9. Larger, faster computers and additional time and effort are necessary for the study of this companion program. Similar statements hold true for rocket and interplanetary space flight problems.

While several dimension-reducers, such as Lagrange multipliers, have already been introduced, more analytic devices are needed to tame the toughest trajectory problems. Some candidates for problem-tamers will be discussed in the sections on numerical analysis in Chapter XII.

Problems can be generalized by means other than state variable expansion. Stochastic elements can and often should be included in the mathematical model. Finally, adaptive techniques where the system learns about its environment and optimally adapts to it must be considered. We shall discuss these matters in the chapter on feedback control (Chapter IX).

24. A Routing Problem

As a further application of these ideas, let us consider the following routing problem which arises in a wide variety of applications. Suppose that we are given N cities, numbered $i = 1, 2, \ldots, N$, in some order, and a set of numbers, (t_{ij}), where

(1) t_{ij} = the time required to travel from the ith city to the jth city.

Starting at the first city, we wish to trace a path to the Nth city which will require a minimum time. We can go directly, or go by way of any of the other cities.

In many situations, there are no connections between two particular cities, in which case we consider t_{ij} to be infinite, or, for digital computer purposes, a very large positive number.

If N is at all large, any direct enumerative solution is impossible. Let us treat the problem by means of functional equation techniques. We consider the general problem of determining the minimum time required to go from the ith city to the Nth city. Let

(2) f_i = the time required to travel from the ith to the Nth city, using an optimal routing policy.

Then the same reasoning we have employed in discussing the preceding trajectory processes leads to the relation

(3) $$ f_i = \min_{j \neq i} [t_{ij} + f_j], \quad i = 1, 2, \ldots, N - 1, \quad f_N = 0. $$

It can be shown without difficulty that this system of equations possesses a unique solution, and thus that the solution of this set is equivalent to the solution of the original problem.

25. Computational Aspects

This equation possesses a feature which we have not previously encountered, namely that the unknown function, f_i, appears on both sides of the equation. Consequently, we possess no immediate iterative scheme for generating the solution.

It is necessary, therefore, to employ some method of successive approximations. We could, for example, set

$$(1) \quad f_i^{(0)} = \min_{j \neq i} t_{ij}, \quad i = 1, 2, \ldots, N - 1, \quad f_N^{(0)} = 0,$$

$$f_i^{(k)} = \min_{j \neq i} [t_{ij} + f_j^{(k-1)}], \quad i = 1, 2, \ldots, N - 1, \quad f_N^{(k)} = 0.$$

This yields monotone convergence from *below*. Or, we can think in terms of policies. Let us consider first those paths that go directly from i to N, then those which make one stop, and so on. This leads to the scheme

$$(2) \quad g_i^{(0)} = t_{iN}, \quad i = 1, 2, \ldots, N - 1, \quad g_N^{(0)} = 0,$$

$$g_i^{(k)} = \min_{j \neq i} [t_{ij} + g_j^{(k-1)}], \quad i = 1, 2, \ldots, N - 1, \quad g_N^{(k)} = 0,$$

which yields monotone convergence from *above*, and, indeed, in a finite number of steps.

Method (1) evaluates the best path of length k starting at city i. However, the equations have the property that N is a sink and if a path reaches N in less than k steps, it can stop there. For any other city, the path cannot stop except after k steps. Hence as k gets large, the paths all tend to go to city N, and the minimization guarantees that they will do this by the best route.

Method (2) assigns to each city at each iteration an attainable, but not necessarily optimal, time. Successive iteration converges to the best path.

This example illustrates the distinction between function-space and policy-space iteration discussed in Chapter II, Section 44. Method (1) gives at each iteration the optimal solution to a problem different from the original problem. Method (2), before convergence, gives a nonoptimal solution to the original problem.

Both techniques are readily suited to hand or machine computation for moderate values of N, i.e., $N \leq 100$, and to machine computation for N of the order of magnitude of several thousand.

26. The *n*th Shortest Path

It is occasionally of interest to determine not only the shortest path, but also the second shortest, the third shortest, and so on. In this way we can ascertain how important it is to use the shortest path, rather than, say, the tenth shortest.

To illustrate the method, let us introduce the sequence of values

$(1) \quad v_i =$ the time required to go from i to N using the second shortest path, $i = 1, 2, \ldots, N - 1$.

In order to obtain a relation for v_i, observe that if the first stop on the way to N from i is at j, then the continuation from j to N must be along either a path which minimizes the time from j to N, or which is a second shortest path from j to N.

Let

(2) $\min_1 w_i =$ the absolute minimum of w_i, $\quad i = 1, 2, \ldots, N$,
$\min_2 w_i =$ the second smallest value of w_i.

Then we have the equations

$$(3) \qquad v_i = \min \left\{ \min_{\substack{1 \\ j \neq i}} (t_{ij} + v_j), \quad \min_{\substack{2 \\ j \neq i}} (t_{ij} + f_j) \right\},$$

$i = 1, 2, \ldots, N - 1$, with $v_N = 0$, and f_j defined as in §24. Similar, but more complex, equations can be derived for the nth shortest path.

27. Conclusions

The aim of this chapter has been to demonstrate to the reader that a number of classes of optimal trajectory problems can be quickly and accurately solved computationally by means of dynamic programming techniques.

The advantage of the dynamic programming approach lies in the fact that realistic equations of motion and realistic constraints are easily incorporated into the solution along functional equation lines.

The principal difficulty with which we must grapple is that of *dimensionality*. How to treat functions of several variables is a problem to which we shall return again.

Comments and Bibliography

§1. A great deal of effort has been devoted to trajectory problems, applying the calculus of variations. For a discussion of some of the results, and references to many other papers, see

J. V. Breakwell, "The optimization of trajectories," *J. Soc. Indust. Appl. Math.*, vol. 7, 1959.

H. J. Kelley, "Gradient theory of optimal flight paths," *Amer. Rocket Soc. J.*, vol. 30, 1960.

§2–§8. The results presented here were originally presented in

S. Cartaino and S. Dreyfus, "Application of dynamic programming to the airplane minimum time-to-climb problem," *Aero. Rev.*, 1957.

§10. The problem was first discussed in

D. E. Okhotsimskii and T. M. Eneev, *J. British Interplanetary Soc.*, January–February 1958,

using variational techniques, and then in

R. Bellman and S. Dreyfus, "An application of dynamic programming to the determination of optimal satellite trajectories," *J. British Interplanetary Soc.*, vol. 17, 1959–60, pp. 78–83,

using dynamic programming techniques.

See also

F. T. Smith, *The Optimization of Multistage Orbit Transfer Processes by Dynamic Programming*, The RAND Corporation, Paper P–2177, 1961.

P. I. Welding and J. Stringer, "A problem in vehicle fuel consumption," *Oper. Res. Q.*, vol. 11, 1960, pp. 197–204.

R. Bellman, S. Dreyfus, and R. Kalaba, *Applications of Dynamic Programming to Space Guidance, Satellites and Trajectories*, The RAND Corporation, Paper P-1923, 1960.

J. N. Franklin, "The range of a fleet of aircraft," *J. Soc. Indust. Appl. Math.*, vol. 8, 1960, pp. 541–548.

S. E. Dreyfus, "The analysis and solution of optimum trajectory problems," *Symposium on Mathematical Optimization Techniques*, Santa Monica, California, 1960.

For a different approach, see

A. E. Bryson, W. F. Denham, F. J. Carroll and K. Mikami, *Determination of the Lift or Drag Program that Minimizes Re-entry Heating with Acceleration or Range Constraints Using a Steepest Descent Computation Procedure*, to appear.

For the use of the Neyman-Pearson lemma and extensions to handle variational problems with constraints, see

R. Bellman, I. Glicksberg, and O. Gross, *Some Aspects of the Mathematical Theory of Control Processes*, The RAND Corporation, Report R-313, 1958.

G. Goertzel, "Minimum critical mass and flat flux," *J. Nuclear Energy*, vol. 2, 1956, pp. 193–201.

§20–§22. These results are due to Ten-Dyke. See

R. P. Ten-Dyke, "Computation of rocket step weights to minimize initial gross weights," *Jet Propulsion*, vol. 28, 1958, pp. 338–340.

§24. This follows

R. Bellman, "A routing problem," *Q. Appl. Math.*, vol. 16, 1958, pp. 87–90.

See also

R. E. Greenwood, "Linear graphs and matrices," *Texas J. Science*, vol. 12, 1960, pp. 105–108.

Many other approaches to this fundamental problem are available. See

R. Kalaba, "On some communication network problems, combinatorial analysis," *Proc. Symposium in Applied Mathematics*, vol. 10, 1960, American Math. Soc.,

and

M. Pollack, "The maximum capacity route through a network," *Operations Research*, vol. 8, 1960, pp. 733–736.

M. Pollack and N. Wiebenson, "Solutions of the shortest-route problems— a review," *Operations Research*, vol. 8, 1960, pp. 224–230,

for further references and extensions, and other techniques.

For a linear programming treatment of related problems, see

L. R. Ford, Jr. and D. R. Fulkerson, "Maximal flow through a network," *Canadian J. Math.*, vol. 8, 1956, pp. 399–404.

§26. A more detailed discussion may be found in

R. Bellman and R. Kalaba, "On k-th best policies," *J. Soc. Indust. Appl. Math.*, vol. 8, 1960, pp. 582–588.

and in the reference by R. Kalaba given in §24.

For some quite different ideas, see

J. Beardwood, J. H. Halton and J. M. Hammersley, "The shortest path through many points," *Proc. Cambridge Phil. Soc.*, vol. 55, 1959, pp. 299–327.

CHAPTER VII

Multistage Production Processes Utilizing Complexes
of Industries

1. Introduction

A problem of fundamental importance in the economic and industrial world is the efficient utilization of a complex of interdependent industries. It is clear that any realistic treatment will present formidable difficulties. Before one can even contemplate optimization, we must grapple with the description of the processes that arise in precise and concise terms, with the recognition of objectives, with the incorporation of stochastic and adaptive features, and with the discovery of feasible, much less optimal, policies.

Here, quite modestly, we wish to study certain simplified models of multistage production processes. Our aim is to show how the functional equation technique enables us to obtain a computational foothold on the solution of classes of problems which preserve some of the aspects of actual economic problems.

The apparently specialized mathematical model is worthy of attention because identical analytic questions arise in many actual areas such as in the field of forestry, in the study of the production and stockpiling of manganese, and in many phases of chemical engineering; as examples of the last group alone, consider problems of isotope separation, catalyst replacement, and any number of other chemical processing problems as well.

We shall very briefly indicate some of the contacts between the results we present here, and the macroeconomic theory of von Neumann, tied in with the theory of games and linear programming. Further results will be found in a number of references given at the end of the chapter.

Often, processes of the type discussed below are called "bottleneck processes," since the behavior of the whole process is governed by the resource or production capacity in shortest supply.

2. A Two-industry Economic Complex

Let us assume that we are examining the operation of a two-industry complex, the "auto" industry and the "steel" industry. Although these appellations are not to be taken too seriously, by using these familar names and relying upon certain intuitive notions, we can hope to obtain a clue to computational and analytic solutions. Alternatively, the solutions which we obtain can be used to provide an intuitive basis for the solution of still more complex models. One of the reasons why it is worthwhile to treat these admittedly over-simplified models in some detail is in the hope of obtaining some picture of the structure of the solution of problems of this nature.

We shall suppose, using the concept of lumped parameters which plays such an essential role in mathematical physics, that the state of each industry at any particular time may be specified by means of two quantities:

(1) (a) the *stockpile* of raw materials required for production,
    (b) the *capacity* of the industry to produce its particular product.

To simplify the formulation and computation in this particular case, we shall assume that auto capacity is arbitrarily large. In short, the production of autos will depend only upon the quantity of steel allocated to the production of autos.

At any particular time, the steel in the steel stockpile may be used for either of three purposes:

(2) (a) to produce additional steel using the existing steel capacity,
    (b) to increase the existing steel capacity,
    (c) to produce autos using the existing auto capacity.

We wish to determine allocation policies which maximize the total quantity of autos produced over a given period of time.

3. A Mathematical Model

At the moment, the process will be taken to be discrete, with allocations made only at times $t = 0, 1, \ldots, T - 1$. At any particular time, $t = n$, the state of the system is determined by the quantities

(1) (a) $x_s(n) =$ amount of steel in the steel stockpile,
    (b) $x_m(n) =$ capacity of the steel mills.

In determining the allocation of available steel at stage n, we introduce the quantities

(2) (a) $z_s(n) =$ the quantity of steel used to produce additional steel,
    (b) $z_m(n) =$ the quantity of steel used to increase steel capacity,
    (c) $z_a(n) =$ the quantity of steel used to produce autos.

We then have the relation

(3) $$x_s(n) = z_s(n) + z_m(n) + z_a(n).$$

In order to introduce some realistic features, we impose two constraints on the z's:

(4) (a) $$z_a(n) \leq a_1 x_s(n), \qquad 0 < a_1 < 1,$$

  (b) $$z_s(n) \leq x_m(n).$$

The first constraint asserts that it is not possible to use more than a fixed percentage of available steel for auto production over any stage, n to $n+1$, while the second states that there is no point to allocating more steel to the steel mills than the maximum capacity of the mills.

We shall choose the units so that the quantity of autos produced in the stage $(n, n+1)$ is $z_a(n)$. Furthermore, the quantity of steel produced in $(n, n+1)$ is proportional to $z_s(n)$ and the increase in steel capacity is proportional to $z_m(n)$. Let the respective coefficients of proportionality be a_2 and a_3.

We are thus assuming that we have a linear model of production. Expressed analytically,

(5) $$x_s(n+1) = a_2 z_s(n), \qquad a_2 > 1, \qquad x_s(0) = c_1,$$
$$x_m(n+1) = x_m(n) + a_3 z_m(n), \qquad a_3 > 0, \qquad x_m(0) = c_2.$$

It is required to choose the quantities $z_s(n)$, $z_a(n)$, and $z_m(n)$, $n = 0, 1, \ldots, T-1$, so as to maximize the total quantity of autos produced over the entire T-stage process.

4. Discussion

The analytic solutions of problems of this genre are complicated by two factors, linearity and the presence of constraints. Nevertheless, a wide variety of variational problems can be solved explicitly.

In continuous form, the variational problem is that of finding a vector y which maximizes the inner product $(x(T), a)$, given that x and y are related by means of the differential equation

(1) $$\frac{dx}{dt} = Ax + By, \qquad x(0) = c,$$

and by a constraint of the form

(2) $$Cy \leq Dx.$$

These problems cannot be treated by means of the classical methods of the calculus of variations. References to papers containing the analytic solution of a number of problems of this type will be found at the end of this chapter.

Turning to the question of obtaining a computational solution, it is clear that the discrete problem may be formulated as a linear programming problem. We must maximize a linear form

$$(3) \qquad L(z) = \sum_{n=0}^{T-1} z_A(n),$$

subject to the constraints of (3.3), (3.4), and (3.5).

In order to examine the feasibility of a solution along these lines, let us count variables, assuming that we are interested in a 30-stage process. With three additional unknowns introduced at each stage, we face a problem involving 90 variables subject to 120 relations. Although not formidable, it is nonetheless sizeable. If we wish to determine the dependence of the solution upon c_1 and c_2, the initial steel stockpile and the initial mill capacity, a direct method of this type may lead to inordinate demands on time.

We wish instead to present a computational method which automatically yields the dependence of the solution upon c_1 and c_2.

5. Dynamic Programming Approach

Let us define, for $N = 1, 2, \ldots,$ $c_1 \geq 0,$ $c_2 \geq 0,$ the function

(1) $f_N(c_1, c_2) = $ total auto production over N stages, starting with initial steel stockpile c_1 and initial mill capacity c_2 and using an optimal policy.

We have

$$(2) \qquad f_1(c_1, c_2) = a_1 c_1,$$

and, generally,

$$(3) \qquad f_N(c_1, c_2) = \max_z [z_a + f_{N-1}(a_2 z_s, c_2 + a_3 z_m)]$$

for $N = 2, 3, \ldots,$ where the maximization is over the region in z-space defined by the inequalities

(4) (a) $\qquad z_a, z_s, z_m \geq 0,$
     (b) $\qquad z_a + z_s + z_m = c_1,$
     (c) $\qquad z_a \leq a_1 c_1,$
     (d) $\qquad z_s \leq c_2.$

In the next section, we shall discuss the numerical determination of the sequence $\{f_N(c_1, c_2)\}$.

6. Search of Vertices

The region in the (z_a, z_s, z_m) plane determined by the inequalities (5.4) has the form shown in Fig. 77.

The vertices, as numbered in Fig. 77, have the following significance in terms of the process:

1. In case mill capacity does not represent a constraint, allocate all available steel to the production of more steel.

237

2. Allocate as much steel as possible to the production of steel; when the mill capacity is met, allocate the rest to the expansion of mill capacity.

3. The allowable percentage of steel stockpile is assigned to auto production, the rest to steel production.

4. This vertex occurs when mill capacity is insufficient to handle all the steel available. It represents an allocation of steel to steel production up to the mill capacity, an allocation to auto production up to the allowable percentage, and an allocation of the remaining steel to the expansion of mill capacity.

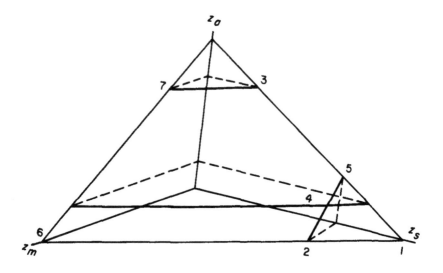

Figure 77. Region of variability of the quantities z_a, z_s, z_m.

5. Allocate as much steel as allowable to steel production and the rest to auto production.

6. Allocate all of the current steel stockpile to the expansion of mill capacity.

7. Produce as many autos as possible and then expand mill capacity with the remaining steel.

Obviously all of these conditions do not occur at once, but depend on steel capacity and steel stockpile, which vary throughout the process.

Of these seven, only the first five are actual possibilities, since vertices 6 and 7 effectively end the process—no new steel being produced.

It may be shown that the maximization over the vertices of the region is either optimal or a very good approximation as the number of stages increases arbitrarily. Here, since we are primarily interested in indicating the general approach to problems of this type, we shall accept maximization over vertices as exact. In any case, a calculation of this type furnishes a useful approximation in policy space.

If we wished to proceed *ab initio* without prejudicing ourselves as to the location of the maximum, we would do the following. The relation in (5.3) may be written

(1) $\quad f_N(c_1, c_2) = \max_{\{z\}} [\min (a_1 c_1, c_1 - z_s - z_m) + f_{N-1}(a_2 z_s, c_2 + a_3 z_m)],$

where the maximization is now over the region

(2) (a) $\qquad\qquad\qquad z_s, z_m \geq 0,$

(b) $\qquad\qquad\qquad z_s + z_m \leq c_1,$

(c) $\qquad\qquad\qquad z_s \leq c_2.$

7. Reduction in Dimension and Magnitude

Let us now show that we can reduce the problem to a sequence of one-dimensional problems and simultaneously introduce "shrinking" transformations. By this we mean that we can ensure that the number of possible states of the system does not increase over time.

It is first of all clear from the linearity of all the constraints and production functions that $f_N(c_1, c_2)$ is a homogeneous function of c_1 and c_2 of the first degree. Hence, for $c_1, c_2 > 0$, we have

(1) $\qquad\qquad f_N(c_1, c_2) = c_1 f_N\left(1, \frac{c_2}{c_1}\right) = c_2 f_N\left(\frac{c_1}{c_2}, 1\right).$

It follows that we need compute only $f_N(1, x)$ or $f_N(x, 1)$. Turning to (5.3), we have

(2) $\qquad\qquad f_N(1, c_2) = \max_{\{z\}} [z_a + f_{N-1}(a_2 z_s, c_2 + a_3 z_m)]$

$$= \max_{\{z\}} \left[z_a + a_2 z_s f_{N-1}\left(1, \frac{c_2 + a_3 z_m}{a_2 z_s}\right) \right].$$

We see, then, that the calculation of $f_N(1, c_2)$ for $c_2 \geq 0$ depends only on a knowledge of $f_{N-1}(1, c_2)$ for $c_2 \geq 0$. This is the required reduction in dimensionality. However, we still face the difficulty of an expanding range for c_2, since the ratio $(c_2 + a_3 z_m)/a_2 z_s$ may be much larger than c_2/c_1.

In order to avoid this difficulty, let us show that we can compute $f_N(1, x)$ and $f_N(x, 1)$ for $0 \leq x \leq 1$, knowing $f_{N-1}(1, x)$ and $f_{N-1}(x, 1)$ for $0 \leq x \leq 1$. It is worthwhile to introduce two functions in place of one in order to preserve a fixed interval of interest.

Referring to (2), we have

$$(3) \qquad f_N(1, c_2) = \max_{\{z\}} \left[z_a + a_2 z_s f_{N-1}\left(1, \frac{c_2 + a_3 z_m}{a_2 z_s}\right) \right]$$

for $a_2 z_s \geq c_2 + a_3 z_m$

$$= \max_{\{z\}} \left[z_a + (c_2 + a_3 z_m) f_{N-1}\left(\frac{a_2 z_s}{c_2 + a_3 z_m}, 1\right) \right]$$

for $a_2 z_s \leq c_2 + a_3 z_m$.

Combining this equation with the foregoing observation concerning the maximization over vertices, we have a quite simple computational scheme.

8. Computational Technique

The simplifications introduced by the transformation technique of §7 represent the most significant contribution of this particular study. With respect to the programming, the results are:

    (a) a reduction in time and space requirements from T^2 to $2T$, and

    (b) a considerable further reduction afforded by the elimination of expanding grid.

Let us elaborate on these two points. Normally, to express all possible states of a system defined by two independent parameters (here c_1, steel stockpile, and c_2, mill capacity), it is necessary to construct a grid of $f_N(c_1, c_2)$ in (c_1, c_2) space, and then to interpolate over this two-dimensional region to determine $f_N(c_1', c_2')$, the steel allocable to auto production during an N-period process in which the initial conditions are c_1' and c_2', where (c_1', c_2') is not a lattice point. This function is necessary for our recursive calculation of $f_{N+1}(c_1, c_2)$. If the intervals $[0, c_1]$ and $[0, c_2]$ are divided into n parts by this grid, we must compute and store n^2 values of $f_N(c_1, c_2)$ for future use. The time requirement becomes even more serious because of the extra logic needed when dealing with a two-dimensional system. This accounts for the savings resulting from the reduction to one-dimensional form.

The possibility of an expanding grid is a serious obstacle in some dynamic programming processes. Nonmathematically, the situation is this: To calculate the conditions at time t, we must know in advance all possible states that might exist at time $t - 1$. In this particular application, to determine auto production over N periods, we must know auto production for $N - 1$ periods for all allowable steel stockpiles and capacities. But after one period of production, either stockpile, or capacity, or both, may be increased. So, to calculate $f_N(c_1, c_2)$, $f_{N-1}(c_1', c_2')$ is needed, where c_1' may be greater than c_1 and similarly for c_2'. Consequently, the region over which $f_N(c_1, c_2)$ can be calculated is smaller than the region over which

$f_{N-1}(c_1, c_2)$ is known. One must therefore begin an N-stage calculation by considering a large region in order to complete the calculation with a modest range of values for c_1 and c_2. The technique of §7, bypassing this obstacle, represents a real and significant advance.

One further innovation in this problem—the optimization over a three-dimensional region—bears mention. Techniques for the solution of general problems of this multidimensional sort have been little investigated. Here, of course, we are saved by the nature of the functions and the nature of our requirement that only the vertices of the region need be considered. The coding technique used in order to determine and evaluate the relevant vertices is diagrammed in Fig. 78.

The remainder of the program is concerned with the calculation of a table of values $f_N(c_1, c_2)$, the block transfer of this table, and its subsequent use in the derivation of a table of $f_{N+1}(c_1, c_2)$.

Table 1 presents the result of an analysis of a typical situation. The calculation generates the optimal choice of vertex at each stage for each initial condition and also lists the total achievable steel allocation to auto production. To display the results to better advantage, a hand calculation was performed, using the policy dictated by the computer; this shows the actual unnormalized, growth of the system as a function of time. The sensitivity of the process was demonstrated by evaluating the return from a policy that was optimal in all but the first decision. An initial choice of vertex 3 resulted in an over-all reduction in productivity of 8 per cent.

9. Steady-state Growth

The question arises as to whether a complex of the type described settles into a regular pattern of growth in which the stockpile and capacity alike grow uniformly over time. If so, we would expect exponential growth.

Thus, for example, considering the differential equation in (4.1), we suspect asymptotic behavior of the form

$$(1) \qquad x \sim e^{\lambda t} w, \qquad y \sim e^{\lambda t} z,$$

where w and z are independent of time. We are led to the relations

$$(2) \qquad \lambda w = Aw + Bz,$$
$$Cz \leq Dw,$$

and to the problem of determining the largest such λ for which these relations hold.

Questions of this nature are part of the theory of linear inequalities. They play an important role in the theory of games and linear programming, the study of the computational aspects of linear inequalities. The problem posed above was first discussed by von Neumann in connection with his study of the possibility of exponentially expanding economy.

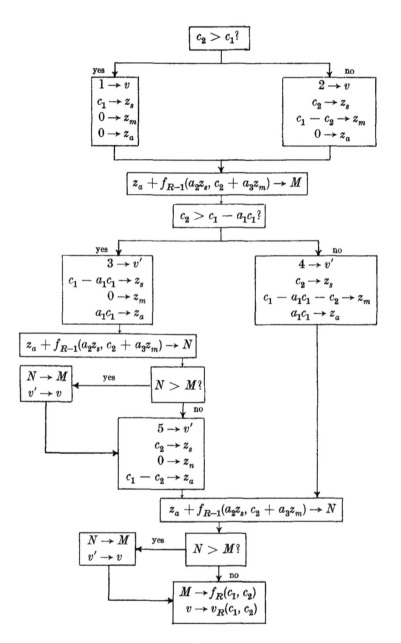

Figure 78

TABLE 1

Analysis of a Typical Bottleneck Situation

Fifteen-stage process, with parameters $a_1 = 0.2$, $a_2 = 2$,
$a_3 = 0.4$, and initial quantities $c_1 = 1$, $c_2 = 1$

	Information Made Available by Calculation		Actual Conditions Using Optimal Policy	
Stage	Normalized Condition (c_1, c_2) at Beginning of Stage	Vertex	Actual Condition at Beginning of Stage	Steel Allocated to Auto Production
1	(1, 1)	1	(1, 1)	0
2	(1, 0.5)	2	(2, 1)	0
3	(1, 0.7)	2	(2, 1.4)	0
4	(1, 0.5857)	2	(2.8, 1.64)	0
5	(1, 0.642)	2	(3.28, 2.096)	0
6	(1, 0.611)	2	(4.192, 2.57)	0
7	(1, 0.626)	2	(5.14, 3.22)	0
8	(1, 0.620)	4	(6.44, 3.988)	1.288
9	(1, 0.588)	4	(7.976, 4.4536)	1.595
10	(1, 0.586)	4	(8.9072, 5.2196)	1.781
11	(1, 0.573)	4	(10.4392, 5.9817)	2.008
12	(1, 0.579)	4	(11.9634, 6.9268)	2.393
13	(1, 0.576)	4	(13.8536, 7.9797)	2.771
14	(1, 0.577)	4	(15.9594, 9.2086)	3.192
15	(1, 0.577)	4	(18.4172, 10.6226)	3.683

Total allocation to auto production   18.853

Important as the question of optimal steady-state behavior is, the problem of approach to steady-state behavior is more important since most applications deal with processes of finite duration.

In our discussion of Markovian decision processes, we shall once again encounter asymptotic behavior and the connection with a linear programming formulation. There we shall present some detailed results.

Comments and Bibliography

§1. The reader interested in further discussion of processes of bottleneck type is referred to Chapters 6 and 7 of *Dynamic Programming*, where more complex models and several analytic solutions are presented.

For applications to forestry, and further numerical results, see

T. Arimizu, "Working group matrix in dynamic model of forest management," *J. Japanese Forestry Soc.*, vol. 40, 1958, pp. 185–190.

For applications to chemical engineering, see

S. M. Roberts, *Dynamic Programming Formulation of the Catalyst Replacement Problem*, (to appear).

R. Aris, R. Bellman, and R. Kalaba, "Some optimization problems in chemical engineering," *Chem. Engr. Progress Symp. Series*, vol. 56, 1960, pp. 95–102.

R. Aris, *The Optimal Design of Chemical Reactors*, Academic Press, Inc., New York, 1961.

§4. A continuous version of the "simplex technique" of linear programming designed to yield solutions of the continuous variational problems described in this section has been developed by Lehman. See

S. Lehman, *On the Continuous Simplex Technique*, The RAND Corporation, Research Memorandum RM-1386, 1954.

§5. These results were given in

R. Bellman, "On bottleneck problems and dynamic programming," *Proc. Nat. Acad. Sci. USA*, vol. 39, 1953, pp. 947–951.

R. Bellman, "Bottleneck problems, functional equations, and dynamic programming," *Econometrica*, vol. 22, no. 4, 1954.

§9. The original paper by von Neumann is

J. von Neumann, "A model of general economic equilibrium," *Review of Economic Studies*, vol. 13, 1945–46, pp. 1–9.

Further results may be found in

M. Morishima, "Economic expansion and the interest rate in generalized von Neumann models," *Econometrica*, vol. 28, 1960, pp. 3,52–363.

J. G. Kemeny, O. Morgenstern, and G. L. Thompson, "A generalization of the von Neumann model of an expanding economy," *Econometrica*, vol. 24, 1956, pp. 115–135.

K. Marx, *Capital*, C. Kerr and Co., Chicago, Illinois, 1933, vol. II, Chapters 20 and 21.

CHAPTER VIII

Feedback Control Processes

1. Introduction

In this and the subsequent chapter we wish to discuss a number of applications of dynamic programming to feedback control processes, and to processes which can be taken to be feedback control processes. As in the chapters treating trajectory processes and the calculus of variations, we will devote ourselves in one chapter to the important tasks of recognition and formulation of problems, and in the following chapter to computational aspects. As we have constantly emphasized, these represent separate but intimately related parts of the complete problem. To divorce them wholly is to seriously handicap any attempt at solutions of the actual physical problems.

We shall begin by discussing the classical control problem, one which is quite different from what we nowadays think of as "control." Following this, we shall consider a mathematical formulation of a typical feedback control problem encountered in electronics. Initially, we shall treat deterministic processes, associated with the usual realistic constraints, nonanalytic and implicit functionals. Subsequently, we shall turn to the more complex stochastic and adaptive control processes, where computational results obtained by Aoki will be given.

It will be clear from what follows that the analytic and computational investigation of this vast domain of intriguing and significant problems has just begun. Consequently, very little has been done in the direction of rigorous formulation, and much remains to be done as far as justification of the techniques that are used is concerned. As usual, we can circumvent some questions of rigor by considering only discrete versions of feedback control problems. We do wish to point out in passing that many interesting analytic problems exist in this general area.

In addition to questions of feedback control problems of rather straightforward nature, we shall discuss a maximum deviation problem arising in the use of nuclear reactors, an implicit variational problem of deterministic type, the "bang-bang" control problem, and implicit variational problems of stochastic type that will be encountered in a "soft landing" on the moon, or another planet, some questions of maximum altitude and maximum range of interest in ballistics, and, finally, some communication processes linked to "information theory."

A number of references to additional applications will be found in the discussion at the end of the chapter.

2. The Classical Control Problem

The idea of feedback control is most commonly associated with the governor used by Watt for the steam engine. Yet, actually, it is older than that, since a governor invented by Huygens for the regulation of clocks was used for windmills and water wheels before the advent of the steam engine. Furthermore, feedback methods appear to have been used in China for several thousand years before the industrial revolution.

Nonetheless, the mathematical analysis of control problems centered about the closely related concept of stability until quite recently. Consider a system ruled by an nth order linear differential equation

$$(1) \qquad \frac{d^n u}{dt^n} + a_1 \frac{d^{n-1} u}{dt^{n-1}} + \cdots + a_n u = 0$$

with constant coefficients. This equation can be considered to arise as the perturbation equation of a more complex nonlinear equation in the course of the investigation of the stability of an equilibrium state.

The system will be considered "stable" provided that all solutions of (1) approach zero as $t \to \infty$. As is well known, this is equivalent to the condition that all the roots of the polynomial equation

$$(2) \qquad \lambda^n + a_1 \lambda^{n-1} + \cdots + a_n = 0$$

possess negative real parts. Necessary and sufficient conditions for this condition were obtained by Routh and Hurwitz, and a great deal has been done on this problem since.

The problem of control was thus taken to be a problem of design. It was necessary to construct the physical system in such a way as to ensure that the foregoing stability condition was satisfied.

This type of analysis is weak in a number of significant ways. In the first place, it is predicated upon *linearity* of the fundamental equations, or equivalently, the assumption of *small deviations* from equilibrium. Secondly, it is not suited to discuss stochastic processes and particularly those of adaptive type. Consequently, we shall not devote any further attention to problems of this nature. The reader interested in these studies will find a number of references at the end of the chapter.

3. Deterministic Feedback Control

Our mathematical models will be built upon the following scheme. Consider the diagram of Fig. 79.

This diagram is to be interpreted in the following way. At time t, the system S emits an output signal $x(t)$. This signal is compared with a desired output signal $w(t)$, in the comparison unit. If there is any significant deviation, a corrective signal $y = y(x, w, t)$ is supplied to S for the purposes of forcing $x(t)$ to correspond more closely to $w(t)$.

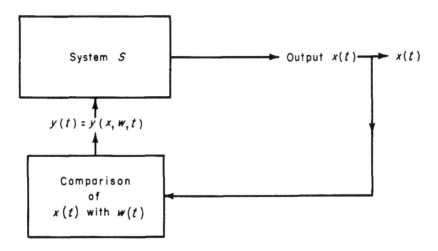

Figure 79

One analytic formulation of a simple feedback control system of this type is the following. In place of the original equation governing the system,

(1)
$$\frac{dx}{dt} = g(x, t), \qquad x(0) = c,$$

we have the new equation

(2)
$$\frac{dx}{dt} = h(x, t; y), \qquad x(0) = c,$$

where y is to be chosen, subject to certain constraints, so as to minimize some criterion function which evaluates both the cost of deviation of $x(t)$ from a desired state vector $w(t)$ and the cost of applying the control vector $y(t)$.

Pursuant to our usual approach to variational problems, we shall consider these problems (which can be posed as questions within the domain of the calculus of variations) to be multistage decision processes of continuous type. However, as mentioned above, for computational purposes, and to avoid rigorous matters, we shall consider only discrete versions.

247

4. Time Lags

In many cases, the use of the auxiliary comparison stage, and the application of the controlling force introduce a delay, or time lag. What this means is that $y(t)$ is actually dependent not upon $x(t)$ and $w(t)$, but rather upon $x(t - \Delta)$ and $w(t - \Delta)$, and, more often, upon more complex forms of the past history of the process. These realistic considerations introduce some quite interesting mathematical complications, which, however, we shall not take up here. References to many papers on the subject will be found at the end of the chapter.

5. Formulation of Variational Problems

Let us suppose that $w(t)$ is the desired state vector and that $k(x(t) - w(t))\Delta + o(\Delta)$ measures the deviation between x and w over the time interval $[t, t + \Delta]$.

The functional

$$(1) \qquad J(y) = \int_0^T k(x - w)\, dt$$

is then taken to be the total measure of deviation. As in most of our studies, we are assuming an additive utility.

There are now two ways of imposing realistic constraints. We can first of all suppose that we have a limited quantity of resources for control, which leads to a constraint of the form

$$(2) \qquad \int_0^T q(x, y)\, dt \le b_1.$$

Secondly, we can impose a set of constraints on the rate at which control is applied,

$$(3) \qquad r_i(x, y) \le 0, \qquad i = 1, 2, \ldots, k.$$

Let us then consider the variational problem of minimizing $J(y)$ subject to the differential equation of (3.2).

The problem has now been formulated in the conventional terms of the calculus of variations.

6. Analytic Aspects

Problems of the foregoing type are of great difficulty, as we have pointed out in Chapter V. Nevertheless, perseverance, ingenuity, and a certain amount of good fortune, enable us to resolve some of these. Unfortunately, the vast majority of the questions which arise even in simplified versions of feedback control processes easily escape the small set of soluble problems.

With these comments in mind, we shall henceforth devote our energies to the determination of algorithms which yield numerical solutions. As we shall see, a great deal of analysis will be required in order to attain this end.

7. Discrete Version

As long as we are going to present a general method, we will do well to consider a general form of the problem. Let us suppose that we wish to minimize the functional

$$(1) \qquad J(y) = \int_0^T g(x, y) \, dt,$$

where x and y are connected by the equation

$$(2) \qquad \frac{dx}{dt} = h(x, y), \qquad x(0) = c,$$

and the constraints

$$(3) \quad (a) \qquad \int_0^T q_i(x, y) \, dt \leq b_i, \qquad i = 1, 2, \ldots, r,$$

$$(b) \qquad r_i(x, y) \leq 0, \qquad i = 1, 2, \ldots, s, \qquad 0 \leq t \leq T.$$

In place of this continuous variational problem, we consider the following discrete problem. Minimize

$$(4) \qquad J(y) = \sum_{k=0}^N g(x_k, y_k),$$

over all y_k satisfying the relations

$$(5) \qquad x_{k+1} = x_k + h(x_k, y_k), \qquad x_0 = c,$$

and the constraints

$$(6) \quad (a) \qquad \sum_{k=0}^N q_i(x_k, y_k) \leq b_i, \qquad i = 1, 2, \ldots, r,$$

$$(b) \qquad r_i(x_k, y_k) \leq 0, \, i = 1, 2, \ldots, s, \qquad 0 \leq k \leq N.$$

We can either regard the vector c and the b_i as state variables, or we can use Lagrange parameters and minimize

$$(7) \qquad J_1(y) = \sum_{k=0}^N g(x_k, y_k) - \sum_{i=1}^r \lambda_i \sum_{k=0}^N q_i(x_k, y_k),$$

or, as we have previously done, consider various combinations of situations. All of this is a review of what we have presented in Chapter V.

8. Functional Equations

Considering, for example, the problem in (7.7), we obtain a recurrence relation of the form

$$(1) \qquad f_N(c) = \min_{r_i(c, y) \leq 0} \left[g(c, y) - \sum_{i=1}^r \lambda_i q_i(c, y) + f_{N-1}(c + h(c, y)) \right].$$

As before, the computational feasibility of a solution along these lines depends upon the dimension of c. We shall discuss various ways in which the method of successive approximations can be utilized in subsequent sections.

9. The "Bang-bang" Control Problem

An interesting problem with an implicit criterion function is the following. We wish to minimize the time required to convert a system from one state into another. This is a problem which occurs in a number of different fields under varied guises.

A particularly simple case is the following. Given the linear system

$$
(1) \qquad \frac{dx}{dt} = Ax + y, \qquad x(0) = c,
$$

where the components of y are subject to the constraints

$$
(2) \qquad |y_i| \le m_i, \qquad i = 1, 2, \ldots, N,
$$

we wish to determine y so as to minimize the time required for x to go from the initial position c to a prescribed state, say $x = 0$.

If the y_i are allowed to assume only the values $\pm m_i$, the problem is called one of "bang-bang" control. A great deal of theoretical work has been done on this problem, using various methods. However, the problem of obtaining simple computational algorithms remains.

If we replace (1) by a nonlinear equation

$$
(3) \qquad \frac{dx}{dt} = g(x, y), \qquad x(0) = c,
$$

then the situation is quite different. Denote the minimum time required to go from c to 0 by $f(c)$. Then we have

$$
(4) \qquad f(c) = \min_y \, [\Delta + f(c + \Delta g(c, v))] + o(\Delta),
$$

which in the limit yields the nonlinear partial differential equation

$$
(5) \qquad \min_y \, (g(c, y), \operatorname{grad} f) = -1,
$$

where y is subject to (2), or to the "bang-bang" condition. We are using a small amount of vector notation: $\operatorname{grad} f$ is the vector whose ith component is $\partial f / \partial c_i$ and $(x, y) = \sum_{i=1}^{N} x_i y_i$ where x_i and y_i, $i = 1, 2, \ldots, N$, are respectively the components of x and y.

A great deal of information can be obtained from this relation, but the general solution is one of some subtlety.

Since the same function appears on both sides of the equation in (4), a computational solution can be made to depend upon either successive approximations, or an approximation in policy space. Another approach is by way of dual problem. In place of the original problem, consider the question of determining y so as to minimize the distance from the origin at the end of time T.

Calling this minimum distance $f(c, T)$, we have the functional equation

(6) $\quad f(c, T) = \min_{y} \left[f(c + g(c, y)\Delta, T - \Delta) \right] + o(\Delta), \qquad f(c, 0) = |c|,$

where

(7) $$|c| = \left(\sum_{i=1}^{N} c_i^2 \right)^{1/2}.$$

The first value of T for which $f(c, T) = 0$ is the function $f(c)$ defined above.

10. Nuclear Reactor Shutdown

When a high flux thermal nuclear reactor is shut down, the presence of a fission product, iodine, which decomposes into xenon-135, can cause the concentration of xenon to rise for many hours. This is quite unsatisfactory since it may postpone for several hours the time at which the reactor may be restarted, with a resultant loss of efficiency. One way of overcoming this defect is by using many times more fuel than that required by the criticality relations. Another procedure is to carefully control the shutdown procedure so as to minimize reactor poisoning. It is this control problem which we wish to discuss.

Using a simplified model of the actual process, we assume that the state of the reactor at any time can be specified by means of

(1) (a) the neutron flux, ϕ,
    (b) the iodine concentration, I,
    (c) the xenon concentration, x.

Let us suppose that we can regulate the neutron flux ϕ. The equations determining I and x are

(2) $\qquad \dfrac{dI}{dt} = a_{11}\phi - a_{12}I, \qquad\qquad\qquad I(0) = c_1,$

$\qquad \dfrac{dx}{dt} = a_{21}\phi + a_{12}I - (a_3 + a_4\phi)x, \qquad x(0) = c_2.$

It is required that the neutron flux be reduced to zero by time b, with the process beginning at time zero. At time b, the state of the reactor will be given by

(3) (a) $\qquad\qquad\qquad \phi(b) = 0,$
    (b) $\qquad\qquad\qquad I(b) = c_3,$
    (c) $\qquad\qquad\qquad x(b) = c_4.$

The quantities c_3 and c_4 are functionals of ϕ. Following the time b, the xenon concentration may rise for several hours due to the xenon concentration imbalance caused by shutdown. The equations governing this phase of the process are then

(4)
$$\frac{dI}{dt} = -a_{12}I, \qquad I(b) = c_3,$$

$$\frac{dx}{dt} = a_{12}I - a_3 x, \qquad x(b) = c_4.$$

The function $x(t)$ for $t \geq b$ will have a graph of the form shown in Fig. 80.

In this case, there is little difficulty in determining the value of t which yields the maximum value of x for $t \geq b$. Let us, however, bypass this

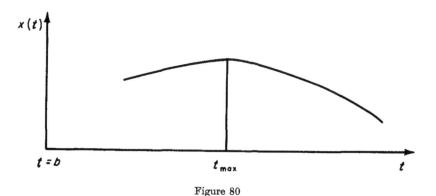

Figure 80

problem for the moment and denote this maximum value by $p(c_3, c_4)$. We shall discuss below the problem of determining $p(c_3, c_4)$ in more general cases where the equations in (4) are nonlinear.

Then we wish to determine $\phi(t)$ over $0 \leq t \leq b$, subject to various constraints such as

(5)
$$\left| \frac{d\phi/dt}{\phi} \right| \leq k_1,$$

so as to minimize $p(c_3, c_4)$. This is a complex variational problem of implicit type, with the usual difficulties.

Writing

(6)
$$f(c_1, c_2, b) = \min_{\phi} p(c_3, c_4),$$

we have the recurrence relation

(7) $f(c_1, c_2, b) = \min\limits_{\phi(0)} [f(c_1 + \Delta(a_{11}\phi(0) - a_{12}c_1),$
$$c_2 + \Delta(a_{21}\phi + a_{12}c_1 - (a_3 + a_4\phi)c_2), b - \Delta)] + o(\Delta).$$

This yields a feasible computational scheme, provided that we possess a digital computer capable of handling functions of two variables.

11. Maximum Deviation

Let us now discuss in more detail the problem of determining the function $p(c_3, c_4)$. Consider the recurrence relation

$$(1) \qquad \begin{aligned} x_{n+1} &= g_1(x_n, y_n), & x_0 &= c_1, \\ y_{n+1} &= g_2(x_n, y_n), & y_0 &= c_2, \end{aligned}$$

and suppose that we wish to determine the quantity $\max_{n \geq 0} |x_n|$. This quantity is clearly a function of the initial values c_1, c_2. Write

$$(2) \qquad f(c_1, c_2) = \max_{n \geq 0} |x_n|.$$

In order to obtain a recurrence relation for this function, let us analyze what we have been doing so far. In studying the linear operator, we set, for $N \geq 1$, and all x_i,

$$(3) \qquad L(x_1, x_2, \ldots, x_N) = x_1 + x_2 + \cdots + x_N,$$

and use the functional equation

$$(4) \qquad L(x_1, x_2, \ldots, x_N) = L(L(x_1, x_2, \ldots, x_{N-1}), x_N).$$

We now observe that the maximum operator

$$(5) \qquad M(x_1, x_2, \ldots, x_N) = \max [x_1, x_2, \ldots, x_N]$$

satisfies the relation

$$(6) \qquad M(x_1, x_2, \ldots, x_N) = M(M(x_1, x_2, \ldots, x_{N-1}), x_N).$$

This observation permits us to treat a number of problems involving the maximum functional by means of essentially the same techniques that we have employed in studying processes characterized by linear utility functions.

For example, the function defined in (2) satisfies the equation

$$(7) \qquad f(c_1, c_2) = \max [c_1, f(g_1(c_1, c_2), g_2(c_1, c_2))].$$

In order to compute $f(c_1, c_2)$ we may have to use a method of successive approximations, based upon an introduction of time, as in §13, or upon some other technique.

12. Maximum Range

There are a number of interesting descriptive processes in which the functional equation technique can be used to furnish a novel analytic approach and an economical computational method. Among these are a number of trajectory processes in which attention is focussed upon the determination of maximum range, minimum miss distance, and so on.

The standard approach to these problems involves the calculation of the entire trajectory, and then the determination of the specific information that is desired. As a simple example of a superior technique based upon the functional equation technique, an approach which yields precisely the desired information and no other, let us consider the following problem.

An object is shot straight up from a flat earth, subject to the retarding forces of gravity and friction. We wish to determine the maximum height that it attains.

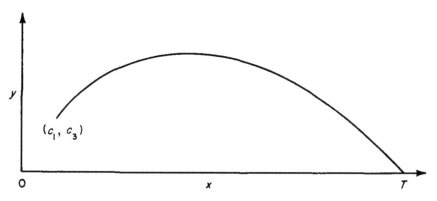

Figure 81

The equation of motion is

(1) $$\frac{d^2x}{dt^2} = -g - h\left(\frac{dx}{dt}\right), \qquad x(0) = 0, \qquad x'(0) = v,$$

where $h(v)$ is the frictional force due to velocity v. Let

(2) $f(v) =$ the maximum altitude, starting with initial upward velocity v.

Regarding Δ as an infinitesimal, we have the equation

(3) $$f(v) = v\Delta + f(v - (g + h(v)\Delta)) + o(\Delta).$$

Expanding and letting $\Delta \to 0$, we obtain the differential equation

(4) $$f'(v) = \frac{v}{g + h(v)}, \qquad f(0) = 0,$$

which yields

(5) $$f(v) = \int_0^v \frac{v_1 \, dv_1}{g + h(v_1)}.$$

(See Fig. 81.)

Similarly, given the two-dimensional path determined by the equations

(6) $$\frac{d^2x}{dt^2} = g_1\left(x, y, \frac{dx}{dt}, \frac{dy}{dt}\right), \qquad x(0) = c_1, \qquad x'(0) = c_2,$$

$$\frac{d^2y}{dt^2} = g_2\left(x, y, \frac{dx}{dt}, \frac{dy}{dt}\right), \qquad y(0) = c_3, \qquad y'(0) = c_4,$$

we can determine the maximum range and altitude in the same fashion. A discussion of this may be found in the references cited at the end of the chapter.

13. Minimum of Maximum Deviation

Consider, finally, a control problem involving the minimization of maximum deviation. Suppose the equation has the form

$$(1) \qquad \frac{d^2u}{dt^2} = g\left(\frac{du}{dt}, u, v\right), \qquad u(0) = c_1, \qquad u'(0) = c_2,$$

and we wish to choose v, subject to the constraint $|v(t)| \le m$, $0 \le t \le T$, so as to minimize the functional

$$(2) \qquad J(v) = \max_{0 \le t \le T} |u|.$$

Write

$$(3) \qquad \min_v J(v) = f(c_1, c_2, T).$$

Then we obtain the approximate functional equation

$$(4) \qquad f(c_1, c_2, T) = \max \left[c_1, \min_{|v(0)| \le m} \left[f(c_1 + c_2\Delta, \right.\right.$$

$$c_2 + g(c_1, c_2, v(0))\Delta, T - \Delta)]] + o(\Delta).$$

This relation permits us to obtain a computational solution of a variational problem.

14. Reduction in Dimensionality

We have previously pointed out that the sole hindrance to a straightforward computational solution of wide classes of variational processes by dynamic programming techniques lies in the dimension of the state vector.

For example, if x and y are N-dimensional, a terminal control process involving the minimization of a functional such as

$$(1) \qquad J(y) = g(x(T)) + \lambda \int_0^T k(y)\, dt$$

over all y where

$$(2) \qquad \frac{dx}{dt} = h(x, y), \qquad x(0) = c,$$

involves the tabulation of functions, $f(c, T)$, of N variables. If $N = 1$, this is a trivial problem; if $N = 2$, this is feasible, but not trivial, and if $N \ge 3$, ingenuity and analytic effort are required, unless we use fairly coarse grids or restrict ourselves to quite small regions of phase space.

Let us now proceed to document the important observation that if (2) is a *linear* equation

(3) $$\frac{dx}{dt} = A(t)x + y, \qquad x(0) = c,$$

and $g(x(T))$ is actually a function of only k of the components of $x(T)$, say $x_1(T), x_2(T), \ldots, x_k(T)$, then this variational problem can be treated by means of functional equation techniques with recourse to functions of only k variables.

The basic idea is that the linearity of (3) enables us to separate the effect of the initial state from the effect of the forcing vector. As is well known, we have from (3) the equation

(4) $$x = X(t)c + \int_0^t X(t)X^{-1}(s)y(s)\, ds,$$

where $X(t)$ is the matrix solution of

(5) $$\frac{dX}{dt} = A(t)X, \qquad x(0) = I.$$

Then

(6) $$x(T) = b + \int_0^T K(s)y(s)\, ds,$$

where b and K depend upon T. From this, we see that the problem is now that of minimizing the functional

(7) $\quad g(x_1(T), \ldots, x_k(T)) + \lambda \int_0^T h(y)\, dt$

$$= g\left(b_1 + \int_0^T \left[\sum_{j=1}^N k_{1j}y_j(s)\right] ds, \ldots, b_k + \int_0^T \left[\sum_{j=1}^N b_{kj}y_j(s)\right] ds\right) + \lambda \int_0^T h(y)\, dt$$

over all y. Let us then consider the new problem of minimizing the functional

(8) $g\left(b_1 + \int_a^T \left[\sum_{j=1}^N k_{1j}y_j(s)\right] ds, \ldots, b_k + \int_a^T \left[\sum_{j=1}^N b_{kj}y_j(s)\right] ds\right) + \lambda \int_a^T h(y)\, dt.$

Call the minimum value $f(b_1, b_2, \ldots, b_k, a)$. Then, using the principle of optimality,

(9) $\quad f(b_1, b_2, \ldots, b_k; a) = \min_{(ya)} \left[\lambda h(y(a))\Delta + f\left(b_1 + \Delta\left[\sum_{j=1}^N k_{1j}y_j(a)\right], \ldots,\right)\right]$
$$+ o(\Delta),$$

a functional equation involving functions of only k variables.

15. Discussion

In addition to the direct application of these techniques, other important uses are possible. In the first place, if the criterion function $g(x(T))$ is quadratic, we know that the variational problem gives rise to a linear Euler equation which can then be treated by means of an explicit solution.

However, the explicit analytic solution of a linear system of large dimension is no simple matter. Consequently, even in this case, it will be far more profitable to employ the functional equation approach. It turns out that the limiting form of (14.9) can be resolved explicitly, since the function $f(b_1, b_2, \ldots, b_k; a)$ will be a *quadratic form* in the b_i with coefficients dependent upon a. These coefficients will satisfy a system of quadratically nonlinear differential equations, of dimension $k(k + 1)/2$ with initial values, as compared to the linear system of dimension $2N$ obtained from the variational equations with two-point conditions.

Secondly, the results of the previous section can be used as the starting point for the method of *successive approximations* in two ways. In the first place, we can approximate to a general criterion function by one dependent upon only k of the N components, and, in the second place, we can approximate to an original nonlinear equation by a linear equation. We shall not discuss these approaches to any further extent here since we have not experimented with these techniques.

16. Stochastic Control Processes

Let us now suppose that the physical system which we are trying to regulate is subject to internal and external forces whose origins and effects are not thoroughly understood. This is, of course, always the actual situation. In many situations, however, the uncertainties produce such small effects that they may be ignored. Let us assume that we are in a situation where this is not the case.

One way to circumvent the apparent roadblock which this ignorance interposes is to introduce the fiction of *"random"* or *stochastic* influences. This very ingenious artifice of the mathematical theory of probability enables us to obtain a number of significant results. It turns out that even in the discussion of many processes where the cause and effect relations are known a great mathematical simplification results from this assumption of stochastic behavior. An outstanding example of this is the Gibbsian theory of statistical mechanics.

In what follows, we shall as before assume that the reader is acquainted with the fundamentals of probability theory and the elementary aspects of the concept of a random variable. In order to avoid complications which are extraneous to the issue we wish to analyze, we shall consider only processes which are discrete in time. In subsequent numerical work in Chapter IX, we shall consider only the simplest discrete distributions. Throughout only the most rudimentary aspects of probability theory will be required.

Consider the recurrence relation

(1)
$$x_{n+1} = g(x_n, y_n, r_n)$$

where x_n is a state vector, y_n is the control vector, and r_n is a random vector representing the random influence applied to the system at the nth stage. To begin with, we shall take the r_n to be independent. Subsequently, we shall show how correlation can be introduced.

Again, as before, we suppose that the effect of a choice of the vector y when the system is in the state x results in a "return" or "deviation," depending upon how we regard the process, of

$$(2) \qquad h(x, y, r)$$

where r is the same random vector occurring in (1).

Taking for the sake of simplicity the case of additive utilities, we have as the total measure of the N-stage process the expression

$$(3) \qquad R_N = h(x_1, y_1, r_1) + h(x_2, y_2, r_2) + \cdots + h(x_N, y_N, r_N).$$

Since this quantity is itself a stochastic quantity, we cannot immediately examine the question of maximizing or minimizing. Indeed, in the study of stochastic processes there is no unique way of introducing a precise optimization problem. One way of doing this is to use the expected value of R_N, taken over the random variables r_n, as the criterion function. We shall do this, while *sotto voce* warning the reader of the arbitrariness involved. Another important criterion function is the probability that R_N will exceed a specified value. One of the advantages of the functional equation technique is that it enables us to use realistic criteria without worrying about analytic expediency.

What makes the use of expected values reasonable is the existence in the mathematical theory of probability of a large body of theorems which assert that in many cases the behavior of the system over a long period of time approximates more and more closely its average behavior. On the other hand, one also knows that in the study of nonlinear systems, this may not be the case. Consequently, linear utility functions, i.e., expected values, must be used with considerable care and caution. The essential point is to keep in mind that we are following only one of many paths. Too often in applications of mathematics to the physical world, particular methods are taken as gospel, and it is often forgotten that other methods exist.

17. What Constitutes an Optimal Policy?

It is rather remarkable that the foregoing discussion does not yet permit us to study optimal control policy. It is still not clear what we mean by an optimal policy.

In order to elucidate this point, let us review some previous remarks. In our study of the calculus of variations and dynamic programming, in the chapter devoted to trajectory problems, and, more generally in all of our previous work on deterministic control processes, we pointed out that we could determine the y_i all at once, or one at a time, as functions of the state vectors. The identity of these two approaches is a consequence of the fundamental duality between points and lines in Euclidean space. Put another way, a curve can be regarded simultaneously as a locus of points and as an envelope of tangents.

When we enter a discussion of stochastic phenomena, the situation changes radically. In general, the two approaches are greatly different, due to the uncertainty of the future.

Borrowing the classical approach, we might pose the following problem. Determine a priori a set of vectors $y_1, y_2, \ldots, y_N$ which minimize the function

$$R(y_1, y_2, \ldots, y_N) = \exp_{r_i} R_N.$$

In this formulation, we reject the possibility of using the actual state of the system at any particular time to guide our decisions. It is easy to see that situations can arise in which this formulation may be the only one available, since the required information may be unattainable.

In place of problems of this nature, we wish to pose one which takes account of *feedback*, which is to say the use of the actual knowledge of some or all of the components of the state vector at each stage of the process. We consider then that the decisions will be made in the following fashion. Starting in state x_1, the decision y_1 is made. The combination of x_1, y_1, and r_1, the random vector, produces by way of (16.1) the new state x_2. Starting with the knowledge of x_2, this process is repeated. We now wish to determine the sequence of vectors y_n which minimizes the expected value of R_N.

It is rather surprising that the first problem, which involves only a minimization over a finite dimensional space, is genuinely difficult, while the second problem, which requires a minimization over function space, the space of the policies $y_1(x_1)$, $y_2(x_2)$, and so on, can be treated by means of the functional equation techniques of dynamic programming.

This is a good example of the fact that more sophisticated and more realistic versions of actual physical processes may be far easier to treat mathematically than the version which has been apparently softened up for mathematical treatment. This is only one of the reasons why it is important to explore many different mathematical formulations of a process before plunging into a sea of equations and a deluge of calculations.

18. Functional Equations

Introducing the function

$$(1) \qquad\qquad f_N(c) = \min_{y} \exp_{r_i} R_N$$

where exp denotes the expected value over the r_n, for a process of feedback type as described above, we can now write some equations of familiar form. We have

(2) $$f_1(c) = \min_{y_1} \exp_{r_1} h(c, y_1, r_1),$$

$$f_N(c) = \min_{y_1} \exp_{r_1} [h(c, y_1, r_1) + f_{N-1}(g(c, y_1, r_1))].$$

Let us suppose that the r_n have a common distribution function $dG(r)$. Then the relations take the form

(3) $$f_1(c) = \min_{y_1} \int h(c, y_1, r) \, dG(r),$$

$$f_N(c) = \min_{y_1} \int [h(c, y_1, r) + f_{N-1}(g(c, y_1, r))] \, dG(r).$$

It follows that apart from the introduction of some average values, the formalism is precisely that given in the deterministic case.

19. Computational Aspects

In order to reduce (18.3) to arithmetical form, we take the distribution for r to be discrete. Then in place of $dG(r)$, we have a set of probabilities $[p_1, p_2, \ldots, p_M]$, with p_i the probability that r assumes the value r_i.

In this case (3) has the form

(1) $$f_1(c) = \min_{y_1} \left[\sum_{j=1}^{M} p_j h(c, y_1, r_j) \right],$$

$$f_N(c) = \min_{y_1} \left[\sum_{j=1}^{M} p_j \{h(c, y_1, r_j) + f_{N-1}(g(c, y_1, r_j))\} \right].$$

It follows that the computational solution for stochastic control processes is almost precisely the same as for discrete processes, although some additional time will be required to perform the averaging operations involved in (1).

20. Correlation

Let us now suppose that the random vectors are not independent. Perhaps the simplest step in the direction of interaction is to suppose that the distribution for r_n depends upon the value of r_{n-1}, but upon no other of the r_i. At the nth stage, we must then add to the state vector the value of r_{n-1}. The vectors x_n and r_{n-1} then constitute the "state" of the system at time n. As we shall see when we come to the study of adaptive control processes, the concept of "state of a system" can be considerably extended beyond this.

Let $dG(r_n, r_{n-1})$ represent the distribution function for r_n, given the value of r_{n-1}. Then we may write

(1) $$f_N(c, r_0) = \min_{y} \exp_{r} R_N,$$

and in place of (18.3) we obtain the relations

$$(2) \qquad f_1(c, r_0) = \min_{y_1} \int h(c, y_1, r_1) \, dG(r_1, r_0),$$

$$f_N(c, r_0) = \min_{y_1} \int [h(c, y_1, r_1) + f_{N-1}(g(c, y_1, r_1))] \, dG(r_1, r_0).$$

The computational solution will be complicated by the introduction of correlation effects if r assumes a large number of values. If, however, r is a scalar taking on two or three different values, say ± 1, or $1, 0$, and -1, then correlation introduces little additional difficulty.

21. An Example Due to Aoki

Let us illustrate this discussion by means of a stochastic control process extensively treated by Aoki. We shall also consider the adaptive version of the process. Detailed numerical results will be found in papers by Aoki cited in the bibliography at the end of this chapter, and some particular cases are discussed in Chapter IX.

Suppose r is a scalar random variable, capable of assuming only the values ± 1. Let c_+ denote the value obtained from a choice of y_1 when $r = +1$ and c_- denote the value obtained when r is -1.

Consider a terminal control process in which we desire to minimize the expected value of a function ϕ of the terminal state x_N. As far as the statistics of r are concerned, let

$$(1) \qquad p = \text{the probability that } r = +1,$$

so that $(1 - p)$ is the probability that $r = -1$.

Then, if we write

$$(2) \qquad f_N(c) = \min \exp \phi(x_N),$$

we have the relations

$$(3) \qquad f_1(c) = \min_{y_1} [p\phi(c_+) + (1 - p)\phi(c_-)],$$

$$f_N(c) = \min_{y_1} [pf_{N-1}(c_+) + (1 - p)f_{N-1}(c_-)].$$

Subsequently, we shall contrast these results with those derived for a corresponding adaptive control process.

22. Games Against Nature

We have attempted to overcome ignorance of precise cause and effect by introducing random variables with known distributions. It is easy to conceive of situations where so little is known that we cannot even assume that the distributions are known. One way of handling this, and a m‑‑‑

pessimistic way indeed, is to suppose that the unknown effects will always occur in the worst possible way. In other words, we can assume that some opponent, which we rather unfairly call Nature, is choosing the probability distributions at each stage in such a way as to maximize our minimum deviation, or to minimize our maximum return.

Thus we conceive of a control process of this kind as a *game against nature*. The type of feedback control process we have treated in the previous pages becomes a multistage game which can be readily treated by the functional equation techniques we have repeatedly used. The reader interested in these matters will find detailed discussion in the references cited at the end of the chapter. We shall pursue a different approach here.

23. Adaptive Processes

So far we have not utilized the multistage character of feedback control to our advantage in our struggle to overcome the handicap of ignorance. Let us see if we can incorporate into our mathematical model the fact that we learn about the structure of the process as time goes on.

A process in which this occurs is called a learning or *adaptive process*. In order to formulate processes of this type in precise analytic terms, we extend the concept of state vector, which has been of such value to us, by the introduction of an *information pattern*.

This information pattern contains not only our exact knowledge, but also all the imprecise information we have gathered. Rather than consider general situations which lead to complexities of various types, let us treat the adaptive version of the terminal control process in §21.

We shall suppose that the probability p is not known initially. Instead, we shall suppose that we possess an a priori probability distribution for p, say $dH(p)$. Furthermore (and this is where the adaptive feature enters), we shall assume that we know how to revise this a priori estimate on the basis of the random effects that are observed.

It has been supposed that r, the random variable, assumes only two values, $+1$ or -1. If a $+1$ occurs, we agree to replace $dH(p)$ by the new distribution function

$$(1) \qquad dH_+(p) = \frac{p \, dH(p)}{\displaystyle\int_0^1 p \, dH(p)},$$

while if a -1 occurs, we replace $dH(p)$ by

$$(2) \qquad dH_-(p) = \frac{(1 - p) \, dH(p)}{\displaystyle\int_0^1 (1 - p) \, dH(p)}.$$

This transformation can be justified on various grounds, but it must be clearly understood that it is not the only transformation possible, or necessarily the best. It is, however, certainly a very plausible one, and quite simple.

The information pattern at each stage of the control process consists of the state vector c and the a priori distribution function $dH(p)$. Given this information pattern, the foregoing rule for adaptation, and the designated criterion function, we wish to determine an optimal adaptive control process.

24. Adaptive Feedback Control

Let us now consider the adaptive version of the process discussed in §21. We denote by $f_N(c, dH(p))$ the expected value of the funtion, $\phi(x_N)$, of the terminal state obtained using an optimal policy. The expected value is taken over the set of a priori distribution functions obtained as the process unfolds.

In place of the probability p, we have the expected probability

$$(1) \qquad \bar{p} = \int_0^1 p \, dH(p).$$

We then have

$$(2) \qquad f_1(c, dH(p)) = \min_y \, [\bar{p}\phi(c_+) + (1 - \bar{p})\phi(c_-)],$$

and, for $N \geq 2$,

$$(3) \quad f_N(c, dH(p)) = \min_y \left[\bar{p} f_{N-1}\left(c_+, p \, dH(p) \Big/ \int_0^1 p \, dH(p)\right) \right.$$

$$\left. + (1 - \bar{p}) f_{N-1}\left(c_-, (1 - p) \, dH(p) \Big/ \int_0^1 (1 - p) \, dH(p)\right) \right].$$

We see then that the same formalism used for deterministic and stochastic control processes can be used to treat adaptive control processes.

25. Computational Aspects

We have worried at considerable length in the foregoing pages about the problem of using functions of many variables for computational purposes. How then can we use functions of functions, of the type appearing in (24.3)? The answer is, of course, that we cannot directly use them. We must, in some fashion, reduce them to functions of a finite number of variables, and, indeed, to a small finite number of variables.

In some cases this can be done easily, in other cases only by use of quite advanced techniques, and, in still other cases no methods exist at the present time. In the present case, we can perform this essential reduction, due to the special structure of the process.

After $m + n$ stages in which $m + 1$'s and $n - 1$'s have been observed, the initial a priori distribution $dH(p)$ has been transformed into

(1)
$$\frac{p^m(1 - p)^n \, dH(p)}{\int_0^1 p^m(1 - p)^n \, dH(p)} \, .$$

Hence, the numbers m and n can be used in place of a distribution function. The information pattern can be replaced by the current state vector and the number of plus and minus ones which have been observed.

The recurrence relation in (24.3) can now be written

(2)
$$f_N(c, m, n) = \min_y [p_{mn} f_{N-1}(c_+, m + 1, n)$$
$$+ (1 - p_{mn}) f_{N-1}(c_-, m, n + 1)],$$

where

(3)
$$p_{mn} = \frac{\int_0^1 p^{m+1}(1 - p)^n \, dH(p)}{\int_0^1 p^m(1 - p)^n \, dH(p)} \, .$$

Although we now have a function of three variables, we face an "expanding grid," since (m, n) goes into $(m + 1, n)$ or $(m, n + 1)$. A discussion of various techniques that can be used to handle this situation will be found in the work of Aoki referred to in the bibliography at the end of the chapter.

26. Communication Theory and Information

A basic problem of our civilization is that of conveying information from one person to another, or from one device to another. Perhaps the most baffling and formidable part of the problem is that of specifying what we mean by *information*, and how we shall agree to measure it.

Fortunately, in some cases, there is a very simple way of resolving this difficulty. In place of attempting to treat information as "a smile of a Cheshire cat," we consider an actual physical process in which the information is being used to make decisions. The value of the information can then be gauged in terms of the effects of the decisions.

Thus the utility of information depends upon the use to which it is put— a most reasonable concept.

Let us view a communication process as composed of three separate elements, a source of signals, a communication channel which transforms the signals emitted by the source into other signals, and a receiver which interprets the signals for an observer. The observer makes decisions on the basis of the signals he receives. These decisions affect the state of another system S.

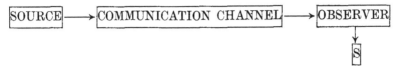

In order to reduce the foregoing to a precise mathematical problem, let us proceed as follows. At any particular time, the source emits one of a set of K different signals, which we denote by the symbols $i = 1, 2, \ldots, K$. The communication channel, due to various internal imperfections and external influences, converts an i-signal into a j-signal, $j = 1, 2, \ldots, M$, with probability p_{ij}. Initially we shall take this to be known.

The observer, upon receiving this signal is required to make a decision which affects the subsystem S. This decision is based upon his knowledge of the probability r_i with which the ith signal is transmitted, the aforementioned set of channel probabilities, p_{ij}, and the state vector of the system x.

The effect of a decision is to transform x into a stochastic vector z, whose distribution is determined by the emitted signal, the received signal, the present state of the system, and the decision.

27. Utility a Function of Use

In order to compare different designs, we must be able to evaluate the performance of a communication system. This evaluation is most naturally carried out in terms of its use. Although in some special cases it is possible to assign figures of merit to transmitters, receivers, or communication channels, without reference to the other components of the system, in general, in realistic and significant processes it is necessary to consider the entire system as one unit.

As we shall see, not only is this description of the problem useful in clarifying our ideas, but it also points us in the direction of the mathematical techniques we shall employ.

28. Dynamic Programming Formulation

Let us suppose that we are dealing with a multistage process at each stage of which a signal is emitted by the source, transformed by the channel, received by the observer, and made the basis for a decision. This process continues for N stages at the end of which the process is evaluated in terms of a prescribed function $\phi(z_N)$ of the final state z_N of the system S.

We introduce the sequence of functions defined by

(1) $f_N(x) =$ the expected value of $\phi(z_N)$ obtained from an N-stage process starting with S in the state x and using an optimal policy,

for $N = 1, 2, \ldots$, and all allowable x.

Let $dG(i, j, x, q; z)$ denote the distribution function for z, where i, j, and x are as above, and q denotes the choice of a decision.

Then, in these terms, we have

(2) $$f_1(x) = \max_q \left[\sum_{i=1}^{K} r_i \left\{ \sum_{j=1}^{M} p_{ij} \int_{-\infty}^{\infty} \phi(z) \, dG(i, j, x, q; z) \right\} \right]$$

and

(3) $$f_N(x) = \max_q \left[\sum_{i=1}^{K} r_i \left\{ \sum_{j=1}^{M} p_{ij} \int_{-\infty}^{\infty} f_{N-1}(z) \, dG(i, j, x, q; z) \right\} \right]$$

for $N = 2, 3, \ldots$.

29. An Adaptive Process

Let us now consider the following process—a relatively simple version of a situation in which we do not have complete information concerning the properties of the communication channel.

Assume that a source is emitting two types of signals, 0's and 1's. Passing through a communication channel, there is a probability p of correct transmission, i.e., that a 0 is transformed into a 0, or a 1 into a 1. The observer, upon receiving the signal, a 0 or 1, wagers a certain sum of money, anything from 0 to the total amount in his possession, that the signal he has received is the same as the signal sent. Let us suppose that there are even odds, a matter of no moment for this discussion. Assuming that this process is repeated N times, we wish to determine the policy which maximizes the expected value of a prescribed function, ϕ, of the final quantity of money.

There are many ways of formulating questions of this nature. We shall begin in the following fashion. Based on whatever information is available, we assume an a priori distribution for p, $dG(p)$, which is not a step-function with a single jump at p_0.

We shall further suppose that a successful wager revises our estimate for p from $dG(p)$ to $p \, dG(p) / \int_0^1 p \, dG$, and an unsuccessful one from $dG(p)$ to $(1 - p) \, dG / \int_0^1 (1 - p) \, dG$.

Under these assumptions we wish to determine the policy which maximizes the expected value of a prescribed function of the final quantity of money.

30. Dynamic Programming Formulation

Let x be the initial quantity of money available, and introduce the function

(1) $f_N(x; m, n)$ = the expected value of $\phi(z_N)$ where z_N is the quantity of money after N stages, starting with a quantity x and using an optimal policy, given the information that there have been m successful wagers and n unsuccessful wagers.

Let us introduce the notation

(2) $$q_{mn} = \frac{\int_0^1 p^{m+1}(1-p)^n \, dG}{\int_0^1 p^m(1-p)^n \, dG}, \quad q_{mn}' = 1 - q_{mn}.$$

We then obtain the following recurrence relations:

(3) $$f_N(x; m, n) = \max_{0 \le y \le x} [q_{mn} f_{N-1}(x+y; m+1, n)$$
$$+ q_{mn}' f_{N-1}(x-y; m, n+1)],$$

$N = 2, 3 \ldots$, with

(4) $$f_1(x; m, n) = \max_{0 \le y \le x} [q_{mn} \phi(x+y) + q_{mn}' \phi(x-y)].$$

Here y is the quantity wagered.

31. Power Law

The problem can be solved explicitly if $\phi(z) = az^b$, $a, b > 0$ or, a limiting case, $\phi(z) = \log z$. Let us consider the power function case first. We have, for $a = 1$,

(1) $$f_1(x; m, n) = \max_{0 \le y \le x} [q_{mn}(x+y)^b + q_{mn}'(x-y)^b]$$
$$= x^b \max_{0 \le y \le 1} [q_{mn}(1+y)^b + q_{mn}'(1-y)^b].$$

It is now easy to prove inductively that

(2) $$f_N(x; m, n) = c_N(m, n)x^b,$$

where the sequence $\{c_N(m, n)\}$ is determined by

(3) $$c_N(m, n) = \max_{0 \le y \le 1} [q_{mn} c_{N-1}(m+1, n)(1+y)^b$$
$$+ q_{mn}' c_{N-1}(m, n+1)(1-y)^b].$$

32. Logarithm Law

Similarly in the logarithmic case, we can show that

(1) $$f_N(x; m, n) = \log x + c_N(m, n)$$

where

(2) $$c_N(m, n) = q_{mn} c_{N-1}(m+1, n) + q_{mn}' c_{N-1}(m, n+1)$$
$$+ \max_{0 \le y \le 1} [q_{mn} \log(1+y) + q_{mn}' \log(1-y)].$$

Although it is not easy to evaluate $\{c_N(m, n)\}$ explicitly, it is easy to determine the optimal policy. We see that

(3) $$y = (2q_{mn} - 1)x, \quad \text{if } q_{mn} > \frac{1}{2},$$
$$= 0 \text{ otherwise.}$$

267

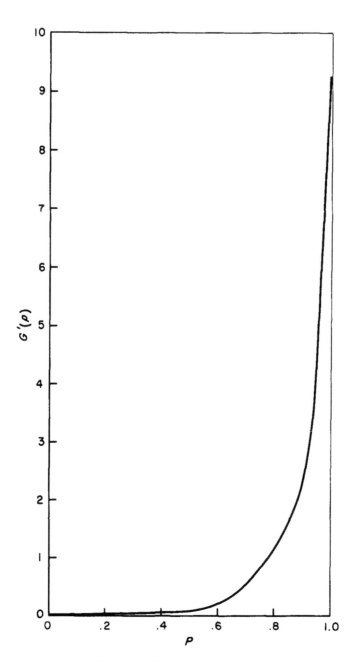

Figure 82. The initial density for p.

33. A Further Simplification, and Numerical Results

If the initial distribution is given in the form

$$(1) \qquad dG(p) = \frac{p^{a-1}(1-p)^{b-1}}{B(a, b)} \, dp, \quad a, b > 0,$$

where $B(a, b)$ is the beta-function, a choice which allows great flexibility in the form of the initial distribution curve, then we can write

$$(2) \qquad q_{mn} = \frac{\displaystyle\int_0^1 p^{m+a}(1-p)^{n+b-1} \, dp}{\displaystyle\int_0^1 p^{m+a-1}(1-p)^{n+b-1} \, dp}$$

$$= \frac{B(m+a+1, n+b)}{B(m+a, n+b)} = \frac{(m+a)}{(m+a)+(n+b)}.$$

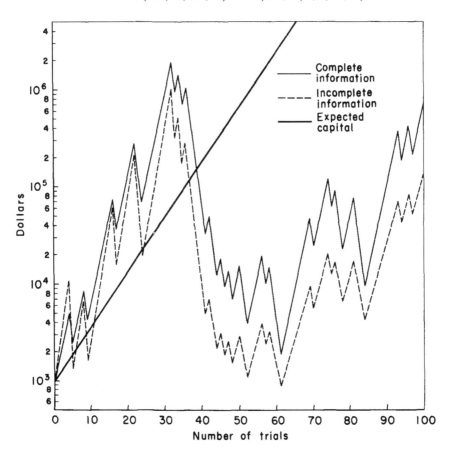

Figure 83

For the logarithmic case this implies that following m wins and n losses the optimal policy is to wager the fraction

(3)
$$\frac{(m + a) - (n + b)}{(m + a) + (n + b)},$$

provided that $q_{mn} > 1/2$, and nothing otherwise. This yields a particularly simple technique for altering the a priori probability of success from trial to trial.

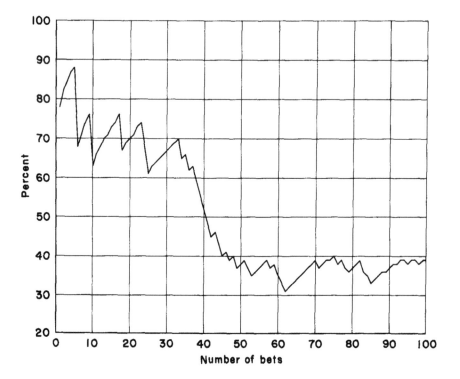

Figure 84

A numerical experiment was carried out for the values $a = 4$, $b = 1/2$, which yields a curve for $G'(p)$ having the shape shown in Fig. 82. It was assumed that the channel has an actual probability of correct transmission given by $p = .75$. Then, using a table of random numbers, sequences of 100 bets were run in two ways: first with knowledge that the underlying p is .75, so that the fraction $1/2$ of the available capital is bet at each opportunity, and then without this knowledge and using the above scheme.

The results are displayed in Fig. 83 from which the appropriateness of the policy may be judged. Figure 84 shows the fraction bet at each stage;

after 100 bets only 68 have been won, so approximately 40 per cent of the available capital is wagered which is still quite a bit below the optimal figure of 50 per cent.

Comments and Bibliography

§1. A detailed discussion of the feedback control concept may be found in

R. Bellman, *Adaptive Control Processes: A Guided Tour*, Princeton University Press, Princeton, New Jersey, 1961.

Extensive references to contemporary literature will be found there.

§2. For further discussion, and many references, see

H. Bateman, "On the control of an elastic fluid," *Bull. Amer. Math. Soc.*, vol. 51, 1945, pp. 601–646.

§4. See the monograph

R. Bellman and J. M. Danskin, *A Survey of the Mathematical Theory of Time Lag, Retarded Control and Hereditary Processes*, The RAND Corporation, Report R-256, 1954,

and the forthcoming book

R. Bellman and K. L. Cooke, *Differential-difference Equations*, Academic Press, Inc., New York, 1962.

§9. See

R. Bellman, I. Glicksberg, and O. Gross, "On the 'bang-bang' control problem," *Q. Appl. Math.*, vol. 14, 1956, pp. 11–18.

J. P. LaSalle, "On time-optimal control systems," *Proc. Nat. Acad. Sci. USA*, vol. 45, 1959, pp. 573–577,

where many further references may be found.

§10. See

M. Ash, R. Bellman, and R. Kalaba, "On control of reactor shutdown involving minimal xenon poisoning," *Nuclear Sci. and Engr.*, vol. 6, 1959, pp. 152–156.

§11. See

R. Bellman, "Notes on control processes—on the minimum of maximum deviation," *Q. Appl. Math.*, vol. 14, 1957, pp. 419—423.

§12. See

R. Bellman, "Functional equations and maximum range," *Q. Appl. Math.*, vol. 17, 1959, pp. 316–318.

§14. See

R. Bellman, "Some new techniques in the dynamic programming solution of variational problems," *Q. Appl. Math.*, vol. 16, 1958, pp. 295–305.

R. Bellman and R. Kalaba, "Reduction of dimensionality, dynamic programming, and control processes," *J. Basic Engr.*, March 1961, pp. 82–84.

C. W. Merriam III, "An optimization theory for feedback control system design," *Information and Control*, vol. 8, 1960, pp. 32–59.

A. T. Fuller, "Optimization of non-linear control systems with transient inputs," *J. Electronics and Control*, vol. 7, 1960, pp. 465–479.

E. L. Peterson, *Recent Soviet Progress in Adaptive and Optimum Control*, Technical Military Planning Operation, SP-121, Santa Barbara, California, 1961.

M. Aoki, "On optimal and sub-optimal policies in the choice of control forces for final-value systems," *1960 IRE National Convention Record*, part 4, pp. 15–21.

R. Pallu de la Barrier, *Controle des Systemes Dynamique*, Faculte des Science, University of Caen, 1961.

M. Aoki, *Dynamic Programming and Conditional Response Extrapolation*, Second Joint Automatic Control Conference, University of Colorado, 1961. Many further references will be found here.

J. Chanugam and G. E. P. Box, *Automatic Optimization of Continuous Processes*, Department of Math., Princeton University Technical Report No. 38, 1960.

L. D. Berkovitz, *A Variational Approach to Differential Games*, The RAND Corporation, Paper P-2205, 1961.

C. M. Kashmar, E. L. Peterson, F. X. Remond, *A General Approach to the Numerical Solution of Multi-dimensional Nonlinear Boundary-valued Problems*, General Electric Co., Santa Barbara, California, 1960.

R. E. Kalaba, *Computational Considerations for some Deterministic and Adaptive Control Processes*, The RAND Corporaton, Paper P-2210, 1961.

For many further results, see

R. Beckwith, *Analytic and Computational Aspects of Dynamic Programming Processes of High Dimension*, Ph.D. Thesis, Purdue University, 1959.

§16. See the book cited above for further discussion and references.

§21. In the following chapter, we present some computational results due to Aoki.

§22. See Chapter 9 of *Dynamic Programming* for a discussion of multistage processes involving two persons, and for further references.

§23–§33. We follow

R. Bellman, "A mathematical formulation of variational processes of adaptive type," *Fourth Berkeley Symposium on Mathematical Statistics and Probability*, to appear.

R. Bellman and R. Kalaba, "A mathematical theory of adaptive control processes," *Proc. Nat. Acad. Sci. USA*, vol. 45, 1959, pp. 1288–1290.

———, "On adaptive control processes," *IRE National Convention Record*, part 4, 1959, pp. 3–11.

———, "Dynamic programming and adaptive control processes: mathematical foundations," *IRE Trans. on Automatic Control*, vol. AC-5, 1960, pp. 5–10.

R. Bellman and R. Kalaba, "On communication processes involving learning and random duration," *IRE National Convention Record*, part 4, 1958, pp. 16–20.

See the book cited in §1 for further discussion and references, and

H. W. Grinnell, *On the Optimum Utilization of Correlated Data by Decision Schemes in Information Channels*, General Electric Company, RM-60-TM-65, Santa Barbara, California, 1960.

For a discussion of some of the ways in which dynamic programming can be applied to chemical process control, see

R. Aris, *The Optimal Design of Chemical Reactors*, Academic Press Inc., New York, 1961.

———, *The Optimum Conditions for a Single Reaction*, Department of Chem. Engr., Univ. of Minnesota, Minneapolis, Minn., unpublished.

———, *The Optimum Design of Adiabatic Reactors with Several Beds*, ibid.

———, *The Optimum Operating Conditions in Sequences of Stirred Tank Reactors*, ibid.

———, *Optimum Temperature Gradients in Tubular Reactors*, ibid.

R. Aris, D. F. Rudd, and N. R. Amundson, "On optimum cross-current extraction," *Chem. Engr. Science*, vol. 12, 1960, p. 88.

G. C. Brown and others, *Unit Operations*, John Wiley and Sons, Inc., New York, 1955.

J. S. Dranoff, L. C. Mitten, W. F. Stevens, L. A. Wanninger, Jr., *Application of Dynamic Programming to Countercurrent Flow Processes*, Technological Inst., Northwestern University, 1960.

S. Dreyfus, "Computational aspects of dynamic programming," *Operations Research*, vol. 5, 1957, pp. 409–415.

J. Happel, *Chemical Process Economics*, John Wiley and Sons, Inc., New York, 1958.

J. J. Hur, *Chemical Process Economics in Practice*, Reinhold, New York, 1956.

R. C. Johnson, W. E. Ball, et al., "Mathematics, computers, operations research, and statistics," *Indust. and Engr. Chem.*, vol. 52, 1960, pp. 359–367.

R. C. Johnson, S. M. Roberts, and C. A. Pfretzschner, *Optimization and its Importance to Chemical Engineering*, AIChE Ann. Meeting, San Francisco, California, December 7–9, 1959.

M. S. Peters, *Plant Design and Economics for Chemical Engineers*, McGraw-Hill Book Co., Inc., New York, 1958.

S. M. Roberts, *Stochastic Models for the Dynamic Programming Formulation of the Catalyst Replacement Problem*, Optimization Techniques in Chem. Engr. Symp., New York University, May 18, 1960.

C. E. Robinson and E. R. Gilliland, *Elements of Fractional Distillation*, McGraw-Hill Book Co., Inc., New York, 1950.

H. E. Schwayer, *Process Engineering Economics*, McGraw-Hill Book Co., Inc., New York, 1955.

R. E. Treybal, *Mass Transfer Operations*, McGraw-Hill Book Co., Inc., New York, 1955.

L. A. Wanninger, *The Application of Dynamic Programming to a Distillation Column*, M. S. Thesis, Northwestern University, August, 1960.

W. F. Gruter and B. H. Messikomer, *Systematische Ausbeuteberechnung fur isotherme Reaktoren im Falle zusammengestetzer Reaktionen*, CIBA, Basel, Switzerland, 1960.

———, "Optimalgesteze in der chemischen Reaktionstechnik," *Helvetica Chimica Acta*, vol. 44, pp. 285–298.

———, "Dynamische Programmierung in derchemischen Technik, die optimierung chemischer Reaktionsaubeuten," *Helvetica Chimica Acta*, vol. 43, pp. 2182–2186.

———, "Optimalgesetze in der chemischen Reaktortechnik," *Chimica*, vol. 14, 1960, pp. 263–264.

S. M. Roberts and J. D. Mahoney, *Dynamic Programming Control of a Batch Reaction*, 1961.

S. M. Roberts, *Dynamic Programming Formulation of the Catalyst Replacement Problem*, 1961.

A. Nomoto, *Dynamic Programming Approach to Brachistochronic Program of Batch Process*, Case Institute of Technology, 1959.

———, *Automatization of Dynamic Testing*, Case Institute of Technology, 1959.

For the study of the asymptotic behavior of control systems, see

D. S. Adorno, *The Asymptotic Theory of Control Systems—I: Stochastic and Deterministic Processes*, Jet Propulsion Lab., Technical Release 34–73, June 30, 1960.

M. Freimer, *A Dynamic Programming Approach to Adaptive Control Processes*, Lincoln Laboratory, No. 54–2, 1959.

———, *Topics in Dynamic Programming—II: Truncated Policies*, Lincoln Laboratory, No. 54G-0020, 1960.

For an intensive study of betting systems, see

L. E. Dubins and L. J. Savage, *How to Gamble if You Must* (to appear).

For a general discussion of the uses of computers, see

P. Armer, *Attitudes Towards Intelligent Machines*, The RAND Corporation, Paper P-2114, 1960.

CHAPTER IX

Computational Results for Feedback Control Processes

1. Introduction

At this point, we wish to present some numerical solutions of typical feedback control processes. One will involve a stochastic control problem connected with the Van der Pol equation

$$(1) \qquad x'' + \mu(x^2 - 1)x' + x = f(t) + g(t),$$

where $f(t)$ is a random disturbing force with known characteristics, and the other will pertain to a vacuum tube affected by random effects of unknown characteristics. The latter we will treat as an adaptive process.

The results of this chapter are based upon the work of M. Aoki.

2. A Discrete Stochastic Process

In place of the differential equation in (1.1), let us use the difference equations

$$(1) \quad \begin{aligned} x_{n+1} &= x_n + \Delta y_n, & x_0 &= c_1, \\ y_{n+1} &= y_n + \Delta[-\mu(x_n{}^2 - 1)y_n - x_n] + f_n + g_n, & y_0 &= c_2, \end{aligned}$$

$n = 0, 1, \ldots$. Here x_n represents the position of the system at time n and y_n the velocity, f_n is the random force, and g_n is the forcing term resulting from the control that is applied.

For the sake of simplicity, the random force is taken to be a stochastic quantity with the stationary distribution

$$(2) \qquad \begin{aligned} f_n &= b \text{ with probability } p, \\ &= -b \text{ with probability } 1 - p. \end{aligned}$$

Let us review briefly the salient facts about the homogeneous Van der Pol equation

$$(3) \qquad x'' + \mu(x^2 - 1)x' + x = 0,$$

with $\mu > 0$. The origin in the phase plane, $x = 0$, $x' = 0$, is an unstable equilibrium point. Consequently, a random perturbation of the system will force the system into periodic oscillation corresponding to the unique limit cycle.

We shall suppose that our aim is to prevent this oscillation and to maintain the system in the equilibrium position. Towards this goal, we shall choose the control variable g_n over $n = 0, 1, 2, \ldots, N$, in such a way as to minimize the expected value of the maximum deviation of the system from equilibrium position over the time-interval $0 \leq n \leq N$.

3. Recurrence Relations

Let us define, as usual, the function

(1) $f_N(x, y) = $ the expected maximum deviation of the point in the phase plane representing the control system from the origin in the N-stage control process, beginning with the initial state (x, y), using an optimal policy.

Measuring the deviation from equilibrium by means of the distance $\sqrt{x^2 + y^2}$, we obtain as in the preceding chapter the relations

(2) $f_1(x, y) = \sqrt{x^2 + y^2}$,

$$f_k(x, y) = \max \left(\sqrt{x^2 + y^2}, \min_g \left[pf_{k-1}(x_+, y_+) + (1 - p)f_{k-1}(x_-, y_-) \right] \right),$$

where we have set

(3)
$$x_+ = x_- = x + y\Delta,$$
$$y_+ = y + [-\mu(x^2 - 1)y - x]\Delta + b + g,$$
$$y_- = y_+ - 2b.$$

We shall use these equations to compute the sequence $\{f_k(x, y)\}$.

4. Choice of Parameters

The numerical results that follow were obtained for a range of values of p over $0 \leq p \leq 1$, and for

(1) $\mu = 1, \quad \Delta = .05, \quad -.25 \leq x, y \leq .25, \quad b = .0625.$

The choice of the control variable g was constrained by the following:

(2)
$$g = \pm 9/128 \quad \text{if } f_k(x, y) < .2,$$
$$g = \pm 1/4 \quad \text{if } f_k(x, y) \geq .2.$$

The sensitivity analysis of $f_k(x, y)$ as a function of p is simplified by the following considerations. Supposing, without loss of generality, that the optimal control is such that $g(-x, -y) = -g(x, y)$, we have

(3) $(-x)_+ = (-x)_- = (-x) + (-y)\Delta = -(x_+) = -(x_-),$

$(-y)_+ = -y + [-\mu(x^2 - 1)(-y) - (-x)]\Delta + b + g = -(y_-),$

$(-y)_- = -y + [-\mu(x^2 - 1)(-y) - (-x)]\Delta - b + g = -(y_+).$

It follows, inductively, that

(4) $$f_k(x, y; p) = f_k(-x, -y, (1 - p)).$$

Hence if we know the optimal policy for p for all x, y in the phase plane, we know the optimal policy for $(1 - p)$. This reduces by one half the problem of determining the dependence upon p.

In limiting the range of x and y to the rectangle $-1/4 \leq x, y \leq 1/4$, we create the problem of specifying suitable conditions for the sequence $\{f_k(x, y)\}$ at the boundary and beyond. There are several different ways of meeting this situation. One way is to set

$$
\begin{aligned}
(5) \qquad f_k(x, y) &= f_k(\tfrac{1}{4}, y), & x &\geq \tfrac{1}{4}, & -\tfrac{1}{4} &\leq y \leq \tfrac{1}{4}, \\
&= f_k(-\tfrac{1}{4}, y), & x &\leq -\tfrac{1}{4}, & -\tfrac{1}{4} &\leq y \leq \tfrac{1}{4}, \\
&= f_k(x, \tfrac{1}{4}), & y &\geq \tfrac{1}{4}, & -\tfrac{1}{4} &\leq x \leq \tfrac{1}{4}, \\
&= f_k(x, -\tfrac{1}{4}), & y &\leq -\tfrac{1}{4}, & -\tfrac{1}{4} &\leq x \leq \tfrac{1}{4}.
\end{aligned}
$$

Another way is to choose the control variable in such a way that the system is always forced into the region $-1/4 \leq (x, y) \leq 1/4$ in the phase plane, whenever it strays outside of it. We shall follow the first method in the calculations which follow.

5. Discussion of Results

Let us henceforth write

$$
(1) \qquad f_k(x, y) \equiv f_k(x, y, p), \quad k = 1, 2, \ldots,
$$

and indicate the specific dependence upon p. It is clear that f_k is non-decreasing as k increases.

In the neighborhood of the origin, it is reasonable to suppose that

$$
(2) \qquad \sqrt{x^2 + y^2} \leq p f_k(x_+, y_+, p) + (1 - p) f_k(x_-, y_-, p).
$$

This is seen to be true in the computational results which follow. As a matter of fact, it is seen that in a narrow strip including the x-axis this result holds.

It is of interest to plot the set of (x, y)-values of equal maximum expected deviation, which is the curve in the (x, y)-plane determined by the equation

$$
(3) \qquad f_k(x, y, p) = c,
$$

for fixed k and p. Typical curves are shown in Figs. 85 and 86.

For sufficiently large $|y|$, the expression $\sqrt{x^2 + y^2}$ is seen to dominate $f_k(x, y, p)$. This is indicated in Figs. 85 and 86 by the fact that for large y, part of the curves are seen to be parts of $\sqrt{x^2 + y^2} = c$.

This can also be shown (Figs. 87 and 88) by taking a cross-section of the function $f_k(x, y, p)$ for constant k, p, and x.

6. A Final Value Problem

As the second problem we wish to treat numerically, let us take a discrete control process governed by the scalar equation

(1) $$x_{n+1} = ax_n + f_n + g_n, \qquad x_0 = c,$$

where f_n is a random forcing term, and g_n is the control variable. We are interested in the case where the distribution function for f_n is not completely known.

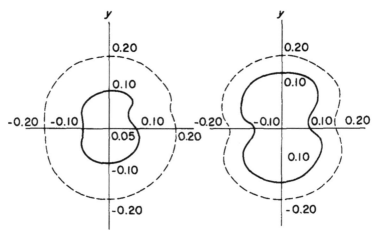

$n = 1.0$
$p = 0.0$
$f_n(x, y, p) = 0.1$ (inner curve)
$f_n(x, y, p) = 0.2$ (outer curve)
$-0.25 \leq x; y \leq 0.25$

$n = 1.0$
$p = 0.5$
$f_n(x, y, p) = 0.15$ (inner curve)
$f_n(x, y, p) = 0.25$ (outer curve)
$-0.25 \leq x; y \leq 0.25$

Figure 85. Contours of equal $f_n(x, y, p)$.

We shall make the following assumptions:

(2) (a) f_n is allowed to assume only two values, $\pm b$, with respective probabilities p and $(1 - p)$, where p is not known.

(b) g_n is allowed to assume only two values, $\pm m$, with $m \geq b$.

(c) The purpose of the process is to minimize the expected value of x_N^2.

7. Stochastic Version

If p is taken as known, we obtain the functional equation

(1) $$h_k(x) = \min_{g = \pm m} [ph_{k-1}(x_+) + (1 - p)h_{k-1}(x_-)], \quad k \geq 2,$$

$$h_1(x) = \min_{g = \pm m} [px_+^2 + (1 - p)x_-^2],$$

278

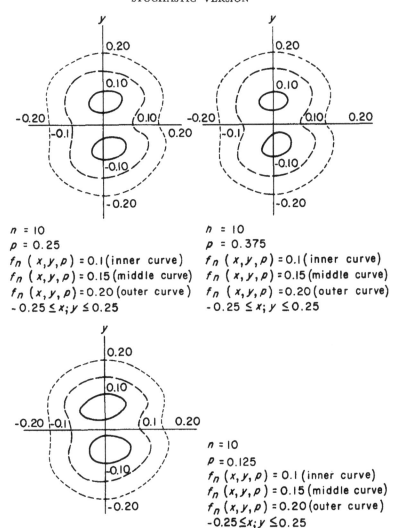

Figure 86. Contours of equal $f_n(x, y, p)$.

for the function $h_N(x) = \min \exp x_N{}^2$. Here

(2) $$x_+ = ax + b + g, \qquad x_- = ax - b + g.$$

This equation can be used to obtain a great deal of information concerning the analytic nature of the optimal policy. It is important to discuss this sequence of functions, $\{h_N(x)\}$, since it is intuitively clear that as the number of trials increases, the adaptive case will approximate more and more closely the stochastic case in which p has been estimated on the basis of the observed frequency of $\pm b$'s.

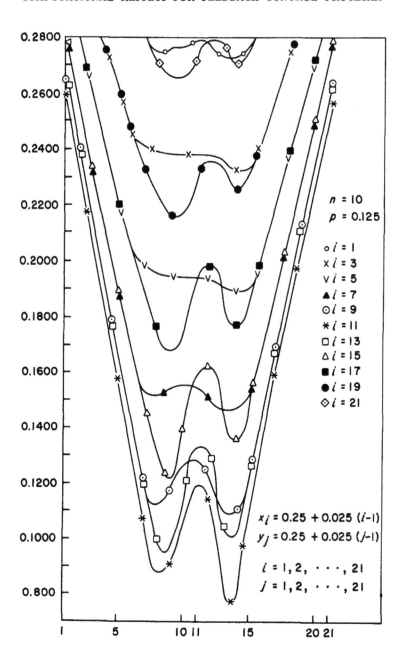

Figure 87. Dependence of $f_n(x, y, p)$ on Y.

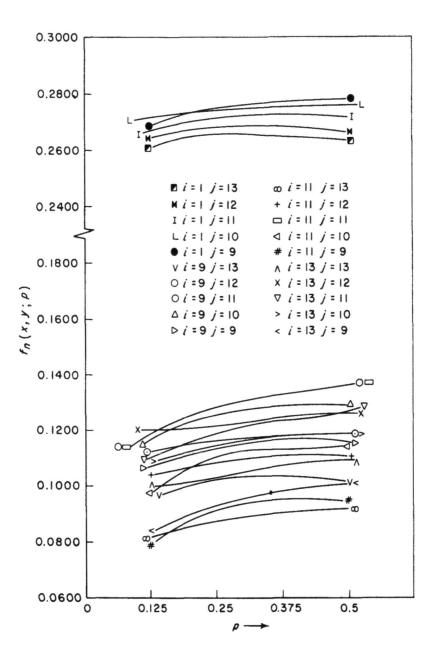

Figure 88. Dependence of $f_n(x, y, p)$ on P.

8. Adaptive Process

Let us now consider a simple adaptive process in the situation where the unknown probability p is either p_1 or p_2, $p_1 > p_2$, with the a priori probability

(1)
$$\Pr(p = p_1) = z.$$

Our assumption will now be that if $f = +b$ is observed, the a posteriori probability will be

(2)
$$z_+ = \frac{zp_1}{zp_1 + (1 - z)p_2},$$

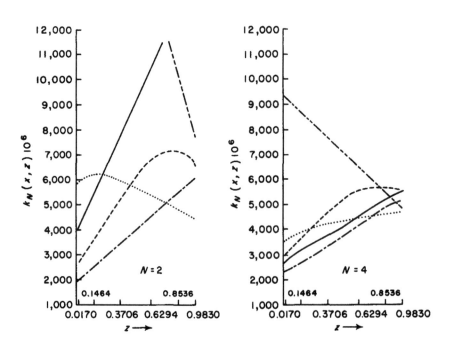

Figure 89. The criterion function, $k_n(x, z)$, as the function of the a priori probability z.

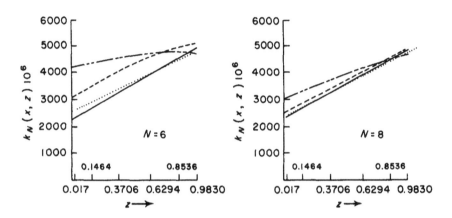

———— $x = 0.25$ $a = 7/8$
— — — $x = -0$ $b = 1/16$
· · · · · · $x = -0.125$ $m = 9/128$
— ·· — $x = -0.25$ $-0.25 \leq x \leq 0.25$

Figure 90. The criterion function, $k_n(x, z)$, as the function of the a priori probability z.

and if $f = -b$, the a posteriori probability will be taken to be

(3)
$$z_- = \frac{z(1 - p_1)}{z(1 - p_1) + (1 - z)(1 - p_2)}.$$

Introducing the functions

(4)
$$k_N(x, z) = \min \exp x_N{}^2,$$

we obtain the functional equations

(5)
$$k_1(x, z) = \min_{g_1} \{[zp_1 + (1 - z)p_2]x_+{}^2$$
$$+ [z(1 - p_1) + (1 - z)(1 - p_2)]x_-{}^2\},$$
$$k_N(x, z) = \min_{g_N} \{[zp_1 + (1 - z)p_2]k_{N-1}(x_+, z_+)$$
$$+ [z(1 - p_1) + (1 - z)(1 - p_2)]k_{N-1}(x_-, z_-)\}.$$

The graphs in Figs. 89 and 90 show the dependence of $k_n(x, z)$ upon z

for various values of N and x. The particular values used for the parameters were

$$(6) \qquad a = \tfrac{7}{8}, \qquad b = \tfrac{1}{16}, \qquad m = \tfrac{9}{128},$$

and the x-range was taken to be $-1/4 \leq x \leq 1/4$. The same technique as before was used to keep the x-interval fixed from stage to stage.

Comments and Bibliography

The material contained in this chapter is taken from the Ph.D. Thesis of Masanao Aoki, Department of Engineering, University of California at Los Angeles, 1960.

CHAPTER X

Linear Equations and Quadratic Criteria

1. Introduction

In the preceding chapters we have focussed our attention in the main upon the derivation of fairly straightforward computational algorithms. Our goal was to obtain methods which would provide numerical solutions regardless of the particular structural features of the individual problems. However, as we have constantly emphasized in the foregoing pages, dimensionality difficulties stymie direct approaches in the majority of cases. Consequently, a certain amount of ingenuity is required. We must combine the specific analytic properties of the process under consideration with the functional equation approach in order to derive feasible techniques, or quicker and more efficient methods.

As we shall see, in a number of cases where the equations describing the process are *linear* and the criterion functions are *quadratic*, we can arrive at computational procedures which are far superior to those yielded by the usual classical techniques. This is the case despite the fact that the classical variational equations are linear as contrasted with the nonlinear equations obtained from dynamic programming.

These results are, of course, important in their own right. In addition, however, they serve as vital steps in a chain of successive approximations to the solution of more complex problems. Finally, the same methods are applicable to stochastic and adaptive control processes, where the conventional methods do not seem at all useful.

In much of this chapter we shall merely sketch the results, referring the reader to original sources for more detailed accounts.

2. A Smoothing Problem

In order to illustrate in simple terms the analytic technique we shall use repeatedly in different contexts, let us return to a "smoothing" process we discussed in Chapter III.

Let us suppose that we wish to determine the values of the x_i which minimize the function

$$(1) \qquad Q(x_1, x_2, \ldots, x_N) = a_1(x_1 - c)^2 + a_2(x_2 - x_1)^2$$
$$+ \cdots + a_N(x_N - x_{N-1})^2$$
$$+ b_1 x_1{}^2 + b_2 x_2{}^2 + \cdots + b_N x_N{}^2.$$

Proceeding in the accustomed fashion, we set

$$(2) \qquad f_k(c) = \min_x \left[a_k(x_k - c)^2 + \cdots + a_N(x_N - x_{N-1})^2 \right.$$
$$\left. + b_k x_k^2 + \cdots + b_N x_N^2 \right],$$

for $k = 1, 2, \ldots, N$. Then, as before,

$$(3) \qquad f_N(c) = \min_{x_N} \left[a_N(x_N - c)^2 + b_N x_N^2 \right],$$

and for $k = 1, 2, \ldots, N - 1$, we have the recurrence relation

$$(4) \qquad f_k(c) = \min_{x_k} \left[a_k(x_k - c)^2 + b_k x_k^2 + f_{k+1}(x_k) \right].$$

Thus far we have not added anything new to our previous discussion. Let us now use the important fact that each of the functions $f_1(c)$, $f_2(c)$, $\ldots$, $f_N(c)$ is a quadratic function of c. Specifically,

$$(5) \qquad f_k(c) = u_k c^2, \qquad k = 1, 2, \ldots, N,$$

where u_k is independent of c. Perhaps the simplest way to establish this is inductively. The result is clearly true for $k = N$, and the relation in (4) shows that this structure perpetuates.

Once we have obtained the result in (5), it is easy to obtain a recurrence relation connecting u_k and u_{k+1}. Combining (4) and (5), we obtain the equation

$$(6) \qquad u_k c^2 = \min_{x_k} \left[a_k(x_k - c)^2 + b_k x_k^2 + u_{k+1} x_k^2 \right].$$

The minimizing value of x_k is easily seen to be

$$(7) \qquad x_k = a_k c / (a_k + b_k + u_{k+1}).$$

Substituting this value in (6), we derive the simple recurrence relation

$$(8) \qquad u_k = \frac{a_k b_k + a_k u_{k+1}}{a_k + b_k + u_{k+1}}, \qquad k = 1, 2, \ldots, N - 1,$$

with

$$(9) \qquad u_N = \frac{a_N b_N}{a_N + b_N}.$$

Having determined the sequence $\{u_k\}$ in this way, we obtain the minimizing values of the x_k from (7).

3. Discussion

The usual method of calculus applied to the minimization problem of the previous section leads to the system of simultaneous linear equations

$$(1) \qquad a_1(x_1 - c) - a_2(x_2 - x_1) + b_1 x_1 = 0,$$

.

.

.

$$a_k(x_k - x_{k-1}) - a_{k+1}(x_{k+1} - x_k) + b_k x_k = 0,$$

.

.

.

$$a_N(x_N - x_{N-1}) + b_N x_N = 0.$$

Although the time required to solve a system of N simultaneous linear equations is usually proportional to N^2, at least, the special form of the matrix associated with the linear system appearing above permits one to use special techniques which make the time proportional to N. In this case, then, there is no particular advantage to using the functional equation approach if only a numerical solution is desired.

4. A More Complex Smoothing Problem

Let us now suppose that we wish to minimize the function

$$(1) \qquad Q(x_1, x_2, \ldots, x_N) = a_1(x_1 - c_1)^2 + a_2(x_2 - 2x_1 + c_2)^2$$
$$+ a_3(x_3 - 2x_2 + x_1)^2 + \cdots$$
$$+ b_1 x_1^2 + b_2 x_2^2 + \cdots + b_N x_N^2.$$

Introducing the sequence of functions

$$(2) \qquad f_k(c_1, c_2) = \min_x [a_k(x_k - c_1)^2 + a_{k+1}(x_{k+1} - 2x_k + c_2)^2$$
$$+ \cdots + b_k x_k^2 + b_{k+1} x_{k+1}^2 + \cdots + b_N x_N^2],$$

we obtain the recurrence relation

$$(3) \qquad f_k(c_1, c_2) = \min_{x_k} [a_k(x_k - c_1)^2 + b_k x_k^2 + f_{k+1}(2x_k - c_2, x_k)],$$

$k = 1, 2, \ldots, N - 2$, with

$$(4) \quad f_{N-1}(c_1, c_2) = \min_{x_{N-1}, x_N} [a_{N-1}(x_{N-1} - c_1)^2 + a_N(x_N - 2x_{N-1} + c_2)^2$$
$$+ b_{N-1} x_{N-1}^2 + b_N x_N^2].$$

It is now simple to show inductively that

$$(5) \quad f_k(c_1, c_2) = u_k c_1^2 + 2v_k c_1 c_2 + w_k c_2^2, \qquad k = 1, 2, \ldots, N - 1.$$

Once this result has been obtained it is easy to obtain a recurrence relation connecting the triple $[u_k, v_k, w_k]$ with $[u_{k+1}, v_{k+1}, w_{k+1}]$, as above.

5. Slightly Intertwined Systems

Let us now consider a generalization 'of the linear system appearing in (3.1).

$$
\begin{aligned}
a_{11}x_1 + a_{12}x_2 + a_{13}x_3 &= c_1, \\
a_{21}x_1 + a_{22}x_2 + a_{23}x_3 &= c_2, \\
a_{31}x_1 + a_{32}x_2 + a_{33}x_3 + b_1x_4 &= c_3, \\
b_1x_3 + a_{44}x_4 + a_{45}x_5 + a_{46}x_6 &= c_4, \\
a_{54}x_4 + a_{55}x_5 + a_{56}x_6 &= c_5, \\
a_{64}x_4 + a_{65}x_5 + a_{66}x_6 + b_2x_7 &= c_6,
\end{aligned}
\tag{1}
$$

.

.

.

$$
\begin{aligned}
b_{N-1}x_{3N-3} + a_{3N-2,\,3N-2}x_{3N-2} + a_{3N-2,\,3N-1}x_{3N-1} + a_{3N-2,\,3N}x_{3N} &= c_{3N-2}, \\
a_{3N-1,\,3N-2}x_{3N-2} + a_{3N-1,\,3N-1}x_{3N-1} + a_{3N-1,\,3N}x_{3N} &= c_{3N-1}, \\
a_{3N,\,3N-2}x_{3N-2} + a_{3N,\,3N-1}x_{3N-1} + a_{3N,\,3N}x_{3N} &= c_{3N}.
\end{aligned}
$$

Systems of this type arise in the treatment of economic and engineering systems in which there is only a small amount of coupling between different subsystems.

Let us now employ a small amount of matrix theory—essentially, only the notation. Introduce the matrices

$$
A_k = (a_{i+3k-3,\,j+3k-2}), \qquad i, j = 1, 2, 3,
\tag{2}
$$

and the vectors

$$
x^k = \begin{pmatrix} x_{3k-2} \\ x_{3k-1} \\ x_{3k} \end{pmatrix}, \quad
c^k = \begin{pmatrix} c_{3k-2} \\ c_{3k-1} \\ c_{3k} \end{pmatrix}.
\tag{3}
$$

Suppose that the matrix associated with the linear system in (1) is positive definite. Then the solution of the linear system is the solution to the problem of determining the minimum of the inhomogeneous quadratic form

$$
\begin{aligned}
(x^1, A_1x^1) + (x^2, A_2x^2) + \cdots + (x^N, A_Nx^N) \\
- 2(c^1, x^1) - 2(c^2, x^2) - \cdots - 2(c^N, x^N) \\
+ 2b_1x_3x_4 + 2b_2x_6x_7 + \cdots + 2b_{N-1}x_{3N-3}x_{3N-2}.
\end{aligned}
\tag{4}
$$

Introduce the sequence of functions $\{f_N(z)\}$, $-\infty < z < \infty$, $N = 1, 2, \ldots$, defined by the relation

$$
f_N(z) = \min_{x_i} \left[\sum_{i=1}^{N} (x^i, A_ix^i) - 2 \sum_{i=1}^{N} (c^i, x^i) \right.
$$
$$
\left. + 2 \sum_{i=1}^{N-1} b_ix_{1+3i}x_{3i} + 2zx_{3N} \right].
\tag{5}
$$

Then we obtain the recurrence relation

(6)
$$f_N(z) = \min_{R_N} [(x^N, A_N x^N) + 2zx_{3N} - 2(c^N, x^N) + f_{N-1}(b_{N-1}x_{3N-2})],$$

where R_N is the three-dimensional region $-\infty < x_{3N}, x_{3N-1}, x_{3N-2} < \infty$.

It is easy to establish inductively that each function $f_N(z)$ is a quadratic function of z:

(7)
$$f_N(z) = u_N + 2v_N z + w_N z^2.$$

Using (6), we readily obtain recurrence relations for the u_k, v_k, and w_k similar to those derived above.

There is no difficulty in using the same techniques to handle the general case where each matrix A_i is of a different dimension.

6. Characteristic Values

The problem of determining nontrivial solutions of the equation

(1)
$$u'' + \lambda\phi(t)u = 0, \quad u(0) = u(1) = 0,$$

can be considered, under reasonable assumptions concerning $\phi(t)$, to be the same as that of determining the relative minima of the functional

(2)
$$J(u) = \int_0^1 u'^2 \, dt$$

subject to the constraints

(3) (a)
$$\int_0^1 \phi(t)u^2 \, dt = 1,$$

(b)
$$u(0) = u(1) = 0.$$

Let us consider only the problem of determining the absolute minimum, the smallest characteristic value of the foregoing Sturm-Liouville problem.

A discrete version of the variational question posed above is that of minimizing the quadratic form

(4)
$$Q(x_1, x_2, \ldots, x_N) = (x_1 - c)^2 + (x_2 - x_1)^2 + \cdots + (x_N - x_{N-1})^2 + x_N^2$$

subject to the constraint

·(5)
$$\sum_{i=1}^N \phi_i x_i^2 = 1.$$

Let us suppose that $0 < a \le \phi_i \le b < \infty$ for all i, and introduce the sequence of functions $\{f_k(c)\}$, $k = 1, 2, \ldots, N - 1$, defined by the relation

(6)
$$f_k(c) = \min_x [(x_k - c)^2 + (x_{k+1} - x_k)^2 + \cdots$$
$$+ (x_N - x_{N-1})^2 + x_N^2],$$

289

where the x_k are subject to the relation

(7)
$$\sum_{i=k}^{N} \phi_k x_k^2 = 1.$$

It is easily seen that

(8)
$$f_{N-1}(c) = \min_{x_{N-1}, x_N} [(x_{N-1} - c)^2 + x_N^2],$$

where

(9)
$$\phi_{N-1} x_{N-1}^2 + \phi_N x_N^2 = 1,$$

and

(10)
$$f_k(c) = \min_{x_k} \left[(x_k - c)^2 + (1 - \phi_k x_k^2)^{1/2} f_{k+1} \left(\frac{x_k}{(1 - \phi_k x_k^2)^{1/2}} \right) \right],$$

where $\phi_k x_k^2 \leq 1$.

The value $f_1(0)$ is an approximation to the lowest characteristic value of the Sturm-Liouville equation.

7. Stochastic Smoothing

Let us now discuss briefly a stochastic version of the smoothing problem discussed in §2. Suppose that we wish to minimize the expected value of the function

(1)
$$Q(x, y) = \sum_{i=1}^{N} (a_i y_i^2 + b_i x_i^2),$$

where

(2)
$$x_{i+1} = d_i x_i + y_i + r_i, \quad i = 0, 1, 2, \ldots, N - 1.$$

Here the r_i are independent random variables with given distributions. Writing, for $k = 1, 2, \ldots, N - 1$,

(3)
$$f_k(c) = \min \exp \left[\sum_{i=k}^{N} (a_i y_i^2 + b_i x_i^2) \right],$$

where $x_{k-1} = c$, we have

(4)
$$f_k(c) = \min_{y_k} \left[a_k y_k^2 + b_k c^2 + \int f_{k+1}(d_k c + y_k + r_k) \, dG_k(r_k) \right],$$

for $k = 1, 2, \ldots, N$, with

(5)
$$f_N(c) = b_N c^2.$$

It is easy to show inductively that each $f_k(c)$ is a quadratic function of c,

(6)
$$f_k(c) = u_k + 2v_k c + w_k c^2,$$

and then to derive recurrence relations similar to those obtained in §2.

8. Linear Control Processes with Quadratic Criteria— Deterministic Case

Consider the problem of determining the control vector $v(t)$ which minimizes the quadratic functional

$$(1) \qquad J(v) = \lambda \int_0^T v^2 \, dt + u(T)^2,$$

where u and v are connected by the relation

$$(2) \qquad \frac{du}{dt} = au + v, \quad u(0) = c.$$

Let us discuss the discrete version. We wish to minimize the quadratic form

$$(3) \qquad Q_N(v) = u_N{}^2 + \lambda \sum_{i=0}^{N-1} v_i{}^2$$

over all v_k where u_k and v_k are connected by the relation

$$(4) \qquad u_{k+1} = au_k + v_k, \quad k = 0, 1, \ldots, N-1, \quad u_0 = c.$$

Writing

$$(5) \qquad f_N(c) = \min_v Q_N(v),$$

we have

$$(6) \qquad f_1(c) = \min_{v_0} [(ac + v_0)^2 + \lambda v_0{}^2],$$

and for $N = 2, 3, \ldots,$

$$(7) \qquad f_N(c) = \min_{v_0} [\lambda v_0{}^2 + f_{N-1}(ac + v_0)].$$

Using the fact that each function in the sequence $\{f_k(c)\}$ is a quadratic function of c, $f_k(c) = u_k + 2v_k c + w_k c^2$, we readily obtain recurrence relations for the u_k, v_k, and w_k.

9. Stochastic Case

Similarly, if

$$(1) \qquad u_{k+1} = au_k + v_k + r_k, \quad u_0 = c,$$

where $\{r_k\}$ is a sequence of random variables with given distributions, we consider the problem of minimizing the expected value of

$$(2) \qquad Q_N(v) = u_N{}^2 + \lambda \sum_{i=0}^{N-1} v_i{}^2.$$

Writing

$$(3) \qquad f_N(c) = \min Q_N(v),$$

where we now minimize over all feedback control policies, it follows, as before, that

$$(4) \qquad f_N(c) = \min_{v_0} \left[\lambda v_0^2 + \int f_{N-1}(ac + v_0 + r_0) \, dG(r_0) \right],$$

where $dG(r)$ is the distribution function for r_0.

It is easy to see inductively that each element of the sequence $\{f_k(c)\}$ is a quadratic in c,

$$(5) \qquad f_k(c) = u_k + 2v_k c + w_k c^2,$$

and once again to derive recurrence relations for the coefficients.

Similar results can be obtained for the adaptive case. References may be found at the end of the chapter.

10. Reduction in Dimensionality

We pointed out in a previous chapter that the problem of minimizing $g(x_1(T), x_2(T), \ldots, x_k(T))$ over all $y(t)$, where

$$(1) \qquad \frac{dx}{dt} = Ax + y, \quad x(0) = c,$$

can be treated in terms of functions of k variables, regardless of the dimension of x. Let us now point out that we can do very much better if g is a quadratic function of its arguments.

The solution of (1) has the form

$$(2) \qquad x = e^{At}c + \int_0^t e^{A(t-s)} y(s) \, ds.$$

Hence the problem is that of minimizing

$$(3) \qquad g\left(c_1' + \int_0^T \left[\sum_{j=1}^N p_{1j}(s) y_j(s) \right] ds, \ldots, c_k' + \int_0^T \left[\sum_{j=1}^N p_{kj}(s) y_j(s) \right] ds \right)$$

where the constants c_i' and the functions $p_{ij}(s)$ are known.

Introducing the new functions

$$(4) \qquad f(c_1', c_2', \ldots, c_k', T) = \min_{\{y\}} g,$$

it is easy to see that f is a quadratic function of the c_i'. If we allow T to be continuous, the functional equation of (14.9) of Chapter VIII yields a set of differential equations for the coefficients $g_{ij}(T)$, in the expression

$$(5) \qquad f = \sum_{i, j=1}^k g_{ij}(T) c_i' c_j'.$$

If we take T to be discrete, we obtain a set of nonlinear recurrence relations.

11. Linear Prediction Theory

The treatment of linear prediction theory due to Kolmogorov and Wiener leads to the problem of minimizing the quadratic form

$$
(1) \qquad D_{N,M} = \sum_{k=0}^{N} (b_k - \sum_{\ell=0}^{M} u_\ell a_{k-\ell}^2)^2
$$

over the real quantities u_k, where the quantities a_k and b_k are given real numbers. We suppose that $a_{-r} = 0$, $r \geq 1$, and that $N > M$. Since a direct approach leads to the problem of solving a system of linear equations, we wish to present a method based upon functional equation techniques which circumvents this.

Following this, we shall consider the minimization of the quadratic form

$$
(2) \qquad \exp_r \left\{ \sum_{k=0}^{N} \left(b_k + r_k - \sum_{\ell=0}^{M} u_\ell a_{k-\ell} \right)^2 \right\}
$$

where the r_k are first independent random variables, then correlated random variables where the distribution of r_k depends only upon r_{k-1}, and then random variables with unknown distributions to be determined on the basis of observation.

12. Deterministic Case

The minimum of $D_{N,M}$ over the u_k is a quadratic form in the b_k,

$$
(1) \qquad \min_u D_{N,M} = (b, Q_{N,M} b),
$$

where $Q_{N,M}$ is a symmetric nonnegative definite $(N+1) \times (N+1)$ matrix defined for $N > M \geq 0$, and b is the $(N+1)$ dimensional column vector whose components are $b_0, b_1, \ldots, b_N$. Write

$$
(2) \quad \min_u D_{N,M} = \min_{[u_0, u_1, \ldots, u_N]} [(b_0 - u_0 a_0)^2 + (b_1 - u_0 a_1 - u_1 a_0)^2
$$
$$
+ \cdots + (b_N - u_0 a_N - u_1 a_{N-1} - \cdots - u_M a_0)^2].
$$

If u_0 is chosen, we see that we face an analogous problem in the determination of $u_1, u_2, \ldots, u_M$ with

(a) $\qquad b_i$ replaced by $b_i - u_0 a_i$, $\qquad i = 1, 2, \ldots, N$,

(3) (b) $\qquad M$ replaced by $M - 1$,

(c) $\qquad N + 1$ replaced by N.

Hence in terms of the function defined by (1), we have

$$
(4) \qquad (b, Q_{N,M} b) = \min_{u_0} [(b_0 - u_0 a_0)^2
$$
$$
+ (b' - u_0 a', Q_{N-1, M-1}(b' - u_0 a'))],
$$

where b' and a' are now $N1$-dimensional vectors with components $a_1, a_2, \ldots, a_N, b_1, b_2, \ldots, b_N$, respectively. Set

$$(5) \qquad P_{N,M} = \begin{pmatrix} 1 & 0 \\ 0 & Q_{N-1,M-1} \end{pmatrix}.$$

Then (4) takes the form

$$(6) \qquad (b, Q_{N,M}b) = \min_{u_0} \; (b - u_0 a, \; P_{N,M}(b - u_0 a)),$$

and it is easy to see that

$$(7) \qquad (b, Q_{N,M}b) = \frac{(b, P_{N,M}a)(a, P_{N,M}a) - (a, P_{N,M}b)^2}{(a, P_{N,M}a)},$$

with the minimizing choice of u_0 given by

$$(8) \qquad u_0 = \frac{(a, P_{N,M}b)}{(a, P_{N,M}a)}.$$

In this way, we obtain a recurrence relation connecting $Q_{N,M}$ with $Q_{N-1,M-1}$. Iterating this relation M times, we reach the problem of minimizing the form

$$(9) \qquad \sum_{k=0}^{N-M} (b_k - u_0 a_k)^2$$

over u_0, a problem with a very simple solution. Starting with this solution, we obtain the solution of the original problem by means of the recurrence relation of (6).

13. Stochastic Case

Consider now the problem of determining the minimum of (11.2) where the r_k are independent random variables with the same distribution function $dG(r)$. Then, if we write

$$(1) \qquad (b, Q_{N,M}b) + 2(b, q_{N,M}) + p_{N,M} = \min_u \exp_r \{\cdots\},$$

we obtain the recurrence relation

$$(2) \qquad (b, Q_{N,M}b) + 2(b, q_{N,M}) + p_{N,M}$$

$$= \min_{u_0} \left[\int \{(b_0 - u_0 a_0 + r_0)^2 \, dG(r_0) \right.$$

$$+ (b - u_0 a, \, Q_{N-1,M-1}(b - u_0 a))$$

$$\left. + 2(b - u_0 a, \, q_{N-1,M-1}) + p_{N-1,M-1}\} \right].$$

From this relation we can readily obtain recurrence relations as before.

14. Correlation

Let us now define r_{-1} to be z and write

(1) $\qquad (b, Q_{N,M}(z)b) = \min_u \left[\exp_r \left\{ \sum_{k=0}^{N} \left(b_k + r_k - \sum_{\ell=0}^{M} u_\ell a_{k-\ell} \right)^2 \right\} \right].$

Then the analogue of (13.2) is

(2) $\quad (b, Q_{N,M}(z)b) + 2(b, q_{N,M}(z)) + p_{N,M}(z)$

$\qquad = \min_{u_0} \left[\int \{ (b_0 - u_0 a_0 + r_0)^2 + (b - u_0 a, Q_{N-1,M-1}(r_0)(b - u_0 a) \right.$

$\qquad \left. + 2(b - u_0 a, q_{N-1,M-1}(r_0)) + p_{N-1,M-1}(r_0) \} \, dG(r_0, z) \right]$

from which once again recurrence relations can be obtained.

15. Adaptive Prediction Theory

Let us now consider the case where the process occurs in the following way. First u_0 is chosen, then $b_0 + r_0$ is observed. Then u_1 is chosen and $b_1 + r_1$ is observed, and so on. We assume that the sequences $\{a_k\}$ and $\{b_k\}$ are known. On the basis of observation of $r_0, r_1, \dots$, we deduce the distribution of r_k. This is an adaptive process as described in Chapter VIII, § 29.

To illustrate the technique we can use to treat problems of this nature, consider the simple case in which each r_k assumes only the values ± 1 with respective probabilities p and $(1 - p)$, where p is not known. Let $dG(p)$ be a given a priori distribution for p and suppose that after observation of $m + 1$'s and $n - 1$'s, we use

(1) $\qquad\qquad dG_{m,n} = \dfrac{p^m (1 - p)^n \, dG(p)}{\displaystyle\int_0^1 p^m (1 - p)^n \, dG(p)}$

as the new a priori distribution.

Write

(2) $\quad f(N, M; m, n; b) = (b, Q_{N,M}(m, n)b) + 2(b, q_{N,M}(m, n)) + p_{N,M}(m, n)$

$\qquad = \min_u \left[\exp_r \left\{ \sum_{k=0}^{N} \left(b_k + r_k - \sum_{\ell=0}^{M} u_\ell a_{k-\ell} \right)^2 \right\} \right],$

assuming that we have already observed $m + 1$'s and $n - 1$'s. Then the recurrence relation

(3) $\quad f(N, M; m, n; b) = \min_{u_0} [p_{m,n} f(N - 1, M - 1; m + 1, n; b - u_0 a,$

$\qquad\qquad + (1 - p_{m,n}) f(N - 1, M - 1; m, n + 1; b - u_0 a)]$

permits us to obtain recurrence relations as above for the matrices $Q_{N,M}$, the vectors $q_{N,M}$ and the scalars $p_{N,M}$. The probability p_{mn} is computed by means of the relation

$$(4) \qquad p_{mn} = \int_0^1 p \, dG_{mn}.$$

Comments and Bibliography

§1. A number of the results of this chapter, together with other results of similar character and additional references, may be found in

R. Bellman, *Introduction to Matrix Analysis*, McGraw-Hill Book Co., Inc., New York, 1960, Chapter 9,

and sprinkled throughout the exercises of *Dynamic Programming*.

§5. A similar technique can be employed to study linear programming problems in which the matrix of coefficients is almost block diagonal. See

R. Bellman, "On the computational solution of liner programming problems involving almost block diagonal matrices," *Management Science*, vol. 3, 1957, pp. 403–406.

§9. A detailed discussion of problems of this nature may be found in

R. Beckwith, *Analytic and Computational Aspects of Dynamic Programming Processes of High Dimension*, Jet Propulsion Laboratory, 1959.

§10. For some further results, see

R. Bellman and R. Kalaba, "Reduction of dimensionality, dynamic programming and control processes," *J. Basic. Engr.*, vol. 83, 1961, pp. 82–84.

§11. For the background of the problem and a treatment by other techniques, see

N. Levinson, Appendix to N. Wiener, *Extrapolation, Interpolation and Smoothing of Stationary Time Series*, Technology Press and John Wiley and Sons, New York, 1949.

The technique given here appeared in

R. Bellman, *Dynamic Programming and Mean Square Deviation*, The RAND Corporation, Paper P-1147, September 13, 1957.

———, *Dynamic Programming and Linear Prediction Theory*, The RAND Corporation, Paper P-2308, May 16, 1961.

For a systematic development of these ideas and further work, see

R. E. Kalman, *New Methods and Results in Liner Prediction and Filtering Theory*, RIAS, Technical Report 61-1, 1960.

CHAPTER XI

Markovian Decision Processes

1. Introduction

As the preceding pages demonstrate, dynamic programming processes assume varied forms. We have examined processes in which the policy variables may vary over a discrete set of values and those in which they may assume a continuum of values. Occasionally, side constraints have limited the range of admissible policy decisions. The state variables describing the system have been discrete or continuous, and the processes themselves deterministic, stochastic, or adaptive.

In the first nine chapters, we presented a uniform computational algorithm, equally applicable to linear or nonlinear criteria, to deterministic or stochastic processes. As a general factotum, it was necessarily not tailored to fit any particular process. In Chapter X, we showed how one could take advantage of the particular analytic structure of a problem to provide simpler computational algorithms than those given by classical or straightforward dynamic programming approaches.

In the pages that follow, we wish to describe some additional ways in which we can take advantage of individual analytic structure to simplify in essential ways the computational solution of the associated optimization problem. In many cases, these problems are only soluble in full generality if we introduce these more sophisticated and ingenious techniques.

We wish now to consider some problems which occupy a favored place in dynamic programming, and, indeed, in all of analysis. These are problems which possess certain *linear* features.

In the art of mathematical model-building, one of the most difficult tasks is that of balancing realistic description against the power of available analytic and computational techniques. Quite often, elaborate solutions are given to problems which have been meaninglessly simplified, and conversely, overly complicated versions of processes have gone unattended because of the mathematical difficulties present.

While it is certainly dangerous to construct linear models of real-world problems, it is difficult to forego the esthetic pleasure involved in obtaining explicit solutions. How to reconcile the two is one of the challenges of model-building.

The computational results of this chapter are based to a large extent upon the work of R. Howard. Many further results will be found in his book cited at the end of the chapter.

2. Markov Processes

Before talking about Markovian decision processes—the particular types of sequential decision processes we wish to discuss in this chapter—it is necessary for us to discuss what we mean by a *Markov process*.

Consider a system which at any particular time is in one of a finite number of states, which we number $i = 1, 2, \ldots, N$, and assume that at the discrete times $t = 0, 1, \ldots$, the system changes from one of these admissible states to another. In place of supposing that this change is deterministic, we assume that it is stochastic, ruled by a transition matrix $P = (p_{ij})$, where

(1) $\quad p_{ij} =$ the probability that the system is in state j at time $t + 1$, given that it was in state i at time t.

We consider here the important case where the transition matrix P is independent of time. This is the most interesting case.

Let us then introduce the following functions:

(2) $\quad x_t(i) =$ the probability that the system is in state i at time t,
$$i = 1, 2, \ldots, N,$$

with t assuming only the values $0, 1, \ldots$. The elementary rules of probability theory then yield the equations

(3)
$$x_{t+1}(j) = \sum_{i=1}^{N} p_{ij} x_t(i), \quad j = 1, 2, \ldots, N,$$
$$x_0(i) = c_i.$$

The theory of Markov processes is devoted to the study of the asymptotic behavior of the functions $x_t(i)$ as $t \to \infty$. If all of the transition probabilities p_{ij} are positive, it is not too difficult to show that these functions converge as $t \to \infty$ to quantities $x(i)$ which satisfy the "steady-state" equation

(4)
$$x(j) = \sum_{i=1}^{N} p_{ij} x(i), \quad j = 1, 2, \ldots, N.$$

That these functions converge as $t \to \infty$ is perhaps not too surprising, in view of the mixing property involved in the assumption that all of the p_{ij} are positive. What is surprising is that in this case, the limiting values are independent of the initial state of the system, the values of $x_0(i)$.

This is the mathematical idea behind the validity of shuffling cards. Actually, most shuffling is done rather carelessly and a great deal of information concerning the play of a bridge hand can be gleaned from a knowledge of the tricks on the previous deal.

3. Markovian Decision Process

We now wish to extend the concept of a Markov process to more general situations in which decisions are made at each stage. Let us suppose that at each stage the transition matrix can be chosen from one of a set of such matrices, and denote the matrix corresponding to policy decision q by $P(q) = (p_{ij}(q))$.

Let us further suppose that not only is there a change of state involved at each stage, but also a return, which is a function of the initial and terminal state and of the decision.

Let $R(q) = (r_{ij}(q))$ represent the return matrix defined in this fashion.

A process of this type we call a *Markovian decision process*. The problem that we wish to consider is that of choosing the sequence of decisions which will maximize the expected return obtained from an N-stage process, given the initial state of the system.

4. Example—A Taxicab Problem

Before entering into any analytic discussion of this type of problem, let us see how problems of this nature enter in a very natural way. To illustrate, let us present a simplified version of the operation of a fleet of taxicabs.

The advantage of an example of this nature is that it enables us to give concrete meanings to such terms as "transition matrix," "alternative decisions," and so on.

Suppose that a taxi driver has an area of operation encompassing three towns. If he is in town 1, he has three alternatives:

(1) (1) He can cruise in the hope of picking up a passenger by being hailed.
 (2) He can drive to the nearest cab stand and wait in line.
 (3) He can pull over to the curb and wait for a radio call.

In town 3, he has the same alternatives, but in town 2, the last alternative is not available since there is no radio cab service in that town.

For any given town and any given alternative within this town, there is a probability that the next trip will go to each of the towns 1, 2, and 3, and a corresponding known return in monetary units associated with each such trip. The probabilities of transition and the returns depend upon the alternative because different customer populations will be contacted under each alternative

Assigning hypothetical numbers, the data for the problem can be shown in Table 1.

As an example of the interpretation of this table, we see from the next to last row that, if the driver is in city 3 and chooses to drive to a cab stand, there is a one-eighth chance he will get a customer who wants to go to city 1, the profit being 6, a three-fourths chance of a trip to city 2 yielding a profit of 4, and a one-eighth chance of a trip within city 3, with a profit of 2 units.

In this problem we have 3 states, i.e., $N = 3$; there are 3 alternatives in states 1 and 3, and 2 in state 2, i.e., $n_1 = 3$, $n_2 = 2$, $n_3 = 3$. There are $3 \cdot 2 \cdot 3 = 18$ possible policies.

TABLE I

State (City)	Alternative	Transition Probability $j = 1$	2	3	Return $i = 1$	2	3
1	1	$\frac{1}{2}$	$\frac{1}{4}$	$\frac{1}{4}$	10	4	8
	2	$\frac{1}{16}$	$\frac{3}{4}$	$\frac{3}{16}$	8	2	4
	3	$\frac{1}{4}$	$\frac{1}{8}$	$\frac{5}{8}$	4	6	4
2	1	$\frac{1}{2}$	0	$\frac{1}{2}$	14	0	18
	2	$\frac{1}{16}$	$\frac{7}{8}$	$\frac{1}{16}$	8	16	8
3	1	$\frac{1}{4}$	$\frac{1}{4}$	$\frac{1}{2}$	10	2	8
	2	$\frac{1}{8}$	$\frac{3}{4}$	$\frac{1}{8}$	6	4	2
	3	$\frac{3}{4}$	$\frac{1}{16}$	$\frac{3}{16}$	4	0	8

After the tools of solution have been developed, we will return to this problem and show its numerical solution.

5. Analytic Formulation

Let us now use functional equation techniques to obtain an analytic formulation of the problem posed in §3. For $i = 1, 2, \ldots, N; n = 0, 1, \ldots,$ let

(1) $f_n(i)$ = expected return obtained from an n-stage process, starting in state i and using an optimal policy.

Note that n represents the *length* of a process, whereas t, used in earlier sections, denoted *time*. The principle of optimality then yields the recurrence relations

$$(2) \quad f_n(i) = \max_q \left[\sum_{j=1}^{N} p_{ij}(q)(r_{ij}(q) + f_{n-1}(j)) \right], \quad i = 1, 2, \ldots, N,$$

for $n = 1, 2, \ldots,$ with $f_0(i) = 0$.

An optimal policy consists of a vector $(q_n(1), q_n(2), \ldots, q_n(N))$, giving the choice to be made in the ith state when n stages remain.

6. Computational Aspects

Although we shall subsequently present some numerical results for a problem of this general nature arising from an equipment replacement process, let us make some general comments at this time.

The computation is complicated not so much by the memory require-ments for the sequences $\{f_n(i)\}$ and $\{g_n(i)\}$, which are negligible, as by the necessity for storing the transition matrices $P(q) = (p_{i,j}(q))$ and $R(q) = (r_{ij}(q))$.

If N exceeds a value such as 1000, these requirements become excessive. To treat really large-scale problems, it is necessary to study the analytic structure of the process and use the information gained in this way to develop approximate techniques. We shall use the linearity of the process and the simple but very important idea that a suitably defined fictitious infinite process affords an excellent approximation to a process of even moderate length. For the study of transient effects, the precise formulation is still necessary.

7. Asymptotic Behavior

The approximation techniques we shall employ are strongly dependent upon the asymptotic behavior of the sequence $\{f_n(i)\}$ as $n \to \infty$. Let us then state the following result.

Theorem 1. Consider the recurrence relation

$$(1) \qquad f_n(j) = \max_q \left[b_j(q) + \sum_{i=1}^N a_{i,j}(q) f_{n-1}(i) \right],$$

where we suppose that

(2) (a) $b_j(q) \geq 0$ and $b_j(q) > 0$ for some j and all q,

   (b) $a_{i,j}(q) \geq d > 0$, $i, j = 1, 2, \ldots, M$, uniformly in q,

   (c) $\qquad \sum_{j=1}^M a_{ij}(q) = 1$, $i = 1, 2, \ldots, M$.

In other words, $A(q)$ is for each q the transpose of a positive Markov matrix.
Assume also that either:

   (a) *The functions $b_i(q)$ and $a_{i,j}(q)$ are functions of finite dimensional vectors q whose components assume only a finite set of values, which, in general, depend upon i and j.*

   (b) *The functions $b_i(q)$ and $a_{i,j}(q)$ are continuous functions of finite dimensional vectors whose components assume values in certain closed, bounded regions in q-space.*

Set

$$(3) \qquad 1 = \begin{pmatrix} 1 \\ 1 \\ \cdot \\ \cdot \\ \cdot \\ 1 \end{pmatrix}, \quad b(q) = \begin{pmatrix} b_1(q) \\ b_2(q) \\ \cdot \\ \cdot \\ \cdot \\ b_N(q) \end{pmatrix}, \quad A(q) = (a_{i,j}(q)).$$

Then as $n \to \infty$,

(4) $$f_n(i) \sim nr, \quad i = 1. 2, \ldots, N,$$

where the scalar value r is determined by the relation

(5) $$r1 = \max_{q} \lim_{n \to \infty} \left[\frac{b(q) + A(q)b(q) + \cdots + A(q)^{n-1}b(q)}{n} \right].$$

A proof of this result will be found in the reference at the end of this chapter. The quantity $b_i(q)$ is the expected return at each stage due to a decision q. The result is intuitively clear when we see that it asserts that we act so as to maximize the *average expected return*.

8. Discussion

The value of this theorem resides in the fact that it assures us that the obvious approach to the determination of an optimal policy is indeed a correct one. Namely, we take a particular policy and use it repeatedly to obtain the average gain. We then choose a policy which maximizes this average gain.

Once this result has been established, the path is open for a number of simple iterative techniques which can be used to obtain the long-term policy in a more efficient way.

As in the theory of Markov chains, there is a considerable difference between the analytic results obtained for the case of positive coefficients, and those valid for merely non-negative coefficients. In most applications, we find ourselves in the situation where a large number of the coefficients are zero. There are several ways around this difficulty. In the first place, we may iterate the matrices a few times until the zeros fill in. The fact that a transition probability is nonzero means that there is a way of going from the ith state to the jth state in any particular stage. The fact that some iterate of the matrix has all positive entries means that there is a way of going from the ith state to the jth state in at most a fixed number of stages.

In most applications, this is actually the case. If it is not the case, this is usually an indication that in some way we have combined two distinct processes into one larger process, at the expense of simplicity.

A second way of circumventing the many fine points that arise in the consideration of Markov chains with zero coefficients in the matrix is to replace these zeros by small quantities. Clearly, if the original physical process is meaningful, small changes in the transition probabilities should have a negligible effect upon the over-all behavior. Having obtained a positive transition matrix in this way, we can then use the corresponding simple theory.

9. Howard's Policy Space Technique

The details of a policy space iterative technique based on the foregoing ideas have been worked out by Ronald Howard. We shall discuss his technique, which furnishes the optimal policy for very long processes (i.e., "steady-state processes") where decisions depend only on the state, and not on the stage. Furthermore, we shall adopt his notation, in order to allow easy reference to his writings.

Defining

(1) V_i^n = total expected return from an n-stage process starting in state i using a *fixed policy*,

one easily sees that V satisfies the recurrence relation

$$(2) \qquad V_i^n = \sum_{j=1}^{N} p_{ij}(r_{ij} + V_j^{n-1}).$$

Also, for large n,

$$(3) \qquad V_i^n = v_i + ng$$

if all states belong to the same chain.[1] This will certainly be the case if all $p_{ij} > 0$, as stated in §7. This equation asserts that return will, in general, be composed of two parts, a steady-state part, ng, resulting from the behavior as $n \to \infty$, and a transient part v_i which depends only on the starting state.

Substitution of the limiting expression (3) in relation (2) yields

$$(4) \qquad v_i + ng = \sum_{j=1}^{N} p_{ij}[r_{ij} + v_j + (n-1)g].$$

Since $\sum_{j=1}^{N} p_{ij} = 1$ by definition, this relation simplifies to

$$(5) \qquad g + v_i = \sum_{j=1}^{N} p_{ij}(r_{ij} + v_j) \quad \text{for} \quad i = 1, 2, \ldots, N.$$

10. The Value Determination Operation

The above is a system of N equations in $N + 1$ unknowns, the N v_i's and g. Observe, however, that the addition of a constant to all the v_i's does not change the equations. This means that only the relative values of the v_i's, rather than their absolute values, are important. Hence one v_i can be arbitrarily designated, leaving N equations in N unknowns. Setting $v_N = 0$, solution of the equations gives the average long term gain, g, and relative values of various starting states, v_i, for a fixed policy.

Howard calls the above generation of the gain and values under a given policy the *value determination operation* (VDO).

[1] The concepts of *chains* are discussed *in extenso* in Howard's book, and may also be found in any comprehensive account of Markov chains.

11. The Policy Improvement Routine

We come now to the central problem. Having guessed a policy, a choice of alternatives for each state, we have shown how to evaluate this policy. On the basis of this information, how are we to generate a better policy? By "better," we mean one possessing a large expected gain, g.

Returning to Equation (9.4), we can solve for g:

$$(1) \qquad g = \sum_{j=1}^{N} p_{ij}(r_{ij} + v_j) - v_i, \quad i = 1, 2, \ldots, N.$$

Recall that p_{ij} and r_{ij} depend on the particular policy we have chosen to pursue.

Using the v's associated with the old policy, we can choose a new policy which maximizes the right-hand side of (1). Calling this new policy k, we choose that k which maximizes $\sum_{j=1}^{N} p_{ij}^{(k)}(r_{ij}^{(k)} + v_j) - v_i$, where $p_{ij}^{(k)}$ denotes the transition probabilities associated with alternative k in state i.

Once g and v have been determined for a given policy, the use of the above rule for generating the new policy is called the *policy improvement routine* (PIR).

One can prove that this rule

(a) leads at each application to a policy of higher, or at least as large, gain,

(b) will eventually lead to the optimal policy.

These proofs depend strongly on the linearity of this simple model. It is, however, not intuitive that a decision dictated by gain and values of one policy will yield a policy with a larger gain.

12. Solution of the Taxicab Problem

Let us return to the taxicab problem of §4 and apply the above rules. As an initial guess, we choose the policy vector

$$D = \begin{bmatrix} 1 \\ 1 \\ 1 \end{bmatrix},$$

which means we cruise in all cities. This is the policy that maximizes the expected immediate return. For this policy we have the transition probability matrix

$$[p_{ij}] = \begin{bmatrix} \frac{1}{2} & \frac{1}{4} & \frac{1}{4} \\ \frac{1}{2} & 0 & \frac{1}{2} \\ \frac{1}{4} & \frac{1}{4} & \frac{1}{2} \end{bmatrix},$$

and immediate return vector

$$\left[\sum_{j=1}^{N} p_{ij} r_{ij} \right] = \begin{bmatrix} 8 \\ 16 \\ 7 \end{bmatrix}.$$

304

Let us denote $\sum_{j=1}^{N} p_{ij} r_{ij}$ by q_i, since the expected return depends only upon i. The value determination equations, with v_3 set equal to 0, are

$$g + v_1 = 8 + \tfrac{1}{2} v_1 + \tfrac{1}{4} v_2,$$
$$g + v_2 = 16 + \tfrac{1}{2} v_1,$$
$$g = 7 + \tfrac{1}{4} v_1 + \tfrac{1}{4} v_2,$$

yielding the solution

$$v_1 = 1.33,$$
$$v_2 = 7.47,$$
$$v_3 = 0,$$
$$g = 9.2.$$

Using a policy of "always cruise," the driver will make 9.2 units per trip on the average.

Returning to the PIR, we calculate the quantities $q_i^k + \sum_{j=1}^{N} p_{ij}^k v_j$ for all i and k:

i	k	$q_i^k + \sum_{j=1}^{N} p_{ij}^k v_j$
1	1	10.50*
	2	8.43
	3	5.51
2	1	16.67
	2	21.75*
3	1	9.20
	2	9.66*
	3	6.75

We see that for $i = 1$, the quantity in the right-hand column is maximized when $k = 1$. For $i = 2$ or 3, it is maximized when $k = 2$. In other words, our new policy is

$$D = \begin{bmatrix} 1 \\ 2 \\ 2 \end{bmatrix}.$$

This means that if the cab is in town 1, it should cruise; if it is in town 2 or 3, it should drive to the nearest stand.

We now have

$$[p_{ij}] = \begin{bmatrix} \tfrac{1}{2} & \tfrac{1}{4} & \tfrac{1}{4} \\ \tfrac{1}{16} & \tfrac{7}{8} & \tfrac{1}{16} \\ \tfrac{1}{8} & \tfrac{3}{4} & \tfrac{1}{8} \end{bmatrix}, \qquad [q_i] = \begin{bmatrix} 8 \\ 15 \\ 4 \end{bmatrix}.$$

Returning to the VDO, we solve the equations

$$g + v_1 = 8 + \tfrac{1}{2} v_1 + \tfrac{1}{4} v_2 + \tfrac{1}{4} v_3,$$
$$g + v_2 = 15 + \tfrac{1}{16} v_1 + \tfrac{7}{8} v_2 + \tfrac{1}{16} v_3,$$
$$g + v_3 = 4 + \tfrac{1}{8} v_1 + \tfrac{3}{4} v_2 + \tfrac{1}{8} v_3.$$

Again with $v_3 = 0$ we obtain

$$v_1 = 3.88,$$
$$v_2 = 12.85,$$
$$v_3 = 0,$$
$$g = 13.15.$$

Note that g has increased from 9.2 to 13.15 as desired, so that the cab earns 13.15 units per trip on the average. Entering the PIR with these values,

i	k	$q_i^k + \sum_{j=1}^{N} p_{ij}^k v_j$
1	1	9.27
	2	12.14*
	3	4.91
2	1	14.06
	2	26.00*
3	1	9.26
	2	12.02*
	3	2.37

The new policy is thus

$$D = \begin{bmatrix} 2 \\ 2 \\ 2 \end{bmatrix}.$$

The cab should drive to the nearest stand regardless of the town in which it finds itself.

With this policy

$$[p_{ij}] = \begin{bmatrix} \frac{1}{16} & \frac{3}{4} & \frac{3}{16} \\ \frac{1}{16} & \frac{7}{8} & \frac{1}{16} \\ \frac{1}{8} & \frac{3}{4} & \frac{1}{8} \end{bmatrix}, \qquad [q_i] = \begin{bmatrix} 2.75 \\ 15 \\ 4 \end{bmatrix}.$$

Entering the VDO

$$g + v_1 = 2.75 + \tfrac{1}{16}v_1 + \tfrac{3}{4}v_2 + \tfrac{3}{16}v_3,$$
$$g + v_2 = 15 + \tfrac{1}{16}v_1 + \tfrac{7}{8}v_2 + \tfrac{1}{16}v_3,$$
$$g + v_3 = 4 + \tfrac{1}{8}v_1 + \tfrac{3}{4}v_2 + \tfrac{1}{8}v_3.$$

With $v_3 = 0$,

$$v_1 = -1.18,$$
$$v_2 = 12.66,$$
$$v_3 = 0,$$
$$g = 13.34.$$

Note that there has been a small but definite increase in g from 13.15 to 13.34.

Trying the PIR,

i	k	$q_i^k + \sum_{j=1}^{N} p_{ij}^k v_j$
1	1	10.57
	2	12.16*
	3	5.53
2	1	15.41
	2	26.00*
3	1	9.86
	2	13.33*
	3	5.40

The new policy is

$$ D = \begin{bmatrix} 2 \\ 2 \\ 2 \end{bmatrix}, $$

but this is equal to the last policy, so that the process has converged and g has attained its maximum; namely 13.34. The cab driver should drive to the nearest stand in any city. Following this policy will yield a return of 13.34 units per trip on the average, almost half as much again as the policy of always cruising found by maximizing immediate return. Summarizing the calculations (to two decimal places),

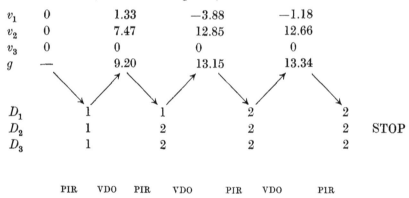

v_1	0	1.33	−3.88	−1.18
v_2	0	7.47	12.85	12.66
v_3	0	0	0	0
g	—	9.20	13.15	13.34

D_1 1   1   2   2
D_2 1   2   2   2   STOP
D_3 1   2   2   2

PIR   VDO   PIR   VDO   PIR   VDO   PIR

Notice that the optimal policy of always driving to a stand is the *worst* policy in terms of immediate return. It often happens in the sequential decision process that the birds in the bush are worth more than the one in the hand.

13. The More General Problem

In the discussion thus far we have required that there be a unique gain, g, associated with the problem. This means that there is only one chain and no matter what policy we choose it is possible to get from any existent state to any other. Taking all the p_{ij} positive is one way of assuring this result.

We would, however, like our technique to be valid for the more general case involving several chains. A transition matrix having this property is shown below:

$$[p_{ij}] = \begin{bmatrix} \frac{1}{2} & \frac{1}{2} & 0 & 0 \\ \frac{1}{2} & \frac{1}{2} & 0 & 0 \\ 0 & 0 & \frac{1}{4} & \frac{3}{4} \\ 0 & 0 & \frac{1}{8} & \frac{7}{8} \end{bmatrix}.$$

Here if we start in state 1 or 2, there is no possibility of transition to states 3 or 4, and conversely. If we have an accompanying return matrix, there will be one long-term average gain associated with starting in states 1 or 2, another for states 3 or 4. This leads to a subscripting of gain, g_1 meaning gain in chain 1, g_2 for chain 2, and so on, in general. With this notation, we proceed to a more general algorithm, which we show schematically.

14. The General Solution (see page 309)

15. Equipment Replacement Problems Revisited

We have, in Chapter III, §12, considered in some detail equipment replacement problems. The technique presented there was to solve a finite duration problem by means of the iteration of a recurrence relation. This allowed us to include cost variations as a function of real time as well as of age.

If the infinite time solution is sought, we can iterate the equation until average return per stage is constant to any degree of accuracy desired, but can rarely by this method categorically assert policy convergence. As an example of this technique we shall consider an industrial replacement problem. Then we shall apply the policy space technique to a similar problem.

16. A Tire Manufacturing Problem

In the manufacture of rubber tires, a machine is used which contains two bladders, and which simultaneously produces one tire on each bladder. If a bladder fails in service, a faulty tire is produced and a cost c_2 is incurred. Further, when a bladder fails, the machine must be stripped down for replacement, a process resulting in a charge c_3 representing the labor cost involved and a cost c_4 representing lost production time. A replacement bladder costs c_1. Once the machine is stripped, the cost of replacing the second bladder is the cost of the bladder alone.

By replacing bladders before failure, the faulty tire expense, c_2, and lost production cost, c_4, can be avoided. However, such a policy will necessarily involve the purchase of more new bladders and require more labor than the replace-after-failure policy, and therein lies the problem.

14. The General Solution

Using the p_{ij} and q_i for a given policy, solve the double set of equations

$$g_i = \sum_{j=1}^{N} p_{ij} g_j,$$

$$v_i + g_i = q_i + \sum_{j=1}^{N} p_{ij} v_j,$$

for all v_i and g_i. The solution will involve as many arbitrary constants as there are independent Markov chains; these constants may be set equal to zero.

For each state i, determine the alternative k which maximizes $\sum_{j=1}^{N} p_{ij}^{k} g_j$ and make it the new decision in the ith state. If $\sum_{j=1}^{N} p_{ij}^{k} g_j$ is the same for all alternatives, the decision must be made on the basis of values rather than gains. Therefore, if the gain test fails, determine the alternative k which maximizes $q_i^{k} + \sum_{j=1}^{N} p_{ij}^{k} v_j$ and make it the new decision in the ith state.

Regardless of whether the policy improvement test is based on gains or values, if the old decision in the ith state yields as high a value of the test quantity as any other alternative, leave the old decision unchanged. This rule assures convergence in the case of equivalent policies.

When this procedure has been repeated for all states, a new policy has been determined and new $[p_{ij}]$ and $[q_i]$ matrices have been obtained. If the new policy is equal to the previous one, the calculation process has converged and the best policy has been found.

17. Dynamic Programming Formulation

Let us begin by defining

$f_N(i, j)$ = total expected cost of producing N additional tires, where bladder 1 has already produced i tires, and bladder 2 has produced j tires, where an optimal replacement policy is used.

We seek $f_N(0, 0)/N$, the expected average cost per tire of producing N tires where we start with new bladders and use an optimal policy. Of even more interest is the corresponding replacement policy. We define p_i, $i = 0, 1, 2, \ldots$, as the probability of successfully producing a tire with a bladder that has already produced i tires and assume that these quantities are known on the basis of experience. Then, recalling the definition of $f_N(i, j)$, we have the recurrence relation

(1)
$$f_N(i, j) = \min \left[\begin{array}{l} \text{Produce:} \\ \quad p_i p_j f_{N-2}(i + 1, j + 1) \\ \quad + (1 - p_i)(1 - p_j)[2c_1 + 2c_2 + c_3 + c_4 + f_N(0, 0)] \\ \quad + (1 - p_i)p_j \min [c_1 + c_2 + c_3 + c_4 + f_{N-1}(0, j + 1), \\ \qquad\qquad 2c_1 + c_2 + c_3 + c_4 + f_{N-1}(0, 0)] \\ \quad + p_i(1 - p_j) \min [c_1 + c_2 + c_3 + c_4 + f_{N-1}(i + 1, 0), \\ \qquad\qquad 2c_1 + c_2 + c_3 + c_4 + f_{N-1}(0, 0)], \\ \text{Replace Bladder } i: \quad c_1 + c_3 + f_N(0, j), \\ \text{Replace Bladder } j: \quad c_1 + c_3 + f_N(i, 0), \\ \text{Replace Both:} \quad\; 2c_1 + c_3 + f_N(0, 0). \end{array} \right]$$

The above equation evaluates the expected costs of each admissible decision as the sum of the immediate cost plus the expected cost of optimally producing the remaining tires after implementing the decision, and chooses the best alternative. The problem is solved by computing the cost of producing one tire, $f_1(i, j)$, and then using Equation (1) to evaluate f_2 using f_1, f_3 using f_2, etc.

18. A Numerical Example

For purposes of illustration, we adopt the following hypothetical figures:

Cost of purchasing a bladder	$c_1 = 50$
Cost of scrap, per scrapped tire	$c_2 = 1$
Labor cost of stripping machines	$c_3 = 2$
Cost of lost production time	$c_4 = 3$

Probability of success:

No. Produced x	0	1	2	3	4	5	6
Probability of Success p_x	1	.9	.8	.6	.4	.2	0

Successive iteration of recurrence relation (17.1) yields the following results:

1. For processes producing more than 15 tires, the optimal policy converges to (a) replace any bladder that has made 6 tires, (b) replace the other bladder at the same time if it has produced 5 or more tires when the machine is stripped due to either policy or failure.

2. The cost of each additional tire converges to 16.94 after about 47 tires have been produced.

19. A Further Example

To show that the optimal policy need not be so simple, let us reduce the cost of a new bladder from 50 to 10 units and calculate a new expected cost and optimal policy.

TABLE II

Table of Results

Average cost per tire: 6.364

Policy:

i / j	0	1	2	3	4	5	6
0	P–1	P–1	P–2	P–2	R–1	R–1	R–1
1	P–1	P–1	P–2	P–2	R–1	R–1	R–1
2	P–2	P–2	P–3	P–3	P–3	R–1	R–1
3	P–2	P–2	P–3	P–3	P–3	P–3	R–2
4	R–1	R–1	P–3	P–3	P–3	R–2	R–2
5	R–1	R–1	R–1	P–3	R–2	R–2	R–2
6	R–1	R–1	R–1	R–2	R–2	R–2	R–2

where P–1 means produce, and if a bladder fails, replace only that bladder.

P–2 means produce, and if the newer bladder fails replace both, if the older fails replace only it.

P–3 means produce, and if either bladder fails replace both.

R–1 means replace the older bladder immediately.

R–2 means replace both bladders immediately.

i is the number of tires previously produced by bladder 1.

j is the number of tires previously produced by bladder 2.

As indicated in the above table, we now follow a radically different policy. The policy yielded by iteration of Equation (1) no longer has the simple form: replace the older bladder when it has made m tires and replace the other bladder at the same time if it has produced more than n tires. Indeed, use of any such policy will yield an average cost greater than 6.364 per tire.

The numerical calculations discussed above each required only one minute of computing time on the Johnniac computer.

20. An Automobile Replacement Problem

Howard's approach affords an alternative approach to problems of this ilk. It is informative to see how one formulates and solves a replacement problem.

In order to fix ideas, let us consider the problem of automobile replacement over a time interval of ten years. We agree to review our current situation every three months and to make a decision on keeping our present car or trading it in at that time. The state of the system, i, is described by the age of the car in three-month periods; i may run from 1 to 40. In order to keep the number of states finite, a car of age 40 remains a car of age 40 forever (it is considered to be essentially worn out). The alternatives available in each state are these: the first alternative, $k = 1$, is to keep the present car for another quarter. The other alternatives, $k > 1$, are to buy a car of age $k - 2$, where $k - 2$ may be as large as 39. We have then forty states with forty-one alternatives in each state so that there are 41^{40} possible policies.

The data supplied are the following:

C_i, the cost of buying a car of age i,

T_i, the trade-in value of a car of age i,

E_i, the expected cost of operating a car of age i until it reaches age $i + 1$,

p_i, the probability that a car of age i will survive to be age $i + 1$ without incurring a prohibitively expensive repair.

The probability defined above is necessary to limit the number of state. A car of any age that has a hopeless breakdown is immediately sent to state 40. Naturally, $p_{40} = 0$.

The basic equations governing the system when it is in state i are: If $k = 1$ (keep present car)

$$g + v_i = -E_i + p_i v_{i+1} + (1 - p_i)v_{40}.$$

If $k > 1$ (trade for car of age $k - 2$)

$$g + v_i = T_i - C_{k-2} - E_{k-2} + p_{k-2}v_{k-1} + (1 - p_{k-2})v_{40}.$$

It is simple to phrase these equations in terms of our earlier notation. For instance,

$$q_i{}^k = -E_i \text{ for } k = 1,$$

$$p_{i,}{}^k = \begin{cases} p_i & j = i + 1 \\ 1 - p_i & j = 40 \\ 0 & \text{other } j \end{cases} \text{ for } k = 1,$$

$$q_i{}^k = T_i - C_{k-2} - E_{k-2} \text{ for } k > 1,$$

$$p_{ij}{}^k = \begin{cases} p_{k-2} & j = k - 1 \\ 1 - p_{k-2} & j = 40 \\ 0 & \text{other } j \end{cases} \text{ for } k > 1.$$

The actual data used in the problem are listed in Table III and in the graph shown in Fig. 91. The discontinuities in the cost and trade-in

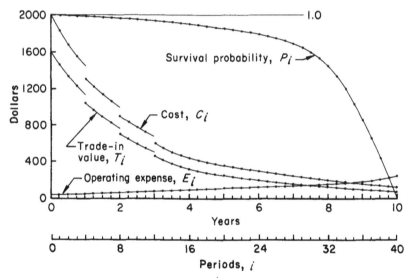

Figure 91. Automobile replacement data.

functions were introduced in order to characterize typical model year effects.

The automobile replacement problem was solved by the simultaneous equation method in seven iterations. The sequence of policies, gains, and values is shown in Tables IV, V and VI. The optimal policy given by iteration 7 is this: If you have a car which is more than $\frac{1}{2}$ year old but less than $6\frac{1}{2}$ years old, keep it. If you have a car of any other age, trade it in on a 3-year-old car. This seems to correspond quite well with our intuitive notions concerning the economics of automobile ownership. It is satisfying

TABLE III

Replacement Problem Data

Age in Periods i	Cost C_i	Trade-in Value T_i	Operating Expense E_i	Survival Probability p_i
0	$2,000	$1,600	$50	1.000
1	1,840	1,460	53	0.999
2	1,680	1,340	56	0.998
3	1,560	1,230	59	0.997
4	1,300	1,050	62	0.996
5	1,220	980	65	0.994
6	1,150	910	68	0.991
7	1,080	840	71	0.988
8	900	710	75	0.985
9	840	650	78	0.983
10	780	600	81	0.980
11	730	550	84	0.975
12	600	480	87	0.970
13	560	430	90	0.965
14	520	390	93	0.960
15	480	360	96	0.955
16	440	330	100	0.950
17	420	310	103	0.945
18	400	290	106	0.940
19	380	270	109	0.935
20	360	255	112	0.930
21	345	240	115	0.925
22	330	225	118	0.919
23	315	210	121	0.910
24	300	200	125	0.900
25	290	190	129	0.890
26	280	180	133	0.880
27	265	170	137	0.865
28	250	160	141	0.850
29	240	150	145	0.820
30	230	145	150	0.790
31	220	140	155	0.760
32	210	135	160	0.730
33	200	130	167	0.660
34	190	120	175	0.590
35	180	115	182	0.510
36	170	110	190	0.430
37	160	105	205	0.300
38	150	95	220	0.200
39	140	87	235	0.100
40	130	80	250	0

TABLE IV

Automobile Replacement Results

State	Iteration 1 Gain Decision	−250.00 Value	Iteration 2 Gain Decision	−193.89 Value	Iteration 3 Gain Decision	−162.44 Value
1	Buy 36	$1373.61	Buy 20	$1380.00	Buy 19	$1380.00
2	Buy 36	1253.61	Buy 20	1260.00	Buy 19	1260.00
3	Buy 36	1143.61	Buy 20	1150.00	Buy 19	1150.00
4	Buy 36	963.61	Buy 20	970.00	Keep	1036.63
5	Buy 36	893.61	Buy 20	900.00	Keep	939.95
6	Buy 36	823.61	Buy 20	830.00	Keep	847.60
7	Buy 36	753.61	Buy 20	760.00	Buy 19	760.00
8	Buy 36	623.61	Buy 20	630.00	Keep	695.44
9	Buy 36	563.61	Buy 20	570.00	Keep	617.26
10	Buy 36	513.61	Buy 20	520.00	Keep	542.04
11	Buy 36	463.61	Buy 20	470.00	Buy 19	470.00
12	Buy 36	393.61	Buy 20	400.00	Buy 19	400.00
13	Buy 36	343.61	Buy 20	350.00	Keep	575.00
14	Buy 36	303.61	Buy 20	310.00	Keep	520.79
15	Buy 36	273.61	Buy 20	280.00	Keep	470.15
16	Buy 36	243.61	Buy 20	250.00	Keep	422.74
17	Buy 36	223.61	Buy 20	230.00	Keep	379.26
18	Buy 36	203.61	Buy 20	210.00	Keep	338.44
19	Buy 36	183.61	Buy 20	190.00	Keep	300.00
20	Buy 36	168.61	Keep	280.00	Keep	263.70
21	Keep	875.93	Keep	213.02	Keep	229.32
22	Keep	801.00	Buy 20	145.00	Keep	196.62
23	Keep	727.97	Buy 20	130.00	Keep	165.60
24	Keep	658.21	Buy 20	120.00	Keep	136.44
25	Keep	592.45	Buy 20	110.00	Buy 19	110.00
26	Keep	529.72	Buy 20	100.00	Buy 19	100.00
27	Keep	469.00	Buy 20	90.00	Buy 19	90.00
28	Keep	411.56	Buy 20	80.00	Buy 19	80.00
29	Keep	355.95	Buy 20	70.00	Buy 19	70.00
30	Keep	306.04	Buy 20	65.00	Buy 19	65.00
31	Keep	260.81	Buy 20	60.00	Buy 19	60.00
32	Keep	218.18	Buy 20	55.00	Buy 19	55.00
33	Keep	175.58	Buy 20	50.00	Buy 19	50.00
34	Keep	140.28	Buy 20	40.00	Buy 19	40.00
35	Keep	110.64	Buy 20	35.00	Buy 19	35.00
36	Keep	83.61	Buy 20	30.00	Buy 19	30.00
37	Keep	54.90	Buy 20	25.00	Buy 19	25.00
38	Keep	33.00	Buy 20	15.00	Buy 19	15.00
39	Keep	15.00	Buy 20	7.00	Buy 19	7.00
40	Keep	0.00	Buy 20	0.00	Buy 19	0.00

TABLE V

Automobile Replacement Results

State	Iteration 4 Gain Decision −157.07	Value	Iteration 5 Gain Decision −151.05	Value	Iteration 6 Gain Decision −150.99	Value
1	Buy 12	$1380.00	Buy 12	$1380.00	Buy 12	$1380.00
2	Buy 12	1260.00	Buy 12	1260.00	Buy 12	1260.00
3	Buy 12	1150.00	Buy 12	1150.00	Buy 12	1150.00
4	Buy 12	970.00	Keep	1002.62	Keep	1072.26
5	Buy 12	900.00	Keep	917.24	Keep	987.22
6	Buy 12	830.00	Keep	836.21	Keep	906.67
7	Buy 12	760.00	Buy 12	760.00	Keep	831.16
8	Buy 12	630.00	Keep	760.54	Keep	760.30
9	Buy 12	570.00	Keep	694.91	Keep	694.73
10	Buy 12	520.00	Keep	632.62	Keep	632.50
11	Buy 12	470.00	Keep	574.05	Keep	573.99
12	Keep	520.00	Keep	520.00	Keep	520.00
13	Keep	463.84	Keep	470.05	Keep	470.12
14	Keep	411.16	Keep	423.84	Keep	423.97
15	Keep	361.55	Keep	381.03	Keep	381.23
16	Keep	314.63	Keep	341.34	Keep	341.61
17	Keep	271.11	Keep	305.57	Keep	305.92
18	Keep	229.67	Keep	272.50	Keep	272.95
19	Buy 12	190.00	Keep	241.97	Keep	242.51
20	Buy 12	175.00	Keep	213.82	Keep	214.46
21	Buy 12	160.00	Keep	187.93	Keep	188.68
22	Buy 12	145.00	Keep	164.19	Keep	165.07
23	Buy 12	130.00	Keep	142.70	Keep	143.73
24	Buy 12	120.00	Keep	123.79	Keep	124.99
25	Buy 12	110.00	Keep	108.60	Buy 12	110.00
26	Buy 12	100.00	Keep	97.25	Buy 12	100.00
27	Buy 12	90.00	Buy 12	90.00	Buy 12	90.00
28	Buy 12	80.00	Buy 12	80.00	Buy 12	80.00
29	Buy 12	70.00	Buy 12	70.00	Buy 12	70.00
30	Buy 12	65.00	Buy 12	65.00	Buy 12	65.00
31	Buy 12	60.00	Buy 12	60.00	Buy 12	60.00
32	Buy 12	55.00	Buy 12	55.00	Buy 12	55.00
33	Buy 12	50.00	Buy 12	50.00	Buy 12	50.00
34	Buy 12	40.00	Buy 12	40.00	Buy 12	40.00
35	Buy 12	35.00	Buy 12	35.00	Buy 12	35.00
36	Buy 12	30.00	Buy 12	30.00	Buy 12	30.00
37	Buy 12	25.00	Buy 12	25.00	Buy 12	25.00
38	Buy 12	15.00	Buy 12	15.00	Buy 12	15.00
39	Buy 12	7.00	Buy 12	7.00	Buy 12	7.00
40	Buy 12	0.00	Buy 12	0.00	Buy 12	0.00

TABLE VI

Automobile Replacement Results

State	Iteration 7 Gain Decision	−150.95 Value	Iteration 7 Values $V_{40} = \$80$, Trade-in Value
1	Buy 12	$1380.00	$1460.00
2	Buy 12	1260.00	1340.00
3	Keep	1160.66	1240.66
4	Keep	1071.93	1151.94
5	Keep	986.93	1066.93
6	Keep	906.43	986.43
7	Keep	830.96	910.96
8	Keep	760.13	840.13
9	Keep	694.61	774.61
10	Keep	632.41	712.41
11	Keep	573.95	653.95
12	Keep	520.00	600.00
13	Keep	470.16	550.16
14	Keep	424.05	504.05
15	Keep	381.36	461.36
16	Keep	341.80	421.80
17	Keep	306.16	386.16
18	Keep	273.24	353.24
19	Keep	242.87	322.87
20	Keep	214.89	294.89
21	Keep	189.19	269.19
22	Keep	165.67	245.67
23	Keep	144.42	224.42
24	Keep	125.80	205.80
25	Keep	110.95	190.95
26	Buy 12	100.00	180.00
27	Buy 12	90.00	170.00
28	Buy 12	80.00	160.00
29	Buy 12	70.00	150.00
30	Buy 12	65.00	145.00
31	Buy 12	60.00	140.00
32	Buy 12	55.00	135.00
33	Buy 12	50.00	130.00
34	Buy 12	40.00	120.00
35	Buy 12	35.00	115.00
36	Buy 12	30.00	110.00
37	Buy 12	25.00	105.00
38	Buy 12	15.00	95.00
39	Buy 12	7.00	87.00
40	Buy 12	0.00	80.00

to note that the program at any iteration requires that if we are going to trade, we must trade for a car whose age is independent of our present car's age. This is just the result that the logic of the situation would dictate.

If we follow our optimal policy, we will keep a car until it is $6\frac{1}{2}$ years old and then buy a 3-year-old car. Suppose, however, that when our car is 4 years old, a friend offers to swap his 1-year-old car for ours for an amount a. Should we take up his offer? In order to answer this question, we must look at the transient values.

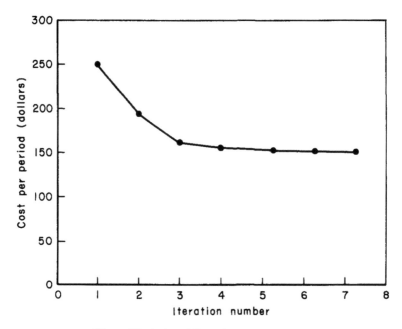

Figure 92. Automobile replacement summary.

In each of the iterations, the value of state 40 was set equal to zero, for computational purposes. Table VI also shows the values under the best policy when the value of state 40 is set equal to $80, the trade-in value of a car of that age. When this is done, each v_i represents the value of a car of age i to a person who is following the optimal policy. In order to answer the question posed above, we must compare the value of a 1-year-old car, $v_4 = \$1,151.93$, with the value of a 4-year-old car, $v_{16} = \$421.80$. If his asking price, a, is less than $v_4 - v_{16} \approx \$730$, we should make the trade; otherwise, we should not. It is, of course, not necessary to change v_{40} from zero in order to answer this problem; however, making $v_{40} = \$80$ does give the values an absolute physical interpretation as well as a relative one.

If the optimal policy is followed, the yearly cost of transportation is about $604 (4 × $150.95). If the policy of maximizing immediate return (shown in iteration 1) were followed, the yearly cost would be $1,000. Thus following a policy which maximizes future return rather than immediate return has resulted in a saving of almost $400 per year. The decrease of period cost with iteration is shown in Fig. 92. The gain approaches the optimal value roughly exponentially. Notice that the gains for the last three iterations are so close that for all practical purposes the corresponding policies may be considered to be equivalent. The fact that a 3-year-old car is the best buy is discovered as early as iteration 4. The model year discontinuity occurring at three years is no doubt responsible for this particular selection.

21. A Simulation Technique

The technique described above involves the solution of simultaneous equations. When these equations are poorly determined or when the number of equations is large, accurate solutions cannot be obtained analytically. To remedy this problem, a simulation approach has been developed.

22. Connection with Linear Programming

A most important feature of the processes we have discussed is the fact that the determination of the asymptotic steady-state behavior can be accomplished by means of linear programming. This is significant since there are now many very efficient algorithms within this theory available for the solution of large-scale problems. Since it would require too much of a digression to present these results, we shall refer the reader to some original papers cited at the end of the chapter.

23. Summary

In this chapter we have presented an application of the technique of "approximation in policy space" particularly suited to the study of Markovian decision processes where the study of asymptotic behavior is meaningful. In many cases, it can be shown that the approach to steady-state behavior is quite rapid. In other cases, only the steady-state behavior is meaningful. Consequently, the results contained in the preceding sections can be applied in a number of ways.

The most difficult problem in this area at the present time is that pertaining to the development of efficient techniques for the treatment of transient states. Here one needs policy approximations of a quite different type.

Comments and Bibliography

§2. Excellent expositions of the fundamentals of the theory of Markov processes may be found in

W. Feller, *An Introduction to Probability Theory and its Applications*, John Wiley and Sons, New York, 1957.

J. G. Kemeny and J. L. Snell, *Finite Markov Chains*, D. Van Nostrand Co., Princeton, 1960.

§3. For the formulation of Markovian decision processes, see

R. Bellman, *Dynamic Programming*, Princeton University Press, Princeton, New Jersey, 1957, Chapter XI,

where references to some papers may be found.

§7. The proof may be found in

R. Bellman, "A Markovian decision process," *J. Math. and Mech.*, vol. 6, 1957, pp. 679–684.

Extensive generalizations, and applications to the optimal inventory problem may be found in the as yet unpublished thesis of Don Iglehart in the Department of Mathematics, Stanford University, 1960.

§9–§14. These results were given by R. Howard in his thesis at Massachusetts Institute of Technology. Many further results will be found in his book

R. A. Howard, *Dynamic Programming and Markov Processes*, Technology Press and John Wiley and Sons, New York, 1960.

§16–§20. These results were first given in

S. Dreyfus, "A note on an industrial replacement process," *Operational Research Q.*, vol. 8, 1957, pp. 190–193.

§21. For discussions of simulation techniques, see

P. Rosentiehl and A. Ghouila–Houri, *Les choix economiques, décisions séquentielle et simulation*, Dunod, Paris, 1960.

R. Bellman, F. Ricciardi, D. Malcolm, C. Clark, and C. Craft, *On Top-Management Simulation*, American Management Assoc., New York, 1957.

§22. A good deal of work has been done by Beckmann, Manne and others on the computational solution of the steady-state equations. For some recent results and other references, see

F. D. Epenoux, "Sur un problème de production et de stockage dans l'aléatoire," *Revue Francaise Recherche Opérationnelle*, no. 14, 1960, pp. 3–16.

We have omitted any discussion of the connection between the results presented here and the theory of sequential machines, and, in particular, the many difficult and significant questions arising in mathematical investigations of medical diagnosis.

See Chapter VIII of

R. Bellman, *Adaptive Control Processes: A Guided Tour*, Princeton University Press, Princeton, New Jersey, 1961,

where many references may be found, and

R. S. Ledley and L. B. Lusted, "Reasoning foundations of medical diagnosis," *Science*, vol. 130, 1959, pp. 9–21.

B. B. Winter, "Optimal diagnostic procedures," *IRE Trans. on Reliability and Quality Control*, vol. RQC-9, 1960, pp. 13–19.

J. E. Overall and C. M. Williams, "Models for medical diagnosis," *Behavioral Science*, vol. 6, 1961, pp. 134–141.

Other references of interest in connection with the foregoing chapter are

D. Blackwell, "On the functional equation of dynamic programming," *J. Math. Analysis and Appl.*, vol. 2, 1961.

H. Raiffa and R. Schlaifer, *Applied Statistical Decision Theory*, Harvard Business School, 1961.

J. L. Fisher, "A class of stochastic investment problems," *Operations Research*, vol. 9, 1961, pp. 53–65.

CHAPTER XII

Numerical Analysis

1. Introduction

In this final chapter, we wish to discuss some matters common to all of the problems we have so far treated. These are questions of accuracy, reduction of computing time, and reduction of dimensionality. Since very little has been done in these areas, our discussion will be necessarily sketchy.

We shall begin with the question of polynomial approximation, presenting both a theoretical discussion and some numerical results. Next we shall consider the use of related techniques for allocation and control processes. Finally, we present a comparison of results obtained by means of the functional equation approach with the exact solution for some simple problems in the calculus of variations.

2. Dimensionality Difficulties—Reprise

Consider the problem of maximizing the function

(1) $$g_1(x_1) + g_2(x_2) + \cdots + g_N(x_N)$$

over all non-negative x_i satisfying the conditions

(2) $$\sum_{j=1}^{N} b_{ij} x_j = c_i, \qquad i = 1, 2, \ldots, M,$$

where $b_{ij} \geq 0$.

As we know, this leads to the recurrence relation

(3) $f_N(c_1, c_2, \ldots, c_M)$
$$= \max_{x_N} [g_N(x_N) + f_{N-1}(c_1 - b_{1N}x_N, c_2 - b_{2N}x_N, \ldots, c_M - b_{MN}x_N)],$$

where

(4) $$b_{iN}x_N \leq c_i, \qquad i = 1, 2, \ldots, M.$$

The solution is readily obtained computationally if $M = 1$, and obtained with a little more difficulty if $M = 2$, using the techniques we have described above. If $M \geq 3$, we must either use a coarser grid or more sophisticated techniques to overcome the memory problem.

3. Polynomial Approximation

Let us now discuss one of the most promising techniques for overcoming the "curse of dimensionality," the approximation of functions by polynomials.

If $f(x)$ is a continuous function defined over the interval $0 \leq x \leq 1$, we can store the function by tabulating the values at grid points

$$x = 0, \Delta, 2\Delta, \ldots, N\Delta = 1.$$

The accuracy of this representation is determined by the value of Δ. However, the smaller the value of Δ, the more values of the function must be computed and stored. Consequently, in any situation we must compromise between the cost due to increased time of computation and that due to inaccuracy of results.

In dealing with functions of several variables, the primary constraint is not cost or time, but the size of the fast memory. If we have a function of four variables, $f(x_1, x_2, x_3, x_4)$, defined over $0 \leq x_1, x_2, x_3, x_4 \leq 1$, even a Δ of .1 for each of the variables leads to a tabulation of 10^4 points for the storage of the function.

What we want then is a far more economical representation of the function. Returning to the case of functions of one variable, let us examine the feasibility of an approximation by means of polynomials,

$$(1) \qquad\qquad f(x) \simeq \sum_{k=0}^{N} a_k x^k.$$

The function is now stored by means of the set of coefficients $[a_0, a_1, \ldots, a_N]$ and the instructions for computing the corresponding polynomial. We can thus obtain the value of $f(x)$ for arbitrary values of x in the interval $[0, 1]$ at the expense of a relatively small amount of storage of information.

4. Orthogonal Polynomials

The problem that now arises is that of determining the coefficients $a_0, a_1, \ldots, a_k$, given the function $f(x)$. Although we may be tempted to use the first $N + 1$ terms of the Taylor expansion of $f(x)$ around $x = 0$, or perhaps $x = 1/2$, we reject this idea for two reasons. In the first place, the Taylor series may diverge outside of a small interval around $x = 0$, or $x = 1/2$. Far more important is the fact that we always view with grave suspicion any method which involves derivatives of functions obtained numerically or graphically.

Let us then retain the polynomial concept, but replace the Taylor expansion by a far more powerful expansion method, expansion in terms of an orthogonal series. For the interval $[0, 1]$, we use Legendre polynomials. To simplify the notation, let us replace the interval $[0, 1]$ by $[-1, 1]$ so that we can use the Legendre polynomials in their usual form.

As we know, the Legendre polynomials, $\{P_n(x)\}$, $n = 0, 1, \ldots,$ $P_0(x) = 1$, form a sequence of polynomials of increasing degree, with the property that

(1)
$$\int_{-1}^{1} P_m(x)P_n(x)\, dx = 0, \qquad m \neq n.$$

Suitably normalizing the polynomials, we can ensure that

(2)
$$\int_{-1}^{1} P_n^2(x)\, dx = 1.$$

It follows purely formally that if we write

(3)
$$f(x) = \sum_{n=0}^{\infty} a_n P_n(x),$$

for $-1 \leq x \leq 1$, we can determine the coefficient a_n by means of the relation

(4)
$$a_n = \int_{-1}^{1} f(x)P_n(x)\, dx.$$

Hence we take as our approximation to $f(x)$ by a polynomial of degree N, the partial sum of degree N,

(5)
$$a_0 + a_1 P_1(x) + \cdots + a_N P_N(x),$$

where the a_N are determined by (4).

This representation of the coefficients has the great merit of depending only upon functional values and not upon derivatives.

5. Gaussian Quadrature

The question arises as to the calculation of the coefficients a_k. If we attempt to derive the values by approximating to the integral in (4.4) by means of a Riemann sum

(1)
$$\int_{-1}^{1} f(x)P_n(x)\, dx = \sum_k f(k\Delta)P_n(k\Delta)\Delta,$$

we find ourselves back in the predicament of tabulating values of $f(x)$ at grid points. If we are going to do this, we may as well do it directly.

We circumvent this difficulty by using a quadrature formula, in this case the Gaussian quadrature formula. In place of using a Riemann sum to evaluate an integral, we use an approximate quadrature formula. The resulting formula has the form

(2)
$$\int_{-1}^{1} g(x)\, dx \simeq \sum_{k=1}^{R} \mu_k g(x_k),$$

where the weights μ_k and the grid points x_k depend upon R. The R quantities $\mu_1, \mu_2, \ldots, \mu_R$, and the R points $x_1, x_2, \ldots, x_R$ can be chosen so that the relation in (2) is *exact* for any polynomial $g(x)$ of degree less than or equal to $2R - 1$.

The coefficient a_n, as determined by integral appearing in (1), will then be evaluated by means of the expression

$$(3) \qquad a_n = \sum_{k=1}^{R} \mu_k f(x_k) P_n(x_k).$$

The quantities $\mu_k P_n(x_k)$, $k = 1, 2, \ldots, R$, $n = 1, 2, \ldots$, are computed ahead of time and stored.

To compute a value of $f(x)$, we now use the expression

$$(4) \qquad f(x) = \sum_{n=0}^{N} a_n P_n(x),$$

where the a_n is determined by (3). The evaluation of $P_n(x)$ for a particular value of x is readily obtained from the three-term recurrence relation

$$(5) \qquad (n+1)P_{n+1}(x) - (2n+1)P_n(x) + nP_{n-1}(x) = 0,$$

valid for the non-normalized Legendre polynomials.

6. A Numerical Example

Let us now see how this technique is applied in practice. Consider the problem of minimizing the function

$$(1) \qquad F_N = \sum_{k=1}^{N} u_k^2 + \sum_{k=1}^{N} v_k^2$$

where

(2) (a) $u_{n+1} = 2u_n - u_n^2 + v_n$, $u_0 = c$,
     (b) v_n must be chosen to keep u_{n+1} within the interval $[-1, 1]$.

Writing

$$(3) \qquad f_N(c) = \min_{\{v\}} F_N$$

for $|c| \leq 1$, we have

$$(4) \qquad f_1(c) = c^2,$$
$$f_N(c) = \min_v [c^2 + v^2 + f_{N-1}(2c - c^2 + v)]$$

for $N \geq 2$. The first six members of the sequence were determined in the usual fashion for a grid of values over $[-1, 1]$.

We then used the technique of polynomial approximation, writing each function in the form

$$(5) \qquad f_N(c) = \sum_{k=0}^{6} a_{k,N} P_k(c),$$

where

$$(6) \qquad a_{k,N} = \int_{-1}^{1} f_N(c) P_k(c)\, dc = \sum_{j=1}^{14} \mu_j f_N(c_j) P_k(c_j).$$

Since the c_j are fixed quantities, independent of N, the sequence of functions $\{f_N(c)\}$ need only be computed at the points $c_1, c_2, \ldots, c_{14}$. To evaluate the expression $f_{N-1}(2c - c^2 + v)$ appearing on the right side of (4), however, we must use the formula

$$(7) \qquad f_{N-1}(2c - c^2 + v) = \sum_{k=0}^{6} a_{k,N} P_k(2c - c^2 + v).$$

To evaluate the quantities $P_k(2c - c^2 + v)$, we employ the recurrence relation of (5.5) and then apply a suitable normalization factor.

A comparison of results is given below. The sequence $\{f_k(c)\}$ was obtained using (4) in a direct fashion, and $\{f_k*(c)\}$ was obtained using (4) and polynomial approximation. As can be seen, the agreement is quite good.

c	$f_6*(c)$	$f_6(c)$
1.0	1.782	1.77
.8	1.370	1.36
.2	.153	.145
0.0	.006	0.0
$-.2$	.202	.20
$-.8$	4.876	4.89
-1.0	8.666	8.67

7. Use of Calculus

In some cases where calculus can be used, we can combine the two techniques, that of continuous variation and that of functional equations, to obtain more efficient algorithms.

Consider the problem of maximizing

$$(1) \qquad F_N = g_1(x_1) + g_2(x_2) + \cdots + g_N(x_N)$$

subject to the constraints

$$(2) \qquad x_1 + x_2 + \cdots + x_N = c, \qquad x_i \geq 0.$$

We obtain the functional equation

$$(3) \qquad f_N(c) = \max_{0 \leq x_N \leq c} [g_N(x_N) + f_{N-1}(c - x_N)].$$

If all of the functions appearing are differentiable, and if we know, in some way or other, that the maximizing point lies inside the interval $0 \leq x_N \leq c$, we obtain from (3) the two relations

$$(4) \qquad g_N'(x_N) - f_{N-1}'(c - x_N) = 0,$$
$$f_N(c) = g_N(x_N) + f_{N-1}(c - x_N).$$

The quantity x_N is determined as a function of c from the first equation. Taking this into account and differentiating the second relation, we have

$$
(5) \qquad f_N'(c) = [g_N'(x_N) - f_{N-1}' (c - x_N)]x_N'(c) + f_{N-1}' (c - x_N)
$$
$$
= f_{N-1}' (c - x_N).
$$

Hence, we have the the the two incremental equations

$$
(6) \qquad\qquad g_N'(x_N) = f_{N-1}' (c - x_N),
$$
$$
f_N'(c) = f_{N-1}' (c - x_N).
$$

We see then that the optimal policy is determined by the marginal returns, the sequence $\{f_k'(c)\}$.

8. Stability

Let us now discuss a problem which we have systematically bypassed in all that has preceded. This is the problem of accuracy of the solution. In treating the typical functional equation that occurs, such as that of (7.3), we introduce two approximations. We first replace a function of a continuous variable by a set of values at discrete grid points, and then replace maximization over a continuous range by maximization over a finite set of values. In some special cases, the original problem is formulated in these terms so that no approximation is made in this fashion. In general, however, we must face the question of comparing the solution of the approximate problem with the solution of the original problem. This is a problem of *stability*. In changing the structure of the equation derived from the physical process in what we hope is a slight way, do we change the structure of the solution in a correspondingly slight fashion?

Questions of this type are notoriously difficult to answer, even in classical theories in which linear equations are paramount. Some work in this area has been done in the field of dynamic programming, but not much. Consequently, we shall attempt to shed some light on these problems by the simple method of comparing the solutions of some problems in the calculus of variations, obtained in exact fashion by analytic techniques, with the solutions obtained computationally by means of functional equation methods.

9. The Brachistochrone Problem

As an initial example, we take one of the first problems attacked by means of the calculus of variations, although posed some time before by Galileo. Indeed, this problem motivated the development of the variational technique.

Given two points in space, we wish to find that path from the higher to the lower along which a particle, under the influence of gravity but without friction, will slide in minimum time.

It is readily seen that along the straight line path shown in Fig. 93, the particle will traverse the minimum distance, but at a low average speed. The curved path results in the particle attaining a high velocity sooner, but travelling a greater distance. The proper balancing of these considerations yields the solution.

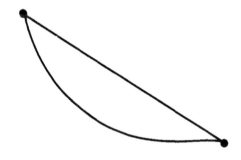

Figure 93

10. Mathematical Formulation

Let us denote the initial point as the origin, and call the final position $(\bar{x}, \bar{y})$ as shown in Fig. 94.

Then, the equations of mechanics tell us that when the particle has fallen a vertical distance y it has velocity $(2gy)^{1/2}$, independent of its horizontal

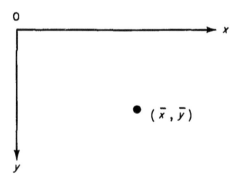

Figure 94

position. Since infinitesimal arc length ds is given by the expression

(1) $$(1 + y'^2)^{1/2}\, dx,$$

the time of descent, the integral of distance over velocity is

(2) $$t(x, y, y') = \int_0^x \left(\frac{1 + y'^2}{2gy}\right)^{1/2} dx.$$

We seek a function $y(x)$ such that $y(0) = 0$, $y(\bar{x}) = \bar{y}$, and t is a minimum.

328

11. Variational Solution

The Euler equation of the calculus of variations states that the solution must satisfy the second order differential equation

$$\text{(1)} \qquad \frac{d}{dx}\frac{\partial t}{\partial y'} - \frac{\partial t}{\partial y} = 0,$$

where t is defined in (2) above.

In this particular case an analytic solution of equation (1) is possible. This rare circumstance accounts for the brachistochrone's lofty position in expositions of the calculus of variations.

Adopting the change of variables

$$\text{(2)} \qquad y' = -\tan\frac{u}{2},$$

the solution has the form

$$\text{(3)} \qquad \begin{aligned} x - a &= b(u + \sin u), \\ y - a &= b(1 + \cos u). \end{aligned}$$

For the boundary points $(0, 0)$ and $(2, 1.8323)$, the constants a and b are easily determined and

$$\text{(4)} \qquad \begin{aligned} x &= \pi + u + \sin u, \\ y &= 1 + \cos u, \\ -\pi &\leq u \leq -.5874, \\ \text{time} &= .4501 \text{ sec.} \end{aligned}$$

It is this solution, and the solution for a related problem with a nonzero initial velocity, which we shall compare with the solution obtained via dynamic programming.

12. Dynamic Programming Formulation

Let us define

(1) $f(x, y)$ = time to fall to the point $(\bar{x}, \bar{y})$ from the point (x, y) following a minimum time trajectory.

Then,

$$\text{(2)} \qquad f(x, y) = \min_{y'}\left[\int_{x}^{x+\Delta x}\left(\frac{1 + y'^2}{2gy}\right)^{1/2}dx_1 + f(x + \Delta x, y + y'\Delta x)\right].$$

The first term of the right-hand side of (2) is the time to traverse an incremental horizontal distance Δx at angle y', and the second term is the remaining time to achieve $(\bar{x}, \bar{y})$. We have assumed that a straight line path is followed during each individual incremental interval. It is important to note that an improved result can readily be obtained by use of a better approximation.

If we make the additional simplification that velocity $(2gy)^{1/2}$ remains constant during each small interval, we obtain the equation

(3)
$$f(x, y) = \min_{y'} \left[\left(\frac{1 + y'^2}{2gy} \right)^{1/2} \Delta x + f(x + \Delta x, y + y'\Delta x) \right].$$

We shall now discuss the numerical solution of this recurrence relation.

13. Computational Procedure

The (x, y) plane was divided into many parts by a grid of width Δx in the x direction and Δy in the y direction, as in Fig. 95.

(0, 0)

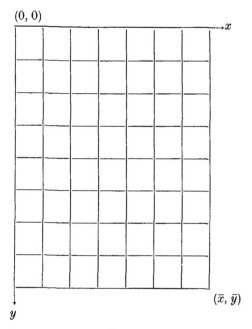

$(\bar{x}, \bar{y})$

Figure 95

Admissible paths are those consisting of straight line segments connecting intersection points of the grid.

The calculation consisted of considering each starting y value for a particular x value, and computing the values of $f(x, y)$ along this vertical line using a recurrence relation of the form of (12.2) or (12.3).

The following simplifications were made:

(1) No path will lie *above* the straight line connecting the initial and final points.

(2) If, starting at (x, y) the optimal value of y at $x + \Delta x$ is $\bar{y}$, then for initial point (x, y^*), where y^* is lower than y, the optimal y is lower than $\bar{y}$.

330

(3) If, as decisions for steeper and steeper descents starting at a given point are examined, the time decreases and then increases, it is assumed that the minimum has been found and no further policy search for that particular starting point is necessary.

These properties of the solution can be established rigorously with some effort.

14. Numerical Results

Since the formulation using a constant velocity fixed at its initial value over an interval results in velocity 0 and hence time ∞ over the first interval, it was decided to use, in this case, the average of initial and final velocity. This formulation is called "Case A," and the exact incremental time case (12.2) is called "Case B." The following results were obtained for initial point (0, 0) and final point (2, 1.8323). The correct minimum time is .4501 seconds.

Case	Δx	Δy	Policy Accuracy	Trajectory Time
A	.25	.09161	.5	.3843
A	.05	.01832	.8	.3976
A	.01	.01832	1.2	.4395
B	.25	.09161	.05	.4546
B	.05	.01832	.02	.4513
B	.04	.01221	.01	.4511

Note that, due to starting at a singularity, approximation A leads to gross errors in policy, but comparatively small errors in time. Approximation B gave as good results as could be hoped for the grid sizes chosen.

A second calculation was performed starting at the point (0, 1.3558), i.e., with initial velocity $(2g)^{1/2}$, and going to (1, 1.8323). The quaint initial and final points chosen were dictated by the trigonometric tables available and the nature of the variable change given by (11.2). For this case, the correct time of descent is .1092. Adopting the above definitions of Cases A and B, we have

Case	Δx	Δy	Policy Accuracy	Trajectory Time
A	.125	.01832	.01	.1092
B	.125	.01832	.01	.1092

We see that, away from the singular point at (0, 0), results are very good.

15. A Problem with Constraints

To evaluate further the accuracy of dynamic programming solutions and to investigate the use of the Lagrange multiplier, let us consider another problem which has been resolved analytically.

We shall seek that curve of specified length connecting two given points such that the area under the curve, and above the axis, is a minimum. We shall further require that the absolute value of the slope be at most equal to 1.

Analytically, we have the problem:

(1)
$$\min_{y(x)} \int_{x_0}^{x_1} y \, dx$$

subject to the constraints

(2)
$$\int_{x_0}^{x_1} \sqrt{1+y'^2} \, dx = c,$$

$$|y'| \leq 1,$$

$$y(x_0) = y_0, \quad y(x_1) = y_1.$$

16. Analytic Solution

An analytic solution was furnished by M. Hestenes. The simplicity of the problem made an exact analysis possible. General problems with constraints possess no straightforward technique of solution.

It can be shown that the optimal solution consists of two (or zero) straight line segments and a circular arc. For end-points $(2\sqrt{2}, 4)$ and $(-2\sqrt{2}, 4)$ and length $4 + \pi$, the solution is

(1) $\quad y = 4 - 2\sqrt{2} + x, \quad \sqrt{2} \leq x \leq 2\sqrt{2}, \quad -2\sqrt{2} \leq x \leq -\sqrt{2},$

$\quad\quad y = 4 - \sqrt{4 - x^2}, \quad -\sqrt{2} \leq x \leq \sqrt{2}.$

17. Dynamic Programming Formulation

We shall adopt the Lagrange multiplier formalism introduced in Chapter II. Then, defining "adjusted area" as area plus λ times length, we let

(1) $f(x, y, \lambda)$ = minimum adjusted area starting at the point (x, y) and going to the fixed final point (x_1, y_1).

This yields the recurrence relation

(2) $f(x, y, \lambda)$

$$= \min_{|y'| \leq 1} \left[\int_x^{x+\Delta x} (y + \lambda(1 + y'^2)^{1/2}) \, dx + f(x + \Delta x, y + y'\Delta x, \lambda) \right],$$

where y' is assumed constant over the interval. Further simplification of the first term on the right yields

(3) $f(x, y, \lambda)$

$$= \min_{|y'| \le 1} \left[\frac{2y + y'\Delta x}{2} + \lambda (1 + y'^2)^{1/2} \Delta x + f(x + \Delta x, y + y'\Delta x, \lambda) \right].$$

Associated with each point (x, y) is the length of the optimal (with respect to the given λ) curve. Calling this quantity $S(x, y, \lambda)$ we have

(4) $\qquad S(x, y, \lambda) = (1 + y'^2)^{1/2} + S(x + \Delta x, y + y'\Delta x, \lambda).$

18. Computational Procedure

We shall consider the problem specified in §16. As in the brachistochrone problem, we divide the space into rectangles by means of grids and consider only paths joining intersections. Since the problem is symmetric about the y-axis, we can consider only the interval $0 \le x \le 2\sqrt{2}$.

The procedure used, for a fixed λ, is to iterate backwards until $f_0(y) \equiv f(0, y), 0 \le y \le 4 - 2\sqrt{2}$, is known. Then the minimum of $f_0(y)$ over all y is determined, and the minimizing y is the starting point for the policy determination phase of the calculation. A little reflection shows that it is this y value that would equal $y(0)$ if the entire interval $-2\sqrt{2} \le x \le 2\sqrt{2}$ were considered.

Once $y(0)$ is determined, for a given λ, $S_0(y(0)) \equiv S(0, y(0))$ gives the arc length. Unless this arc length is the desired one, one adjusts λ and reperforms phase one of the calculation, the determination of the new $f_0(y)$, without bothering to determine the optimal policy, phase two. This means that during the iterations necessary to determine the correct λ, policy data need not be stored or used.

As discussed in Chapter II, §24, the following linear extrapolation rule was used to determine λ:

$$\lambda = \frac{S - S_0}{S_1 - S_0} (\lambda_1 - \lambda_0) + \lambda_0,$$

where λ_0 and λ_1 are the previous guesses, yielding lengths S_0 and S_1 respectively, and S is the desired length.

Since a choice of $\lambda = 0$ implies no length restriction, this would result in a solution with length 8 (Fig. 96). This information was used to initially evaluate λ_0 and S_0. A guess of λ_1 then began the computation.

Summarizing, the computation cycle consisted of: an educated guess of λ; the backward iteration of equation (17.3); the simultaneous evaluation of length via (17.4); the determination of y such that $f_0(y)$ was minimum; and the recalculation of λ dependent upon $S_0(y)$.

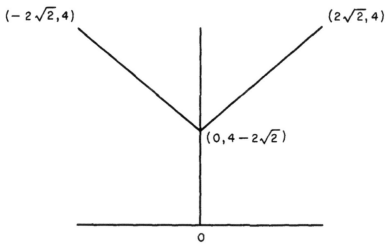

$(-2\sqrt{2},4)$　　　　　　　　　　　　　　　$(2\sqrt{2},4)$

$(0,4-2\sqrt{2})$

O

Figure 96

19. Numerical Results

Results are shown below:

	No. 1	No. 2
Δx	.4	.03
Δy	.05	.01
initial λ	1.4	1.5
final λ	2.034	2.0121
no. of iterations	4	3
max policy error	.03	.01
area error	.01	.01

20. Approximation by Piecewise Linear Functions

In many situations it is convenient to approximate to a function $g(x)$ over an interval $[a, b]$ by means of a piecewise linear function

(1)　　$g(x) = a_j + b_j x, \quad u_{j-1} \leq x \leq u_j, \quad j = 1, \ldots, N-1,$

where $u_0 = a$, $u_N = b$. The constants a_j, b_j and the intervals $[u_{j-1}, u_j]$ can be determined conveniently by the condition that

(2)　　$F(a_1, a_2, \ldots, a_{N+1}; b_1, b_2, \ldots, b_{N+1}, u_1, u_2, \ldots, u_N)$

$$= \sum_{j=1}^{N+1} \int_{u_{j-1}}^{u_j} (g(x) - a_j - b_j x)^2 \, dx$$

is minimized. If approached in a direct fashion this minimization problem leads to a complex computational problem. Dynamic programming furnishes a simple numerical algorithm for obtaining the a_j, b_j and u_j.

21. Basic Recurrence Relation

Let us write, for fixed a and $b \geq a$,

(1) $\qquad f_N(b) = \min_{[a_i, b_i, u_i]} F(a_1, \ldots a_N; b_1, \ldots, b_N; u_1, \ldots, u_N)$.

Then

(2) $\qquad f_1(b) = \min \left[\int_a^{u_1} (g(x) - a_1 - b_1 x)^2 \, dx \right.$

$$\left. + \int_{u_1}^b (g(x) - a_2 - b_2 x)^2 \, dx \right],$$

where the minimum over $-\infty < a_1, a_2, b_1, b_2 < \infty$, $a \leq u_1 \leq b$. This function is readily determined since we can compute the minima over the a_i and b_i and then minimize over u_1 by means of a discrete search.

It is easy to see that for $N \geq 2$ we have

(3) $\qquad f_N(b) = \min_{0 \leq u_N \leq b} \left[\min_{[a_N, b_N]} \int_{u_N}^b (g(x) - a_N - b_N x)^2 \, dx + f_{N-1}(u_N) \right]$.

This is a particular application of the principle of optimality. Since the minimum over a_N, b_N can be calculated explicitly we can write (3) in the form

(4) $\qquad f_N(b) = \min_{a \leq u_N \leq b} [h(u_N b) + f_{N-1}(u_N)]$.

A computational solution along these lines requires a few seconds per stage, where N is the number of stages.

22. Extensions

It requires very little additional effort to approximate to $g(x)$ by quadratic polynomials, or by polynomials of any fixed degree. Similarly, we can compute the minimum of

(1) $\qquad \sum_{j=1}^{N+1} \int_{u_{j-1}}^{u_j} (g(x) - h(x, a_j, b_j))^2 \, dx$,

provided that we know how to minimize the function

(2) $\qquad \int_{u_N}^b (g(x) - h(x, a_N, b_N))^2 \, dx$

over a_N and b_N, or the minimum of

(3) $\qquad \sum_{j=1}^{N+1} \max_{u_{j-1} \leq x \leq u_j} |g(x) - h(x, a_j, b_j)|$.

Comments and Bibliography

§1–§6. We follow the discussion in

R. Bellman and S. Dreyfus, "Functional approximation and dynamic programming," *Math. Tables and Other Aids to Computation*, vol. 13, 1959, pp. 247–251.

§3. For a systematic use of polynomial approximation to resolve dimensionality difficulties, see

C. W. Merriam, III, "An optimization theory for feedback control system design," *Information and Control*, vol. 3, 1960, pp. 32–59.

For examples of the way the technique is used in mathematical physics, see

S. Chandrasekhar, *Radiative Transfer*, Oxford Univ. Press, 1948.

R. Bellman, R. Kalaba, and M. Prestrud, *Invariant Imbedding and Radiative Transfer—I: Plane Parallel Slabs of Finite Thickness*, The RAND Corporation, to appear.

§8. For a discussion of the concept of stability as it pertains to differential equations, see

R. Bellman, *Stability Theory of Differential Equations*, McGraw-Hill Book Co., Inc., New York, 1954.

Many further references will be found there. There is a brief discussion of stability of solutions of the functional equations we have been considering in Chapter 1 of *Dynamic Programming*.

On a Transcendental Curve

BY O. GROSS

The following discussion is concerned with the inflection points of a family of curves defined by the relationship

$$(1) \qquad f(z) = [1 - e^{-x/(y+z)}]^y + \lambda z, \qquad z \geq 0,$$

with the parameters satisfying $y \geq 1$, $x > 0$, $\lambda > 0$.

1. The Number of Inflection Points

We assert that each member of the family has at most one point of inflection. To show this, it is sufficient to verify that the extended curve on the range $z > -y$ has exactly one. We proceed to do this.

Note that, for the foregoing result, the presence of λ in (1) is inessential. Also, since nonsingular linear transformations preserve the number of points of inflection, we can set $z = xw - y$. The condition $z > -y$ is then equivalent to $w > 0$ and the problem thus reduces to determining the number of points of inflection of

$$(2) \qquad \phi(w) = (1 - e^{-1/w})^y, \qquad w > 0.$$

From (2) we get

$$(3) \qquad \frac{-\phi'(w)}{y} = (1 - e^{-1/w})^{y-1} e^{-1/w} \frac{1}{w^2}.$$

Now, the inflection points of (2) correspond to the relative minima and maxima of the function (3). But since the transformation $w = 1/u$ is a homeomorphic mapping of $(0, \infty)$ with $dw/du < 0$, we see that the inflection points of (2) correspond to the relative interior minima and maxima of

$$(4) \qquad X(u) = (1 - e^{-u})^{y-1} e^{-u} u^2, \qquad u > 0.$$

These, in turn, are included in the set of positive roots of $X'(u) = 0$. Now, since $e^{-u} u^2$ has exactly one interior local maximum ($u = 2$) and no interior local minima, we can assume that $y > 1$. Thus, from (4) we get

$$(5) \qquad \begin{aligned} X'(u) &= 2u(1 - e^{-u})^{y-1} e^{-u} - (1 - e^{-u})^{y-1} e^{-u} u^2 \\ &\quad + (y - 1)(1 - e^{-u})^{y-2} e^{-2u} u^2 = 0. \end{aligned}$$

Since
$$u(1 - e^{-u})^{y-2}e^{-u} \neq 0,$$
from (5) we obtain
$$2(1 - e^{-u}) - u(1 - e^{-u}) + (y - 1)ue^{-u} = 0,$$
or
$$2 - u + e^{-u}(uy - 2) = 0.$$
Now since $y > 1$, $u = 2$ is not a root of the above equation, and we obtain

(6)
$$e^u = \frac{uy - 2}{u - 2}, \quad 2 \neq u > 0.$$

Since $e^u > 1$ if $u > 0$, and $(uy - 2)/(u - 2) < 1$ if $0 < u < 2$, we see that there is no root in $(0, 2)$. On the other hand, e^u strictly increases to infinity while, for $u > 2$, $(uy - 2)/(u - 2)$ strictly decreases from ∞ to a finite value. Thus, we see that there is exactly one positive root of the above equation. Since the order of contact is clearly zero, it follows that this root corresponds to a unique inflection point of (2) and our assertion is proved.

2. A Necessary and Sufficient Condition for Convexity

We observe from (1) that the term not involving λ is positive and tends to zero as $z \to \infty$. The presence of the unique inflection point on the extended curve then guarantees that f is eventually convex. It follows that a necessary and sufficient condition that f be convex on the range $z > 0$ is that the inflexion point, z, on the extended curve satisfy $z \leq 0$, i.e., in accordance with the order of the transformations of §1, $xw - y \leq 0$, or $x/u - y \leq 0$, where, from (6),
$$e^u = \frac{uy - 2}{u - 2}.$$
Solving this last equation for y in terms of u, we obtain

(7)
$$y = e^u + \frac{2}{u}(1 - e^u) = F(u).$$

Now, noting that the right-hand side of (6) is a strictly increasing function of y for $u > 2$ and that e^u is strictly increasing, we see that the root u is a strictly increasing function of y, and thus we see that a necessary and sufficient condition that $x/u - y \leq 0$, i.e., that $u \geq x/y$, is $y \geq F(x/y)$. In other words,
$$y \geq e^{x/y} + \frac{2y}{x}(1 - e^{x/y}).$$
The boundary curve $y = F(x/y)$ of course can be parametrized as follows:

(8)
$$x = tF(t),$$
$$y = F(t), \quad t \geq 2,$$

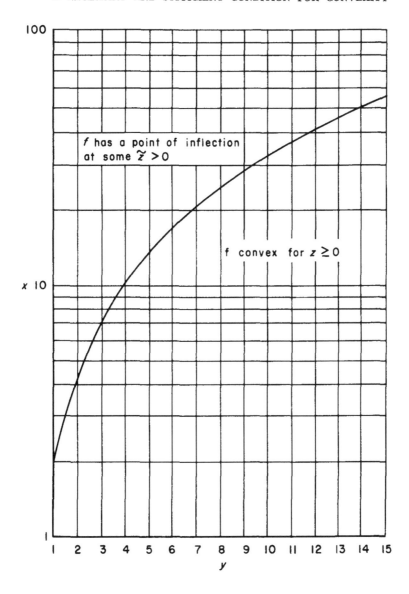

Figure 97. Region of convexity of the function $f(z) = [1 - e^{-x(y+z)}]^y + \lambda z$, $\lambda > 0$, for $z \geq 0$ with parameters satisfying $y \geq 1$, $x > 0$.

where

$$F(t) = e^t + \frac{2}{t}(1 - e^t).$$

We thus obtain the region in the (x, y) plane in which f is convex, as shown in Fig. 97.

339

A New Approach to the Duality Theory
of Mathematical Programming

S. DREYFUS and M. FREIMER

1. Introduction

In this appendix we shall develop a technique in which we imbed a mathematical programming problem in the more general problem in which the optimal return is considered to be a function of the available input commodities. This optimal return function is central to our method. A simple characterization of its properties leads directly and intuitively to the duality theory of linear programming and also to the Kuhn-Tucker [1] results for quadratic programming. Furthermore, this approach yields immediate economic interpretation of the quantities involved.

2. The Dual Linear Programming Problem

The typical linear programming problem requires us to find a vector

$$(1) \qquad x = \begin{pmatrix} x_1 \\ x_2 \\ \cdot \\ \cdot \\ \cdot \\ x_n \end{pmatrix}$$

which maximizes the linear objective function

$$(2) \qquad c'x,$$

subject to the inequality constraints

$$(3) \qquad Ax \leq b$$

and

$$(4) \qquad x \geq 0,$$

where the components of

$$(5) \qquad c = \begin{bmatrix} c_1 \\ c_2 \\ \cdot \\ \cdot \\ \cdot \\ c_n \end{bmatrix}$$

$$(6) \qquad A = \begin{bmatrix} a_{11} & a_{12} & \cdots & a_{1n} \\ a_{21} & a_{22} & \cdots & a_{2n} \\ \cdot & \cdot & & \cdot \\ \cdot & \cdot & & \cdot \\ \cdot & \cdot & & \cdot \\ a_{m1} & a_{m2} & \cdots & a_{mn} \end{bmatrix},$$

and

$$(7) \qquad b = \begin{bmatrix} b_1 \\ b_2 \\ \cdot \\ \cdot \\ \cdot \\ b_m \end{bmatrix}$$

are given.

Let $f(b)$ be the maximum value of the objective function (2), considered as a function of the right side of the constraint (3). If x^0 is an optimal solution to the problem, then

$$(8) \qquad f(b) = c'x^0.$$

In order to study the behavior of f, consider the element $x_j{}^0$ of the optimal solution. If we were to increase $x_j{}^0$ by ϵ, then we might have to replace the right side of (3) by $b + \epsilon A^{(j)}$ in order to still satisfy the restriction, where

$$(9) \qquad A^{(j)} = \begin{bmatrix} a_{1j} \\ a_{2j} \\ \cdot \\ \cdot \\ \cdot \\ a_{mj} \end{bmatrix}$$

is the jth column of A. We are thus led to considering $f(b + \epsilon A^{(j)})$, which is the maximum value of $c'y$ subject to the restrictions

$$(10) \qquad Ay \le b + \epsilon A^{(j)}$$

and

$$(11) \qquad y \ge 0.$$

Since

$$(12) \qquad y = \begin{bmatrix} x_1{}^0 \\ \cdot \\ \cdot \\ \cdot \\ x_j{}^0 + \epsilon \\ \cdot \\ \cdot \\ \cdot \\ x_n{}^0 \end{bmatrix} = x^0 + \epsilon e^j,$$

where e^j is the unit vector in the jth direction, satisfies inequalities (10) and (11) and yields a return of

$$(13) \qquad c'(x^0 + \epsilon e^j) = f(b) + \epsilon c_j,$$

we see that

$$(14) \qquad f(b + \epsilon A^{(j)}) \geq f(b) + \epsilon c_j \qquad\qquad \epsilon > 0, \text{ all } j.$$

Expanding[1] the left side in powers of ϵ, we obtain

$$(15) \qquad f(b) + \epsilon \sum_{i=1}^{m} \frac{\partial f}{\partial b_i} a_{ij} + \text{ higher order terms } \geq f(b) + \epsilon c_j$$

Taking ϵ small enough and > 0, we see that for all j

$$(16) \qquad \sum_{i=1}^{m} \frac{\partial f}{\partial b_i} a_{ij} \geq c_j$$

Now suppose that $x_j{}^0 > 0$. Then we can allow ϵ to be negative in the above analysis, provided it is close enough to zero (so that y as defined in (12) satisfies inequality (11)). But, since $\epsilon < 0$, we conclude from (15) that

$$(17) \qquad \sum_{i=1}^{m} \frac{\partial f}{\partial b_i} a_{ij} \leq c_j \qquad \text{if} \qquad x_j{}^0 > 0.$$

Therefore

$$(18) \qquad \sum_{i=1}^{m} \frac{\partial f}{\partial b_i} a_{ij} = c_j \qquad \text{if} \qquad x_j{}^0 > 0.$$

We next observe that

$$(19) \qquad \frac{\partial f}{\partial b_i} \geq 0, \qquad \text{for all } i.$$

This follows, for the problem as stated above, from the fact that changing the problem by increasing b_i (which is usually thought of as the available amount of some commodity) cannot lead us to choose an optimal solution worse than the original one, but may allow us to improve on the previous optimal value of the objective function.

Inequalities (16) and (19) lead us to consider vectors

$$(20) \qquad u = \begin{bmatrix} u_1 \\ u_2 \\ \cdot \\ \cdot \\ \cdot \\ u_m \end{bmatrix}$$

---

[1] There may be some values of b for which this expansion is mathematically impossible. We can get around this difficulty by the simple trick of choosing a well-behaved b infinitesimally close to the given one. We shall omit any discussion of this procedure here, since it contributes nothing to the understanding of our approach to duality.

which satisfy the inequalities

(21) $$u'A \geq c'$$

and

(22) $$u \geq 0.$$

Combining inequalities (3), (4), (21) and (22) we have

(23) $$c'x \leq (u'A)x = u'(Ax) \leq u'b,$$

which holds for any x and u satisfying (3), (4), (21) and (22). In particular, if we choose x^0 and u^0, where

(24) $$u_i^0 = \frac{\partial f}{\partial b_i},$$

then the two inequalities in (23) become equalities. For, by equation (18) we have $x_j^0 = 0$ or $c_j = \sum_{i=1}^{m} u_i^0 a_{ij}$ (or both), while the very definition of f shows that if $\sum_{j=1}^{n} a_{ij}x_j^0 < b_i$ then $u_i^0 = 0$. (This last statement follows from the fact that if a commodity is not used to capacity, then changing the supply of the commodity slightly will not change the optimal return).

We have now shown that

(25) $$c'x \leq c'x^0 = u^{0'}b \leq u'b,$$

for all x and u satisfying constraints (3), (4), (21) and (22). We have thus derived the *dual problem*: minimize $u'b$ subject to constraints (21) and (22). We have introduced the variable u_i for $\frac{\partial f}{\partial b_i}$ to conform to conventional terminology. The meaning of the imputed value $\frac{\partial f}{\partial b_i}$ is evident, and is used, throughout the derivation. Usual derivations of duality introduce u as Lagrange multipliers and, after formal manipulation to derive the duality results, observe that u has economic significance.

It is interesting to observe how the particular statement of the problem affects our conclusions. If the inequality in the constraint set (3) were reversed, then our conclusion (19) about the sign of the dual variable would be reversed. Equality in (3) would imply nothing about the sign of the dual variables. (Since all of commodity i would be consumed by any feasible program, an increase in b_i might result in either increased or decreased return). Changing the problem from one of maximizing a linear form to one of minimizing would reverse the sense of the inequalities in equations (14), (15), (16), and (17) and, ultimately in (25) and the conclusions based upon it. In this case, of course, one would define $f(b)$ as the minimum obtainable value of the objective function.

We present in Table 1 some primal and related dual problems. The reader can easily verify these results using the above considerations.

TABLE 1

	Objective, $c'x$	max	min	max	min	max	max
PRIMAL	Constraints, Ax	$\leq b$	$\leq b$	$\geq b$	$\geq b$	$\leq b$	$= b$
	Variables, x	≥ 0	≥ 0	≥ 0	≥ 0	unrestricted	≥ 0
	Objective, $b'u$	min	max	min	max	min	min
DUAL	Constraints, $A'u$	$\geq c$	$\leq c$	$\geq c$	$\leq c$	$= c$	$\geq c$
	Variables, u	≥ 0	≤ 0	≤ 0	≥ 0	≥ 0	unrestricted

3. The Kuhn-Tucker Equations: Quadratic Case

The typical quadratic programming problem requires us to choose the vector x so as to maximize the quadratic objective function

$$(1) \qquad p'x - \tfrac{1}{2}x'Cx,$$

subject to constraints (2.3) and (2.4). Here x, A, and b are as in Section 2, and the components of

$$(2) \qquad p = \begin{bmatrix} p_1 \\ p_2 \\ \cdot \\ \cdot \\ \cdot \\ p_n \end{bmatrix}$$

and

$$(3) \qquad C = \begin{bmatrix} c_{11} & c_{12} & \cdots & c_{1n} \\ c_{21} & c_{22} & \cdots & c_{2n} \\ \cdot & \cdot & & \cdot \\ \cdot & \cdot & & \cdot \\ \cdot & \cdot & & \cdot \\ c_{n1} & c_{n2} & \cdots & c_{nn} \end{bmatrix}$$

are given. Furthermore, C is assumed to be positive definite.

Let $f(b)$ be the maximum value of the objective function. If x^0 is an optimal solution then

$$(4) \qquad f(b) = p'x^0 - \tfrac{1}{2}x^{0\prime}Cx^0.$$

We again consider $f(b + \epsilon A^{(j)})$, which is now the maximum value of

$p'y - \frac{1}{2}y'Cy$ subject to constraints (2.10) and (2.11). As before, $y = x^0 + \epsilon e^j$ satisfies (2.10) and (2.11), now yielding a return of

(5) $p'(x^0 + \epsilon e^j) - \frac{1}{2}(x^0 + \epsilon e^j)'C(x^0 + \epsilon e^j)$

$$= f(b) + \epsilon\left(p_j - \sum_{i=1}^{n} c_{ji}x_i^0\right) + \frac{1}{2}\epsilon^2 c_{jj}.$$

Thus

(6) $$f(b + \epsilon A^{(j)}) \geq f(b) + \epsilon\left(p_j - \sum_{i=1}^{n} c_{ji}x_i^0\right) + \frac{1}{2}\epsilon^2 c_{jj}.$$

Expanding the left side in powers of ϵ, we obtain

(7) $f(b) + \epsilon\sum_{i=1}^{m}\frac{\partial f}{\partial b_i}a_{ij} + \frac{1}{2}\epsilon^2\sum_{i=1}^{m}\sum_{k=1}^{m}\frac{\partial^2 f}{\partial b_i \partial b_k}a_{ij}a_{kj} + \text{higher order terms}$

$$\geq f(b) + \epsilon\left(p_j - \sum_{i=1}^{n} c_{ji}x_i^0\right) + \frac{1}{2}\epsilon^2 c_{jj} \qquad \epsilon > 0, \text{ all } j.$$

Taking ϵ small enough we see that

(8) $$\sum_{i=1}^{m}\frac{\partial f}{\partial b_i}a_{ij} \geq p_j - \sum_{i=1}^{n} c_{ji}x_i^0 \qquad \text{all } j$$

or, in vector notation,

(9) $$A'u^0 \geq p - Cx^0.$$

Now suppose that $x_j^0 > 0$. Then we can allow ϵ to be negative in the above analysis, obtaining the opposite inequality to (8). Combining this with (8) we have

(10) $$\sum_{i=1}^{m}\frac{\partial f}{\partial b_i}a_{ij} = p_j - \sum_{i=1}^{n} c_{ij}x_i^0 \qquad \text{if} \qquad x_j^0 > 0.$$

In order to make (8) an equality for all j, we introduce the vector

(11) $$v = \begin{bmatrix} v_1 \\ v_2 \\ \cdot \\ \cdot \\ \cdot \\ v_n \end{bmatrix},$$

which is defined by the equation

(12) $$A'u^0 = p - cx^0 + v.$$

It is then clear that

(13) $$v \geq 0,$$

and that

(14) $$v_j = 0 \qquad \text{if} \qquad x_j^0 > 0.$$

345

As in Section 2,

(15) $$u^0 \geq 0$$

follows from the definition of f.

The equations (12), (13), (14), and (15) are the *Kuhn-Tucker optimality conditions* for the above quadratic programming problem.

Combining equations (7) and (10) we find that

(16) $$\sum_{i=1}^{m} \sum_{k=1}^{m} \frac{\partial^2 f}{\partial b_i \partial b_k} a_{ij} a_{kj} \geq c_{jj} \quad \text{if} \quad x_j^0 > 0,$$

the interpretation of which we leave to the reader as an exercise.

4. The Kuhn-Tucker Equations: General Case

Suppose that we are required to maximize an arbitrary function $\phi(x)$, subject to constraints (2.3) and (2.4). Defining $f(b)$ to be the maximum value of the objective function, and x^0 to be an optimal solution, we apply our usual argument to obtain

(1) $$f(b + \epsilon A^{(j)}) \geq \phi(x^0 + \epsilon e^j) \qquad \epsilon > 0, \text{ all } j,$$

(2) $$f(b + \epsilon A^{(j)}) \geq \phi(x^0 + \epsilon e^j) \qquad \epsilon < 0, \text{ if } x_j^0 > 0.$$

Since the expansions of f and ϕ are

(3) $$f(b + \epsilon A^{(j)}) = f(b) + \epsilon \sum_{i=1}^{m} \frac{\partial f}{\partial b_i} a_{ij} + \tfrac{1}{2}\epsilon^2 \sum_{i=1}^{m} \sum_{k=1}^{m} \frac{\partial^2 f}{\partial b_i \partial b_k} a_{ij} a_{kj} + \cdots$$

(4) $$\phi(x^0 + \epsilon e^j) = \phi(x^0) + \epsilon \frac{\partial \phi}{\partial x_j} + \tfrac{1}{2}\epsilon^2 \frac{\partial^2 \phi}{\partial x_j^2} + \cdots$$

and

(5) $$\phi(x^0) = f(b),$$

we conclude (as in Section 3) that

(6) $$\sum_{i=1}^{m} \frac{\partial f}{\partial b_i} a_{ij} \geq \frac{\partial \phi}{\partial x_j} \qquad \text{all } j,$$

(7) $$\sum_{i=1}^{m} \frac{\partial f}{\partial b_i} a_{ij} = \frac{\partial \phi}{\partial x_j} \qquad \text{if } x_j^0 > 0,$$

(8) $$\sum_{i=1}^{m} \sum_{k=1}^{m} \frac{\partial^2 f}{\partial b_i \partial b_k} a_{ij} a_{kj} \geq \frac{\partial^2 \phi}{\partial x_j^2} \qquad \text{if } x_j^0 > 0.$$

346

If we replace $\dfrac{\partial f}{\partial b_i}$ in equations (6) and (7) by u_i, we obtain the *Kuhn-Tucker optimality conditions* for the general programming problem stated above.

Bibliography

1. H. W. Kuhn and A. W. Tucker, "Nonlinear programming," *Proc. Second Berkeley Symposium on Mathematical Statistics and Probability*, University of California Press, Berkeley, 1951, pp. 481–492.

A Computational Technique Based on Successive Approximations in Policy Space

S. DREYFUS

1. Introduction

In this appendix we wish to present the elements of a theory of numerical solution of optimization problems that holds great promise of breaking the dimensionality barrier. The technique is basically one based upon gradients in which the approach to an optimal policy is by successive steps. Our method of derivation employs the familiar concepts and techniques of dynamic programming. These results have also been obtained by Bryson and Kelley[1],[2], using more complicated derivations. Bryson has obtained in this way numerical solutions of variational problems involving up to eight state variables, and there seems to be practically no limit to the generality of the method.

The drawbacks to this method of breaking the bonds of dimensionality are twofold. In the first place, there is the possibility of converging to an extremal which does not yield the absolute minimum or maximum. Consequently, for problems of low dimensionality there is much in favor of the usual technique emphasized in the foregoing pages of this book. For problems of high dimensionality, however, the simplicity and practicality of the method compensate for the danger of local optimality. Secondly, inequality constraints on the state and decision variables cause considerable difficulty. These can to some extent be taken into account in the successive approximations, but not in any routine fashion. Recall that in the conventional dynamic programming algorithm constraints merely limit the range of decision space that must be searched and thus are desirable rather than inconvenient.

2. The Problem

We shall restrict ourselves throughout this appendix to a discrete analogue of the type of variational problem that bears the name "Problem of Mayer" (see § 22 of Chapter V). This represents no loss of generality since to begin with any variational problem can be transformed into a Mayer problem, and since, secondly, discretization is necessary for the digital computation of the numerical solution of continuous variational problems. Furthermore, the reader has probably realized by now that almost all dynamic programming problems can be viewed as variational problems, and conversely.

Our problem can be stated in the following form.

We wish to minimize a function ϕ of the state variables $y_1, \ldots, y_n$ and time t at some unspecified future time T where T is the first time that a certain "stopping relation"

$$(1) \qquad \psi(y_1, \ldots, y_n, t) = 0$$

is satisfied. The y_i's are determined by their initial values

$$(2) \qquad y_{1_0}, \ldots, y_{n_0}$$

and the difference equations

$$(3) \qquad y_i(t + \Delta t) = y_i(t) + g_i(y_1(t), \ldots, y_n(t), z(t), t) \; \Delta t$$

where $z(t)$ is the decision variable and is to be chosen optimally.

That is, we wish to choose that sequence of numbers $\{z_k\}$, where $z_k = z(k \; \Delta t)$, so that as the state variables y_i develop with time we encounter the stopping condition $\psi = 0$ with minimum ϕ.

Minimum time problems can be considered to be special cases of this general problem where $\phi = t$. Alternatively, if the final time is required explicitly to be T_F, then

$$(4) \qquad \psi = t - T_F = 0$$

is the stopping condition.

In order to avoid treating t as a special variable, we shall let $y_{n+1} = t$ and $g_{n+1} = 1$.

3. The Recurrence Equations

We begin by guessing a presumably nonoptimal sequence of decisions $\{z_0, z_1, \ldots, z_k, \ldots\}$ where $z_k = z(k \; \Delta t)$ and compute the curve generated by these decisions in conjunction with equations (2.2) and (2.3).

We define the nonoptimal return function

$$(1) \qquad f(y_1, \ldots, y_{n+1}) = \text{the value of } \phi \text{ at stopping condition } \psi = 0$$
$$\text{where we start in state } y_1, \ldots, y_{n+1} \text{ and use}$$
$$\text{the guessed policy } \{z_k\}.$$

The function f is immediately seen to satisfy the recurrence relation

$$(2) \qquad f(y_1, \ldots, y_{n+1}) = f(y_1 + g_1 \; \Delta t, \ldots, y_{n+1} + g_{n+1} \; \Delta t)$$

where the g's are evaluated using the guessed $\{z_k\}$ and associated trajectory.

In order to discover the first order effect of a change in the decision variable at time t we seek to evaluate $\dfrac{\partial f}{\partial z}\bigg|_t$ where this notation means

$\partial f/\partial z$ evaluated in terms of the state and decision variables at time t. By partial differentiation of (2) with respect to z we see that

$$(3) \qquad \left.\frac{\partial f}{\partial z}\right|_t = \left\{ \sum_{i=1}^{n+1} \left(\left.\frac{\partial f}{\partial y_i}\right|_{t+\Delta t}\right) \left(\left.\frac{\partial g_i}{\partial z}\right|_t\right) \right\} \Delta t.$$

To evaluate this expression we see that we need to know $\left.\dfrac{\partial f}{\partial y_j}\right|_{t+\Delta t}$. A recurrence relation for this quantity is obtained by partial differentiation with respect to y_j of (2)

(4)

$$\left.\frac{\partial f}{\partial y_j}\right|_t = \left\{ \sum_{i=1}^{n+1} \left(\left.\frac{\partial f}{\partial y_i}\right|_{t+\Delta t}\right) \left(\left.\frac{\partial g_i}{\partial y_j}\right|_t\right) \Delta t \right\} + \left.\frac{\partial f}{\partial y_j}\right|_{t+\Delta t}, \qquad j = 1, \ldots, n+1.$$

Both equations (3) and (4) have obvious verbal interpretations. Equation (3) states that the rate of change of f with respect to z at time t equals the rate at which the state of the system at time $t + \Delta t$ changes as z varies multiplied by the rate at which f changes as the state of the system changes at time $t + \Delta t$. Equation (4) adds the change in f due to the effect of a change in y_j on the g_i to the direct effect of the change in $y_j(t)$ on $y_j(t + \Delta t)$ to obtain the net change in f.

Equation (4) is seen to be the discrete analogue of the Multiplier Rule

$$(5) \qquad \frac{d}{dt} f_{y_j} + \sum_{i=1}^{n+1} f_{y_i} \frac{\partial g_i}{\partial y_j} = 0$$

derived in Chapter V, § 22, equation (10). If $\partial f/\partial z \equiv 0$ no improvement is possible and the nominal curve is optimal. This observation leads to equation (6) of § 22, Chapter V.

We now have two ordinary recurrence relations, (3) and (4), that permit us to evaluate the effect of a change in z at any time upon the final objective function ϕ. We determine the boundary conditions for the recurrence relations by observing that a change in a state variable at the final time T has two effects, the immediate change in ϕ and the change in ϕ due to the change in the final time determined by $\psi = 0$. Applying this reasoning we have

$$(6) \qquad \left.\frac{\partial f}{\partial y_j}\right|_T = \left.\frac{\partial \phi}{\partial y_j}\right|_T - \left(\left.\frac{\dot{\phi}}{\dot{\psi}}\right|_T\right) \left(\left.\frac{\partial \psi}{\partial y_j}\right|_T\right), \qquad j = 1, \ldots, n+1.$$

We have derived, by two simple differentiations, expressions evaluating the first order effect of a decision change at any time upon the final value of ϕ. These results can be thought of as "influence functions," or adjoint equations, and are usually derived from theorems concerning the representation of solutions of linear differential equations.

The manner in which these results can be used most efficiently for the successive improvement of a nonoptimal solution is largely an experimental matter in the realm of numerical analysis. In the following section we shall present one seemingly very efficient way of using these results due to Bryson.

4. The Means of Improvement

We postulate the rule

$$(1) \qquad z_{\text{new}}(t) = z_{\text{old}}(t) + \delta z(t)$$

for adjusting z and seek an expression for δz. We start by adopting the reasonable policy (there are alternatives), of changing z at each time t proportionally to the quantity

$$\sum_{i=1}^{n+1} \frac{\partial f}{\partial y_i} \frac{\partial g_i}{\partial z}$$

evaluated at time t. That is, where the potential payoff rate $\partial f/\partial z$ is greater we will act more decisively. Writing

$$(2) \qquad \delta z = k \sum_{i=1}^{n+1} \frac{\partial f}{\partial y_i} \frac{\partial g_i}{\partial z},$$

we conclude from (3.3) that

$$(3) \qquad \Delta\phi = \sum_{t=0}^{T} \frac{\partial f}{\partial z} \delta z = k \sum_{t=0}^{T} \left(\sum_{i=0}^{n+1} \frac{\partial f}{\partial y_i} \frac{\partial g_i}{\partial z} \right)^2 \Delta t$$

where $\Delta\phi$ is the change in the final value of ϕ due to the changes in $z(t)$ of $\delta z(t)$ at all times $0 \leq t \leq T$. The summand in the expression for $\Delta\phi$ is easily computable along a given trajectory by means of the recurrence relations (3.3) and (3.4).

If we desire an improvement of $\overline{\Delta\phi}$ in the value of ϕ, we choose

$$(4) \qquad k = \frac{\overline{\Delta\phi}}{\sum_{t=0}^{T} \left(\sum_{i=1}^{n+1} \frac{\partial f}{\partial y_i} \frac{\partial g_i}{\partial z} \right)^2 \Delta t}$$

and use, for the next iteration, the new decision function given by

$$(5) \qquad z_{\text{new}}(t) = z_{\text{old}}(t) + \frac{\left(\sum_{i=1}^{n+1} \frac{\partial f}{\partial y_i} \frac{\partial g_i}{\partial z} \right) \overline{\Delta\phi}}{\sum_{t=0}^{T} \left(\sum_{i=1}^{n+1} \frac{\partial f}{\partial y_i} \frac{\partial g_i}{\partial z} \right)^2 \Delta t}.$$

We would be well advised to seek only a modest improvement $\overline{\Delta\phi}$ at each successive iteration since our analysis is first order and only accurate for small changes.

Let us now introduce some notation and recapitulate results before deriving successive approximation techniques for more complicated problems. We shall write $\lambda_{y_i}(\phi)$ for $\partial f/\partial y_i$, remembering that $\lambda_{y_i}(\phi)$ can be interpreted as the effect of a change in y_i on the value of ϕ at the final time. For $\sum_{i=1}^{n+1} \dfrac{\partial f}{\partial y_i}\dfrac{\partial g_i}{\partial z}$ we write $\lambda_z(\phi)$. In this notation, the technique of successive improvement is:

(1) Guess $z(t)$.
(2) Integrate the equations of motion (2.3).
(3) Evaluate $\lambda_{y_i}(\phi)$ at the final time T by means of (3.6).
(4) Determine $\lambda_{y_i}(\phi)$ along the nominal trajectory by backwards recursion of (3.4) and simultaneously compute $\lambda_z(\phi)$ and $\sum_{t}^{T} (\lambda_z(\phi))^2 \, \Delta t$ from (3.3).
(5) Determine z_{new} for a specified small $\overline{\Delta\phi}$ by (4.5).
(6) Return to step (2).

Suppose now that an additional relationship

(6) $$\theta(y_1, \ldots, y_n, t) = 0$$

must be satisfied at the stopping time. The same arguments as in the preceding paragraphs allows us to compute the influence of a change in z on the final value of θ by means of the formulas

(7) $$\lambda_{y_j}(\theta)\big|_t = \left(\sum_{i=1}^{n+1} \left(\lambda_{y_i}(\theta)\big|_{t+\Delta t}\right)\left(\frac{\partial g_i}{\partial y_j}\bigg|_t\right) \right) \Delta t + \lambda_{y_j}(\theta)\big|_{t+\Delta t},$$

(8) $$\lambda_z(\theta)\big|_t = \sum_{i=1}^{n+1} \left(\lambda_{y_i}(\theta)\big|_{t+\Delta t}\right)\left(\frac{\partial g_i}{\partial z}\bigg|_t\right),$$

(9) $$\lambda_{y_j}(\theta)\big|_T = \frac{\partial\theta}{\partial y_j}\bigg|_T - \frac{\dot{\theta}}{\dot{\psi}}\bigg|_T \frac{\partial\psi}{\partial y_j}\bigg|_T.$$

We now let δz have the form

(10) $$\delta z = k_1\lambda_z(\phi) + k_2\lambda_z(\theta),$$

and conclude

(11) $$\Delta\phi = \sum_{t=0}^{T} \lambda_z(\theta) \, \Delta t \, \delta z,$$

(12) $$\Delta\theta = \sum_{t=0}^{T} \lambda_z(\theta) \, \Delta t \, \delta z.$$

If the nominal trajectory, due to either numerical roundoff, nonlinearity, or difficulties in finding an initial feasible trajectory, does not satisfy the auxiliary condition (6) we choose $\overline{\Delta\theta}$ as minus the deviation for the desired final condition. If the nominal trajectory is feasible, $\overline{\Delta\theta}$ is taken to be zero.

We now solve the simultaneous linear equations

$$(13) \qquad \overline{\Delta\phi} = \left[\sum_{t=0}^{T} \lambda_z(\phi)^2 \right] k_1 \, \Delta t + \left[\sum_{t=0}^{T} \lambda_z(\phi)\lambda_z(\theta) \right] k_2 \, \Delta t,$$

$$(14) \qquad \overline{\Delta\phi} = \left[\sum_{t=0}^{T} \lambda_z(\phi)\lambda_z(\theta) \right] k_1 \, \Delta t + \left[\sum_{t=0}^{T} \lambda_z(\theta)^2 \right] k_2 \, \Delta t$$

for k_1 and k_2 to be used in equation (10) to achieve an improvement $\overline{\Delta\phi}$ in the objective function and a correction $\overline{\Delta\theta}$ in the final value of the subsidiary condition.

The above device can be used to include any reasonable number of auxiliary final conditions.

In an unpublished paper, Bryson has extended the above technique so that one can ask for the maximum improvement in the objective function given a specified value for

$$(15) \qquad \sum_{t=0}^{T} (\delta z)^2$$

and has also developed techniques that prevent one from asking for incompatible changes in the objective and auxiliary conditions. The analysis, however, is beyond the scope of this discussion.

Bibliography

1. A. E. Bryson, F. J. Carroll. W. F. Denham, and K. Mikami, "Determination of the lift program that minimizes re-entry heating with acceleration or range constraints using a steepest descent computation procedure," *J. Inst. Aerospace Sciences*, to be published in 1961.

2. H. J. Kelley, "Gradient theory of optimal flight paths," *ARS Journal*, vol. 30, no. 10, October 1960.

On a New Functional Transform in Analysis: The Maximum Transform

RICHARD BELLMAN and WILLIAM KARUSH

1. Introduction

We have seen in Chapter I how frequently one encounters in mathematical economics and operations research the problem of determining the maximum of the function

$$(1) \qquad F(x_1, x_2, \ldots, x_N) = f_1(x_1) + f_2(x_2) + \cdots + f_N(x_N)$$

over the region R defined by $x_1 + x_2 + \cdots + x_N = x$, $x_i \geq 0$. Under various assumptions concerning the f_i, this problem can be studied analytically; cf. Karush[1],[2], and it can also be treated analytically by means of the theory of dynamic programming[5], and, of course, computationally, as we have seen in what has gone before.

It is natural in this connection to introduce a "convolution" of two functions f and g, $h = f * g$, defined by

$$(2) \qquad h(x) = \max_{0 \leq y \leq x} [f(y) + g(x - y)].$$

For purposes of general study, it is more convenient to introduce instead the convolution $h = f \otimes g$ defined by

$$(3) \qquad h(x) = \max_{0 \leq y \leq x} [f(y)g(x - y)].$$

It is easy to see that the operation $\otimes$ is commutative and associative provided that all functions involved are nonnegative. By analogy with the relation between the Laplace transform and the usual convolution, $\int_0^x f(y)g(x - y) \, dy$, it is natural to seek a functional transform

$$(4) \qquad M(f) = F$$

with the property that

$$(5) \qquad M(f \otimes g) = M(f)M(g),$$

that is,

$$(6) \qquad H(z) = F(z)G(z)$$

where H, F, G are the transforms of h, f, g respectively.

We shall show that M exists and has a very simple form. In addition, M^{-1} has a very simple and elegant representation in a number of cases.

2. The Maximum Transform

Let a transform (1.4) be defined by the equation

$$(1) \qquad F(z) = \max_{x \geq 0} [e^{-xz}f(x)], \qquad z \geq 0.$$

It will be assumed that $f(x)$ is continuous and nonnegative for $x \geq 0$. Furthermore, since $F(z)$ is unchanged when f is replaced by its monotone envelope, we shall consider (1) only for monotone nondecreasing f.

It is now a straightforward matter to prove (1.5) by the method used in the usual convolution. We have

$$(2) \qquad H(z) = \max_{x \geq 0} [e^{-xz} \max_{0 \leq y \leq x} [f(y)g(x-y)]]$$

$$= \max_{x \geq 0} \max_{0 \leq y \leq x} [e^{-xz}f(y)g(x-y)] = \max_{y \geq 0} \max_{x \geq y} [\qquad]$$

$$= \max_{y \geq 0} [f(y) \max_{x \geq y} [e^{-xz}g(x-y)]]$$

$$= \max_{y \geq 0} [e^{-yz}f(y) \max_{w \geq 0} [e^{-wz}g(w)]]$$

$$= \max_{y \geq 0} [e^{-yz}f(y)] \cdot \max_{w \geq 0} [e^{-wz}g(w)] = F(z)G(z)$$

as desired.

To ensure the existence of $F = M(f)$ for $z > 0$, it is sufficient to assume that f satisfies a relation of the form $f(x) = 0[x^c]$ for $x \geq 0$ where $c \geq 0$. The transform F is decreasing and continuous for $z > 0$; if $c = 0$, this holds for $z \geq 0$.

3. Inverse Operator

The determination of the existence and uniqueness of M^{-1} is of some complexity, and at this time we shall consider only special cases. If for $z > 0$, the maximum of $f(x)e^{-xz}$ can be found by differentiation, we have the maximizing value the equation $f'(x) - zf(x) = 0$. Suppose that this equation possesses a unique solution $x = x(z)$ with $dx/dz \neq 0$ (and hence < 0). For this value of x, we have $F(z) = e^{-xz}f(x)$. Differentiating this relation with respect to x, we have

$$(1) \qquad F'(z)\frac{dz}{dx} = (f'(x) - zf(x))e^{-xz} - xf(x)e^{-xz}\frac{dz}{dx}$$

$$= -xf(x)e^{-xz}\frac{dz}{dx}.$$

Hence,

$$(2) \qquad x = -F'(z)/F(z), \qquad \text{or} \qquad F'(z) + xF(z) = 0.$$

355

But this is precisely the relation which gives the z minimizing $F(z)e^{xz}$, for fixed x. Hence, we have

$$(3) \qquad f(x) = \min_{z \geq 0} e^{xz} F(z),$$

the required inversion relation.

A simpler way to obtain this relation is the following. By (2.1), we have, for $x \geq 0$,

$$(4) \qquad F(z) \geq e^{-xz} f(x),$$

whence $F(z)e^{xz} \geq f(x)$. If there is a one-to-one correspondence between x and z values, we have $\min_{z \geq 0} F(x)e^{zx} \geq f(x)$, with equality for one value, whence (3).

4. Application

Let

$$(1) \qquad f(x) = \max_{R} [f_1(x_1)f_2(x_2) \cdots f_N(x_N)],$$

where R is as in (1.1). Then, inductively,

$$(2) \qquad M(f) = \prod_{i=1}^{N} M(f_i), \qquad \text{or} \qquad F(z) = \prod_{i=1}^{N} F_i(z),$$

whence formally

$$(3) \qquad f(x) = \min_{z \geq 0} \left[e^{xz} \prod_{i=1}^{N} F_i(z) \right].$$

Similarly, if we have a "renewal" equation

$$(4) \qquad f(x) = a(x) + \max_{0 \leq y \leq x} [f(y)g(x - y)],$$

we have a formal solution

$$(5) \qquad f(x) = \min_{z \geq 0} \left[\frac{e^{xz} A(z)}{1 - G(z)} \right],$$

where $A = M(a)$, $G = M(g)$.

Bibliography

1. W. Karush, "A queuing model for an inventory problem," *Operations Research*, vol. 5, 1957, pp. 693–703.

2. ———, *A General Algorithm for the Optimal Distribution of Effort*, to appear.

3. R. Bellman and W. Karush, "On a new functional transform in analysis: the Maximum Transform," *Bull. Amer. Math. Soc.*, vol. 67, 1961, pp. 501–3.

4. R. Bellman and W. Karush, *The Maximum Transform*, to appear.

5. R. Bellman, *Dynamic Programming*, Princeton University Press, Princeton, New Jersey, 1957.

The RAND Johnniac Computer

STUART DREYFUS

The majority of the computations reported in this book were performed on the Johnniac computer at The RAND Corporation. Since reference is occasionally made to computing times and other data peculiar to a particular computer, we shall briefly sketch the vital statistics of Johnniac as it existed at the time of our dynamic programming research.

The machine, built on the basic Princeton design and named after John von Neumann, contained 4000 high-speed magnetic core memory cells, a magnetic drum capacity of 12,000, and no tape storage facility. Input was by punched card and output by 900 line/minute printer on punched cards. Each word of storage held 40 binary digits and contained either numerical data or two single-address instructions. The fixed point addition of two numbers required about .000080 seconds and multiplication or division consumed up to .001500 seconds. Floating point operation was obtained by means of interpretive programming and slowed the computation by a factor of about ten.

The performance of the Johnniac, on the whole, was comparable to its contemporary, the IBM-701 computer.

To convert, in a rough way, computing time quoted in the text to numbers applicable to present (circa 1960) machines, divide by 10.

NAME INDEX

Adorno, D. S., 274
Alchian, A., 147
Allen, S. G., 150
Amundson, N. R., 273
Aoki, M., 245, 261, 264, 272, 275, 284
Arimizu, T., 244
Aris, R., 244, 273
Armer, P., 274
Aronszajn, N., 70
Arrow, K. J., 37, 102, 146, 149
Ash, M., 271

Ball, J. E., 273
Barankin, E. W., 148
Bateman, H., 271
Beale, E. M., 149
Beardwell, J., 233
Beckenbach, E. F., 99
Beckmann, M., 150, 320
Beckwith, R., 272, 296
Bellman, R., 37, 38, 99, 100, 101, 102,
  146, 147, 148, 149, 150, 179, 205, 206,
  231, 232, 233, 244, 271, 272, 296, 320,
  335, 336, 354, 356
Berkovitz, L. D., 272
Blackwell, D., 321
Bliss, G. A., 186, 204
Bolza, O., 186
Bonessen, T., 99
Bowman, E. H., 146
Box, G. E. P., 179, 272
Breakwell, J. V., 231
Brock, P., 37, 102
Brown, G. C., 273
Bryson, A. E., 101, 180, 232, 348, 351,
  353
Buras, N., 38

Cahn, A. S., 148
Cahn, J. W., 101, 147
Caplygin, S., 101
Carroll, F. J., 232, 353
Cartaino, T., 231
Chandrasekhar, S., 336
Chanugam, J., 272
Charnes, A., 146, 148
Clark, C., 37, 102, 320
Collatz, L., 206
Cooke, K. L., 271
Cooper, W. W., 146, 148
Courant, R., 204

Craft, C., 37, 102, 320

Danskin, J. M., 271
Dantzig, G. B., 38, 70, 100, 146
de Guenin, J., 38
Denham, W. F., 232, 353
Denny, J., 148
Desoer, C. A., 206
Dorfman, R., 37, 100
Dranoff, J. S., 273
Dreyfus, S., 38, 99, 100, 147, 148, 149,
  205, 206, 231, 232, 273, 320, 335, 340,
  348, 357
Dubins, L. E., 38, 274
Dvoretzsky, A., 149, 178

Eggleston, H. G., 99
Eneev, T. M., 231
Epenaux, F. D., 320
Euler, L., 182, 186

Feller, W., 319
Fenchel, W., 99
Fisher, J. L., 321
Fleming, W. H., 205, 206
Flood, M. M., 70, 100
Ford, L. R. Jr., 70, 100, 232
Fox, L., 206
Franklin, J. N., 232
Freimer, M., 99, 274, 340
Fukao, T., 100, 147
Fukuda, Y., 148, 150
Fulkerson, D. R., 70, 100, 232
Fuller, A. T., 272

Gaddum, J. W., 149
Gale, D., 37
Galileo, G., 327
Gauss, K. F., 202
Ghouila-Houri, A., 37, 320
Giffler, B., 150
Gilliland, E. R., 273
Gleason, A., 178
Glicksberg, I., 100, 146, 149, 205, 206,
  232, 271
Gluss, B., 179
Goertzel, G., 232
Gomory, R., 38
Gradwohl, A. J., 150
Greenwood, R. E., 232
Grinnell, H. W., 273

359

Gross, O., 58, 100, 146, 149, 152, 178, 205, 206, 232, 271, 337
Gruter, W. F., 274

Hacker, T., 206
Hadley, G., 149
Hahn, F., 146
Hall, W. A., 38
Halton, J. H., 233
Hammersley, J. M., 233
Happel, J., 273
Harris, T., 149
Hestenes, M., 332
Hilbert, D., 186, 204
Hitchcock, F. L., 100
Hoffman, A. J., 146, 149
Holt, C. C., 37
Howard, R. A., 37, 298, 303, 312, 320
Hur, J. J., 273
Hurwicz, L., 102, 246
Huygens, C., 246

Iglehart, D., 150, 320
Ingarden, R. S., 204

Jacobs, W., 146, 149
Johnson, R. C., 273
Johnson, S., 146, 150, 152, 178
Jorgenson, D. W., 147

Kalaba, R., 101, 149, 206, 232, 233, 244, 271, 272, 296, 336
Kalman, R. E., 296
Kantorovich, L. V., 70, 100
Karlin, S., 37, 146, 149
Karreman, H. F., 102
Karush, W., 37, 146, 354, 356
Kasegai, T., 150
Kashmar, C. M., 272
Kasugai, H., 150
Kaufman, A., 37, 148
Kelley, H. J., 231, 348, 353
Kemeny, J. G., 244, 320
Kiefer, J., 149, 178, 179
Kikuchi, R., 101, 147
Kimura, S., 147
Kolmogorov, A. N., 293
Koopmans, T. C., 100
Kuhn, H. W., 340, 344, 346, 347

Lagrange, J. L., 186
LaSalle, J. P., 205, 206, 271
Ledley, R. S., 179, 320
Lefkowitz, B., 149
Lefschetz, S., 206
Lehman, S., 244

Levinson, N., 296
Levitan, R. E., 148
Lusted, L. B., 179, 320

Magee, E. J., 179
Mahoney, J. D., 274
Malcolm, D. G., 37, 102, 320
Manne, A., 320
Mantel, N., 179
Marks, B. J., 147
Marschak, J., 101, 149
Marx, K., 244
Mayne, A. J., 38
McGuire, C. B., 102
McNaughton, R., 148
Mellon, B., 146
Merriam, C. W., III, 271, 336
Messikomer, B. H., 274
Mikamic, K., 232, 353
Mitten, L. C., 273
Modigliani, F., 37, 146
Moran, P. A. P., 150
Morgenstern, O., 244
Morin, F., 147
Morishima, M., 244
Motzkin, T. S., 100
Mullin, A. A., 38
Muth, J., 37

Nakeshima, I., 151
Newman, D. J., 179
Nomoto, A., 102, 274
Norris, R. C., 179

Okhotsimskii, D. E., 231
Osborn, H., 205, 206
Overall, J. E., 320

Pallu de la Barrier, R., 272
Peters, M. S., 273
Peterson, E. L., 272
Pfretzschner, C. A., 273
Phelps, E. S., 151
Pollack, M., 232
Pontryagin, L. S., 206
Prager, W., 149
Prestrud, M., 336

Radner, R., 102, 147, 148
Raiffa, H., 321
Reiter, S., 100
Remond, F. Y., 272
Ricciardi, F., 37, 102, 320
Robbins, H., 178
Roberts, S. M., 244, 273, 274
Robinson, C. E., 273

SUBJECT INDEX

OTHER RAND BOOKS

COLUMBIA UNIVERSITY PRESS, NEW YORK, NEW YORK

Bergson, Abram, and Hans Heymann, Jr., *Soviet National Income and Product, 1940-48*, 1954
Galenson, Walter, *Labor Productivity in Soviet and American Industry*, 1955
Hoeffding, Oleg, *Soviet National Income and Product in 1928*, 1954

THE FREE PRESS, GLENCOE, ILLINOIS

Dinerstein, Herbert S., and Leon Gouré, *Two Studies in Soviet Controls: Communism and the Russian Peasant; Moscow in Crisis*, 1955
Garthoff, Raymond L., *Soviet Military Doctrine*, 1953
Goldhamer, Herbert, and Andrew W. Marshall, *Psychosis and Civilization*, 1953
Leites, Nathan, *A Study of Bolshevism*, 1953
Leites, Nathan, and Elsa Bernaut, *Ritual of Liquidation: The Case of the Moscow Trials*, 1954
The RAND Corporation, *A Million Random Digits with 100,000 Normal Deviates*, 1955

HARVARD UNIVERSITY PRESS, CAMBRIDGE, MASSACHUSETTS

Bergson, Abram, *The Real National Income of Soviet Russia Since 1928*, 1961
Fainsod, Merle, *Smolensk under Soviet Rule*, 1958
Hitch, Charles J., and Roland McKean, *The Economics of Defense in the Nuclear Age*, 1960

THE MACMILLAN COMPANY, NEW YORK, NEW YORK

Dubyago, A. D., *The Determination of Orbits*, translated from the Russian by R. D. Burke, G. Gordon, L. N. Rowell, and F. T. Smith, 1961.
O'Sullivan, J. J. (ed.), *Protective Construction in a Nuclear Age*, 1961
Whiting, Allen S., *China Crosses the Yalu: The Decision To Enter the Korean War*, 1960

MC GRAW-HILL BOOK COMPANY, INC., NEW YORK, NEW YORK

Bellman, Richard, *Introduction to Matrix Analysis*, 1960
Dorfman, Robert, Paul A. Samuelson, and Robert M. Solow, *Linear Programming and Economic Analysis*, 1958
Gale, David, *The Theory of Linear Economic Models*, 1960
Janis, Irving L., *Air War and Emotional Stress: Psychological Studies of Bombing and Civilian Defense*, 1951
Leites, Nathan, *The Operational Code of the Politburo*, 1951
McKinsey, J. C. C., *Introduction to the Theory of Games*, 1952
Mead, Margaret, *Soviet Attitudes toward Authority: An Interdisciplinary Approach to Problems of Soviet Character*, 1951
Scitovsky, Tibor, Edward Shaw, and Lorie Tarshis, *Mobilizing Resources for War: The Economic Alternatives*, 1951
Selznick, Philip, *The Organizational Weapon: A Study of Bolshevik Strategy and Tactics*, 1952
Shanley, F. R., *Weight-Strength Analysis of Aircraft Structures*, 1952
Williams, J. D., *The Compleat Strategyst: Being a Primer on the Theory of Games of Strategy*, 1954

THE MICROCARD FOUNDATION, MADISON, WISCONSIN

Baker, C. L., and F. J. Gruenberger, *The First Six Million Prime Numbers*, 1959

NORTH-HOLLAND PUBLISHING COMPANY, AMSTERDAM, HOLLAND

Arrow, Kenneth J., and Marvin Hoffenberg, *A Time Series Analysis of Interindustry Demands*, 1959

FREDERICK A. PRAEGER INC., NEW YORK, NEW YORK

Dinerstein, H. S., *War and the Soviet Union: Nuclear Weapons and the Revolution in Soviet Military and Political Thinking*, 1959
Speier, Hans, *Divided Berlin: The Anatomy of Soviet Political Blackmail*, 1961
Tanham, G. K., *Communist Revolutionary Warfare: The Viet Minh in Indochina*, 1961

PRENTICE-HALL, INC., ENGLEWOOD CLIFFS, NEW JERSEY

Dresher, Melvin, *Games of Strategy: Theory and Applications*, 1961
Hsieh, Alice L., *Communist China's Strategy in the Nuclear Era*, 1962
Newell, Allen (ed.), *Information Processing Language-V Manual*, 1961

PRINCETON UNIVERSITY PRESS, PRINCETON, NEW JERSEY

Baum, Warren C., *The French Economy and the State*, 1958
Bellman, Richard, *Adaptive Control Processes: A Guided Tour*, 1961
Bellman, Richard, *Dynamic Programming*, 1957
Brodie, Bernard, *Strategy in the Missile Age*, 1959
Davison, W. Phillips, *The Berlin Blockade: A Study in Cold War Politics*, 1958
Ford, L. R., Jr., and D. R. Fulkerson, *Flows in Networks*, 1962
Hastings, Cecil, Jr., *Approximations for Digital Computers*, 1955
Smith, Bruce Lannes, and Chitra M. Smith, *International Communication and Political Opinion: A Guide to the Literature*, 1956
Wolf, Charles, Jr., *Foreign Aid: Theory and Practice in Southern Asia*, 1960

PUBLIC AFFAIRS PRESS, WASHINGTON, D.C.

Krieger, F. J., *Behind the Sputniks: A Survey of Soviet Space Science*, 1958
Rush, Myron, *The Rise of Khrushchev*, 1958

RANDOM HOUSE, INC., NEW YORK, NEW YORK

Buchheim, Robert W., and the Staff of The RAND Corporation, *Space Handbook: Astronautics and Its Applications*, 1959

ROW, PETERSON AND COMPANY, EVANSTON, ILLINOIS

George, Alexander L., *Propaganda Analysis: A Study of Inferences Made from Nazi Propaganda in World War II*, 1959
Melnik, Constantin, and Nathan Leites, *The House without Windows: France Selects a President*, 1958
Speier, Hans, *German Rearmament and Atomic War: The Views of German Military and Political Leaders*, 1957
Speier, Hans, and W. Phillips Davison (eds.), *West German Leadership and Foreign Policy*, 1957

STANFORD UNIVERSITY PRESS, STANFORD, CALIFORNIA

Kecskemeti, Paul, *Strategic Surrender: The Politics of Victory and Defeat*, 1958
Kecskemeti, Paul, *The Unexpected Revolution: Social Forces in the Hungarian Uprising*, 1961
Kramish, Arnold, *Atomic Energy in the Soviet Union*, 1959
Leites, Nathan, *On the Game of Politics in France*, 1959
Trager, Frank N. (ed.), *Marxism in Southeast Asia: A Study of Four Countries*, 1959

UNIVERSITY OF CALIFORNIA PRESS, BERKELEY, CALIFORNIA

Gouré, Leon, *Civil Defense in the Soviet Union*, 1962

THE UNIVERSITY OF CHICAGO PRESS, CHICAGO, ILLINOIS

Hirshleifer, Jack, James C. DeHaven, and Jerome W. Milliman, *Water Supply: Economics, Technology, and Policy*, 1960

JOHN WILEY & SONS, INC., NEW YORK, NEW YORK

McKean, Roland N., *Efficiency in Government through Systems Analysis: With Emphasis on Water Resource Development*, 1958

www.ingramcontent.com/pod-product-compliance
Ingram Content Group UK Ltd.
Pitfield, Milton Keynes, MK11 3LW, UK
UKHW022010180125
453918UK00004B/190